TESTING
CLIENT/SERVER
SYSTEMS

OTHER McGRAW-HILL CLIENT/SERVER BOOKS

Testing
Client/Server
Systems

Kelly C. Bourne

McGraw-Hill, Inc.
New York · San Francisco · Washington, D.C.
Auckland · Bogotá · Caracas · Lisbon · London
Madrid · Mexico City · Milan · Montreal · New Delhi
San Juan · Singapore · Sydney · Tokyo · Toronto

Library of Congress Cataloging-in-Publication Data

Bourne, Kelly C.
    Testing client/server systems / Kelly C. Bourne.
        p.   cm.
    Includes index.
    ISBN 0-07-006688-4
    1. Client/server computing.   2. Computer software—Testing.
I. Title.
QA76.9.C55B69   1997
005.2'76—dc21   97-22888
                                                           CIP

McGraw-Hill

*A Division of The **McGraw·Hill** Companies*

ISBN 0-07-006688-4

*The sponsoring editor for this book was Steve Elliot, the editing supervisor was
Sally Glover, and the production supervisor was Tina Cameron. It was set in Vendome
ICG by Tanya Howden of McGraw-Hill's Professional Book Group composition unit,
Hightstown, N.J.*

Printed and bound by Quebecor/Fairfield.

McGraw-Hill books are available at special quantity discounts to use as premi-
ums and sales promotions, or for use in corporate training programs. For more
information, please write to the Director of Special Sales, McGraw-Hill, 11 West
19th Street, New York, NY 10011. Or contact your local bookstore.

This book is printed on recycled, acid-free paper containing
a minimum of 50% recycled, de-inked fiber.

Dedicated to my family. They have been both an inspiration and a continuous source of support.

CONTENTS

vii

Contents

INTRODUCTION

The transition from a mainframe, flat-file, batch-oriented environment to client/server, graphical user interface (GUI) systems represents an enormous transformation in the software development landscape. Software developers, and their management, need to recognize that this transition must be accompanied by an equally large shift in how systems are tested. Testing techniques and tools which were satisfactory for procedural or batch-oriented systems don't test client/server systems adequately.

Why This Book Is Needed

This book is an attempt to illustrate the differences between testing traditional, procedural systems and client/server systems. The most obvious difference is that client/server systems are almost always associated with a graphical user interface (GUI), while traditional systems have a character- or line-oriented user interface. This single difference is immense but represents only the tip of the iceberg between the two contrasting approaches. Other, equally significant, differences are listed in Chapter 1.

For developers who have begun their software development career in a client/server, GUI environment, this book may be their first introduction to testing as a planned and methodical activity. For others it will be primarily an introduction to client/server-style testing. In either case, it is hoped that the reader will become more familiar with tools and techniques to successfully test client/server systems.

A number of specialized software tools have been developed to test client/server systems. This book will introduce many such tools. No attempt is made to review any particular tool or vendor. Rather, the emphasis is on highlighting major categories of tools and providing examples of several representative products in each category.

The Audience for This Book

The intended audience for this work includes a variety of professionals with an interest in developing client/server software. Developers, of course, should be familiar with the concepts in this book.

Managers of developers must have a very complete grasp of the software-testing process. Without such a grasp they will allow testing to be incomplete, inadequate, and inefficient.

Quality Assurance (QA) personnel also have a vested interest in testing client/server systems completely and efficiently. The tools which are described in this book have become (or are quickly becoming) predominant in the testing world.

Last, but not least, the user community must participate in the testing process at a much higher level than they did in the past. Users have the most to lose. They are the group who pays for systems in more than one way. If the resulting system is inefficient or difficult to use, the users are the ones who have to work with it.

What Is Included

Part 1 presents an overview of client/server testing, especially why it is different enough from traditional, procedural-based systems to warrant a new approach to testing. The different goals of testing are outlined, and a brief introduction to the background of automated testing tools is presented.

Part 2 outlines how and when test planning should be done. It lists and describes the different types of testing. Tools which can provide significant assistance in this area are outlined. Methods and tools for handling errors once they have been discovered and corrected are presented, and a discussion on knowing when adequate testing has been performed is put forth.

Part 3 gets to the heart of the testing process. It outlines the primary tools used to test client/server systems. Examples based on market-leading tools are used.

Part 4 covers aspects of client/server testing which are all too frequently overlooked. In the turmoil of developing and deploying a system, it's easy to overlook the items listed here, but doing so is definitely opening the door for problems at a later time. Some examples of items covered in this section are testing SQL code, security, and system performance. All too often these items aren't addressed until systems have been developed and deployed. Corrections at this stage of the project are extremely expensive, time-consuming, and embarrassing.

The final chapter attempts to predict the future of client/server systems and testing. As in all fields, predicting trends in client/server systems and testing is risky. Certain trends, though, are fairly obvious. Internet and Web-based systems are becoming indispensable to corporations. Better performance from any system, client/server included, is always desirable. It's a safe bet that future client/server systems will be more complex. Distributed and replicated databases are becoming the norm, as are client/server systems built to access them. Like all predictions, the ones made in this chapter may be off the mark, but I am fairly confident that most of them will be reasonably accurate.

PART 1

Client/Server Testing

An Overview

CHAPTER 1

Client/Server Systems Are Different from Traditional Systems

A "traditional" computer system consists of a single, large computer and a number of "dumb" terminals. All of the intelligence in the system resides in the one computer. This piece of hardware was usually, but not always, a mainframe computer. The users interact with the computer via the character-based terminal. Frequently, the user interface consists of entering obscure codes and receiving back fairly simplistic screens of data. People normally associate applications running on traditional systems with languages like CICS and COBOL.

A client/server system consists of one or more client computers connected to one or more server computers by a network. The network might be a *local area network* (LAN) or a *wide area network* (WAN). A significant amount of computer power resides at both the client and server levels of the system. Users interact with the system via a *graphical user interface* (GUI). The interface provides the user with a mouse, keyboard control, and objects such a pull-down list boxes, buttons, radio buttons, menus and graphics. The applications are written with tools such as PowerBuilder, Visual Basic, C++, and Developer/2000.

To explain what is different about testing client/server systems, it's necessary to impress upon the reader how truly different client/server systems are from traditional computer systems. Only with this background in place can the differences in testing procedures be outlined and discussed.

1.1 The GUI Interface

The most conspicuous difference between client/server systems and traditional, procedural-based systems is that client/server systems are almost always associated with a graphical user interface (GUI). Traditional systems have a character or line-oriented user interface. A client/server architecture provides sufficient computing power at the desktop level to allow the generation and manipulation of a graphical interface. Terminals generally employed by traditional systems are frequently referred to as being "dumb." They have no independent computational functionality. Without such a capability, it isn't feasible for a terminal to depend on the mainframe to provide a graphical interface.

A GUI interface presents users with a wide array of objects (i.e., controls) on the screen. Menus, command buttons, picture buttons, dropdown list boxes, tool bars, grids, scroll bars, graphs, help screens, and MDI sheets are only some of the objects which users can choose from. Table 1.1 presents a list of object types commonly available with popular client/server development tools. Contrast this variety with the previous generation of systems in which users could enter only data or commands at an input prompt. Frequently the commands in traditional systems were abbreviations or obscure codes.

The existence and variety of graphical objects associated with client/server systems has been a boon to the user. Graphical objects make applications much easier and more intuitive to use. Training costs and requirements for new systems are significantly less than with traditional systems. Unfortunately, what is a boon to users imposes additional testing burdens upon the developer and testing personnel. Each object on every window must be thoroughly tested before the product can be released to the user community. Complicating the testing process is the fact that each object on a window can (and frequently does) affect or control other objects on the window. The effort to test all permutations of objects on a window increases geometrically with the number of objects.

Figures 1.1 and 1.2 demonstrate a trivial example of how one window object can affect another. The set of radio buttons can be used to determine what objects (labels, fields, buttons, menu items) are displayed to the user. Selecting a button requires that the application

TABLE 1.1

Common Object Types

Command Buttons

Picture Buttons

Static Text

Data Windows

Grids

Multiline Edit Fields

Pictures

Single-line Edit Fields

Edit Masks

List Boxes

Drop-Down List Boxes

Check Boxes

Radio Buttons

Scroll Bars

Menus

Figure 1.1
Example Screen
When First Radio
Button Is Selected

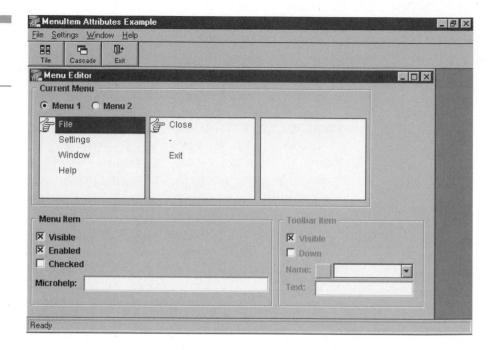

make one set of labels, tool bar buttons, and menu items invisible yet another set of objects visible. Figure 1.1 represents what the user sees when the first radio button is selected. Figure 1.2 is a screen shot of what is presented when the second button is selected.

The above example is fairly simple. A more complicated example of different objects affecting each other could involve multiple windows. Say the first window displays a data window or grid with master records. Double clicking on a row might bring up a second window with related detail records. To further complicate the scenario, a user could be allowed to modify or delete contents of the detail window and these changes would be reflected back on the master window.

As these cursory examples show, the interdependencies between objects can become very complicated very quickly. A client/server system designed and built to handle a real-world problem will contain hundreds, if not thousands, of such interdependencies. Each of these relationships must be identified, documented, and tested. Testing not only must be done once, but each relationship will need to be retested should objects change or additional objects be added to the mix.

A graphical interface represents an enormous difference between client/server and traditional systems, but it represents only the tip of the iceberg between the two contrasting approaches of system architecture. Other notable differences are highlighted in the following sections.

1.2 Event-Driven Logic Versus Procedural Programming

The programming languages and logic in traditional system were invariably procedural. A *procedural language* is one in which the computer executes statements in the sequence specified in the program's source code. Line one of the code is executed and then line two of the code is executed. The only variation of sequencing of this logic is when values in the data cause different looping or change in controls to occur.

Client/server, GUI systems aren't procedural; they're event driven. This means that the computer executes statements in response to events which occur. The events referred to here are actions taken by the user. Examples of events are keyboard activity, mouse movements, mouse button clicks, and button clicking. Event driven systems are more difficult to test because the sequence of the events isn't known in advance.

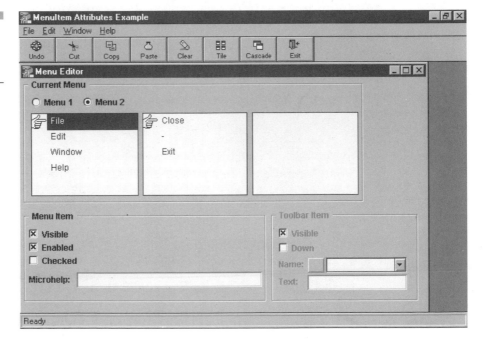

Figure 1.2
Example Screen
When Second Radio
Button Is Selected

The developer can't know which button or menu item a user will activate next. This being the situation, the application must be ready to properly handle any and all possible events at any given moment.

Obviously, every control on a form doesn't necessarily impact all other controls on the form. Most label or static text-type fields have no impact on any objects. Data-entry fields are normally fairly passive, but this isn't always the case. Many check boxes as used to simply flag a value being on or off.

In addition to potentially many objects or controls being placed on a window, a large number of events exist for each of the controls. In PowerBuilder 4.0, a picture button has a total of 11 standard events, while a form has 41 standard events. Custom events for each object type in PowerBuilder can be defined by the user. Command buttons in Visual Basic 3.0 also have 12 standard events, while a Visual Basic form has 22 events. Code written for events associated with each form, object, or control must be thoroughly tested.

Testing all possible combinations of event sequences can quickly become a logistical nightmare. Simply keeping track of which sequence combinations have already been tested and which remain to be tested becomes a Herculean chore in itself. For a system with a large number of windows and objects on them, it becomes almost statistically impossible to test all permutations.

To complicate testing of client/server systems even further, a single user action (e.g., pressing a key) can initiate numerous events. For example, a PowerBuilder user pressing the Tab key could generate the following events:

- Modified event in object with current focus.

- LoseFocus event in object with current focus.

- GetFocus event in object getting focus.

A mouse click on a field could generate the same set of events. Obviously, each distinct event needs to be tested.

1.3 GUI Application Navigation Is Significantly More Complex

Navigation within a client/server GUI application can become almost Byzantine. There is nothing specific about the client/server or GUI paradigm which causes this, but the ease with which new screens can be presented to the user certainly contributes to this phenomenon. Most GUI development packages allow screens to be brought up as a result of a menu item selection, a command button click, double clicking on a row in a grid, or clicking a tool bar icon.

The most frequent cause of complex application navigation is probably poor application design. Many applications and their navigation evolved, instead of being designed. Neither the client/server paradigm nor specific GUI tools can be blamed for a shortcoming in time and effort spent in the design phase of the project.

Complexities in application navigation certainly place additional responsibilities on those brave souls performing the testing. All conceivable navigation paths within an application must be tested. Special care needs to be taken to test possible dependencies between screens. Testing must also sufficiently stress applications by going deep within the application. This is where memory leakage or resource limitations can be found.

Testing must also be done to be certain that circular pathing isn't inadvertently allowed. An example of a circular path would be if form "B" could be called from form "A." Form "C" could then be reached from "B." If form "C" allows the user to call form "A" then a circular path has been allowed. In an application with only three forms, it would be easy to spot. An application consisting of scores or hundreds of forms would be considerably more difficult to correct. The problem with circular pathing is that it consumes system resources and inevitably will lead to a general protection fault (GPF) or other type of crash.

1.4 Inheritance

Inheritance is one of the primary tenets of object oriented programming (OOP). A working definition of inheritance is that attributes of ancestors can be passed onto descendants. New attributes can be defined for descendants. An example would be that an ancestor window could include buttons for "Add," "Delete," and "Modify." Descendants inheriting capabilities from this ancestor would not need to duplicate code to provide these functions.

The primary advantage of inheritance is to achieve increased reusability of code, the "Holy Grail" of software development. Writing basic functionality a single time and inheriting this functionality greatly decreases the amount of code which needs to be written. Besides saving the time and resources of writing the code only once, there is the side benefit of having less code to test. Less code to test means fewer resources need be devoted to the testing process and testing can be completed quicker.

A secondary advantage of inheritance is that it helps to maintain appearance consistency and functionality among objects within applications and suites of applications. This may not seem like a significant advantage to the developers down in the trenches, but it makes user training much simpler.

Inheritance's impact on testing client/server systems is twofold. First, since inherited objects are heavily relied upon, their reliability and adherence to requirements must be without question. These objects must be tested early and thoroughly. Ancestor objects would most likely be developed very early in a development project. There must be sufficient time devoted to testing them before descendants are created.

The second effect inheritance has on testing is *regression testing*. Regression testing is testing which must be done to be certain that changes to existing code haven't inadvertently introduced bugs into otherwise correct code. When inheritance is used in a system, regression testing becomes even more crucial. This is because may objects rely upon a small number of ancestors. Changes to any ancestor, if done incorrectly, can corrupt large portions of a system. Any modifications or enhancements to an ancestor object, no matter how trivial they appear to be, must be accompanied by stringent regression testing of all descendent objects.

Not all GUI development environments allow inheritance. Those that do have differing degrees of how inheritance can be used. PowerBuilder 4 and 5 both enable developers to exploit inheritance. Types of objects which inheritance can be used with are windows, menus, and user objects. Delphi also allows inheritance. The object types in Delphi which can be inherited are very similar to the objects in PowerBuilder. Visual Basic 4.0 doesn't allow developers to inherit functionality from an ancestor object.

1.5 Differences Between Flat Files and RDBMS Systems

There are a number of significant differences between flat files and a relational database system. Many of these differences will have an impact on how client/server testing needs to be done. Some differences between these different data storage techniques are outlined in the following sections.

1.5.1 How They Are Accessed

One of the most noticeable differences between flat files and a relational database management system (RDBMS) is that users interact directly with a flat file system while they must go through the database engine to access the data in an RDBMS. Flat files can be opened, read, written to, and closed. Data is read from flat files one record at a time. Application programs do this by making calls to system functions.

Applications needing to obtain data from a relational database open a connection to the database. The overwhelmingly used language for accessing relational databases is the structured query language (SQL). Data within a RDBMS is accessed a set at a time.

1.5.2 Who Owns Them

The owner of a flat file is whichever account is marked as the owner of the individual disk files. Other users can have read and/or write access to these files. Any other granularity of security must be imposed by the application programs themselves.

One account owns a relational database. Frequently this account is the "dbo" or database owner account. The majority of tables and other objects in the database are also owned by the dbo, but individual users can own tables. The owner of each table can grant access to that table to other users. Access can be granted in the form of read, insert, update, and delete privileges. Security in a client/server RDBMS system can be completely imposed separate from the applications themselves.

1.5.3 Where They Are Stored

Flat files are stored on disk drives which are connected to the main-frame computer. The application program must know exactly where the flat files are located and what their names are. Without this specific information, the program won't be able to access the flat files.

A relational database is also stored on disk drives. Usually these drives are connected with the database server. Relational databases can also be divided between multiple servers. One-half of the database might be in Omaha and the other half might be in Kansas City. The application doesn't necessarily know that the database is split between multiple locations.

1.5.4 Security

Security in a traditional system is frequently imposed by the application programs themselves. On a client/server system, security can be built into the database, imposed at the application level or some combination of the two. It is most efficient and secure to impose security by building it into the database. This is the norm for client/server systems.

1.5.5 Data Dependence Versus Data Independence

An application in a flat file system needs to know a great deal about how the data is stored in the files. It must know the names and locations of the files and the record layout of each table. If there is a change in the location or name of the files, the application must be changed so it correctly names and identifies the flat files. If the record layout changes within a flat file, it will have severe repercussions on the application. The area into which the record is read must be resized to fit the new record length. Variables will have to be changed so they will be associated with the current position of fields in the record. It would be accurate to say that an application using flat files is very dependent on the record layout of the flat file.

In contrast, applications which access data via a relational database have a very high degree of data independence. The tables they are using can be moved from Omaha to Kansas City and the application need not know about it. Columns can be reordered within tables and it won't affect the applications. Columns can be added or dropped from tables and applications needn't be modified. Columns can even be moved from one table to another and this can be masked from the user by use of a view.

1.6 Object Class Libraries

An *object class library* is a collection of tested, reliable objects. Examples of the types of objects which compose a typical library are windows, menus, and user objects. These objects can be inherited to provide quick, consistent, bug-free components in an application. Having a broad range of objects which can be inherited can significantly speed up the development of a client/server system. It brings the developer one step closer to the dream of snapping together preexisting software components to build an application.

While the above statements represent the ideal situation, the problem facing the vast majority of development projects is how to achieve this state of nirvana. The two choices for acquiring and using an object class library are to 1) build it yourself or 2) purchase a library from a vendor. As occurs so many times in both life and software development, each alternative has its own distinct pros and cons.

The advantages of purchasing an object class library are that it's immediately available, fully developed, adequately tested, and supported by the vendor. Addressing each of the above points and comparing them to the alternative of internal development provides an idea of the vast differences between the two approaches. Purchasing an object class library means you can start learning and using it as soon as it arrives and is installed. Compare this with the time it takes to realistically develop an in-house library. The first step would be to determine requirements which are common across the entire system. These are the initial candidates for the library. The next step is to design, code, and thoroughly test these objects. Once built, the objects must be documented so other developers know they exist and how to use them. Obviously, these steps are going to take substantially longer than choosing and ordering a library from a vendor.

The primary advantage of an internally developed library is that it will be a custom fit instead of an off-the-rack solution. It can be developed to precisely fit your needs instead of one-size-fits-all. Time and energy won't be spent developing functionality not required in your circumstances. The underlying assumption is that the developers know what is needed. This may sound trite, but until they have been through a few client/server GUI development projects, developers aren't likely to know exactly what they should be building. This being the case, there will be a lot of corrections and additions made late in the effort.

Another area where long-term planning needs to be thought out is in the area of support. Support of an internally developed library will be an ongoing responsibility. New releases of the development tool may precipitate significant changes to the object library. Moving to a different operating system (e.g., Windows 3.11 to Windows 95 or Windows NT) won't be easy or automatic. Maintenance fees of a third-party vendor would hopefully eliminate these problems for a vendor-provided solution.

The cost of an object class library should be measured carefully. The total cost of the library needs to be clearly identified. Total costs over the expected life of the library should be measured instead of adding up just the acquisition costs. Total costs for a third-party product need to include the initial licensing cost, annual maintenance fees, and training costs. Training costs must reflect both dollars and hours to take classes and the hours needed for developers to become effective with the tool. Total costs for an in-house development effort should include resources spent designing the library, building and testing the library, documenting and publicizing it, and ongoing support. Failure to accurately address total costs will likely result in unrealistic expectations and results.

An aside to the topic of inheritance and ancestor objects would be that many software shops are choosing to purchase object class libraries developed and marketed by third-party vendors. While the objects in such libraries should already have been adequately tested, you might want to perform testing before committing to any specific library. It would be extremely disruptive to have spent significant time, training, and money on a third-party library only to find out that it wasn't sufficiently tested and remains buggy. At that point your choices would be to hope the vendor will clean up its product or start over with another class library. Neither alternative will help you meet your development schedule or inspire the confidence of your management and users.

1.7 MDI Versus SDI Applications

The Windows 3.11 environment allows developers to produce multiple document interface (MDI) applications. Essentially this means that multiple windows (called sheets) can be opened within the application. The user can quickly and easily move between the different sheets. Individual sheets can reference each other, allowing data shown on one sheet to affect data on other sheets.

Single document interface (SDI) applications are those where only a single window at a time is active. The user can't work on more than one document at any one time. Traditional applications are generally SDI in nature, while client/server GUI applications are more likely to be MDI. This is true largely because recent development tools (PowerBuilder, Visual Basic, Delphi, etc.) simplify the creation of MDI applications. Another pressure in producing MDI applications is that Windows literate users have become accustomed to MDI applications and expect and demand this level of functionality.

Examples of applications of each type are easily provided. All mainstream word processor programs (such as Microsoft Word and WordPerfect) are MDI applications. Most spreadsheets (such as Lotus 1-2-3 and Microsoft Excel) are as well. The user can open multiple documents in Word and work on each of them individually. Moving between them is easily accomplished by selecting the desired document under the "Window" menu item.

Examples of SDI applications in the Windows environment are Notepad and CardFile. Notepad allows only a single document to be open at any given time. To open a different document, the first must be closed. CardFile is similar in that only a single data file can be opened. To open a second file containing names and addresses, the first must be closed.

Testing an MDI application is significantly more difficult than testing an SDI application. The reason for this is that it enables users to open multiple documents, which places greater stress on an application. Resource usage is pushed much higher when multiple sheets are active. Greater resource usage causes problems to occur which likely would have gone unnoticed at a lower resource usage level.

Additionally, each sheet in an MDI application is essentially a different "thread." The existence of numerous threads leads to the possibility that the application will mistake one thread for another. This possibility doesn't exist in a single-threaded (SDI) application. Stress testing must be performed to make certain the application will properly handle more than one thread.

1.8 Partitioned Processing

Referring to the "partitioning" of an application is just a way of describing where the components of the application reside and execute. The possible locations where components can exist are on a client machine or on one or more server machines. There are three different partitioning approaches which can be taken. Figure 1.3 graphically presents the three different partitioning approaches. Each approach is described in the following sections.

In the one-tiered approach, the user interface (client) software and the database software both reside on a single computer. This approach

Figure 1.3
Application
Partitioning

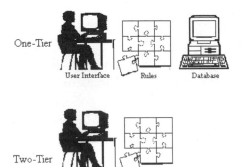

One-Tier

User Interface   Rules   Database

Two-Tier

User Interface   Rules   Database

Three-Tier

User Interface   Rules   Database
CLIENT   MIDDLE TIER   SERVER

doesn't represent a true client/server architecture. It would be used for single-user stand-alone applications.

A two-tiered partitioning approach involves two computers: a client machine and a server machine. The client machine which executes the user interface software is likely a desktop PC. The client machine probably contains the logic or business rules of the application. The server machine holds the data and is dedicated to processing database requests made by the client.

A three-tiered or n-tiered approach consists of at least three machines. The client machine executes the user interface software. As is done in the two-tiered approach, the database server holds the data and processes database requests made of it. A third computer is a server which processes logic or business rules for the system. Both the client and the application server make requests for data from the database server.

The two primary reasons for partitioning an application are 1) to improve performance and 2) increase flexibility. Isolating a system's business logic from presentation logic has the effect of both publicizing and clearly stating the business rules. When rules are embedded in the user interface, there is a tendency to overlook them. Extracting them enables designers, users, and developers to clearly address business logic.

The ability to develop multitiered architectures is becoming more and more common among client/server development products. PowerBuilder

5.0 allows users to develop applications in this manner. Oracle's Developer 2000 goes so far as allowing logic to be moved from one tier to another via a drag-and-drop method. Visual Basic provides hooks to develop multitiered applications as well. Within a short time the ability to partition applications will become an expected feature in development tools.

Multitiered architectures can significantly improve the performance of a client/server system. The reason for this is that additional computing power is introduced into the system. More importantly, separating business rules onto their own server allows these rules to be implemented more efficiently. Instead of being shoehorned into the presentation layer, they can be coded in an efficient manner.

Partitioning an application has the effect of making it more difficult to test. The reason for this is that now there is an additional level of machines to include in the testing process. The development tool and/or languages at each different level can be different. This would require developers to acquire skills in additional languages. Until they become proficient in these languages, their skills and accuracy are suspect.

Tests must now specifically address each level of hardware and the software it contains. It's quite possible that the chosen testing tools aren't available on each hardware platform and software environment. This requires developers and testers to use and learn additional test products. This also leads to a lessening of productivity and accuracy.

One of the advantages of a partitioned system is that logic can be moved from one partition to another if it is determined that this constitutes a better implementation. Unfortunately, moving logic represents a major alteration to the system. When logic is moved in this manner, a significant amount of regression testing must be performed. This regression must encompass the logic which was relocated and any functions which depend on it.

1.9 RAD

Rapid application development (RAD) and joint application development (JAD) are paradigms in which development is done in sessions attended jointly by software developers and user representatives. The fundamentals of RAD are to jointly design the screens in the system. The developer then quickly codes minimal functionality on these screens and presents them to the user. The users and developers then review the screens to assure that they meet the user's needs. This cycle continues until the fundamentals of the system have been defined. Once the design is accepted by the users, the developer completes the code needed to fully implement the screens.

The RAD approach has a number of extremely positive aspects. Because high-leverage development tools are used, the developer can very quickly design basic screens for the system. Screens can be roughed out in a matter of only minutes. Navigation within the system can also be put together quickly.

RAD allows users to gain insight into what the system will look like much earlier in the development cycle. In traditional development projects, voluminous specifications were written and presented to the users. Unfortunately these specifications were very dry and not always easily understood by end users. Frequently they agreed to the specifications not fully understanding them.

While RAD development has many advantages, it also has significant disadvantages. One primary downside is that project schedules frequently omit a dedicated testing phase. Testing, like on traditional development projects, is often overlooked or given an unrealistically small amount of time and resources.

One other way in which RAD contributes to the concept of minimal testing is that the users see prototypes of the application but don't really understand that the prototype isn't a completed system. Users often tell developers that they'll accept the prototype "as is." This has the effect of rushing developers to get something in the hands of the users, resulting in minimal (or no) testing.

Another fundamental difference between RAD and traditional software development projects is that with RAD the system is released in stages. A traditional project generally is released in a single piece, also known as the "big bang." Stage-released projects generate a large number of interim releases or builds. Each release must be built and tested before it can be distributed to users.

1.10 Heterogeneous Hardware

Traditional systems are built of fairly homogeneous hardware. It likely consists of a single mainframe computer and a fairly "vanilla" variety of dumb terminals. Client/server systems conversely consist of very heterogeneous hardware. The database server is likely to be a SUN or Hewlett-Packard (HP) computer running a version of the UNIX operating system. The application server can be a UNIX server, or possibly an Intel-based machine.

The client machines are where the real heterogeneous nature of client/server systems comes into play. Relatively few projects enjoy the luxury of purchasing new workstations for all intended users of the system. More frequently, client/server systems are deployed onto client machines already acquired and in place on the users' desktops. When this is the case, the client/server system must work with machines of varying ages and capabilities. Some of the machines may be 80486s, others might be Pentium-based products, and still others might be laptop machines. A project might be further complicated by having to deploy the application onto Apple Macintosh machines, X-terminal-based computers, and UNIX workstations.

As well as encompassing machines of different generations, it is almost certain that the client machines will have been purchased from different vendors. Some will be IBM, others will be Compaq, and others might be Gateway machines. Although all of these different machines might appear to be similar, there are significant ways in which they differ. Buses, interrupt request queues (IRQs), CPU speeds, memory speeds, port assignments, and video adapters are just a few ways in which they will differ. Each of the differences can be significant enough to prevent a client/server application from running on a machine without a significant amount of tweaking.

Two PCs which appear to be identical on the outside will differ greatly if the case is removed. The hard drives may be different makes and sizes. Amounts of memory and its manufacturer may also differ. The network cards may differ in make, model, or version. Each of the probable differences are enough to cause problems and make testing and deployment a nightmare.

Testing on each different type of computer in the system must be performed to instill confidence that the system will function as advertised. The time and resources to perform adequate testing shouldn't be underestimated. Testing in a multiple platform environment will be made even more difficult if the test tools being used aren't available for all of the platforms. Choosing test tools which will work on all the different hardware devices is extremely important.

1.11 Multiple Software Vendors

The number of software vendors involved in a client/server system is much greater than the number of software vendors in a traditional project. In a client/server system it is extremely likely that each major piece of software has been purchased from a different vendor. Some of the major software components and representative vendors are listed in Table 1.2.

Obtaining software from such a large number of vendors entails a significant amount of risk. There will very likely be incompatibilities. Product "A" won't be certified to work with one of the others.

One area where incompatibilities are extremely common are DLLs (*dynamic link libraries*). These are files which contain executable Windows code. This code is called by the vendor's programs. DLLs are dynamically loaded and linked at run time. The code in a DLL can be shared by multiple applications. Very frequently each vendor's installation process assumes the responsibility of overwriting DLLs. Even though the DLL in question may be used by many different vendors' applications, the offender considers it to be its own personal property. When this happens, an installation or upgrade of one product may disable other applications which had previously functioned. This is enough to make one pull one's hair out.

On a fairly regular basis, software vendors release new versions of their products. Most new versions include significant changes. Other times the new version simply addresses problems and is called a maintenance release. Ideally, installing the new version of a vendor's product should trigger a significant amount of regression testing on the client/server system. This is a prudent approach to a change being made to a fundamental component of the system. Testing a single vendor's new versions isn't by itself an overwhelming responsibility, but what if each of your eight software vendors issues two new releases each year? Are you prepared to perform regression testing 16 times a year on each client/server system? Your staff could exhaust a significant portion of their careers simply installing upgrades!

TABLE 1.2

Major Software
Components and
Potential Vendors

O/S on Client Workstations—Windows 3.11, Windows 95, Windows NT, OS/2, UNIX

O/S on Database Server—Windows NT, OS/2, UNIX

O/S on Application Server—Windows NT, OS/2, UNIX

RDBMS - Oracle, Sybase, or Informix

Network Software—Novell, Banyan, Microsoft, one of many TCP/IP flavors

Development Package—PowerBuilder, Visual Basic, Delphi, Developer/2000, JAM, C++

Shrink Wrapped Applications—Any number of vendors

When the inevitable problems crop up, the real bane of dealing with multiple software vendors exposes its ugly head. The name of this predicament is "finger pointing." Each software vendor is very likely to explain away the problems (and responsibility) by pointing to another vendor as the cause of the predicament. Contacting the second vendor will likely get you a similar answer, except that yet another vendor will be implicated as the root of the problem. This process continues until you get tired of playing the game or until you obtain indisputable proof of the problem child.

When initiating a client/server system project, one role which most project managers don't realize they are undertaking is that of general contractor. Each hardware and software vendor becomes a subcontractor to you. It becomes your responsibility to manage each subcontractor and make certain it completes its facet of the system. This is in addition to managing the development of the applications by in-house developers.

2

Testing Concepts and Goals

2.1 Testing Concepts

The topic of testing is one area in which a good deal of commonality exists between traditional systems and client/server-based systems. In both situations the objective is to deliver a system which does what is required without errors. The significant differences between the two types of systems may require that the approach to testing be different, but the basic goals are the same.

2.1.1 What Is an Error?

In a traditional system, errors were frequently defined as errors in output or calculations. Since traditional systems had minimal user interfaces, there wasn't as much room for errors in the area of the interface. Client/server systems, on the other hand, include more complex, robust user interfaces. More complex interfaces allow much more room for errors or omissions to occur. Examples of typical errors in the user interface are listed in Table 2.1.

From the user's perspective, the definition of an error is a bit broader than that of a developer. To a user, an application which is awkward to use, poorly documented, or inefficient isn't error-free. The implementation method may work, but it is unclear or requires users to perform extra, unnecessary, steps to get the work done. Examples of such ineffective user interfaces are listed in Table 2.2.

Some of the items listed in Table 2.2 may appear to be relatively trivial to developers. To users they appear anything but trivial. Users spend

TABLE 2.1 Examples of User Interface Errors	Incorrectly defined datatypes for input fields (e.g., character instead of date)
	Incorrect edit masks applied to input fields
	Application navigation which won't allow users to reach a desired window
	Nonfunctional menu items or control buttons
	Drop-down list boxes which don't populate correctly
	Improperly sized controls (e.g.; don't show the entire field)
	Controls which aren't visible or invisible at appropriate times
	Controls which aren't enabled or disabled at appropriate times
	Incorrectly labeled buttons or data entry fields
	Incorrect data being presented in a datawindow, table, or grid

TABLE 2.2 Examples of Ineffective User Interface	Poorly worded or confusing message boxes and pop-up windows
	Error messages which are unintelligible or overly cryptic
	Navigation which requires users to perform extra, unnecessary steps to reach desired windows
	Requiring users to enter data which the application could have provided
	Forcing all system users to share a single set of user preference settings
	Window controls which aren't properly aligned
	Allowing significant changes to be made to data without confirming it with the user

much more time dealing with the interface than either developers or testing personnel. Seemingly insignificant points can grow and grow until they overshadow the useful aspects of the application. Even something as trivial as controls being out of alignment can be distracting enough to draw attention to them each time the window appears.

The types of errors listed in Tables 2.1 and 2.2 are ones which can occur in client/server systems, but for the most part, don't occur in traditional systems. Developers and testers must be alert to identify and correct errors such as these before they ever reach the user.

As well as the above types of errors, client/servers fall prey to the same types of errors which traditional systems are subject to. Client/server systems have calculation errors, update errors, errors in reports, etc. Developers and testers have to prevent and correct these more traditional errors as well.

2.1.2 Severity of Errors

Just as in traditional systems, errors in client/server systems come in a wide variety of sizes and severity. The most severe of these require developers to drop everything and correct them right away. Less severe errors can be addressed as time and resources permit. Table 2.3 lists the spectrum of errors and a description from the most severe to least severe.

2.1.3 Error Taxonomy

In addition to being categorized by severity, errors can be divided by technical category. Table 2.4 lists categories of errors. This category list is not meant to be definitive by any means. Different individuals and project teams would define them differently. They might combine multiple

TABLE 2.3

Error Severity

Catastrophic	An error which can potentially cause the destruction of property or cost lives.
Severe	Errors which have the potential to destabilize the system, including the database.
Damaging	Errors causing erroneous results leading to inadvisable business actions or decisions.
Performance	Accuracy is not endangered, but system performance and response time is hindered.
Moderate	Inaccurate output, but not considered exceptionally damaging.
Convenience	Error doesn't allow the system to be used as conveniently as possible.
Cosmetic	Buttons or labels with misspelled words, improper capitalization, etc.

categories into a single one or divide one of these categories down into subcategories providing greater detail.

The purpose of breaking errors down into classifications is to help identify, control, and hopefully prevent future occurrences of errors. By gathering statistics on the distribution of errors encountered, it's possible to improve one's focus on that type of problem. This can result in additional education, testing, or training on that particular aspect of the system to reduce the number of bugs. Gathering and analyzing these statistics is described in Chapter 7, Handling Software Errors and Corrections.

2.1.3.1 Functional Errors. Errors in this category are associated with the functional requirements which the system is designed to provide. If a requirement listed in the specifications is not included in the delivered system, for whatever reason, it would be categorized as a functional error. Functional errors can be caused by omission of a requirement, incomplete specifications, an ambiguous description of a requirement, or requirements which are contradictory.

The omission of a requirement is usually much easier to recognize and address than when requirements have been misunderstood, are ambiguous, or contradict each other. Functional errors of this ilk aren't likely to be noticed by developers. Since the developers aren't the intended users of the system, they don't have the expertise to notice such transgressions. This type of problem is usually noticed by users or a user representative.

Testing for functional errors can be effectively performed by close comparison of the specifications document and the system design or completed system. A checklist or spreadsheet can assist in this task. It can be developed to map system requirements with the window, menu, stored procedure, and/or report where the functionality is provided. Only by producing this mapping can there be assurance that the system has indeed fulfilled all functional requirements. Obviously, it would be preferable to catch functional errors before the system is completed.

2.1.3.2 System Errors. System errors are errors which reside in, or are caused by, hardware or software outside the scope of the client/server system being developed. Some examples of the types of software in which system errors can occur are operating systems, database systems, communications software, printer drivers, Windows DLLs, file compression utilities, and report subsystems. Hardware which can cause system errors includes graphics adapters, memory chips, disk drives and controllers, network adapter cards, tape backup units, floating point coprocessors, cables, and connectors.

The current generation of hardware has become increasingly powerful, less expensive, and extremely reliable compared to previous generations of computer equipment. This is certainly a factor bolstering the move to client/server systems. Unfortunately, the move to client/server systems has increased the amount of hardware involved. Servers now routinely include multiple processor units. Single disk drives have been replaced by RAID (redundant arrays of inexpensive drives) units. Tape backup units have evolved into jukebox storage arrays. CD-ROM drives are deployed in jukebox arrays as well. Network cards and cabling are much more complicated than previous generations. Client machines frequently sport 16—32MB of memory, gigabit capacity drives, 17-inch color monitors, modems, and many other accoutrements. The reliability of each individual piece of hardware is admirable, but when the array

TABLE 2.4	Functional Errors
Error Categories	System Errors
	Communications Errors
	Logic Errors
	User Interface Errors
	Data Errors
	Coding Errors
	Testing Errors

of hardware increases to such high levels, the likelihood of one piece malfunctioning climbs rapidly.

Errors in calls to the software listed (in the above paragraph) would not be considered a system error. For example, an improperly written SQL query can't be considered a system error. If incorrect data returned by the operating system was caused by omitting a parameter on a Windows API call, it couldn't be considered a system error either.

System errors can be extremely difficult to identify and pin down to a specific part or software module. Even when the offending module has been identified, it may be very difficult to do anything about it. If a network card is malfunctioning, it can simply be replaced by an operational card. Unfortunately, the solution isn't as simple if the offending component is a piece of software. Even when the software vendors will acknowledge that the problem belongs to them, it can be a long time before a new version which addresses the problem is developed and released.

The only feasible choices available in many system-error situations are 1) workarounds and 2) selecting a different vendor. If you absolutely must stick with this particular vendor, e.g., your entire shop uses the "XYZ" database package and it contains the problem, then you will probably need to find a way to endure until a patch or new version becomes available. Frequently, vendors will work with you to find a workaround solution or help minimize the error's impact until a fix becomes available. If the vendor isn't providing the desired level of assistance, the user community can be enlisted for their solutions, suggestions. An active user group or an online forum can be of tremendous value in this situation.

It may be that the software in question might be a component which is readily available from more than one vendor. If, for example, the problem is in the ODBC driver and the vendor isn't being responsive to requests for assistance, you could simply obtain another ODBC driver from a different vendor. Some additional effort might be required to install and convert to the new component, but if the error in question is a show stopper, then there isn't much choice.

System errors are more prevalent in client/server development projects for the simple reason that more vendors are involved than in traditional systems. The number of distinct components (both hardware and software) in a client/server system dwarfs comparable numbers in traditional systems. This is an area where client/server systems have proven to be significantly more complicated to develop and maintain than the previous generation of systems.

Another cause for the increased number of system errors in client/server systems is the heightened rate at which new releases of software are issued. The software industry is undergoing dramatic changes and vendors are releasing new versions of their products to meet the changing demands and requirements of the customers. The result is that products are being produced, updated, and made obsolete in record time. Unfortunately this trend is unlikely to change. If anything, it will likely accelerate.

Combining the two above-mentioned trends yields an almost geometric increase in the number of changes a client/server system undergoes. Assume a client/server system has 25 distinct software products embedded in it or significantly affecting it. Further assume that each vendor releases a new release, patch, or update on a quarterly basis. The result is 100 software revisions will be installed on the system per year, roughly two changes per week. How many bugs will be inadvertently included in these 100 releases? How many errors will be made while installing these 100 changes?

2.1.3.3 Communications Errors. While all types of computer systems communicate with somebody or something, the amount of communication involved in client/server systems is significantly higher than other environments. The entire client/server paradigm is built upon the concept of dividing processing between different levels. Having the system separated in this manner demands that communications between the levels be easy, quick, and accurate. When communications between levels begin to falter, a client/server system becomes dysfunctional very quickly.

Communications errors could appropriately have been grouped with system errors. They are addressed separately for a couple of reasons. The first is that communications are critical for client/server systems. Another reason is that communications errors as a group are fairly common in client/server systems.

The ways in which communications can fail are so diverse as to be almost unpredictable. A few examples of how these errors manifest themselves are provided in Table 2.5. This list starts with examples at the client end of the system and progresses toward the server end. The examples provided here are not intended to represent the entire spectrum of communications possibilities.

There are many ways of troubleshooting a communications problem. One would be to see how widespread the problem is. If it affects a single client machine, then it's likely to be either hardware or software in that

TABLE 2.5

Error Categories

Network card is bad

Poorly connected cable

Bad communications cable

Communications software is bad

Invalid user login

User privileges are inadequate

Backbone cable is bad or cut

Router is down or bad

Addressing problem

Server communications equipment is bad

machine. If all users in the same area are affected then it might be cabling or a router problem. If no users whatsoever can access the server, then the problem is likely to be found in the server itself.

2.1.3.4 Logic Errors. This category of error occurs when code is written to meet system requirements. If the program doesn't perform as the requirements dictate, the result is a logic error. The responsibility for logic errors rests entirely in the hands of the developers. Some techniques for minimizing the number of logic errors are described here.

Program variables should always be declared and typed. Some development environments don't require that all variables be declared. When variables aren't declared, a typographical error can inadvertently create a new variable. Referencing this new variable will almost certainly create a logic error. As an aside, project standards should demand that all variables be declared and documented at the top of the code module.

Don't assume that a variable will be initialized to a known value. Always initialize a variable within the code to be certain it has the value the code expects it to have.

Complicated IF..THEN..END IF should be written with great care. It is easy to make mistakes in this type of coding. If the CASE statement is available, it can significantly simplify the processing logic.

2.1.3.5 User Interface Errors. User interface errors are an area where client/server GUI systems have broken new ground. These interfaces have provided examples of both exceptional as well as dreadfully poor user interfaces. Systems which combine pictures, graphs, grids, audio, and video components can translate an enormous amount of information to users very quickly. On the flip side, it can also enable the developer to produce a system which is complex, confusing, and extremely slow. It's up to the design team and the developer to determine which type of system will be produced.

Objects on windows which don't function as expected are certainly included in the rolls of user interface errors. Drop-down list boxes which don't display all the expected data are errors. Edit masks and validation checks on input fields which don't format or validate user input are also errors.

Many GUI applications share data between windows. When data is modified or updated in one window, the values displayed in a related window are refreshed to reflect the new values. This aspect of a GUI application needs to be thoroughly tested.

Inconsistency is an interface error which becomes extremely frustrating to users and isn't always grasped by developers. It isn't likely to be something which is severe enough to prevent a system from being used, but it can certainly prevent users from liking a system.

Inconsistently labeled fields and controls are a prime example of this type of error. In some windows the button to leave the window might be labeled "Exit," while in others it is labeled "Return." A button which writes changes to the database might be titled "Save" or "Update" in different windows. The label for the customer number field might vary between "Cust#," "Customer No.," and "Customer Number" within a system.

Inconsistently available functionality is another form of interface error. If one window has a certain functionality, all similar windows should provide the same functionality. For example, the ability to sort a grid or datawindow on columns dynamically chosen by the user is one feature which should be available throughout the client/server system. Another example is the ability to print out (to a printer or a file) the contents of every datawindow or grid in the system. If functionality like the above is available in some windows, but not others, users won't likely feel comfortable with the system. As they attempt to use a function which isn't always available, they will become frustrated very quickly.

2.1.3.6 Data Errors.   Data errors are errors which occur when accessing the database. In many ways these errors are indistinguishable from logic or coding errors. The rationale behind listing them separately is that most client/server systems interact with relational databases. Access to relational databases will almost certainly be via SQL (structured query language). SQL, for all its advantages, presents distinct challenges for developers. It is relatively easy to become familiar with SQL. Fundamental statements such as SELECT, INSERT, DELETE, and UPDATE are relatively easy to pick up and use. So far so good. It is only when developers move up to the next level of SQL complexity that they start running into problems. Multitable joins, unions, complicated inserts, aggregates, and subselect statements can be deceptively difficult. Sad to say, most developers don't get sufficient SQL training. Nor does everyone become a master of the language even with long-term exposure to it. In reality, many GUI developers write just enough SQL code to make themselves dangerous.

Being a very high level language, SQL packs a lot of power into relatively few statements. It also packs an enormous amount of danger! Combining a powerful language with inadequately trained developers makes for a hazardous situation. An unlimited number of rows can be accessed, inserted, modified, or deleted with a single SQL statement. One incorrectly written SQL statement can drag a database system to its knees. It could quickly obtain locks on commonly used tables and prevent other users from accessing them. Worse yet, it could delete an enormous amount of valuable data.

The solution to this predicament is twofold. First, make sure that developers get adequate SQL education. Training classes can be held in-house and taught by knowledgeable SQL veterans. It could also take the form of a computer-based training (CBT) package. Even less formal could be self-taught lessons utilizing one of the many excellent SQL books on the market. The route taken to achieve SQL proficiency doesn't really matter. What is important is that your development team reaches a level of competency.

A second solution to avoiding SQL database problems is to have a cadre of SQL experts either write or approve all SQL code included in the system. This approach has both advantages and disadvantages. It is probably more efficient and generates fewer errors if the "experts" handle all the code. The disadvantage of this approach is that the entire project is dependent on a small number of individuals. Should they be less competent than necessary or if they transfer, retire, die, or quit, the project would be in dire straits.

The best solution is probably a combination of both approaches. First, make sure all developers receive adequate training. As stated previously, this doesn't have to be either expensive or time-consuming. Second, encourage and enforce the practice that all SQL code must be examined by someone other than the author before it can be moved to production. This solution provides the best of both worlds.

Some aspects of SQL coding which need to be specifically examined are listed in the following. There are certainly items not included, but the major areas are addressed.

The error code returned must be checked after every SQL query. Error checking shouldn't be limited to just statements which alter data; it should be done after select statements as well. This is probably an area where most development teams could use improvement. Before code is accepted into the configuration management system, this logic should be examined.

Updates have the capability of altering entire tables with a single statement. Having this capability, they must be carefully examined to be certain that only the expected data set gets changed. Again, the idea of requiring at least one other developer inspecting SQL code applies here.

Stored procedures are sets of SQL statements which reside in the database and execute when called. There are numerous advantages associated with the use of stored procedures. The primary advantage is that stored procedures execute faster because the database system has already compiled their query plan. Stored procedures are also advantageous because they can be reused by multiple developers. This reduces the amount of code written. Since stored procedures are so powerful and widely used, it is essential that they be efficient and accurate. Stored procedures should be written by the most experienced SQL programmers and carefully examined before being moved into production.

Triggers are a specialized type of stored procedure. Triggers are associated with a specific activity on a specified table. For example, when an insert is made into the "class" table, a trigger can be written to make a corresponding insert into the "rooms" table. Like stored procedures, triggers should be developed by an experienced SQL programmer or database administrator (DBA).

A *null* is a special value indicating that no specific data is present in the field. Assume the field "gender" exists in the employee table. Normal values are "M" or "F." What if the data entry clerk doesn't know the gender of the applicant because that field wasn't completed? It would be better to store a null than guess at the gender. Users of the system would realize that the null value indicates that this information isn't known. Use of nulls has a definite advantage, but they complicate the database significantly. All code in the system which handles null values needs to be carefully scrutinized to be certain that the logic has been implemented correctly.

Deleting data from a database needs to be handled with a great deal of care. Obviously, any function which deletes data is one which potentially has a tremendous impact on the system. The code which actually performs the delete operations should be examined very closely. As an aside, users should always be required to confirm a delete operation. A pop-up window needs to present an unambiguous warning that data is about to be deleted, and users should indicate their agreement by clicking the "OK" button.

Delete operations need to be reviewed especially in light of the concept of *referential integrity* (RI). RI implies that data in one table references data in another table. For example, assume a database has a customer table and an order table. Data in the order table would include references to which the customer placed the order. If customer "X" is deleted from the customer table, what should be done with rows in the order table which document orders placed by "X"? Many database packages allow the DBA to define in advance how the RDBMS system will handle deletes from related tables. Decisions made in advance will have an enormous impact on the system. These decisions must be extremely well-thought out and consistently made.

A *join* is the ability to retrieve data from more than one table in a relational database. An example would be to join a table listing customers and a table listing their orders to list all orders made by a specific customer. Joins which involve two or three tables are fairly easy to understand. However, if they reference a large number of tables, then they become increasingly difficult to understand and code correctly. The consequences of incorrectly written joins can range from very poor response time to an incorrect answer being returned to the user.

One of the detriments of SQL and relational database systems is that it is exceedingly easy to be deceived by incorrect results. The query may look correct and the result set may appear legitimate, but in fact both may be wrong. This is especially true if the test environment includes a database with a minimal amount of data. Aggressive, probing testing against a realistic database must be performed on all but the simplest of SQL statements.

Many database systems allow developers to define their own user data types (UDTs). Creating datatypes specifically for the system can be a useful, efficient decision. UDTs can be created to represent the data in a manner particular to how the company carries out its business. This decision carries along with it a great deal of responsibility. In some cases the user must also write the code to perform logical operations on UDTs. When this is the situation, a significant amount of planning and testing must be done to be certain they have been implemented correctly.

Security is an important factor for most client/server systems. As crucial business functions are moved onto client/server systems, the need to protect this data grows in importance. Security in a client/server system can be implemented at numerous levels. One such implementation is accomplished by restricting which users can access data and what level of access (read, write, delete, update) they have. If security is implemented at the database level, then a significant amount of design and planning effort needs to be done when the database is being designed and implemented. An improper security solution can allow invalid access to critical data and deny legitimate access attempts.

A *schema* is a subsection of the database organized by the owner. The accounting department may be the owner of a number of tables, and the human resources (HR) department may own their own collection of tables. Each of the groups of tables comprise a schema. Schemas allow more than one table to exist with the same name. The full, formal name of database tables usually is in the following format, "database_name"."owner"."table_name", but a table can be referred to with just the table name alone.

This naming convention allows the developer to be as specific or general as he or she desires. If just a table name is specified, the RDBMS package usually searches the schema of the user. If a table is found in that schema, it terminates the search, another table with the same name in a different schema wouldn't be discovered or used. If no table with the specified name is found in the default schema, the schema of the database owner (dbo) is searched. Normally widely used tables are owned by the dbo, while individuals own only temporary tables.

While the concept of schemas and escalating search patterns is very powerful, it requires a certain degree of knowledge and sophistication on the part of the developer. The developer could very easily create a local version of a particular table. Should the intent be to access the dbo table and a local table is accessed instead, database errors will almost certainly result from this oversight.

Dates are probably the most complicated and cumbersome of the common types of data handled in client/server systems. The primary reason for this is that no two relational database systems seem to handle dates in the same way. Additional date-related complications can develop if the client/server system has to interact with multiple RDBMS systems.

Some of the ways in which dates are handled differently between database packages are described in Table 2.6. Specific examples are provided for in some of the more common database systems.

TABLE 2.6

Date
Representation In
RDBMS Systems

Date ranges - acceptable ranges of values differ drastically among packages. A Sybase SQL Server smalldatetime field ranges between 1/1/1900 and 6/6/2079 while date in Microsoft Access can range between 1/1/100 and 12/31/1999.

Internal Storage Representation - CA/Ingres stores dates as tenths of seconds since a base date. Sybase SQL Server stores dates as the number of days since a base date

Base Date - CA/Ingres's base date is 1/1/1970. Sybase SQL Server's base date is 1/1/1900. Microsoft Access's base date is 12/30/1999.

Size of Date - Sybase SQL Server smalldatetime requires 4 bytes while CA/Ingres requires 12 bytes. Many other packages dates require 7 or 8 bytes.

Default Input Format - the expected input format for Microsoft Access is "MM/DD/YY." Oracle's default format is "DD-MMM-YY."

2.1.3.7 Coding Errors.   While client/server development packages such as Visual Basic and PowerBuilder require that significantly less code be written, a certain amount of source code must still be generated. Any time a programmer writes code, there is a chance for errors to occur. Some errors are violations of syntax and will quickly be caught by the compiler. Many development packages provide additional help for the developer in this area. PowerBuilder, for example, won't allow the script for an event to be saved if it has errors which prevent it from being compiled. Developers aren't always particularly fond of this feature, but it certainly brings the error to their attention in a hurry.

Beyond such automatic syntax checking, the code for client/server systems needs to be checked just as closely as the code in traditional systems. Checking for coding errors can be done via self-inspection, structured walk-throughs, or informally having developers check each other's code. Different development shops have experienced varying levels of success with each method. A number of studies have found that code reviews are a more effective method of finding errors than testing. A study at NASA's Software Engineering Laboratory found that code reading unearthed almost twice as many errors per hour of effort as testing did.

2.1.3.8 Testing Errors.   Everyone in the testing effort seems to greatly enjoy finding and isolating a software error. Most developers and testers seem to intuitively sense that a system has only a finite number of errors, and each one which is found and extinguished moves the project that much closer to completion. In the afterglow of identifying an error, it is extremely important to properly catalogue the error. It's equally crucial to make sure that the error is correctly fixed and the correction is propagated to all appropriate locations. There are few greater frustrations in the testing world than finding and fixing an error only to run across it again later in the testing process. It makes you feel like all your efforts are for naught!

Gathering and analyzing statistics on the types of errors must be an ongoing activity. Statistics at any given moment provide a snapshot of that point in time. The development environment and errors encountered are constantly changing and statistics must be constantly updated. As increased training or improved techniques diminish (or eradicate) one particular error type, other types will become proportionally more prevalent. Out-of-date statistics wouldn't accurately indicate what has become the most prevalent type of error.

There are numerous others factors which change the development environment and proportion of error types. Changing from one development tool to another, e.g., changing from C++ to PowerBuilder, would likely affect the types of errors introduced. It might, for instance, cut down drastically on the number of coding errors. Migrating to a different development or deployment hardware or software platform would influence the types of errors. Changing relational database management systems (RDBMS) is likely to have an effect. A significant change in the experience level of development personnel could increase the number of errors in systems as well as the error type distribution.

Organizations which are just beginning their client/server development efforts are at a disadvantage compared to other groups because they don't have background data on the distribution of various kinds of errors. Sage advice to them would be to thoroughly study trade journals for articles and papers on this topic. Attempts to network with client/server-experienced organizations could also be very informative.

Unfortunately, the experience level with client/server system development is limited industrywide. As the level of experience grows, hopefully the knowledge base regarding errors will be captured and taken advantage of.

2.1.4 Testing versus Debugging

There is a fundamental difference between the testing and debugging processes. Testing is a process of executing a program with the intent of finding an error. It can be done by the original developer, a test team member, a member of the quality assurance (QA) team or an end user. The tests being performed can be rigid and formal or very unofficial.

No matter who is doing the testing or exactly what is being tested, the goal is the same—finding errors.

Debugging is the process which begins with an identified error and continues by trying to find out how it is possible for the error to occur. The error may have been caused by any of the error categories listed in Table 2.4. It could have been a misunderstanding of the functional specifications, a system error, a communications errors, etc. In some extreme situations the error might have been caused by the conjunction of more than one error type. It may, for instance, have been caused when a systems error and a communications error occurred simultaneously. Errors of this type can be extremely difficult to resolve.

2.1.5 Designer versus Tester

Testing can be successfully performed by a variety of individuals. Developers, quality assurance personnel, or users can all be productive in the testing process. Debugging, in contrast, can only be effectively performed by developers or analysts. Only they have the knowledge of and experience with both the development environment and the system as it was designed and built.

Unfortunately this introduces a significant problem. Developers are all too often placed in situations where they are the primary (or only) people testing a system. Even worse, they are frequently assigned to test their own code. Developing and testing are innately different types of activities. Development is an act of creating or building something, e.g., a module or an entire system. The sole objective of testing is to prove that the module doesn't work. There is a fundamental conflict between these activities. It isn't wise to assume that a single individual can perform effectively in fulfilling two diametrically opposing roles. With this caveat in mind, it is better to limit the involvement of developers in the testing effort. The most appropriate role for them to fill is to perform testing at the lowest level possible, unit testing.

2.1.6 Test Case Design

Tests don't just appear like Aphrodite out of the surf; they must be built. Exemplary tests must be designed, documented and polished to the same degree that programming code is. Developers and management are inept or fooling themselves if they think that effective testing can be done without planning. Successful testing without design is just as likely as successful client/server system building without any design being done.

The concept of testing without planning reminds me a lot of school yard pickup football games. The standard "play" called during those games was "everybody block somebody and go out for a pass." This play seldom worked, and if it did, it was pure luck. Testing without designing and laying out test cases, and assignments, is like playing football without designing plays. There is very little chance that without the necessary groundwork your testing will be complete, effective, and reproducible. Chapter 5, "Test Management," discusses how to design test cases, assign resources, and schedule the testing effort to improve the odds of a successful client/server system.

2.1.7 Areas Which Deserve Specific Focus During Testing

The analogy of comparing errors with bugs does our industry a disservice. "Bugs" in computer systems are mistakes, nothing more and nothing less. They exist in systems because everyone involved in the development process is a human being and human beings by our very nature make errors. To euphemistically call them "bugs" is to deny both our humanity and responsibility. I have made a concerted effort to avoid the use of the term "bug" throughout this entire book.

After making my soapbox presentation in the above paragraph, there is one apt analogy between software errors and the creepy, crawly type of bugs. When dealing with bugs you can count on two things. One, they're hiding in areas you avoid looking and two, when you find one you're likely to find more in that same vicinity.

Software errors are very much like this. Errors have a tendency to crop up in certain areas, areas which developers tend to hurry through. These areas deserve more forethought, planning, and respect. Some areas in which errors tend to crop up are listed in the following sections.

Also like crawly bugs, software errors tend to cluster together. This could be because developers tend to make the same types of mistakes over and over throughout their careers. It could be because the schedule pushes them to hurry through the code, and consequently a lot of mistakes are made in certain areas. It could also be because people don't always work as hard or as diligently as they should. Whatever the reason, it is usually the case that where one error occurs you're bound to find others. Keep this in mind during your testing efforts.

2.1.7.1 Input Validation Testing.   One of the many corollaries to Murphy's Law is that if you make the input validation of a system idiot-proof, an imaginative idiot will figure a way to get bad data past all the checks. It may seem that this "law" is overstated, but there are times it seems to be accurate.

Input validation in client/server systems is both more and less complicated than the same process in traditional systems. How can it be both more and less complicated? It's more complicated because the user has a great deal more flexibility in how, when, and where data can be input into a GUI system. Being ready to properly validate this barrage of data makes the validation process more complicated. But it's less complicated because of the tools that most development packages and RDBMS systems bestow onto developers.

The tools being referred to are rules in the database packages and edit checks which can be built into the front ends. PowerBuilder, for example, allows developers to create validity checks once, name them, and assign them to many input fields in an application. This enables the development team to create a single edit check for a database field and apply it in every window where that value can be entered. A significant amount of coding can be avoided by using edit checks.

Relational database systems like Sybase allow validity checking to be applied at an even lower level. There are two methods of enforcing validity restrictions at the individual column level: rules and triggers.

A rule can be created which specifies values that can exist in the affected column. Each time an SQL statement is executed which inserts or updates a value, the database engine checks the value against any rules created for that column. If the value doesn't pass the criteria specified in the rule, the SQL statement is rejected.

A trigger is a specialized stored procedure which is fired (executed) when an insert, update, or delete statement is applied to the affected table. Triggers can be used to enforce data entry or update validity checking. While rules and triggers can both perform validity checking, triggers enable more complex data checking to be performed. A trigger could, for example, verify that the order number specified in the insert statement exists in the order table. Rules cannot enforce validity checking of this nature.

Rules and triggers can help relieve developers from checking data many times throughout an application. If rules or triggers have been created, developers don't even need to be aware of the validity checks being enforced. Unfortunately these tools don't do the work by themselves. Developers or DBAs must design, code, and implement validation checking at the column level and employ it uniformly across the entire client/server system.

2.1.7.2 Path Testing. A path is any possible sequence of instructions which lead from the beginning of a module to its end. Depending on the number of control statements in the module, there can be from one to an almost infinite number of paths in a module. Examples of control statements which affect the path count are IF..THEN..ELSE, CASE, FOR..NEXT, etc. Each control statement causes the number of paths to be multiplied by the number of junction points within the control statement. A list of control statements and the number of possible paths they generate is listed in Figure 2.1.

Figure 2.2 shows a PowerScript code snippet from a PowerBuilder application. This relatively small module has **60** possible paths. This value is calculated in the following manner. The CASE statement results in five possible paths, one for each case plus one if none of the case statements is true. The "IF i_iReportType = 3 OR i_iReportType = 4" statement has three possible paths, the first IF, plus the ELSEIF, plus the condition

Figure 2-1
Control Statements
and The Number of
Paths They Generate

Control Statement Type	Number of Paths
IF..END IF	2
IF..ELSE..END IF	2
IF..ELSEIF..END IF	3
IF..ELSEIF..ELSE..END IF	3
IF..ELSEIF..ELSEIF..END IF	4
IF..ELSEIF..ELSEIF..ELSE..END IF	4
CASE statement with x cases and CASE ELSE	$x+1$
CASE statement with x cases and no CASE ELSE	$x+1$
FOR..NEXT	2
DO WHILE..LOOP	2
DO UNTIL..LOOP	2

```
i_iReportType = message.DoubleParm


// Set Title Bar

CHOOSE CASE i_iReportType

   CASE 1

      this.title = "Report - Monthly Expense"

      dw_criteria.dataobject = "d_submitted_report"

   CASE 2

      this.title = "Report - Travel Expense"

      dw_criteria.dataobject = "d_submitted_report"

   CASE 3

      this.title = "Graph - Expense by Department"

      dw_criteria.dataobject = "d_start_end_date"

   CASE 4

      this.title = "Report - Expense by Account"

      dw_criteria.dataobject = "d_start_end_date"

END CHOOSE


// Initialize external datawindow

dw_criteria.InsertRow(0)


// For reports 3 and 4, insert a row and set default values

IF i_iReportType = 3 OR i_iReportType = 4 THEN
```

Figure 2-2
Code Example
Demonstrating Paths

```
// Default start date to first of this month and end date to last

// of this month

dw_criteria.SetItem(1, "start_date", Date(Year(Today()),Month(Today()), 1))

IF Month(Today()) = 12 THEN

    dtEndDate = Date("12/31/" + String(Year(Today())))

ELSE

    dtEndDate = RelativeDate(Date(Year(Today()),Month(Today()) + 1,1), -1)

END IF

dw_criteria.SetItem(1, "end_date", dtEndDate)

dw_criteria.SetColumn("Start_date")

ELSEIF i_iReportType = 1 OR i_iReportType = 2 THEN

    // For monthly and travel expenses, retrieve the dddw of submitted reports.

    datawindowchild dwc

    dw_criteria.GetChild("report_number", dwc)

    dwc.SetTransObject(SQLCA)

    // i_iReportType = 1 for monthly and = 2 for travel

    IF dwc.Retrieve(g_w_mdi.i_nEmployee, i_iReportType) > 0 THEN

        dw_criteria.SetText(dwc.GetItemString(1, "descr"))

    END IF

END IF
```

Figure 2-2
Continued

where neither is taken. The "IF Month(Today())" statement has two possible paths, one for the first IF, plus one for the ELSE condition. The "IF dwc.Retrieve(g_w_mdi_" statement has two possible paths, one if the condition is true and one if the condition is false. Calculating the total number of paths is achieved by multiplying the number of possible paths of each control statement. For this code the calculation is $5 * 3 * 2 * 2 = 60$.

Path testing refers to the process of testing the paths through a module. Ideal test conditions would be to test each possible path. Achieving the ideal isn't usually practical. The above relatively simple code yielded 60 paths. Assume each window has 7 scripts as complicated as it. If the system being tested has 100 windows, then the system has $60 * 7 * 100$ or 42,000 possible paths. This represents a moderately sized application and the calculation doesn't even take into consideration code in functions. How long would it take to design and execute 42,000 test cases? It's not realistic that any project will ever perform that many tests.

Since complete path testing isn't likely to be achieved, is it still worthwhile to perform path testing? The answer here is an unqualified "yes." It becomes necessary then to reduce the objective from testing all possible paths to testing enough paths to gain a high level of confidence in the module. The minimum set of paths (call this the fundamental set of tested paths) which needs to be tested must assure that:

- Every decision statement is taken at least once in each direction.
- Each statement is executed once as a minimum.

Applying the concept of testing, the fundamental set of tested paths to the code in Figure 2.1 yields a minimum of five paths. Figure 2.3 details how five paths cover the fundamental set of tested paths for the above code example. While this set of paths to be tested isn't inconsequential, it is significantly easier to achieve than 14,000 tests cases.

2.1.7.3 Transaction Testing. From a design point of view, a transaction is a distinct unit of work. From an RDBMS standpoint, a transaction is a set of SQL operations which are executed together or not at all. From a user's perspective, a transaction is likely to be an operation she performs which is completely successful or entirely removed. A classic example is a bank customer's attempt to transfer $100 from his savings account to his checking account. This transaction consists of two distinct actions, deduct $100 from the savings account in question and add $100 to the appropriate checking account. If for some reason the client/server system can't successfully perform both actions, then it shouldn't execute either.

```
Test #    Values required for this test    Code executed by this test case

1         i_iReportType = 1                CASE 1, ELSE portion of outer IF block

          dwc.Retrieve result <>= 0

2         i_iReportType = 1,               CASE 1, ELSE portion of outer IF block and

          dwc.Retrieve result > 0          the final IF statement

3         i_iReportType = 2                CASE 2

4         i_iReportType = 3                CASE 3, IF portion of outer IF block and

          Month(Today()) = 12              IF portion of "IF Month(Today())" block

5         i_iReportType = 4                CASE 4, IF portion of outer IF block and

          Month(Today()) != 12             ELSE portion of "IF Month(Today())" block
```

Figure 2-3
Cases To Explicitly
Test Paths

Transaction testing is the process of identifying and testing all transactions in the system. While this sounds forbidding, it isn't quite as bad as it appears. First of all, most operations in client/server systems are read oriented. Pure read operations are atomic, i.e., each select is a transaction in and of itself. The transactions which need to be identified and examined are those which:

- Enter data (rows) into multiple tables.
- Enter data (rows) into a single table and update rows in one or more other tables.
- Update rows in more than one table.

Transactions such as these shouldn't be easy to find because they will almost certainly require special coding. In many cases the development tool can automatically handle transactions which affect a single table. DataWindows in PowerBuilder are an example of this. PowerBuilder can generate the SQL for select, update, and delete operations. However, when multiple tables are involved, PowerBuilder can't generate the code. It must be written by the developer. A greater than normal amount of handwritten SQL is a very good indicator that a complex, multitable transaction is being processed. Test cases to thoroughly test such transactions should include:

- Enter a legitimate, complete record. Verify that the transaction is executed correctly.

- Enter a record and deliberately omit a required data item. Verify that neither table was changed.

- Enter a record and deliberately include data which won't pass validation checks. Verify that neither table was changed.

- Enter a record which refers to a nonexistent reference in a second table, i.e., an order with a nonexistent part number. Verify that neither table was changed.

- Enter a legitimate, complete record. Before the transaction completes attempt to abort the operation. Verify that all involved tables were changed or none were changed.

Transaction testing should also verify that there is no possibility of "user think time" being included within a transaction. An example of this would allow a user to begin a transaction and enter a row into one table and delay indefinitely until a record is inserted into a second table which completes the transaction. Allowing a situation like this isn't an error in the traditional sense, but it certainly opens the door very wide to allow deadlocks and performance problems.

When updating database records, there is the possibility of losing a transaction. Assume user A selects the details on client XYZ. Shortly after that, user B also selects the details on the same client. User A modifies the client's telephone number and writes the record to the database. Shortly after that, user B changes the client's zip code and writes the record to the database. What happens to the telephone number? Will the new value written by A be retained, or will it be overwritten because B had an outdated value on her screen and updated from it? Actually the correct answer is either. It depends on how the developer programmed it. Testing must be performed to be certain that updates such as these aren't lost.

2.1.7.4 Loop Testing.   A *loop* is a statement (or group of statements) which allow a block of code to be executed zero, one, or many times. The exact number of times which the loop iterates depends on the loop control variable. All GUI development tools allow a number of methods for creating and executing loops.

Testing loops is a specialized type of path testing. It deserves special mention because loops are a bit more complicated than most statements. The chance of errors is significantly higher in loops than other code constructs. The testing for any given loop should include test cases which specifically test each of the following conditions:

- The loop is not executed at all.
- A single execution of the loop.
- Two iterations of the loop.
- A number of iterations which reflects typical execution of the loop.
- One less than the maximum number of iterations if a maximum number exists.
- The maximum number of iterations.
- More iterations than the maximum number.

Each of the above cases represents a situation which will certainly occur once the system has been put into production. If testing doesn't include each of these conditions, then there is no assurance that it will be properly handled. Special attention should be paid to "For" loops which increment or decrement by a number other than one (i.e. –1, 0.5, 1.5, etc.). Since programmers only infrequently increment by a value other than one, there is a higher likelihood of this being done incorrectly.

Many development tools allow loops to be nested, i.e., an inner loop completely resides within an outer loop. This technique is frequently used in sorting arrays of values. Nested loops require an even higher degree of attention during the testing process. The number of times through the logic increases geometrically when nested loops are involved. For example, if the outer loop iterates 100 times and the inner loop also iterates 100 times, the total number of times the statements inside the inner loop will execute is 10,000. It isn't practical to generate and execute this many test cases. The answer is to test smarter, not harder. Test conditions which should be included are:

- Set the outer loop to its minimum value and run the inner loop through all possible cases.
- Set the inner loop to its minimum value and run the outer loop through all possible cases.

- Run a test with all loop values at their minimum.
- Run a test with all loop values at their maximum.
- Set the outer loop to its maximum value and run the inner loop through all possible cases.
- Set the inner loop to its maximum value and run the outer loop through all possible cases.

2.1.7.5 Boundary Value Testing. Boundary value testing refers to tests specifically designed to test system reaction when values referenced in conditional statements are at or near boundaries. The best example of the statements being tested are "IF_Then..Else_End If" blocks. An example of such a statement is:

```
IF a <= 123 Then
    b= 1
ELSEIF a >= 123 Then
    b= 2
ELSE
    b= 3
END IF
```

Boundary test cases for the above block should include at least the following values for a: 122, 123, 124. By the way, what will be the value of b if a equals 123? Will it be 1 or 2?

The first IF clause will be executed and variable b will be set to 1.

2.1.7.6 Date Testing. Dates are a complicated enough data type that they deserve special mention. The input format of date values was covered in an earlier section. Here the testing aspects of dates are mentioned. Date arithmetic operations can be very convoluted. Most client/server tools don't allow these operations to be performed directly on date variables. Most require a function call to add or subtract a unit of time to a date value. For example, the following statement would add 30 days to a date value.

```
Tickle_date = RelativeDate(Today(), 30)
```

Code to calculate the number of days until the end of the month, or the date of the next work day, can be fairly complicated and error prone. Unfortunately, most client/server development tools provide a proprietary set of date-related functions. The experience and knowledge gathered in one tool is not directly applicable in other tools. Test cases should be contrived which thoroughly test all date arithmetic.

2.1.7.7 Export Testing.   Most client/server systems export data in one format or another. The export may be a hard copy suitable only for reading. It may be electronic output which becomes input to another system. Sometimes the export is an ASCII file, an electronic copy of a report, a comma-delimited file, or a spreadsheet file.

The export process might allow users to specify that only certain data be exported. Examples of this might be orders posted between two user-supplied dates or orders going to a certain client. Testing needs to verify that the export includes only the data which meets specified criteria.

Each type of export needs to be tested. It is also necessary to test what might happen if there is no data to be exported, if an incorrect output device has been specified, or if the output device is full.

2.1.7.8 Security.   Security is always important in a client/server system. In some systems, such as financial systems, it is of primary importance. Testing security is extremely important and often an overlooked area of the testing process. Security can be implemented in a number of ways. It may be imposed via application navigation. The principal behind this concept is that users are locked into certain paths through an application depending on the ID. The windows in their paths allow them to access only the data they need to see. Security may also be imposed at the database level. Users are granted rights to access certain tables, views, columns, rows, etc.

Test cases to check security will rely heavily on how security was implemented. If security has been implemented via application navigation, then special attention must be paid to be certain that users are truly restricted to the windows they need to see. Verify that buttons and menu items which would allow them additional application access are properly disabled or made invisible. Tests must also be developed which attempt to break out of the restrictions.

Security that is based on database grants being created give each user grants to the necessary tables. A user could also be added to a group which has the access she requires. Tests to verify that grants have been properly distributed will lean towards trying to access data which hasn't been granted to the tester.

Testing must also be made to verify that access to the database doesn't totally bypass the application. Attempts could be made to access the database directly via an interactive SQL session. Application navigation won't prevent this type of illegal access. Nonusers could also attempt to access files containing logins and passwords. Initialization files (*.INI) frequently contain information of this nature.

2.1.7.9 Login and Logout Testing. Logging into a system is the gateway to the system. This gate must be as safe as possible without overly taxing the users. Tests should be performed to verify that only legitimate users can access the system. Excessive login failures can indicate an intruder is attempting to gain access to the system. When this occurs special precautions should kick in. Among these precautions are:

- That particular client machine should not be allowed to connect until a security officer permits it.
- The user ID should be disabled until a security officer re-enables it.
- A log of the possible intrusion attempt should be made.
- A security officer should be contacted via e-mail, pager, etc.

Testing should be done to verify that all appropriate precautions are being taken after the prescribed number of login failures.

Login Ids and passwords are normally the keys to user access. Users should be forced to change their passwords frequently. Their new password should not be allowed to be the same as the previous password or some slight derivation of their previous password. Test cases should include attempts to violate password restraints.

Many client/server systems are considered sensitive enough that idle client machines are automatically logged off. If the user hasn't moved the mouse or touched the keyboard in a certain period of time, the application is either locked or exited. If the system being tested has this requirement, this capability must be carefully tested. Is it possible that a screen-saver type program might cause an idle situation to be missed? The method of logout implementation must take into consideration that the user may be in the middle of a transaction. Will such a transaction be aborted or committed?

2.2 Testing Goals

The goal of testing both traditional and client/server systems is to verify that the finished product performs as expected and demanded by the customer. It really doesn't matter whether the system in question is a batch program running on a mainframe or the latest in GUI packages running on a Pentium PC, if it doesn't perform as the user expects it to, it's a failure. The task in the testing phase of the development effort is to assure that the system is everything the customer requires.

The statement that a system should "meet customer expectations" is pretty general. Like many general statements, it's hard to defend or refute until some specifics are provided. Some specific goals of testing are outlined in Table 2.7.

2.2.1 Ensure That the System Meets Published Functional Specifications

One area where there is absolutely no difference between testing different types of systems is that published specifications must exist for all systems! The client/server system must perform all the requirements in the specifications. Each window, report, input screen, batch process, pick list, etc., must perform as laid out in the specifications. Tests must be designed, built, and executed to verify that the completed system adheres to the specifications.

A developer who works on a system may think that a lack of functional specifications will work to his advantage. After all, if nothing has been agreed to, how can the client (internal or external) claim that the system isn't complete? In reality, it doesn't usually turn out this way. A lack of specifications will almost certainly cause a problem at the end of the project. The client will claim that the system isn't complete, while the developer will state the contrary. If a developer or vendor cares about his reputation, then attempting to hoodwink a client in this matter is a big mistake. At best the client will trash your reputation among all their acquaintances. At worst, you will end up in court. In either situation the lack of functional specs won't allow you to easily avoid delivering a fully functional system. Do yourself and your client a favor and make sure specifications exist at the onset of the effort. Then endeavor to deliver a system that meets them.

Rapid application development (RAD) projects frequently are ones which tend to "overlook" specifications. The iterative joint design, development, demonstrate cycle isn't conducive to laying out specifications in advance. It would be easy to allow RAD to be an exception

TABLE 2.7	Ensure the System Meets Published Functional Specifications
Testing Goals	Verify Performance Requirements Have Been Met
	Stress Testing Confirms the Application Can Handle the Required Load
	Certify That the System Functions on Required Hardware and Software Platforms

to the principle requiring specifications be defined. This would also be a serious mistake. RAD development should concentrate on building the visible user interface of a system which has already had functional specifications defined. The RAD part covers screen design, objects on screens and navigation within the application. Fundamental concepts, such as what the system should accomplish, should already be defined. The boundaries of what the system does and doesn't do needs to be established long before developers sit down with user representatives.

2.2.2 Verify That Performance Requirements Have Been Met

Whether the user community articulated it or not, they have certain expectations concerning performance in mind. If users expect most screens to be completed and usable in two seconds and the system averages five seconds, there are going to be discontented users. A couple of seconds might seem inconsequential to the developer during testing, but that lag can be annoying (or infuriating) to users. The difference in attitude can be attributed chiefly to the number of times the window or function is used by each. The developer brings up the screen a few dozen times during the testing process, while users might access the same screen hundreds of times a day for years. Whose perceptions of performance are more accurate when the problem is examined from this angle?

Being a developer by training and background, the reader might assume I would take the side of developers on this issue. This isn't the case. For most installations on which I've worked, the performance demands of users were realistic and achievable. That isn't to say that they wouldn't like response time to be instantaneous for all displays.

Many developers think that if performance expectations were overlooked, they are off the hook in this area. This isn't the case! Even though the users may have forgotten to mention performance (and developers "forget" to bring up this point), users will certainly have unspoken performance expectations. If the system doesn't meet these standards, users will demand that it meet them. Worse case, they will sabotage or outright reject the system.

Another way in which systems developers occasionally try to play games with performance specifications is by defining when a screen is "available." Available may be defined to be when the first character of a screen is displayed on the monitor. Never mind that it takes 30 seconds for the rest of the display to be loaded. It isn't advisable to start playing semantic games like this. The users aren't going to be fooled by such chicanery. Both sides know that a window isn't truly available until it is fully populated and the user regains control of the mouse or keyboard. Getting into a battle on a losing point such as this just gives the development team a bad reputation among the user community.

2.2.3 Stress Testing Confirms That the Application Can Handle the Required Load

Unless stress or performance testing is performed on an application before it is deployed to the users, no one really can predict what the performance of the client/server system will be.

Testing a system with only one or two users or running it against a minimal database won't allow accurate prediction of the performance in a production environment. Most client/server systems or applications will run quickly when only a single user is utilizing it. Such a system undergoes no contention for system resources. An absence of proper indexing won't be evident and neither will a poor distribution of the database across the available disk drives. Only when stress testing is performed will flaws of this nature be exposed.

2.2.4 Certify That the System Functions on Required Hardware and Software Platforms

Traditional mainframe systems existed in a relatively stable, homogeneous environment. There was a limited diversity of hardware and software. The hardware platforms consisted primarily of a mainframe or midrange computer and a number of dumb terminals. The software environment could be equally straightforward on a mainframe system.

A client/server system, on the other hand, includes a conglomeration of hardware and software. The CPU which the RDBMS runs on is likely to be manufactured by one company. The client hardware will probably consist of a CPU manufactured by another company. In fact, it's almost certain that client hardware will include workstations from a number of manufacturers. Some will be Intel-based workstations and some will be RISC based.

Software in the client/server environment is even more diverse. Generally there is one operating system for the database server and another one for the client machines. The network software is likely to be produced by another vendor. At the client machine level, it's almost certain that each workstation will have a unique combination of software loaded onto it. One user's machine will have the latest version of a word processor, while another user will have a version several generations out of date. Even something as trivial as the autoexec.bat file will assuredly be different on each workstation.

The client/server system must work on the above described collection of hardware and software. To verify that it does function as required, it must be tested. It isn't valid to assume that the application will work on each of the components; testing is mandatory!

2.3 Differences in How Testing Goals Are Achieved

One way in which the testing procedure has changed substantially is that on traditional systems, hands-on time on the computer was at a premium and the turnaround for test results was far from instantaneous. Consequently, the analyst spent significantly more time checking code before submitting it. It was unproductive and disheartening to submit a job, wait half an hour, and find out that a typographical error prevented the program from compiling. As a result, developers spent substantially more time desk-checking the code before submitting it.

Turnaround time ("dead" time) between when a program was submitted and when the results were done printing off of the line printer was frequently spent desk checking the code or designing the next test. This use of "dead" time was a very productive use of time which would be unproductive otherwise.

In contrast, the development environment of client/server systems provides almost instantaneous compilation and execution of applications. If it takes more than a few seconds to compile the latest changes made to a GUI application, it's unusual. The explanation for this is that the power of developers' workstations is enormous compared to a first-generation mainframe computer. Additionally, all of this power is available exclusively to the developer. As a result, developers have less reason to be as careful before compiling a module or executing an application. Current sentiment seems to be that since the compiler is so fast, why not let it do your syntax checking for you. Unfortunately, this can lead to sloppy thinking and coding. Sloppy coding practices are indicative of sloppy design and sloppy testing.

The "dead" time—which had previously been devoted to analysis of the code and the next test to be performed—no longer exists. With the demise of these time blocks, less time is spent doing this valuable preparatory work.

Printouts of modules or entire systems on green-bar, 132-column paper were commonly produced when working on traditional systems. Few client/server projects today have analogous printouts of the entire system. This is partly because the client/server, GUI development environments and their use of event-driven programming break the program logic into smaller, more focused segments of code. The level of code modules seen by developers is almost always at the event level. There might be hundreds of such scripts making up a single screen. The entire system might be built from scores of screens.

Another reason developers seldom see the big picture in a single printout is that a significant amount of code is partitioned throughout the system. Many development platforms allow objects to inherit attributes from ancestor objects of the same class. The code for events in ancestor objects is likely to be stored in another library or source file. Stored procedures, which are commonly used for performance or security purposes, reside in the database at the database server level. Triggers, rules, and table constraints also reside at the database server level. It's difficult to pull together code for objects which reside in such diverse locations.

One last reason for diminished reliance on printouts is the ascension of excellent editing tools. In the bad old days, the typical terminal displayed 24 or 25 lines of display area. Each line contained only 80 columns or characters. Terminals were monochrome. Editors were quite simple and were character oriented. With editors and monitors like this, there were very good reasons for printouts of programs instead of viewing them online. Current WYSIWYG (what you see is what you get) editors are much more powerful and convenient.

3

Testing Tools

3.1 What Are Test Tools?

Client/server systems have become significantly more capable and more complex as they have evolved. As they have grown in complexity, it has become more difficult to test them thoroughly. As more and more organizations build client/server systems upon which their businesses depend, the importance of well-tested software is becoming critical. Test tools to assist the developer and quality control group in the testing process are becoming widely available. The features and capabilities of these tools are growing to match the evolution in the client/server development environments.

3.2 Overview of Tools Useful in Testing Client/Server Systems

There is a great diversity of tools available to assist in testing client/server systems. Some tools are used early on in the testing process, while others come into play much later. The platform on which tools execute ranges from the client workstation to the server. Users of the specific tools also vary greatly. Some tools are used exclusively by developers, others by both developers and QA-ers, and yet others by project management.

The following sections provide a brief overview of tools which are available in the testing process. The order in which they are listed roughly parallels the chronology of when they are used in the development project.

3.2.1 Planning and Management Tools

The first tools encountered when testing client/server systems are most likely ones which assist in designing and laying out the tests needed by the project. Planning tools allow the team to define the testing strategy, estimate the resources which will be required, schedule tests, and allot the resources each requires.

Once testing has begun in earnest, most test management tools provide the ability to document and report on the progress of the testing effort. Reports and graphs are available to detail what has been tested and what testing remains to be done. This enables management to control the effort and estimate when it will be completed.

Also included in management tools are packages used to track software defects. Once a software error has been identified, defect-tracking tools allow it to be catalogued, prioritized, and assigned. This tool helps to assure that each error will be debugged and corrected. Assigning errors to individuals will cut down enormously on instances of them falling through the cracks and being forgotten.

3.2.2 Source Code Control

There may not be unanimous agreement that source code control products should be classified as test tools. Many developers would just as soon that they never be used at all. Realistically, though, what is the use of testing, finding, debugging, and correcting errors if the fix doesn't get installed everywhere it is required?

Client/server systems especially can benefit from source code control for the simple reason that there are more computers involved. Software code changes required to correct an error may need to be made to more than one machine. One part of the change may be on the server, and another portion of the code change might be implemented on workstations. A source code control system will guarantee that all changes will be made.

Another aspect of client/server systems which benefits from source code control is that such systems are deployed to a wide diversity of client workstations. A typical corporatewide client/server might include users with PCs, Macs, and UNIX-based client machines. Software changes to each type of workstation are likely to be different.

Even within the category of PCs there are likely to be differences from one user's machine to another. Users will probably be running PCs with a variety of operating systems. The major choices are Windows 3.11, Windows 95, Windows NT, and O/S2. Different executables and different source code exist for each of these installations. A source code control system in place will make it more likely that corrections will be properly made to each set.

3.2.3 Debuggers

Debuggers make it possible to step into the source code of the system and take a good look at what's actually going on. A debugger allows the developer to suspend execution of an application and examine it from the inside. The developer can examine and set variables and attributes used by the application.

Developers are the only members of the development team likely to employ debuggers. They frequently use a debugger during unit testing. Before releasing the module, developers will undoubtedly discover and fix errors. Debuggers are prime tools used to correct these errors.

Another time when developers are presented with errors which might require a debugger is much later in the project. If a test uncovers an error, it will be assigned to someone, undoubtedly a developer, to identify and correct. The developer will most likely use the debugger.

Most client/server GUI development packages include a debugger. In most cases these debuggers provide all of the functionality required to get the job done. Third-party vendors also market debuggers as well.

3.2.4 Database Generators

In order to have a high degree of confidence in your testing, the system must be running against a realistically sized database. Testing against an unrepresentative database has a number of shortcomings. Potential performance problems won't be apparent if the tables contain only a handful of rows. Concurrency and locking problems won't surface either unless the database is realistic.

Unfortunately, testing likely begins long before users have started entering data. So that source of data isn't viable. It's not safe to assume that developers will create data in either the required volume or variety. Normally they create as little data as they can get away with. The data that developers do insert isn't always representative of the production environment.

The situation might be much better if the client/server system is replacing an existing system. When this is the case, data can be exported from the old system and imported into the client/server system. If the client/server system is a completely new system, there is no chance of obtaining such historic data.

To get an adequately sized database, a database generator can be employed. Tools of this nature allow any amount of data to be generated and inserted into the database. Developers can design data with customized characteristics in each column. Generated data may consist of alphabetical characters, digits, or a mixture of both. Data can be created which meets the dependencies between columns in database tables.

3.2.5 Testing Database Objects

Some extremely advantageous features of relational databases include stored procedures, triggers, and rules. These can be used to enforce consistent, systemwide entry validation and referential integrity. Another advantage of using database objects is that they can provide a significant improvement in database performance.

Testing components which reside at and execute at the database server level can be difficult. There isn't an easy way to interact with and test objects at the database level. Test tools exist which allow these components to be debugged much like applications. Tools of this nature can be useful to ease the testing of these useful objects.

3.2.6 Capture and Playback Testing

Anyone who has been involved in testing client/server systems will readily admit that the process can be slow and manually intensive. Running lengthy test processes once is tiring and time-consuming. Running them multiple times can be frustrating and mind-numbing. Fortunately, a class of tools has been developed to assist in this area. The generic description applied to these tools is "capture and playback." These tools allow the tester to execute the application and have her actions captured into a script file. Scripts can be played back at a later time, and all actions taken by the user are duplicated. This fundamental capability can be exploited in a number of ways to assist in the testing process.

3.2.7 Unattended Testing

Scripts created via capture and playback tools can be utilized to perform unattended testing. Unattended testing is made viable when a test tool is capable of capturing responses from the client/server system and storing them. The tool also must be able to distinguish between tests which have passed and those that have failed. They store this information in the repository. Test team members can later view these results to see the test outcome.

One of the most productive aspects of this unattended testing is that the work doesn't have to stop at the end of the day. An unattended test script can be kicked off late in the day and run all night. Since no one needs to be in attendance, there is no reason testing can't be performed every night of the week and each weekend. Setting up a test session to run every test in the system could and should be done. This might be the system's regression test, and it could be run unattended after every build of the system.

Another advantage of unattended testing is that it can be shifted to later shifts to reduce its impact on system performance. By running tests after hours two benefits are realized. First, developers and other users aren't impacted by the testing activity. This enables them to be more productive as well as reduce resentment toward the system being tested. Second, if testing is the only activity going on, then it will be easier to reproduce anomalies which occur during tests.

3.2.8 Load Testing

Load or stress testing is achieved by simulating a large number of users and their actions on the system. The purpose of this form of testing is to determine what the performance of the client/server system will be when a realistic number of users are simulated. Load testing can be accomplished by test tools which coordinate the execution of test scripts on multiple client workstations.

There are at least two ways to implement load testing. One method is accomplished by installing agents on each client workstation involved in the test. A test controlling program on one workstation communicates with all workstations via their agent programs. The test to be executed is passed to the agent. When the test is completed, the agent communicates with the controlling program. The controller at this point may have additional testing for the agent, or its tasks may be done.

Another technique for performing load testing is to have a single workstation simulating a number of client workstations. A test program, running on a workstation, simulates the activity of a number of user workstations. This is possible because normal interaction between a client and the server includes relatively little communication interspersed by a lot of pauses. The test program needs to keep the individual client sessions with the server isolated.

3.2.9 Concurrency Testing

Concurrency is the ability of the client/server system to handle multiple simultaneous user sessions. Handling concurrent users is a prerequisite of every client/server system. If the system wasn't properly designed and built to handle concurrent users, then when the second or third user logs in, the system will start to degrade. Symptoms of this degradation can range from a severe performance drop to a situation where the system completely locks up.

This type of testing is absolutely necessary, and it isn't normally addressed by unit and system testing. Developers frequently have a very myopic view of the system they are developing. When their unit tests function correctly, the thought is everything's fine. It takes someone with a higher-level view of the system to focus on concurrency testing.

Concurrency testing can be difficult to accomplish because it requires a high level of coordination among multiple client workstations. Manually doing concurrency testing involves a large number of testers, client workstations, and a carefully choreographed test scenario. Each tester is required to run her tests at the same moment that other test personnel are running their scripts. Should the collective timing of the test personnel be off, the testing hasn't been effective.

Concurrency testing is enormously simplified by the use of automated test tools. Test scripts are prepared and launched from multiple client workstations. Concurrency test tools include the capability to accurately control the timing of tests run on individual workstations. This allows the test team to have a great deal of confidence that they have in fact thoroughly tested the ability of the system to allow concurrent users.

3.2.10 Object-Oriented Testing

An object is an entity which provides data and functionality in a program. Each object has attributes, events, and functions. Attributes are what the object knows about itself. Examples of attributes which a window object has include height, width, a title, and a name. Events occur and scripts associated with the object are executed. Examples of events are a control button object that has a clicked event, a double-clicked event, and a drag event. Functions are the work that an object can do. Examples of functions for a window are that it can be hidden or shown.

All client/server, GUI development environments include varying levels of object-oriented programming. Windows, control buttons, list boxes, menus, combo boxes, radio buttons, sliders, spin boxes, tabs, etc., are examples of objects common to most development environments. Test tools customarily recognize and can interact with all of these common types of objects.

Some development environments have evolved to offer additional, more complex types of objects. Examples of these objects are VBXs and OCXs in Visual Basic and DataWindows in PowerBuilder. Once a development tool and its more complex objects have gained sufficient marketplace momentum, test tools are frequently enhanced to specifically address and handle them. For example, SQA Suite recognizes and allows testing of PowerBuilder DataWindows, Centura Table Windows, and Visual Basic custom controls (ActiveXs/OCXs and VBXs).

3.2.11 Wizards

Testing tools, like so many other types of software products, provide *wizards* to guide users through commonly performed tasks. Wizards are specialized software assistants that provide a self-guided, visual interface for specifying test requirements and test cases. The capabilities of wizards range significantly from tool to tool. One tool's wizard generates a test plan to ensure that all the components of the application are tested. Another wizard assists the user in pulling together test scripts to thoroughly test new builds of a client/server system.

3.2.12 Automatic Test Generation

Some test tools have made the leap from being a tool to assist in generating test cases to having the ability to generate test cases themselves. Tools of this nature don't claim to completely automate the testing effort. Instead they create a first version of test scripts to be refined and enhanced by the test team.

Rapid Test, a script wizard included in WinRunner by Mercury Interactive, learns an application by navigating its way through it. Rapid Test opens every menu, and menu item, dialogue box in the application. Scripts are created for testing every object and window in the application. The resulting scripts can be used and reused to test the application.

3.2.13 Sniffer Programs

Sniffer programs are used to determine what communications packets are moving across a network. A tool of this nature can be invaluable in helping to determine why a client/server system's performance is below expectations. Frequently the knowledge of what packets are moving across the network (and the number of them) provides valuable insight into the performance.

3.2.14 Profiler Test Tools

Profiler programs help identify where resources, primarily CPU time and disk I/Os, are being utilized. This knowledge enables developers to expend resources where they are most likely to achieve the highest returns. In most cases the infamous "80/20" rule applies. Eighty percent of the benefits will be achieved by addressing only twenty percent of the code.

One area which can significantly affect performance in a client/server system is the SQL statements used to interact with the database. The difference between a good SQL statement and a really bad one may be only a few words or lines, but the performance impact can be devastating! Profiler and analysis tools can be used to monitor the SQL queries sent to the database server. Once the most "offensive" statements have been identified, the DBA or developers can use their expertise to tune them. A small amount of tuning can significantly affect the overall performance of a system.

3.2.15 Memory Leakage

Memory management isn't a problem in all client/server development environments, but it certainly is a factor in systems developed with C and C++. When developing in these environments, a tool which automatically handles memory deallocation and loose pointers can be of enormous value. Failure to properly handle memory management can result in errors which occur intermittently. Errors of this nature are notoriously hard to pin down and debug because they can neither be predicted nor easily recreated.

3.3 Advantages of Using Test Tools

The previous section provides a list of some of the capabilities of advanced test tools. Capabilities are meaningless if they can't be translated into direct improvements in the testing process. The improvements which using tools can bring are very concrete. The following sections list a number of efficiencies experienced through using test tools.

3.3.1 Testing Is Formalized

In too many situations testing is designed and performed in a very informal, almost ad hoc manner. Under such conditions the details of testing are frequently left to the discretion of individuals on the test team. While most developers and testers go about their tasks with the best of intentions, some don't. Even among those who do their best, there may be a lack of true understanding concerning how testing should be done.

Testing systems of any nature needs to be a formal and rigorous process. Putting in place a test management planning package puts rigor and backbone into the testing proceedings. By designing and planning tests from the beginning of the process, there is less likelihood that significant parts of the testing process will be overlooked, forgotten, or conveniently eschewed.

3.3.2 Test Progress Is Readily Documented

Test management tools all provide the capability of producing reports and graphs which document the progress of testing efforts. Reports can be produced showing which components have been tested and which have not. Other reports will document which tests have passed and those which have failed and need to be rerun. This capacity can be of great use to the test team. It gives them the ability to recognize what testing has been completed and what needs to be the focus.

As the project gets closer and closer to its deadlines, upper management will increasingly pester the project management team for progress reports. If no ready answer to these queries exists, a significant amount of time and energy will be consumed pulling together details in order to respond. The ability of the test management tool to produce progress reports of this nature is invaluable.

3.3.3 Formal Test Plans Can Be Reused

A formal, complete test plan is a document which can be extremely valuable to an organization. It can readily be adapted to and reused on subsequent projects. Such a test plan can be polished and improved upon with each successive usage. If each project team which uses it includes more corrections and additional details, it will become more complete with age.

In addition to becoming more thorough, it can enable project management to more accurately estimate the time and resources that testing will require. If metrics are kept during each project, the estimates of how long each testing phase takes will become more and more accurate.

3.3.4 Defect Tracking

Developers may not truly understand it (or want to admit it), but finding errors is the goal of the testing process. The objective isn't to "prove" that there are not errors. It isn't possible to prove that a computer system has no errors in it. The best manner to improve the system is to find as many errors as possible and eradicate them.

However, what is the use of discovering an error if it never gets fixed? Defect tracking enables project management to make certain that defects, once identified, get corrected. Tracking software allows an error to be assigned and tracked to make sure it doesn't get overlooked.

3.3.5 Using Test Scripts Is Efficient

Utilizing test scripts is an extremely efficient way to automate testing. Since test tools impose almost no additional time or effort to generate, there is no downside in producing them. On the plus side, scripts can be rerun numerous times. The effort to rerun a test based on a test script is only a fraction of the time and effort that the test originally took.

Each module within a client/server system must be tested many times during the overall testing process. If a developer finds an error and fixes it in unit testing then the module must be tested over again. This process is repeated until the developer completes unit testing. A module might be tested dozens of times during this testing phase. Is it more efficient to have the developer perform each repetition manually or via a test script?

Increased reliance on inheritance in client/server systems forces a requisite reliance on regression testing. Some of the fundamental objects may be ancestors to scores of descendents. Any change to such an ancestor necessitates regression testing on each and every one of the modules. Is it realistic to assume that project management has the people to perform testing of this magnitude? Utilizing test scripts for regression testing is the only practical solution.

3.3.6 Reproducible Test Results

Performing a test on a GUI-based system can involve a significant number of steps. A trivial example might be to open an application, bring up a specific window, specify a number of search criteria, and execute a search. Each step must be performed in exactly the same order. If any step is done incorrectly or out of sequence, the validity of the test has been jeopardized. For the test to be performed identically from one iteration to the next, either the tester must have a photographic memory or be following a script with the most minute details laid out. There aren't too many people around with the former quality and just as few who will perform the latter in the minute detail required.

A script-based test, on the other hand, will be executed identically each time it is run. As long as no one meddles with the test script, the test is guaranteed to run the same steps in the exact same sequence. Some test tools even allow the pauses between actions to be controlled. There is no comparison between the fidelity of tests run subsequent times by individuals versus tests run by a script.

3.3.7 Regression Testing

Once test scripts have been written to automate testing of the system, they can be used for multiple purposes. One excellent use of test scripts is to perform regression testing in an automated manner. If the test tool allows scripts to be strung together, a single script can be assembled which tests the entire system. Using such a script, complete regression testing of the entire system can be performed unattended.

3.3.8 Load Testing

Test scripts built to test the system's accuracy and functionality can also be employed to perform load testing. Running a number of test scripts concurrently can simulate the actions and load of a number of users.

Since the scripts were already in place, load testing can be seen as a cost-free by-product of using an automated test tool.

3.3.9 Extended Period Testing

A fairly common occurrence is for a newly developed software system to run smoothly initially. After the application has executed for a considerable period of time without being restarted, problems occur. The errors might be caused by overflow in counters, inability to recognize a change in date, accumulated memory leakage, or other similar problems. The result could be a significant reduction in performance, inaccurate calculations, or potentially a total shutdown of the system.

One extremely treacherous example of this type of problem occurred with the Patriot antimissile batteries during the Gulf War. The missiles worked fine initially. They successfully destroyed Iraqi Scud missiles. Unfortunately, some of the Patriots weren't cycled down after extended periods of time. When later Scuds appeared, some Patriot batteries were ineffective. They weren't able to successfully target the incoming Scud missiles. This occurred because time-related values in the software had overflowed. Periodically recycling the other systems had cleared the fields and prevented the problem from occurring. While this is perhaps one of the most extreme examples of the need for extended testing, it's very likely that at least some problems will surface if extended testing is performed in every system.

A fairly easy way to test for this potential problem is to once again re-use test scripts. The test scripts can be joined together and repeated to keep the system running for an indefinite period. As a minimum, this form of testing should extend across midnight. Testing in excess of 24 hours straight is also an excellent idea. Finally, the system time should be manipulated to simulate month-end, quarter-end, and year-end scenarios. These final tests are especially important when a significant amount of specific processing is required at those times and dates.

3.3.10 Graphical Test Tools

One of the most significant departures that client/server GUI systems made from traditional systems was the addition of a graphical interface. A GUI interface is easier for users to understand, remember, and interact with. The success of graphical interfaces in applications foreshadowed the same types of interfaces appearing in test tools. These tools are now as graphical as the systems they were built to test. Virtually all of them include control buttons, MDI sheets, menus, and tool bars.

3.3.11 Easy to Use

The graphical interface has done a great deal to make test tools easier to use. Most tools allow capture recording to be started with the click of one or two buttons. Replaying a test script is not much more difficult than creating the test script. Standardized reports that document testing progress can often be generated with very little effort.

This ease of use makes it possible for nondevelopers (i.e., users) to participate to a much greater extent in the testing process. The advantages of this increased participation are twofold. First of all, it relieves the developer from a significant amount of the testing effort. Developers are freed to fix errors or continue the development activity.

Secondly, enabling users to partake more heavily in the testing gives them an opportunity to become familiar with the system and gain a sense of ownership in the system. Their feeling of ownership will be invaluable when the time comes for system acceptance. If they have a sense of ownership, there will be less of a tendency to criticize the system and compare it unfavorably to the system it is replacing.

3.3.12 Common Repository

As client/server projects grow in size and complexity, they require more people to participate in the testing process. A detrimental aspect of adding developers to a project is that software tends to become scattered across developers' machines and servers. Source code may reside on each developer's PC, and source SQL statements for stored procedures might be on the DBA's PC. Test scripts may be housed on still other machines. Keeping track of all system components in a major project can be a time-consuming job.

Another problem is that multiple copies of objects are frequently created. If there is more than one copy of a test script, how do you know which one was used for a specific test run? Can you be certain that the current copies of scripts aren't being inadvertently deleted? A significant amount of effort is often spent simply keeping track of where these objects are maintained and which are the most current version of each.

Test tools can come charging to the rescue if this becomes a problem. Most tools are built upon the concept of a shared repository. This means that test plans, scripts, test results, reports, etc., are kept in a single place. This place is normally a database on the server. The advantages of a shared repository are many. The location of all test-related objects is known and available to everyone (project management, DBAs, developers, QA personnel, user representatives) involved in the project. Everyone who requires it can be granted access to test objects. Only a single copy of each object is maintained in the repository. Since all objects are in one place, it becomes easier to ascertain that objects are being backed up regularly.

3.4 Disadvantages of Using Test Tools

While most test tools are extremely useful and help to make the project team more productive, you shouldn't be misled into thinking they are a panacea. Like any other type of software product or tool, they have their shortcomings. Some of the disadvantages are fairly minor, but a realistic look must be taken on both sides of the coin.

3.4.1 Expense

Tool vendors are in business to make a profit just like all other software vendors. These products, as a rule, aren't cheap. Test suites which offer management planning, error tracking, automated testing, etc., cost significantly more than products which cover only a single facet of the testing solution. While buying a suite is cheaper (and more likely to be successful) than purchasing pieces separately from individual vendors, the overall cost can be steep. Pricing is affected by the type and number of platforms on which the product runs. Generally, products which run on UNIX systems are more expensive than similar tools that run on Windows-based machines.

Another factor in the pricing strategy is the number of user licenses purchased. Single user licenses are less costly than multiuser licenses but could be extremely limiting for a large scale project. Purchase enough licenses to allow all your developers to be productive. Saving a few hundred dollars in license costs, but having idle staff doesn't make good business sense.

Added to the purchase price of the test tool must be other, less-visible costs. Like many software products, test tools frequently have an annual maintenance or support expense. Before users of the test tool can become proficient, they will need to be trained. Training costs come in two flavors, hard and soft. Hard costs are dollars expended for the cost of training courses and the travel and lodging needed to get there. Other training costs are softer, such as the time users spend educating themselves on how to use the tools. Soft costs might not seem consequential, but they can mount up quickly. No matter how training is done, the time required for it must be built into the schedule.

Once the testing package is obtained it must be installed. This certainly requires someone's time. That "someone" is frequently a LAN administrator, DBA, or another technical specialist. Costs for individuals with these skills can be significant. Installation of the test tool may require that additional hardware or software be acquired. After installation is complete, an internal help desk might be needed to support users.

Only when all associated expenses (including the nonobvious ones) are summed up will the true costs of using the tool be known. Management must then estimate the value of using the test tool on the project. Unfortunately, estimating these figures is extremely difficult. The number of hours spent testing can be estimated to a reasonable degree. But how can an estimate be put on completing the project on time or error free? Project management must decide whether the advantages of using test tools outweigh the expenditures.

3.4.2 Someone Else's Methodology

No matter how well packaged and implemented it is, using any third-party software package entails some degree of compromise. Each user of the package can probably think of at least one thing which they would change if they were given the opportunity. Test tools are no different in this regard.

Each product out on the market has its strengths and its weaknesses. Your project team won't like the way any test product does everything. Even the best product is likely to have a few inconveniences. In some cases the matter goes beyond cosmetics to the very fundamentals of how testing is done. The group which chooses a test tool must be certain that the approach used by the tool is compatible with your shop's approach to things. This is where obtaining and using a demo copy for 30, 60, or 90 days is invaluable. If you've had an opportunity to test drive the package, you're much less likely to be dissatisfied with it.

3.4.3 No Silver Bullets

When applied consistently and appropriately, test tools can help to produce world-class software in a timely manner. Unfortunately, test tools are neither a cure-all or a silver bullet. If you, or worse yet your management, is foolish enough to believe that simply purchasing a test tool will guarantee error-free software, then you would be better off to simply return it now for a full refund. Even with the best tools, testing is still hard work. It requires planning, time, effort, and experience. Any vendor which promises otherwise is best avoided.

3.4.4 Test Suites

Most test tools within suites are extremely tightly interconnected. Choosing one product from a vendor frequently forces you to use only components from their suite for the rest of your test tools. Using company X's capture and replay tool limits you in that only their reports will produce documentation on testing failures. If you want to run reports on the progress of the testing effort, you will have to use their test planning package.

The test tool software market hasn't evolved to the point where customers can purchase the "best of breed" in each category and put them all together. That day may someday arrive, but it isn't here yet. The unfortunate reality is that you will almost certainly need to select a single test suite and stick with it.

3.4.5 Test Databases

Databases used specifically for running tests must be created and supported. In some situations, a number of test databases will need to be maintained. The reason for this requirement is fairly simple. When a test script is executed for the first time with the capture tool running, a baseline for the test is created. Every piece of data on all the screens is recorded. Later, when the test is repeated, the playback tool looks for differences between this execution and the baseline. When a variance is found, it is logged and declared as a likely software error. If the database has been changed in the interim, there will be differences which are due to database changes instead of software errors. If nothing else, digging through the variations to determine which are software errors and which are database changes is a time-consuming job.

3.4.6 Platform Variation

Each test tool has limitations on what hardware and software platforms it can function on. If your client/server system must be deployed across an unusually wide breadth of platforms, your choice of test tools may be somewhat limited. In fact, you may not have any choices at all. In the worst case, an organization may be forced to use different test products to perform similar functions on different platforms.

3.5 Choosing and Acquiring Test Tools

Congratulations! Your organization has decided that using advanced test tools will help improve the quality of your client/server systems. Now the decision must be made regarding which of the many test tool(s) on the market will be chosen for your projects. The best approach to this decision is one based on logic and reason.

3.5.1 Analyze Testing Requirements

The first step in deciding which tool(s) would be beneficial to an organization's needs is to define what testing needs are required. Table 3.1 is a checklist of potential testing requirements. This list should be modified to represent your organization's needs.

Developers will certainly need a debugger to allow them to step through applications. A debugger most likely was included in the development tool.

The ability to capture and replay test scripts is absolutely fundamental to an advanced test plan. Many pieces of your test plan will be dependent on this capability. Without this ability, it would be impossi-

TABLE 3.1	Test Plan Manager
Test Requirements	Debugger
	Capture / Playback
	Database Objects
	Load Testing
	Stress Testing
	Regression Testing

ble to perform unattended testing. It would be difficult or at least require more people to run load testing and regression testing without a capture and replay capability.

Some client/server systems are more dependent on database objects such as stored procedures, triggers, and rules. If your system is one of them, then obtaining a tool specifically assigned for testing these objects makes sense. Be certain that the tool acquired is compatible with the database back-end package being used.

3.5.2 Hardware and Software Platforms

The second step is to write down the hardware platforms and software products which the client/server system will be deployed on. For instance, the system might be a PowerBuilder GUI running on Windows 95 PC accessing an Oracle database which resides on a Sun SPARC server. Any test tools being seriously considered had better function on those platforms. Table 3.2 is a checklist of potential hardware platforms and software environments. This list should be modified to represent your organization's requirements.

Future expansion of the client/server system also needs to be taken into account when evaluating test tools. For example, there might be a strong possibility that the system will be deployed to other types of client machines in the future. Perhaps the marketing department will use the system in the future and there are a significant number of Apple Macintoshes in that department. If and when the system is deployed to Macs, it makes sense to reuse the test scripts which have already been built. When this is the case, the selection of test tools should be whittled down to tools which run on both Windows and Macs. If the chosen tool doesn't run on Macs then completely new test scripts would have to be

TABLE 3.2

Hardware
Platforms
and Software
Environments

Hardware Platforms	Software Environments
Intel PCs	Windows 3.11
PowerPCs	Windows 95
Macintoshes	Windows NT
Sun Workstations	UNIX
Laptop Computers	MacOS

developed to test on this new platform. Not utilizing existing test scripts would be extremely wasteful.

3.5.3 Gathering Data about Test Tools

You know what testing you need to do and what platforms you'll need to do it on. Now you need to know which of the myriad tools meet those requirements. Where can detailed information about tools be found? It would be wonderful if this type of information could be included in a book. Sadly, as soon as a book has been printed everything it says would likely be outdated. The computer industry in general, and client/server development in particular, is changing too quickly to allow timely, accurate knowledge to be current for long.

The best sources for information on test tool products come from the companies themselves. They are happy to send out marketing information and technical details. If you contact them, they will flood your mailroom with brochures, white papers, press releases, and articles praising their wares. Frequently they will send demonstration copies of their products.

Finding out which companies produce test tools is a more difficult assignment. One excellent way of keeping tabs on testing products and their vendors is to read the computer trade press on a regular basis. Publications which cover the entire industry, such as *Computer World*, *Datamation*, and *Information Week*, frequently have articles on testing client/server systems. Journals dedicated to software development, client/server systems, or database systems are even more likely to cover these topics. Examples of such publications are *Database Programming & Design*, *DBMS*, *Client/Server Computing*, and *Client/Server Journal*.

Almost every issue of the above periodicals will include advertisements of testing tools. You can quickly compile a list of company names and phone numbers and a brief description of their product. Most magazines include a "bingo" card which makes it easy to request information from companies which advertise in the publication. Always beware of the slant which advertising inherently contains. Frequently, advertisements pitch their products as the biggest, best, whiz-bang test tool ever invented. Take all advertising claims with a large grain of salt.

Industry trade shows are another good source for information on test tool vendors. At a single trade show it should be possible to gather data on numerous products. The likelihood of being able to view a display of different products is also good at an exhibit. The latest and greatest versions of products are normally being displayed at these shows.

Probably the best source for extremely current information on test tool vendors, as well as almost everything else, is the Internet. The majority of vendors have home pages on the Web. By going to their home page you can get the most recent details on their products. Some of the areas typically found on vendor home pages include press releases, what's new, training, product information, and white papers. Some vendors will allow a demo version of their product to be downloaded from the Web.

Vendors will be happy to put you on their mailing list (e-mail or USPS). This will keep you informed of their press announcements regarding new releases and new features. If you have a particular interest on a specific product, then this is probably one of the best ways of keeping up on what is new. Beware. Sometimes the amount of information will be overwhelming.

3.5.4 Evaluating Test Tools

Testing requirements for your organization have been compiled. Information on each of a number of testing products has been gathered. You're ready to make the decision. What's next? The next step is to determine which of the products meet your requirements. This phase will most likely make a significant reduction in the number of products being considered. Table 3.3 illustrates some configuration-oriented points which should be considered.

Once your evaluation team becomes familiar with the test tools available, they will start to develop opinions about what they see as desirable features. Their preferences will sway them when choosing between tools which meet the fundamental requirements. Table 3.4 is a preliminary list of technical capabilities available in some test tools. This table should be expanded by your evaluation team to meet your requirements. Each

TABLE 3.3

Configuration
Issues

What hardware platforms does the tool run on?

What software environments does the tool run under?

What development packages is the tool integrated with?

  VB

  PowerBuilder

  Oracle Developer/2000

  Delphi

  Gupta SQLWindows

  C++

What networks is the tool compatible with?

  Novell

  Banyan

  Microsoft LAN Manager

What protocols is the tool compatible with?

  TCP/IP

  IPX/SPX

  NetBIOS/NetBEUI

What back-end databases will it run with?

  Informix

  Oracle

  Sybase

  Access

  Rdb

  DB2

  CA OpenRoad Ingres

tool being evaluated should be checked against this list to see what percentage of capabilities it provides.

Other issues which should be considered before purchasing a test tool are of a corporate nature. These are more likely to be evaluated and decided upon by the project manager than the development team.

Table 3.5 lists some of these corporate issues. Again, this list needs to be customized for each organization's particular needs and concerns.

3.5.5 When to Acquire the Tool

When should testing tools be acquired? You would be wise to follow the advice of one politician who advised his supporters to "vote early and often." The earlier you acquire your test tool, the earlier the staff can become competent with it. The earlier you acquire your test tool, the earlier you can begin to develop a test plan for your client/server project.

TABLE 3.4

Technical Issues

Does the tool recognize standard GUI objects (datawindows, grids, control buttons, data entry fields, menus, tool bars)?

Is the scripting language proprietary or based on a standard? (Two common languages which scripting languages are based on are Visual Basic and C.)

Are test scripts primarily created via capture or by hand writing them?

Can test scripts created by capture technique be edited?

Can test scripts be written from scratch?

Can test scripts be randomly executed or are pre-existing scripts always executed?

Are scripts and test plans stored in files or a database?

Are the names of test objects limited to eight characters? (Very hard to be descriptive in eight characters.)

Can test scripts be concatenated to create a single, longer test script?

How much control over concurrently executing threads is possible?

Will the tool gather execution time performance statistics?

Does the tool come with demonstration applications?

How are the tool's help facilities?

Is the tool suitable for users?

Can multiple applications be tested simultaneously?

How does the tool handle tests which fail or crash?

Do any changes *whatsoever* need to be made to the application in order to test it? One test tool requires that a subroutine call be included in the source code. Another requires that OSF/Motif applications bind their product to the applications to use it.

TABLE 3.5

Corporate Issues

Is it possible to obtain a demonstration of the product for 30, 60, or 90 days?

Does the vendor have a support phone line?

Are there any user groups for this product? (Any branches in your area?)

How long has the vendor been in business?

How many licenses have been sold?

What percentage of the market does the vendor represent?

Is their market share percentage growing, shrinking, or stable?

Are classes/training available? Is in-house training available?

How much does the product cost?

Is there an annual maintenance fee and if so what is it?

Is there an extra cost for a support license?

3.6 Test Tool Matrix

Table 3.6 is a compilation of features that are available in client/server test tool packages. Realistically, it isn't possible to build a "complete" list because features are continuously added to products. It's an attempt to present an overview of what features were available at one point in time. It can be used to roughly judge where each tool being evaluated falls in the spectrum. Some offer very few features, while others offer nearly all features.

TABLE 3.6

Test Tool
Feature List

Test Plan Manager

Reports

Test Scripts

Capture and Replay

Unattended Testing

Web Pages

Test Script Concatenation

Object Comparator

    What can it compare?

        Bitmaps

        Text fields

        Numeric fields

Automatic Test Generators

    What is automatically tested?

Stress/Load Testing

    How many client workstations can be controlled?

    How many sessions can run from a single client workstation?

Testing Practices

4

Test Planning

Test planning is the process of defining the testing effort of a project so that it can be properly measured and controlled. It comprises a set of activities for collecting information. This information is then used in other phases of the testing cycle. Test planning will also establish resource requirements for the test effort, test scheduling, and the test deliverables.

4.1 Testing Phases

Actual testing activity can be broken down into three distinct and equally essential phases:

- Unit testing.
- Integration testing, also called build testing.
- System testing.

A fourth testing phase can also be included in the testing effort. Acceptance testing is similar in nature and scope to system testing. The essential difference between system testing and acceptance testing is that the former is internal while the latter is controlled by the "customer." Other differences between them are explained in Section 4.1.4.

4.1.1 Unit Testing

Unit testing represents the beachhead of the testing effort. It's where the action starts. But to really define and understand what unit testing is, it becomes necessary to define what a unit is.

4.1.1.1 What Is a Unit?   A unit of software defines a piece of software at a very low level. The absolute lowest ("atomic") level of software in the client/server GUI environment would be a GUI control. This "atom" of the code would include all of the code written for the events associated with a control. An example of this would be a button control. The events associated with the button (e.g., click, double click, and drag) and the code behind each event are atomic. They cannot be divided into any smaller, usable pieces.

A software unit is one level higher than a control. An example of a unit could be a window in PowerBuilder or a form in Visual Basic.

Other examples of units in a client/server system are functions, menus, reports, or stored procedures.

4.1.1.2 Attributes of a Unit. Some distinctive attributes of a unit include:

- It normally is developed by a single person. Continuing on with the example of a window as a unit, it wouldn't be easy or efficient to have two developers simultaneously working on a single window. They would simply get into each other's way.
- The functionality of a unit has been documented in the system specifications. At a minimum, the following details have been documented:
  - Input which the unit handles.
  - Database tables queried by the unit.
  - Overall appearance of the module for units which interface with users.
  - Navigation to the unit.
- Units can be separately compiled or assembled.

4.1.1.3 Who Performs Unit Testing? The person who has developed a particular software unit knows more about it than anyone else does. Having such an intimate level of knowledge puts this person in the best position to perform unit-level testing. By applying her knowledge, the developer can quickly and thoroughly test a unit.

If an independent tester were to be brought into the loop to do the unit testing, there would be a number of consequences. First it would increase the personnel costs. Adding testers at the unit testing level would be a significant increase in the size of the project team. The efficiency of both the developer and tester would suffer. A major amount of the developer's time would be spent explaining to the tester how and why the unit was developed the way it was. A high degree of resentment would likely be felt by the developer towards the tester. The developer would feel (and rightly so) that someone was constantly looking over his or her shoulder. At this level of detail, the developer expects to execute a certain degree of freedom on how he or she implements the design. Having to constantly explain oneself to a tester would impinge on this autonomy.

Yet there are drawbacks to having the developers test their own software. While they are serious and should not be overlooked or discounted, they aren't serious enough to change personnel involved in unit testing. These drawbacks are described in the following sections.

Having worked long and hard to create an "error-free" software module, the developer may not be emotionally ready to find flaws in his or her own work. Finding an error in a just-completed module is an admission that the developer isn't perfect. No one likes to admit such an ugly truth. The reluctance to find errors and acknowledge one's imperfection may exist at a conscious or subconscious level, but it is real. The ultimate outcome may be that developers do not try as hard as they could (or should) to find their own errors.

Development is inherently a creative process, while testing is viewed as being basically "destructive." Software developers have moved into this particular profession at least partly because they like to build things. They are inherently a creative lot. Testing, on the other hand, is viewed as tearing down things. People who want to be builders aren't likely to have it in their hearts to work aggressively at tearing down things.

A single individual may be an excellent developer but a lousy tester. These two roles require substantially different skills. A developer needs to be creative, positive, and maybe even a little artistic. Skills or attributes required by a good tester include an ability to track details, tenacity, slyness, and perhaps even a dash of ruthlessness. It stands to reason that not all developers will possess the spectrum of skills and personality traits essential to fulfill both roles. If a developer doesn't possess the skills needed to be a good tester, then no matter how hard she tries, her work won't be flawless.

A developer's "eye" or mindset towards a unit and how it is to be used is likely to become ossified by continuously working with it. One definition of ossify is "to become rigid or inflexible in habits and opinions." This describes to a "T" how developers adapt to a module (e.g., a window) during the development effort. While working on the window they tend to perform the same steps, in the same order, time and time again. This rigid sequence of steps may represent one legitimate approach when using the window, but it isn't likely to represent the variety of how users will interact with the screen. They are almost certain to vary both their steps and their sequencing of them. Users will also make mistakes. This is something the developer is less likely to do.

Once developers make the mental leap from development mode to testing mode, is it likely that they will significantly change their approach to the module? Not very likely. Isn't it more realistic to assume that they will continue testing the same controls in the exact same way?

This approach may assist them during a building phase, but it isn't robust enough for unit testing.

Within the developer grows a certain amount of bias. This bias includes the assumption that he has done a good job and has properly addressed everything that needs to be done. Such a disposition would be expected of any intelligent worker as he went about a project. If the developer has overlooked or misunderstood some aspect of the unit's requirements, then such a bias may well blind him to the omission. He may thoroughly test what the module does but be completely blind regarding what the module has omitted. A tester taking a fresh look at the module may quickly notice an oversight of such a nature.

Very few software development projects, client/server or otherwise, are ahead of schedule. This being the predominate situation, it is safe to assume that the project is either on time or behind schedule. When a project is behind schedule, it is not unheard of for developers to feel pressure to advance through their assignments as quickly as possible. A developer may be coerced to gloss over testing the current unit in order to begin developing the next unit. Should this happen, then the quality of unit testing performed on the module would be questionable.

These aforementioned problems associated with developers performing unit testing shouldn't be overlooked or discounted. Despite the drawbacks, developers are best suited for this job. Perhaps if the potential problems are discussed with the development team, it will result in an improvement of the unit testing quality.

4.1.1.4 Black Box Tests or White Box Tests. Quite often articles, books, or discussions on testing contain the phrases "black box testing" or "white box testing." The context takes for granted that all readers are familiar with the meanings of these phrases, but that is not always the case. These two forms of testing apply to software testing as well as testing other engineering products. Definitions and descriptions for each of the phrases are included for clarity here.

Black box testing assumes that the internal details of the module being tested are not known or available to the tester. This may be by design or dictated by circumstances. Testing is restricted to verifying that the module functions as demanded by the specifications document. For a software module, one example would be a test to show that each control on a window responds in the manner required.

It probably won't come as a great surprise that white box testing assumes the tester is privy to internal details of the module being tested. Since the tester has detailed knowledge of how the module was coded, tests can be specifically designed to test unique parts of the code. Such tests can zero in on a particular complicated part of the module.

Depending on the phase of testing being performed, software testing emphasizes differences between the two testing types. Testing at the unit is almost always exclusively white box testing. A mix of black and white testing approaches is employed at the integration level. Once testing progresses to the system level, the testing approach shifts to strictly black box testing.

The rationales behind the above mix of black box versus white box testing has a very logical explanation. Unit testing is primarily performed by the unit's developer. The developer has access to and complete understanding of the code used to create the software module. Integration testing is performed by a combination of developers and QA personnel. Some of these individuals have a technical background and will understand the code within the module, and other members of the group won't. This explains the mixture of black box and white box testing. Once testing moves to the system level, almost all of the testers are user representatives or QA team members. It is doubtful that they will have the technical capability or physical access to the code. Their function is strictly to determine whether or not the system functions as required. If the system doesn't comply, they don't need to know and probably don't care why. They simply mark that particular test as having failed.

The above discussion of when black box versus white box testing should be used applies generically to the software development landscape. Testing client/server systems doesn't differ significantly from this traditional approach. The significant advancements that occurred from traditional systems to client/server changed a lot of things, but not this. Developers still perform unit testing and white box testing. Users and QA personnel are involved in integration, system, and black box testing.

4.1.1.5 Unit Test Plan.   Test plans must be designed and documented before a unit can be formally tested. The amount of documentation should be in sufficient detail to allow another developer to perform the unit testing if necessary. This might actually become necessary if the developer is transferred, promoted, or leaves the organization for another reason.

Other reasons for clear test documentation is that unit tests can be heavily mimicked or outright copied during integration and system testing. Understandable documentation will also be of great use to the testers during these later phases. In some cases the original developer may be involved in integration testing. If a considerable period of time has elapsed, the documentation will be needed to refresh her memory as much as anyone else's. No one can be expected to remember all the details of multiple test plans for any considerable period of time.

The unit test plan document should include the following:

- The name and description of the unit as well as the larger entity to which it belongs. This entity might be an application or other high-level entity.

- A short description of the module and its purpose.

- Other modules and system capabilities which this unit is dependent upon.

- A list of the tests that comprise the complete unit test. This requirement may be fulfilled by the name of a test script that calls all of the lower-level tests.

- A separate sheet outlining each individual test run as a part of the unit test. These sheets contain the test identifier and style (path test, validation test, etc.)

- Outcomes for each of the tests being executed.

All test plans should be reviewed before being put into place. This review must be by someone other than its developer before it can be accepted. Ideally, each unit test plan would be reviewed twice. The first review would be by the developer's immediate supervisor, mentor, or peer. These individuals would be looking primarily for technical problems with the test plan. Specifically they are looking for testing thoroughness, gaps, and oversights.

The second review of a unit test plan needs to be by a member of the quality assurance group. This review is less technical in nature than the first review. The primary objective of it is to make certain that the test plan meets the published requirements and objectives for all unit test plans. If the plan is insufficient on any grounds, it should be returned immediately to the developer. Second occurrences of deficiencies for a test plan should not occur.

4.1.1.6 When to Perform Unit Testing.   Unit testing is the first form of testing performed during client/server development. In fact, the sooner unit testing is performed, the more valuable its results. The earlier in the development cycle errors are uncovered, the less it costs to

Figure 4.1
Costs of Fixing Errors
in Various Phases

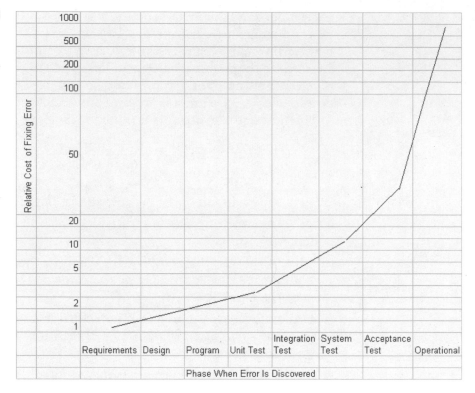

correct them. Figure 4.1 is a chart that displays the relationship between when an error is discovered and relative costs to fix it. As the chart clearly shows, errors caught in the unit testing phase are among the least expensive to amend. The later an error is caught, the more it costs to correct it.

Correcting errors earlier is cheaper than fixing them later, and this is true for a number of reasons. Because of inheritance, this is the case when developing client/server systems. If an error is discovered which is either in an ancestor code script or requires an ancestor to be modified, then a number of descendents will be affected. Finding this early on reduces the number of descendents affected. Fewer descendents depending on the ancestors translates into fewer descendents that might be affected or require additional testing.

Another reason why it is important to discover errors early on is because errors introduced in one module by a developer are likely to be repeated in other modules developed by that same individual. The earlier this pattern of errors is discovered, the fewer modules he will have infected. Fewer modules to be fixed translates into less time and energy spent on this effort. With any luck, the developer will actually learn something from this experience and generate better code in the future.

Unit testing can be performed in parallel. If a large number of developers are involved in a client/server development project, there is no reason why they cannot all be performing unit testing simultaneously. Since each software unit is independent of all others, parallel testing by one developer won't negatively impact other testers.

4.1.1.7 Types of Tests Performed during Unit Testing. Certain types of testing can only be done in a white box testing scenario. It is essential to have access to the code to adequately test it. Examples of forms of testing which have to be done under these conditions include:

- Path testing.
- Declaration testing.
- Loop testing.
- Boundary testing.
- Interface testing.

Path testing involves verifying that all possible paths in a module are exercised. It goes without saying that a test designed to verify all paths can only be done when the code is available.

A significant number of errors are caused when variables have not been declared or have been improperly declared. Part of unit testing involves checking that all variables have been declared. Many development tools will automatically assign an undeclared variable to a default data type. Allowing default declarations represents sloppy design and error-prone coding practices, which should be avoided at all costs.

Loop testing could conceivably be done without access to source code. As a practical matter, though, the truly important aspects of loop testing involve testing boundary conditions. For example, does the code properly handle situations where the loop variable is just below, at, or just above values that determine whether a loop occurs? Cases such as these cannot be tested without seeing the code and designing the test to fit the loop's specific conditions.

Boundary testing ascertains that the code doesn't fail at any internal boundary. One example of an internal boundary is when the nth row of an n-dimensional grid is processed. An SQL-related example of boundary testing would be determining whether or not the correct data set is being returned when the user has been allowed to dynamically build a "where" clause. Like loop testing, boundary testing must verify that the software functions properly, just below, exactly at, and just above boundary conditions. Also like loop testing, it wouldn't be feasible to perform boundary testing without having access to the software.

Interface testing entails checking that data flowing in and out of a module is correct. Modules that do not correctly handle data at its boundaries are so severely flawed that other testing is pointless. A short checklist of interface facets that should be examined include:

- Does the number of input parameters match the number of declared arguments?
- Do the declaration types of parameters and arguments match?
- If applicable, are the order of parameters and arguments the same?
- Are "by value" parameters altered within the unit?
- Are global variables properly defined and used?
- Is the caller properly assigning values returned by all functions called?

Other types of testing can be done under a white box or black box scenario. These also need to be performed in unit testing. Some of these test scenarios are:

- Data validation.
- Transaction testing.

Data validation only tests whether the application rejects invalid values. It might be of interest to see the code, but it isn't necessary. In actuality, this validation might be enforced at the database level by triggers, rules, or stored procedures. When this is the case, there is no application level code to see.

A transaction is a logical unit of work. Unless the user aborts an operation, it isn't immediately apparent where the transaction begins and ends. For this reason it would be desirable to see the code, although it isn't really imperative.

4.1.1.8 Special Considerations of Unit Testing.   Unit testing represents something of a coming out party for a software module. Prior to unit testing, the unit "belongs" to the developer. No one else in the development project has access to it. No one else can see it, judge it, or use it. It is a private piece of software. The developer is free to make any changes he wants to the unit. No one can interfere with his decisions.

After a unit has undergone unit testing, the developer releases the module to the outside world. The unit is handed over to a group which is responsible for it. This group is frequently referred to as "configuration management." From this point on, the unit belongs in the public domain and is no longer the property of the developer. Other developers will now be able to see the module and potentially include calls to the module in their software. Changing of the module by other developers is not allowed. In fact, if the original developer wants to make a change to a unit after it has been released, he must obtain permission from configuration management.

Any errors found before unit testing are "private" errors in the sense that no one but the developer knows about them. Once a unit has made the transition into the public domain, any errors are very public. If errors or other problems in a module are found, the prospect for embarrassment is quite real. Due to this potential, there is a certain reluctance on the part of some developers to release their software modules to configuration management. Project management has to understand this hesitancy and handle it delicately. It isn't reasonable to allow a developer to delay this event indefinitely, but on the other hand, it doesn't help matters to push him to release units prematurely. As in so many situations, there is a fine line which needs to be respected.

4.1.2 Integration Testing

One definition in the *Random House Webster's College Dictionary* (1992) for integration is "the organization of the constituent elements of the personality into a coordinated, harmonious whole." When the word "system" is substituted for "personality," we have a perfect description of system integration. It's the act of putting together a number of software units, which have up until this point been independent, into a coordinated whole.

It would be delightful if this assembly process could be done without any complications. In a perfect world all the pieces would fit together like a jigsaw puzzle you've assembled many, many times. There would be no missing pieces, no gaps, and no distortion in the overall picture. Of course, this isn't the way it works in the real world. Integration testing is the effort to find and correct the problems that occur when all the pieces don't fit together neatly.

At first glance, one could assume that integration testing might be unnecessary. After all, if unit testing has successfully been completed on

TABLE 4.1

Integration
Problems Which
Slip Past Unit
Testing

Miscommunication about data formats. Developer A thinks a field is date, while developer B has made the assumption that it is date/time. Possibly one developer has declared a field as long, while another has declared it as integer. The integer-declared fields will quite likely experience an overflow error.

Missing, extraneous, or differently typed parameters being passed between modules.

Name collision, i.e., two developers have independently selected the same name for a module, table, function, or stored procedure. Changing either name forces code to be modified. Which one should be changed?

Global variables—too many, name collision, differently typed.

Different security approaches taken in different modules. For example, developer A may assume security is implemented via grants to tables, while developer B has combined security into application navigation.

Gaps in functionality can occur when developers assume someone else was to provide a vital function. An oversight like this isn't likely to turn up until integration testing.

Overlapping functionality can occur if multiple developers provide similar capabilities. While this may not seem bad, it has a number of potential problems. Among them are that results from two functions may not always be the same. When results differ, which one is correct? Also, if there are multiple functions providing the same or similar services, there will be twice as much code to maintain.

Application navigation problems won't be visible until units are integrated. Frame A should contain an ability to call Frame B. If the developer forgets to include this call, then Frame B may be unreachable.

Counters or pseudo-keys can be assigned and used inconsistently. Developer A may assume the key value represents the current counter, but developer B might assume the key value is the next available value. This misunderstanding can result in either values being duplicated or skipped.

One tactic for avoiding deadlocking of relation tables is for all users to acquire tables in the same order. If all developers have not incorporated the same technique, then deadlocks can spontaneously occur. This won't turn up in unit testing because a single unit can never experience deadlock.

Improper table locking and database transaction handling won't usually turn up in unit testing. Only during integration testing (or later) will it rear its ugly head.

all the involved modules, what could possible go wrong? The more experienced developer knows that plenty can go wrong. Table 4.1 provides just a few quick examples of problems which could occur.

4.1.2.1 Who Performs Integration Testing?   Integration testing lies right at the cusp where individual software modules combine to form a complete system. It's not strictly unit level testing, yet it's not entirely system-functional testing. In reality it's a combination of the two. Integration testing combines aspects of both unit testing and system testing.

The ambiguousness surrounding integration testing also applies to who should perform this type of testing. Integration testing requires participants with an intimate knowledge of the modules' internal details as well as participants with a much higher-level view of the system. As a consequence, the team which performs integration testing should contain people from both of these backgrounds.

4.1.2.2 Black Box Tests or White Box Tests. The section of this book on unit testing outlined the fundamentals of black box testing, white box testing, and the differences between them. Unit testing is virtually all white box testing, while system testing is almost completely black box testing. Integration testing, as you might expect, is a mixture of both black and white box testing. Some of the tests are done with the knowledge of the underlying code, while others are performed not knowing what lies below the surface.

4.1.2.3 Integration Test Plan. Table 4.2 provides an outline for an integration test plan document. The details for an integration test plan need to be filled in. The testing description and scope summarize the characteristics of the system which are to be tested. The test plan outlines the overall strategy for integration testing.

4.1.2.4 When to Perform Integration Testing. Certain systemwide fundamental requirements must be in place before integration testing can be initiated. These fundamental requirements include the installation of the development tool (e.g., PowerBuilder, Visual Basic, etc.) and the ability to generate executables of the code being tested; a database which, although not completely "frozen," has reached a reasonably stable position; communications software and other support pieces which allow applications to connect to the database; workstations which are configured very much like those that the system users will be utilizing. The workstations just referred to should not belong to, or be configured like, development machines.

Once the fundamental requirements have been fulfilled, productive integration testing can begin as soon as enough modules in the same functional area pass unit testing. If modules that have nothing to do with each other are ready, it wouldn't make sense to "integrate" them. For example, an invoice input screen, a sort option, and a code table lookup window might have passed unit testing but are completely unrelated.

Integration testing is easier and goes more smoothly when a certain critical mass of the system is functional. This core system would

TABLE 4.2

Integration
Test Plan

1. Testing Description and Scope

2. Test Plan

    a. Test Stages

    b. Testing Schedule

    c. Supporting Software

    d. Required Resources

3. Test Procedure

    a. Description of Test Stage n

       1) Order of integration

       2) Purpose and modules to be tested

       3) Special tools or techniques

       4) Overhead software description

       5) Test case data

    b. Expected outcome for test stage n

4. Actual Test Outcome

5. References

6. Appendices

include the means of creating valid input records, viewing and editing existing records, and deleting records. The ability to produce output reports would also be a useful compliment to the ability of inputting data.

Many client/server systems being developed encompass a number of functional areas, e.g., accounts payable, invoicing, timekeeping, human resources, etc. Integration testing can be started on one area well before the others are ready. As soon as unit testing on the core of functionality has been completed, integration testing can be initiated.

4.1.2.5 Types of Tests Performed during Integration Testing.
One examination a module should undergo during integration testing is to verify that any documented design and programming standards have been met. This particular test shouldn't be done at the unit level because it would be like letting the fox guard the hen house. The developer was supposed to conform to established standards when developing the module. If he didn't then either he a) didn't know about the stan-

dards, b) doesn't understand them, c) conveniently ignored them or d) defied them. No matter which is the case, it isn't realistic to assume that now he will verify that his code complies with the standards. Someone else must check the unit for adherence to standards and report any failure. Another time when standard compliance can be tested is during peer reviews or structured walk-throughs. These concepts are discussed in Section 4.2.

4.1.2.6 Special Considerations of Integration Testing.   There are two opposing methods of performing integration testing. One is to perform integration on every unit at the same time. This can be considered the "big bang" approach. The alternative is an incremental approach. This consists of testing a relatively few number of units. When all integration testing has been successful with these units then several more units are added and integration testing continues.

It might be a matter of personal opinion, but I feel that the big bang approach is more difficult, more confusing, and ends up taking more time than an incremental approach. If errors occur during integration testing (and they will), it will be more difficult to isolate the offending module if every module in the system is a potential culprit. Better to test in an incremental fashion and know that when a new error occurs, it must be due to a newly integrated module.

Approaching integration testing in an incremental fashion is much more straightforward. Test a small core of modules. Correct any resulting integration errors. Add a small number of additional modules to the system, rebuild the executable, and repeat the integration tests. If errors occur, they will almost certainly be located in one of the recently added modules. Correct them and repeat the process. It may seem like this approach will take more time, but by using automated testing they can go very quickly.

4.1.2.7 Top-down Versus Bottom-up Integration.   Once the decision has been made to take an incremental approach to integration testing, you are faced with another decision. Should the testing start at the top and work downwards or should it start at the bottom and work upwards? The former is call "top-down" integration and naturally enough the latter is called "bottom-up" integration.

Top-down integration typically starts with the window which launches various subsystems within the application. This window is thoroughly tested and debugged. The next testing stage is the top level of each subsystem. These windows are completely tested. Attention then shifts to the next lower level in each subarea. This process continues until the lowest-level windows, i.e., those which don't call any other windows, are tested.

Bottom-up testing by definition is done in just the opposite order. The first parts of the system tested are the low-level windows. Usually these are the screens where users actually enter new data, modify existing data, and generate reports. Once this level has been tested and corrected, then attention shifts upward to windows which call the low-level ones. This process continues until the window which launches all subsystems is reached.

Which is better? Like most of life's imponderables, there is no easy answer. Each has advantages and disadvantages. Overall, I feel the advantages of the bottom-up approach exceed those of top-down. With a bottom-up approach, the core functionality of a system can be focused on. This normally consists of being able to input records, view them, modify them, delete them, and generate reports based on them. Once this basic functionality has been thoroughly tested, the system has a base stable enough to allow the testing to be expanded to other areas and functionality.

Another advantage of a bottom-up approach is that it lends itself more readily to parallel testing. Two or more teams can perform integration testing simultaneously. Each test group would normally concentrate on a different subarea of the application. The ability to perform parallel testing can have a significant positive impact on the project's testing schedule. Testing can be completed significantly faster if multiple subareas of the application are being tested simultaneously.

4.1.2.8 Regression Testing and Integration Testing.   In many situations integration testing will seem to be a case of "two steps forward and one step backwards." It might actually seem like one step forwards and two steps backwards. Errors will occur which require changes to previously integrated and tested software modules. Any change to a software module should cause that module to undergo unit testing again. After the unit testing has been successful, then the integration testing which uncovered the error can be rerun. It the problem still exists, then it's back to the drawing board because the whole cycle must be repeated.

The gist of what I'm saying is that integration testing will require a significant amount of regression testing. It isn't safe to assume that a fix made to a module is correct. Many times, changes to a system made during the testing phase introduce bigger problems than the original problem being addressed. All changes made to units must be thoroughly tested to prevent this possibility. Fortunately, all of the test scripts generated during the unit testing phase have been saved and are available for reuse. A test cycle built to rerun all unit tests for a module can be quickly executed. The amount of actual, manually performed regression testing should be minimal if test scripts were generated during the unit testing phase.

4.1.3 System Testing

System testing represents the summit of the testing activity. It isn't begun until all development, unit testing, and integration testing have been concluded. All of the development and testing activity up until this point has been focused at producing a functioning client/server system. At this point in time the test team may draw a breath of relief and think they are done. Sorry, folks; this isn't the case. The system now exists, but its accuracy and completeness must be determined. Determining whether the system is both accurate and complete is the focus of system testing.

Past experience has shown that when system testing begins, approximately one-half of the testing and quality assurance work remains to be done. What could be left to test, asks the gentle reader? Table 4.3 provides a list of the areas which need to be addressed during the system testing phase. Each of them constitute a significant amount of work.

4.1.3.1 Functional Verification Testing. The development of the system has been completed. All of the modules in the system passed unit testing with flying colors. All of the modules were successfully integrated. Everything looks great. The system must be done. What could possibly be wrong?

You can't test functions which have been inadvertently left out of the system. Normally, features of the system are omitted because of a misunderstanding of the specifications, poorly written specifications, or a lack

TABLE 4.3

Facets of
System Testing

Functional Verification Testing

Stress Testing

Performance Testing

Configuration Testing

Recovery Testing

Security Testing

of understanding of the requirements on the part of the developers. Verification testing checks that all of the functionality required by the system design specifications have been included in the completed system. This testing involves stepping through the specifications documents and cross-referencing them with modules in the system which fulfill these requirements.

This cross-reference system can be as complicated as a computerized database or as simple as a rolodex file. All that it must accomplish is to associate each functional requirement identified with the window, function, and/or stored procedure which fulfills that requirement. Once all of the requirements have been listed, it should be relatively simple to identify which ones haven't yet been implemented. The requirements which haven't yet been satisfied are pointed out to developers as system deficiencies.

Verification testing tends to be less of a problem with client/server systems than traditional systems. The reasoning behind this is that in traditional systems the users didn't ordinarily see the system during the development process. Typically the developers spent months (or years!) writing code. Users were shown the system only at the end of the process. RAD, in contrast, typically is more of a collaboration between developers and users. The users see and critique the system as it is being developed, instead of only at the completion.

4.1.3.2 Stress Testing. Stress testing involves "pushing" the system to see how it can handle extreme situations. If the system can handle these situations, that's great. Otherwise, the tests will allow developers to identify problem conditions and modify the system to better handle them. Examples of extreme situations which should be contrived are listed in Table 4.4.

The first two stress situations can be produced in at least two manners. The first method would be to pull together a large number of

TABLE 4.4

Stress Tests

Simulating more online users than the system is designed to handle

Each simulated user interacts with the system at a higher rate than normal

Inputting data into the system at a much higher rate than production will experience

Reducing available system resources (free disk space, memory) while the system runs

Exercising the system for periods of time which exceed normal production conditions

Generating a significant amount of background network traffic

Requesting a number of large reports be produced at one time users and client workstations. Their interaction with the system would then need to be carefully planned and coordinated. The combined activity allows the system to be placed under the desired stress. This method is unreliable, difficult to orchestrate, expensive in terms of manpower and hardware, and not readily reproduced.

A second method to stress test a client/server system is to employ the same test tools used in previous test activities. The first test can be accomplished by reusing previously built test scripts and executing them to simulate a greater number of terminals. The second test is achievable by modifying test scripts to take out the pauses or "user think time." With delays removed, the scripts can subject the system to significantly greater throughput rates.

The advantages of the second, automated method over the manual process are noteworthy. Automated testing can be done much easier and cheaper. It involves fewer people and hardware resources. Additionally, the results are reproducible. This advantage becomes very important if the system fails the initial round of stress testing and requires corrections and retesting.

4.1.3.3 Performance Testing. Once the client/server system has been developed and passes all the functional tests, it undergoes perhaps the ultimate (and least forgiving) test of all. This test is whether the performance of the system meets the documented requirements and/or the users' expectations. If a system doesn't pass this test, it diminishes the success of all previous testing. A system perceived as being too slow won't be tolerated by the user community. They will complain about it, undermine it, and sabotage it in an effort to make the system fail.

Correcting performance shortcomings, unfortunately, isn't as easy as correcting a simple error. Frequently the cause of performance problems is rooted deep within the system. The basis might be a poor database table design, inefficient application code, inadequate indexing, excessive network traffic, or a similar cause. None of these are amenable to a quick fix. They are all likely to take considerable effort to find and correct.

The sooner performance problems are found, the better. The reasons for this statement are many. The earlier that a performance problem is known about, the more time there is to identify and correct it before the system is scheduled to go into production. If performance problems are discovered early, the less code there is to scour for the cause and less code there will be to correct. Finally, time needs to be allowed to acquire faster hardware if the performance-related problem can't be corrected by a software fix.

4.1.3.4 Recovery Testing. All computer systems are likely to fail at one time or another. Some typical causes of system crashes include hardware failure, disk failures, lightning strikes, power surges, and communications problems. The causes for system failures are legion. A failure frequently involves a combination of threats which by themselves wouldn't cause a problem.

Loss of power is probably the most commonly perceived threat to continued system operation. Many systems employ a battery backup which allows a graceful shutdown in the event of a power failure. This solution helps, but it doesn't guarantee power indefinitely. Even systems with backup generators have crashed because their generators eventually ran out of fuel.

If it is accepted that all systems can crash, the process of restoring the system to an operational state becomes crucial. Recovery procedures must be developed during system design for all conceivable types of failure. These procedures must outline what needs to be done in clear and concise steps. Operations personnel will likely be in a panic trying to restore the system, so the clarity and accuracy of the recovery procedures are paramount.

It isn't enough to simply have recovery procedures; they must be tested. Whether the recovery is completely automatic or requires human intervention, it must be tested. The best guinea pigs to test system recovery on are the operational personnel who will be supporting the system. Since they are the ones who will actually be there to recover the system, they should be involved in tuning and testing these procedures.

4.1.3.5 Security Testing. It should be apparent that any data an organization puts on a computer system (client/server or otherwise) must be worth something to that organization. It's also a sad but true fact that any data worth acquiring and storing is a potential target. Computer criminals could be hackers simply trying to beat the system for a challenge, dishonest employees who see a chance to make an illegal buck, or competitors intent on gaining a competitive advantage. These criminals may want to read, alter, delete, or destroy the data. They might simply want to prevent rightful users from accessing it in a timely manner. No matter what their intentions, the client/server system must be designed to protect its contents.

The distributed nature of a client/server system is one element which increases its security exposure. Messages sent across the LAN or WAN can potentially be intercepted or blocked. If the LAN or WAN is large enough that it can't be physically secured, then thought should be given to encrypting the data.

Security testing is an attempt to assure that the client/server system is safeguarding its data in an appropriate manner. The tester must play the role of a criminal intent on accessing the system. He or she should try any and every trick to gain access to the system. Tests to breach security should include attempts to obtain passwords, access idle terminals, imitate valid users, and guess at passwords. To adequately test a system's security, the testing personnel must be as wily as the criminals they are trying to thwart.

4.1.3.6 Configuration Testing. Configuration testing attempts to verify that all of the system's functionality works under all hardware and software configurations. This form of testing is significantly more important and complex for client/server systems than for traditional systems. This is because client/server systems typically are deployed using a much greater variety of hardware configurations than are traditional systems. Each of the configurations requires thorough testing to be certain that no errors occur under just that configuration.

The hardware platforms involved in a typical client/server system involve, at a minimum, one computer acting as a server and one computer in the client role. Normally there will be significantly more than a single client machine. For some systems the number of client machines will reach into the thousands. It's also likely that the hardware being used for the client workstations is heterogeneous. Some of the workstations will be 486-based PCs, others will be Pentiums, and still others will be Pentium Pro machines. There is also a strong likelihood that some of the workstations will be Macintoshes, UNIX-based workstations, or X-terminals. Configuration testing requires that each of these platforms be completely tested. The value of utilizing previously built test scripts in this scenario should be obvious!

4.1.3.7 Who Performs System Testing. System testing is performed by a quality assurance (QA) team, user representatives, or a group composed of both. These team members will focus exclusively on whether the system meets the documented requirements. They don't care about excuses, apologies, or explanations. Either the test in question passes or it doesn't.

If the client/server system is being developed internally, then the system test group may be a little less formal. It might be composed exclusively of user representatives. The reason for this is that in-house projects typically have an assurance of ongoing corrections and enhancements. Systems developed by a third party commonly include a defined period in which system problems must be discovered and reported. Any errors discovered after this period are not covered under the warranty. When this is the situation, there needs to be a more formal, concentrated effort to detect and report errors before the time runs out.

One group that is noticeably absent from the system test team is developers. Since system testing focuses exclusively on functional testing (all of it is black box testing), there is no need for developers. Problems that occur during system testing will be referred back to developers. As participants in the actual testing, developers aren't involved.

4.1.3.8 System Test Plan. The system test plan is the grand finale of testing. There are no "stubs" for modules whose design hasn't been finished. There are no "we'll finish that later" excuses allowed. System testing doesn't start until everything is complete. In a system test, everything is loaded. All of the parts of the system are exercised to make certain that they work in unison as well as they worked individually in early tests.

4.1.3.9 When to Perform System Testing. The time to perform system testing comes after all unit testing and integration testing have been completed. Since system testing relies upon all components of the system, it isn't correct to begin before the development has reached this point.

Design work on the system test plan needs to be started very early in the life cycle of the project. It may seem unnecessary to begin planning a test that early, but there are legitimate reasons for doing so. First of all, it will take more time that expected to produce this plan. Be prepared to put a significant amount of time and detail into this plan. A second reason for starting so early is that many people need to sign off on the system test plan. The representative of the user community must agree that this test satisfies them. The head of software development must agree that the test is complete. The quality assurance group must concur that the plan tests everything that the system was designed to deliver.

4.1.3.10 Special Considerations of System Testing. During system testing, people will attempt to shift the blame. Typically, when system testing uncovers errors, it isn't immediately apparent which subsystem is causing the error. It might not be immediately apparent which computer the error is occurring on. This being the case, each developer claims that his or her subsystem is innocent. This phenomenon can be avoided (or at least minimized) by fostering an atmosphere which avoids blaming people for errors. When developers don't feel threatened, they're likely to expend less time avoiding the blame and more time correcting their errors.

4.1.4 Acceptance Testing

The line between system testing and acceptance testing is blurry. The reason is that many development shops consider system testing and acceptance testing to be essentially the same activity. The significant distinction between these two is that system testing is performed by the organization which developed the system, while acceptance testing is equivalent testing performed by the customer.

The two forms of testing are most likely to exist when there is a very clear-cut line between the developing group and the group accepting the system. A perfect example of this would be if corporation XYZ contracted with a consulting company to develop a new client/server system. The consulting company would perform its own internal system testing. Once the system testing was complete, the customer would run the newly developed system through its acceptance testing. Both forms of testing are intent on assuring that the system meets the formal specifications.

If corporation XYZ had its MIS department develop a similar client/server system, there would probably be no acceptance testing. The system testing performed by the MIS department would be the final testing of the system.

4.1.4.1 Who Performs Acceptance Testing. Acceptance testing is performed exclusively by customer representatives. This might include the customer's own QA team, user representatives, or consultants engaged specifically to perform this job. There should be no one from the development team involved in acceptance testing, whatsoever! The purpose of acceptance testing is to provide a completely independent testing phase proving to the customer's satisfaction that the system does what it was contracted to do. Development personnel included in acceptance testing foils the whole idea of an independent confirmation.

4.1.4.2 Acceptance Test Plan. The format of the acceptance test plan is identical to that of the system test plan. Each of these tests attempts to corroborate that the client/server system fulfills all required capabilities. The only difference between them is who performs them. Since the purpose of both tests is identical, there is no reason why the same general test plan can't be used.

4.1.4.3 When to Perform Acceptance Testing. Acceptance testing marks the end of the trail. It's done after everything else. Once acceptance testing is complete, all that is left is to deploy the system.

4.1.4.4 Special Considerations of Acceptance Testing. This series of testing represents the customer's last chance to be certain that the system does what the customer said it needed to do. If it doesn't fully address the requirements, then there will be no later chance to do additional testing. Because of this, the people who write the acceptance test plan must be alert that it addresses all concerns. Questions they have about certain aspects of the system must be addressed now.

4.2 Desk Checking, Peer Review, and Code Inspections

Not all corrections to a system being developed need to come about as a result of formal testing. Development teams also employ techniques to check the quality of modules long before they get to the point of being tested. These techniques go by a number of names. The most common among them are desk checking, peer reviews, and code inspections.

4.2.1 Desk Checking

Desk checking is the manual process of reading the programming code to verify that it does what it is intended to do. The origins of desk checking date back to the days when the turnaround time for each compile was measured in hours. Under those conditions, a significant amount of time was spent waiting for a compilation to complete. During these periods, programmers made productive use of their time by examining or checking code modules. In his book *Software System Testing and Quality Assurance*, Boris Beizer states that meticulous desk checking can catch up to 30% of all errors.

Compile times on modern workstations and current development tools now measure in seconds instead of minutes and hours. Developers no longer have significant periods of dead space while waiting for their compilations to complete. Just because the dead time periods are no longer available, the concept of desk checking hasn't lost its value. Activities which should be included on the agenda for desk checking by all developers are:

■ Examine all uses of global type variables. Is it essential that they be global in nature or would a more limited scope be sufficient?

Certain values do require the breadth of a global-type variable, but using global variables has potential dangers. It's possible for any module in the system to inadvertently modify values in global variables. This can cause unexpected results to occur later in the application. If the global is referenced throughout the system, it can be very difficult to pinpoint where the modification is being performed. A value whose access is limited is much safer in a variable with a more limited scope.

■ Verify the type and value of every constant being declared. Is it necessary? Is it correct? Confirm that constants are being used everywhere it is feasible to use them.

■ Calls to all functions.(local, global, and system) should be closely examined. Specifically, the number of parameters being passed, their order, and return values need to be scrutinized. Attention needs to be given as to whether these parameters are being passed by reference or by value. Using the wrong choice can result in unpredictable errors.

■ Error messages displayed to the user should be examined to make certain they are clear, understandable, and accurate. Users have little tolerance for messages which are cryptic, misleading, or provide no instruction on what must be done to correct the situation.

■ Return codes from every SQL query must be examined for error conditions. Every error returned by an SQL statement must be properly handled. The appropriate response might be to retry the query, abort the operation, or inform the user of the failure. This checking is especially true for deadlock errors. If such a problem occurs, the user must be informed whether their changes were made or not.

■ All code must be examined to assure that it conforms to existing programming standards and naming conventions. This should be verified in integration testing, but each developer should be held accountable for failing to comply with published standards.

■ Every module needs to be documented internally. Many developers balk at documenting their code by saying it is "self-documented," but in most cases that's bunk. This requirement is for the good of the developer as well as anyone who must support the system in the future. Each developer needs to develop the personal and professional responsibility to perform this task, whether they like doing it or not.

- Most development environments use an item called a *database transaction object* to communicate with the database. Many tools allow a developer to create and utilize more than one such object. While this capability is essential in many situations, it opens the door for a number of problems. Developers can inadvertently reference an incorrect object, drain resources by using them to excess, or forget to delete objects when they are done using them. Use of these objects needs to be closely monitored.

- Finally and most importantly, developers need to read their code. It's amazing how many errors can be picked out by simply reading the code. Developers quickly improve their skills as they gain experience with a given development package. After even a few months of using a tool, they can look back on their earliest code and notice both errors and room for improvement. If they don't read their own code, then this possibility for improving the system can't occur.

4.2.2 Peer Reviews

The concept of peer reviews is pretty simple. The more eyes that examine a module, the more likely it is that errors and inefficiencies will be discovered and corrected. A peer review can be as simple or formal as the group wishes to make it.

The simplest form of peer review is when developers ask co-workers to look over their code. This happens all the time during development projects. Developers bang their heads against a problem until they can't stand it any longer. They ask a co-worker to look at a section of code. More often than not, the co-worker quickly finds the problem. It isn't that the co-worker was "smarter" than the first. The first developers had certain expectations (or delusions) concerning their code. They convinced themselves that the error was in a certain area or wasn't in another area. Being free of these mental blinders, the co-worker is able to zero in on the error easily.

A more formal method of peer review would be for one developer to ask another to examine an entire unit once it has been completed. This relationship develops when developers feel that their counterparts are technically competent and willing to help each other. The co-worker looks over the code and comments on what he or she sees as errors, inefficiencies, or potential problems. After marking up the printout, he or she returns it to the original developer. The original developer is then free to follow or ignore the criticism.

Frequently, developers will work out an arrangement to look over each other's code. In other development shops, management may require that every module must undergo examination by someone other than the developer. While this is ultimately good for the project, there is frequently reluctance to mandate from above. Management should take care to stress the mutual advantages of peer reviews when instituting the requirement.

There is one ground rule which must be followed for peer reviews to be effective. This condition is that while reviewing a module, all comments are directed toward the code and not the developer. If this isn't followed, then comments and criticism can become personal. Once this happens, people are apt to become defensive or vindictive. Without an environment of cooperation and sensitivity to others' feelings, peer reviews become an empty, worthless exercise.

The flip side of this coin is that developers might withhold criticism because they want to be "nice." The reviewer sees problems but is afraid to mention them because it might be misconstrued as being unfriendly. Management should strive to assure all reviewers that they can be honest without hurting anyone's feelings.

4.2.3 Code Inspection

Code inspection, also called a structured walk-through, is a formal process of inspecting the code in modules. Each module in the client/server system which undergoes an inspection follows the same procedures. The inspection process is described in the following paragraphs.

■ When a developer feels a module is ready for unit testing, an inspection is scheduled. Each inspection is expected to take approximately two hours. If more time is required, then multiple module inspections should be scheduled.

■ The developer is responsible for arranging a time and location which enables all attendees easy access. Any supporting material (e.g., screen prints, code listings, function definitions, etc.) needed for the inspection must be distributed by the developer.

- There should be from three to six participants at the inspection. Each organization should develop its own procedures for assigning attendees. All attendees should have a technical background and experience with the appropriate tool or language. At least one attendee should be senior to the developer.

- Each attendee is expected to spend time reviewing the module prior to the formal inspection. The time spent should be two hours or less.

- The most senior individual is assigned the role of leader. Another attendee is responsible for recording comments and results of the inspection.

- The inspection should take no more than two hours. Meetings which last longer than this have likely deviated from the subject at hand.

- During the inspection, comments or critiques should be directed towards the code and not the author. Each participant should feel free to comment on the code, its style, and efficiency.

- Consensus must be reached on whether the module is accepted or not. A module can be accepted with the suggestion that certain changes be made to it. The suggestions should be listed on the formal inspection sheet.

- The inspection leader is responsible for verifying that specified changes to the module are actually made. He or she should coordinate with the developer to review these changes.

Each formal code inspection requires that certain information be gathered and retained—details such as the name of the module, who participated, and the output of the inspection. Figure 4.2 is an example of the inspection sheet which might be employed during a technical review. The person acting as recorder is responsible for filling out the sheet. Completed copies need to be forwarded to all attendees as well as the project librarian.

4.2.4 Advantages of These Techniques

The advantages of desk checking, peer reviews, and structured walk-throughs are many. First of all, it helps detect errors early in the development process. Earlier errors are cheaper errors to fix. By finding and fixing these even before the unit testing stage, the unit tests will go faster and won't need to be rerun.

Figure 4.2
Technical Review
Inspection Sheet

Code Inspection Summary

Inspection Identification:

Project: Inspection Number:

Date: Time: Location:

Module Identification:

Module under Inspection:

Module Author:

Module Description:

Inspection Team:

Name & Position   Signature:

1. _____   _____

2. _____   _____

3. _____   _____

4. _____   _____

5. _____   _____

6. _____   _____

Inspection Results:

Accepted: as is ( )   with alterations ( )

Rejected: major changes required ( )   minor changes required ( )

Inspection incomplete: (explanation must be attached)

Supporting Material:

Screen Shots ( )

Table Layouts ( )

Application Navigation ( )

Other ( )

Issues To Be Addressed:

All three of the techniques described above have an educational aspect. Whether developers look at their own code or someone else's, the practice of reading code will make them better developers. This advantage is especially apparent when developers scrutinize each other's work. They will each be exposed to different techniques of using the system. During the review, the best techniques will be recognized and all developers can begin using them. Overall, it will hopefully elevate the proficiency of everyone at the organization.

Code inspection enforces code consistency throughout the project. This is advantageous because consistent code is easier to debug and maintain. It's easier to test for errors in similar code because everyone who looks at it is already familiar with the programming style. Errors are more likely to stick out. The same concept carries through to maintaining the system. If all modules are programmed in a similar style, then the person charged with maintaining the system only has to learn a single style of programming.

Like most good things, these approaches can become disadvantages if they are taken to the extreme. You know you've gone over the edge when more time is spent preparing for, inspecting, and dissecting code than actually writing code. If this point is reached then any potential advantages are outweighed by the time spent doing the inspections.

4.3 Testing Personnel

There has been a tendency endemic in the software development industry to assign personnel with the least experience (i.e., "new hires") to the role of testing the product. Other people assigned to the testing area typically include people who aren't productive developers or those who don't fit into other teams. This practice is extremely shortsighted. Skills needed to effectively test client/server systems aren't any less demanding than those needed to develop the software. In fact, test personnel benefit from an extremely wide experience base. They encounter situations and problems which developers won't likely be presented with.

4.3.1 Attributes of an Ideal QA Team Member

Somewhere there is a software professional who is a testing machine. He or she does a quality job each and every day at the office by rooting out errors, obscure and obvious alike. Unfortunately, it's unlikely that this individual is employed by your organization. While few of us have all the skills needed to make us perfect in a testing capacity, it's worthwhile to list the skills such a person would have. These skills would include:

- Communication skills. An ideal tester has to communicate with both ends of the spectrum. They need to be able to talk to users as well as with developers. Unfortunately these two groups don't have the same jargon. Discussions with users focus on what the system does or doesn't do right. This information must then be translated and relayed to the development staff. Someone in QA must be able to communicate with each group equally well.

- Empathy. Everyone involved in developing a client/server system has fears and concerns. Users are afraid they'll be stuck with a system which doesn't fulfill their needs. Developers are afraid they haven't been told what the users really want and will have to rebuild the entire system. Management is afraid the whole project will collapse and they will catch the blame. Testers deal with each of these groups and must understand and sympathize with each. By being empathetic, testers will be able to minimize confrontation and hostility.

- Technical skill. Developers as a group have very little respect for people they perceive as technically illiterate. The first time someone from QA makes a claim which is unsound, their credibility goes out the window. A tester must have technical knowledge in client/server concepts as well as experience with the tools being used on the project. Several years of hands-on programming experience should be a prerequisite.

- Self-confident. Testers must have the self-confidence to stand their ground when they are accused of being wrong. If they allow themselves to be talked or bluffed out of every position, they won't accomplish much.

- Diplomatic. It takes a great deal of diplomacy to tell someone that they are wrong. Testers must be able to diplomatically inform developers when their software has errors. If the approach taken is confrontational the tester may "win the battle but lose the war" in terms of future cooperation from the development staff.

- A sense of humor. Many tricky situations can be defused by a well-timed humorous comment.

- A great memory. How many times have you had the nagging feeling that you've seen a similar problem before? You just can't remember where or when. An ideal tester would have the ability to dredge these facts out of her memory. This skill is invaluable during the testing process because so many problems turn out to be minor alterations of already discovered errors.

- Perseverance. Someone in a QA position has to have an incredible degree of perseverance. Sometimes it takes an amazing amount of time and effort to isolate, identify, and assign an error. This position isn't for someone who gives up easily.

- Skepticism. Developers will try to explain away any error they can. This is to be expected. Testers must listen to everyone but be skeptical until they look into things for themselves.

- Self-motivating. In this type of position, it would be easy to slack off. Only someone with the ability to self-motivate will be able to throw themselves into their job every day.

4.3.2 Hostility and Resentment

There is no getting around the fact that QA people aren't popular with the developer team. Since the fundamental responsibility of QA people is to demonstrate that developers made mistakes, this shouldn't really come as a surprise. QA personnel should be aware of this reality when they come into the job. New testing personnel should be able to deal with resentment and hostility. In the best of circumstances, outright acts of hostility can be avoided, but it will always exist right under the surface.

4.3.3 Rotation

Being in the role of quality assurance can be very draining for a number of reasons. It's hard to keep up one's enthusiasm indefinitely. The best resolution is to rotate people from development positions to QA positions and back on a regular basis. There are several advantages to this. First of all, it gives QA people a chance to recharge their batteries by moving back to a less stressful position. A rotation cycle introduces fresh blood into the QA area on a regular basis. It exposes everyone to what being in QA is like. It can serve to make developers realize that QA members are human beings after all. Perhaps most importantly, being in a QA position will enable developers to be more proficient testers when they rotate back to that position.

4.3.4 Budget

Quality costs money. This is a reality which can't be denied. It takes time and costs money to test software. It costs money to purchase test tools and test hardware. Some of the expenses required to adequately test client/server systems are described in the following sections.

4.3.4.1 Software. The QA department must be adequately funded. Client/server system development testing requires considerably more expenditures on software packages than traditional systems ever did. Types of software needed include development tools, database engines, and communications packages. Typically, these packages include a base cost, a cost per seat, and an annual maintenance fee. It isn't cheap, but client/server systems can't be done without these packages.

Testing software is just as essential as the previously mentioned types of software but is frequently misunderstood or overlooked. Implementing client/server systems is a complex undertaking. To be successful, productive, and efficient, the quality assurance group needs up-to-date testing tools as well as training in how to use them.

4.3.4.2 Hardware. Another necessity for a quality assurance department is enough hardware to assemble a testing lab. Such a lab may require multiple server machines and a number of client workstations. Although it may seem like a luxury to have such a facility, there are a number of very valid reasons why this test bed is a necessity and not a pipe dream.

Testing doesn't end once the system goes into production. Even after this momentous occasion, there will still be many situations when testing is required. It isn't safe, logical, or rational to perform testing on a live system. The cost of a company's critical system going down is too great a chance to take. Security of the data might also preclude developers from working on the real system.

If users discover an error on the production system, it must be reproduced on a test system. The cause will be analyzed and a fix will be implemented on the test system. If the coding change corrects the problem and regression testing proves the fix hasn't created any new errors, then the modification can be implemented on the production system. Oftentimes, modifying the online system must be scheduled and coordinated with production personnel.

Another reason for having a test platform is to evaluate new releases of underlying software. New versions of the operating system, database management system, GUI tool (e.g., PowerBuilder, Visual Basic, etc.), and communications software are issued on a regular basis. It wouldn't be advisable to install this new software without some initial testing to verify that errors won't be introduced.

One more use for a test system is to test new hardware platforms. A useful client/server system is a growing client/server system. Growth will frequently involve deploying the system onto a totally new hardware platform. Using a test system instead of the production system will isolate online users from any possible problems. Once the new hardware has been "certified," then it can be brought into the production system.

4.3.4.3 Training.   Training for everyone in client/server development is an absolute necessity, not a boondoggle! Client/server is so new and growing so fast that if developers aren't frequently being trained, they are falling behind. Without proper training there are too many false paths which developers can wander down. All of the above statements are just as true for quality assurance team members as they are for developers.

Training can take many forms. It can be a class put on by one of your vendors, either on-site or off-site. If a national or local user group exists for packages used in-house, they can provide invaluable opportunities for networking and information gathering. Training might take the form of computer-related degrees or classes at a local university or community college. Attending a seminar by a third-party vendor can also provide valuable knowledge about upcoming changes. Thoroughly scanning trade journals can allow personnel to keep a handle on changes in the industry overall.

Management might not want to hear it, but attending national user group conferences can be extremely valuable. Too often, management and jealous co-workers, assume that attendees are simply on a vacation. Nothing could be further from the truth. A diligent employee can stay busy all day attending pertinent sessions at a user conference.

Developers and testers need to be in a constant state of education. The days of relying on a static skill set are long gone in this industry. This is even more true in the client/server arena. If skills aren't kept up to date the quality and the very success of client/server systems are at risk.

When calculating the training budget for the quality assurance unit or the entire client/server development team, it's important not to overlook any cost components. The obvious costs are hard dollars required to have personnel attend classes. The dollars go towards travel, lodging, meals, and class entry costs. Other hard dollar costs are tuition reimbursement when applicable. Less obvious is the cost of time not spent on system development during classes, seminars, and user groups. While these costs are harder to calculate, they are still important. Schedules should be developed with training time estimates factored into them. Otherwise, developers and testers will feel that they are being penalized for being trained.

4.3.4.4 Summary. Each of the areas previously described costs money. Quality software costs money. What isn't always so obvious is that the lack of quality costs even more money! What does it cost per day, per hour, per minute for your company's mission-critical systems to be down? If system throughput is half of what it should be, what does that cost? Is the cost in lost sales, irritated customers, and frustrated employees ever known? Quality costs, but the alternative is much worse.

4.4 Testing Metrics

Metrics pertains to the science of measurement. If this book were about developing client/server systems, this section would be extremely long and complicated. The practice of developing client/server systems hasn't advanced to the point where metrics are widely agreed upon. Metrics which are measurable, reliable, and accurate haven't yet been standardized.

4.4.1 Percent of Testing Complete

There are several metrics which need to be monitored when testing client/server systems. The first measurement which management always wants to know is what percentage of the testing has been successfully completed. This statistic will be requested on a regular basis. Management and users alike will eagerly watch this measurement creep toward the magical "100%" value.

Most of the test management information products include the ability to answer this basic question. The status of tests must be documented as each test is run. When this is adhered to, then current reports showing testing completion statistics will be both readily available and accurate. It obviously follows that the more finely defined the testing details are, the more accurate testing completion reports can be. Chapter 5 describes test management products and their capabilities.

4.4.2 Code Coverage

Code coverage measures how much code has been executed during the test compared to how much code there is left to execute. Code coverage can either be based on control flows or data flows. In control flow coverage, the aim is to test lines of code, paths through the code, branch conditions, and other elements of the software's flow. In data flow coverage, the aim is to test that data states remain valid through the operation of the software—for example, assuring that a data element is defined before it is used.

4.4.3 Corrected Errors

Another metric to watch is the number of discovered errors which have been successfully corrected. Users, especially paying clients, have an expectation that all errors discovered while testing the system will be corrected and retested before the system is released. This report will also be requested on a regular basis.

Since users (and probably managers as well) are going to be watching this area, there needs to be a convenient method of providing them with the information. The normal method is a "Corrected Errors" report. This management tool needs to be able to provide at least the information listed in Table 4.5. Chapter 7 addresses tools which track software errors

TABLE 4.5

Correct Errors Report

All discovered errors

Status (critical, etc.) assigned to each error

Developer assigned to fix each error

Status of each error

Release in which errors were corrected

Estimated time of completion for errors not yet corrected

4.5 GUI Controls and Suggested Tests

This section provides a list of typical GUI objects and controls and specific tests which should be performed on them. It is an extensive list, but isn't intended to be definitive. Custom controls specific to a single environment aren't included here. Objects and some tests which should be performed on them are:

Object Type	Specific Attribute to Testing
Windows	Is the title bar text accurate?
	Does a menu bar exist?
	Does the menu contain appropriate items?
	Is the Help menu item functional?
	Is the System Menu Box visible? Should it be?
	Are Minimize/Maximize buttons visible? Should they be? Do they function?
	If a window is maximized, are objects on it (grids, datawindows) properly adjusted?
	If the window is minimized, is an appropriate icon displayed?
	Are horizontal and/or vertical scrolls bars visible? Should they be?
	Is the window modal (application modal, system modal)?
	Is the window resizable? Should it be?
	If a window is resized, are objects, grids primarily, on it automatically adjusted?
	Is the window moveable? Should it be?
	Is the window background the correct color and pattern?
	Will users find the tab sequence logical and/or convenient?
	Does the system recognize idle terminals?
	If changes to a window are made, is the user prompted before losing them?
	Do the foreground and background colors result in easily read text?
	Do visual cues inform users which fields are required versus optional?

Object Type	Specific Attribute to Testing
Menus	Are menu items grouped together logically?
	Do menu groups follow industry (i.e., Microsoft) standards?
	Are accelerator keys defined? Do they work?
	Are speed keys (mnemonic keys) defined? Do they work?
	Are separator lines in menu lists used consistently?
	Do active items get checkmarked where appropriate?
	Are cascaded menu items identified with a right arrow?
	Are cascaded menus used only where absolutely necessary?
	Are cascaded menus limited to two levels of cascade?
	Are menus designed consistently throughout the system?
	Is an ellipsis used to identify menu items which bring up a dialog box?
	Are inactive menu items dimmed out?
	When an inactive menu item becomes active, is it still dimmed out?
Dialog Boxes	Does every dialog box include a meaningful title?
	Are dialog boxes modal?
	Are buttons on dialog boxes clearly labeled?
	Do all dialog boxes offer a clear opportunity to abort the current operation?
	Is text on dialog boxes clear and understandable?
	Are dialog box borders thicker than normal to draw attention to the box?
	Are dialog boxes moveable? Should they be?
Static Text	Is all static text protected from modification by users?
	Are consistent font sizes applied to static text fields?
	If static text is dynamically changed by the application, is it being done correctly?
	Is the text foreground color legible against the window background color?
Control button	Are all control buttons (also called command buttons) clearly labeled?
	Do they have borders which emphasize the fact that they are buttons?
	When the button is clicked, is the user presented with a visible cue or change in the button?

Object Type	Specific Attribute to Testing
	Are control buttons on windows consistently aligned?
	Do all control buttons on a window have the same font type and size?
	Does every control button perform the intended action?
	Is the default action (i.e., Enter Key executes it) assigned rationally?
	Is the cancel action (i.e., Esc Key executes it) assigned rationally?
Radio Button	Are all radio buttons on a window mutually exclusive?
	Are radio buttons on a window logically grouped? Does this work as desired?
	Are radio buttons clearly labeled?
	Is the most common choice the default?
	If radio buttons are clicked, do related fields change appropriately?
Check box	Are any check boxes mutually exclusive? If so, radio buttons should be used.
	Are all check boxes clearly labeled?
	Are check boxes properly initialized?
	Does a box surround related check boxes to emphasize their relationship?
Edit Box	Can users enter or change text in all edit boxes?
	Are all edit boxes large enough to contain values entered by users?
	If data potentially requires it, are multiline edit boxes employed?
	Are all edit boxes properly initialized when the window comes up?
	Are values entered into all edit boxes validated?
List Boxes	Is the list box single selection or multiple selection? Has this been tested?
	Are all list boxes properly initialized when the window comes up?
	Are values entered into all list boxes validated?
	If an invalid value is entered, is the user informed immediately?
	Do all list boxes contain horizontal and vertical scroll bars when appropriate?
Combo Box	Is the combo box editable? Should it be?
	Are combo boxes properly initialized or loaded?
	Are values entered into all combo boxes validated?

Object Type	Specific Attribute to Testing
	If an invalid value is entered, is the user informed immediately?
	If a combo box contains a long list, can the first letter or two of a value be entered?
Pictures	Are images loaded into picture controls always available?
	If an image isn't available, what fills the picture control?
	Are picture controls appropriately sized?
	Are picture controls resizeable? If so, does the image resize to fill the control?
	Are picture controls moveable? Should they be?
Drop & Drag	What objects on a window can be dragged?
	What objects on a window recognize a drop operation?
	Is the cursor icon changed during a drag operation?
	Do all objects which recognize a drop handle it correctly?
Grids	Are grids (also known as datawindows or tablefields) properly initiated?
	Are horizontal and vertical scroll bars visible when required?
	Is a command button available to clear all grids?
	If split scrolling is possible, is it provided?
	Have all grids been tested to verify that they display valid, accurate rows?
	Are grid headers clear and understandable?
	If grids are editable, is this fact clear?
	Is a command button to save the grid visible?
Edit Masks	Are edit masks used in all appropriate situations?
	Are they consistently used, e.g., all phone number fields use the same mask?
	If an invalid character is entered, is an understandable error message listed?
	Do edit masks provide enough space for all the largest possible legitimate values?

4.5.1 Navigation Testing

While navigation isn't an object placed on a window, it fulfills a crucial element of an application. Without navigation it wouldn't be possible to move from one window to another. Navigation needs to be specifically examined when testing a client/server system. The appropriate time to inspect navigation is during integration testing and again during system testing.

The tester must follow each possible link or path off of a window. These links may be brought about in a number of ways. Clicking a control button, tool bar icon, or a menu option are by far the most common methods of initiating a move to another window. Double clicking an object, such as a grid, is a different means of moving to another window. Accelerator keys and speed keys are two more ways of initiating a move to other windows.

The number of links in a system tend to grow very quickly. If a client/server system has 100 windows and each window has links to 5 other windows, there are a total of 500 links. Navigation can become even more complicated if menus are dynamically modified to enforce security. When this is the case, there are no additional links, but determining which links should be executable at what time becomes very complicated. The effort to test the navigation aspect of the application isn't trivial and should never be discounted.

4.6 How RAD Affects Testing

RAD development has a significant effect on the testing process. Projects developed under more traditional techniques didn't begin to address testing the system until much later in the project. RAD projects, in contrast, must confront testing much earlier in the project cycle. Some of the ways in which RAD affects testing are described in the following sections.

4.6.1 Numerous Builds

The RAD development cycle emphasizes an iterative approach to software development. Developers and users meet to outline what the application does and how it should function. The developer then creates screens to meet these requirements. An executable or "build" is created and demonstrated to the user. The user and developer then collaborate to identify corrections and enhancements needed. The developer once again goes off to implement the changes requested. This cycle continues until the user community is satisfied with the interface and functionality of the application.

Each build (i.e., intermediate release) of the system must be relatively error free. If users are distracted by new errors each time they see the system, they won't be able to focus on advancing the project. They will also expect errors they noticed in the last iteration to be corrected. This combination of numerous builds and minimal number of errors requires that testing be done early and often.

Each new build must undergo regression testing to be certain errors haven't been introduced along with the desired enhancements. This heightened emphasis on regression testing forces the use of an automated test tool. Developers simply don't have the time, patience, or accuracy to repeat regression testing for every build in the development cycle.

4.6.2 Testing Must Be Designed in Parallel with Development

The test life cycle must start at the same time that development starts. The design and development process for tests is as elaborate and arduous as for applications being tested. If not started early enough, the tests won't be adequate or will cause a long testing schedule to be appended to the development schedule, defeating the rapid aspect of RAD.

Another reason to start testing early is that the earlier testing is started, the earlier gaps or flaws in the application requirements are exposed. The earlier these are identified and addressed, the lower the cost and impact on the project schedule.

4.6.3 RAD Emphasizes What's Visible

One of the idiosyncrasies of RAD is that it focuses almost exclusively on what the user can see. Development sessions tend to dwell on the appearance of screens and navigation within the application. Since users can't see functions and processing of the data, they tend to overlook it. The result is that developers must be especially careful to fully test these frequently overlooked aspects of the application.

4.6.4 Users Will Want What They See

Another quirk of RAD-developed applications is that users tend to assume the project is done once the screens have been built. They don't grasp the concept that a significant amount of foundation-level functionality hasn't been built yet. Some examples are the code for error checking, backups, restoration, data integrity, help screens, data validation, etc. Since these capabilities aren't visible to the users' eyes, they must not be very important. Developers must constantly inform users that what is being developed during RAD sessions is only the interface, not the entire application. If the developer doesn't strive to educate them, users will have unrealistic expectations about how close to completion the project is.

4.6.5 Inheritance

Most client/server development tools claim to be compatible with the RAD paradigm. One of the foundations of their technology which allows them to make this claim is that their packages allow inheritance. Developers can create (or purchase) object classes and place them in an object class library. The "normal" objects (windows, menus, etc.) then inherit from ancestor objects in this library. The capabilities in the ancestor object automatically become available to all descendents.

Inheritance truly represents a two-edged sword to development projects. One edge is that a well-developed object class library can have enormous advantages for a client/server system project. The most significant impact is the improvement in the development time of a client/server system. By building the client/server system upon a well-designed foundation, most of the functionality can be inherited from ancestor objects. This allows descendents to contain a minimum of code. Less code to be developed usually translates into faster development.

The down side of this proposition comes into play if errors or missing capability is discovered in ancestor-level objects. Any changes made to the ancestor objects will impact practically every object in the system. If an error is found in an ancestor object and a correction is made to it, then all objects which inherit from it are questionable. To be certain that they still function as required, all such objects must be retested. This retesting, called *regression testing,* is likely to represent an enormous amount of effort.

The obvious solution to this conundrum is that ancestor objects must function perfectly from the beginning. This solution is easily stated but much less easily implemented. To assure that this level of quality is achieved, two things must be done. First, ancestor objects need to be developed well in advance of all other objects. This will allow sufficient time for thorough design and testing. Second, ancestor objects need to be tested to a much higher level than other objects. Only by guaranteeing the quality of the object class library can the benefits of inheritance be attained.

4.6.6 Heightened User Participation

Traditional software development techniques isolated developers from the user community. The point of contact between MIS and users was normally an analyst. The analyst would then hand the design over to the developers. If the developer had questions or needed an interpretation of the specifications he or she would go to the analyst. At that point the analyst would either answer the question or confer with the users. Eventually a response would work its way back to the developer.

RAD is a cooperative effort between developers and user representatives. This represents a potential improvement in the communications process. First of all, without the middle person, there is less of a chance for misunderstandings to occur. Explanations and descriptions which go through a third party are more likely to be garbled or portions dropped.

Without the interface, the turn-around will be significantly faster. Details flow directly from the user representative to the developer. If questions arise, they can be settled more quickly and more accurately if the developer is able to directly question the user about it. A quicker turnaround has a very positive impact on the testing process. Many "errors" discovered during the integration and system testing process are in fact subject to debate. More than one way of interpreting the requirements leave a significant gray area. When a direct channel of communication exists between users and developers, these types of errors can be resolved more satisfactorily.

All of the above sounds great. Unfortunately, the impact of increased user participation isn't exclusively positive. Many technical people in the MIS area don't have particularly good communication skills. A significant number of people in this field chose it because they don't enjoy working with people. Now RAD techniques require that they be adept at the very skill they may have been running from. To effectively participate in RAD, people on both sides of the table might need some training in effective communication skills.

Another question which crops up during RAD is, who actually represents the user community? Management may appoint one person to be the liaison between users and MIS. There's no guarantee, regretfully, that this individual understands or represents the needs of all users. One project I was involved with had four users in succession designated as the representative of the user community in less than two years. Each person had a significantly different outlook on how the system should function. Needless to say, there were a number of unproductive zigs and zags during that effort.

4.7 Developing a Test Plan

The information needed to formulate a Test Plan includes:

- Test strategy.
- Test requirements to be verified.
- Required resources.

The deliverable of the test planning effort is a test plan document. The steps required are:

1 - Define the testing strategy

Test Strategy Item	Example
Stage of testing	System
Testing type	Function
Technique	75% automated test procedures, 25% manual testing
Completion Criteria	95% of Test cases passed. No high-priority defects unresolved
Testing constraints	Test can't occur during 8 A.M.–6 P.M. time frame

2 - Decompose the software into test requirements

Analyze what business functions the system is supposed to do

When defining test requirements, the goal is to rigorously test each application feature. To do so, you need to decide which set of inputs to a feature will provide the most meaningful test results.

3 - Estimate the testing effort

For each type of test requirement defined in step 2, estimate effort needed to design, develop, execute, and evaluate the test.

Estimate the number of tests that are needed to validate each test requirement.

Count the total number of test requirements of each type.

Sum up all estimated test efforts.

4 - Identify resources

List staff requirements for testing effort.

List system resources, hardware and software, requirements for testing effort.

5 - Create the project test schedule

List each task along with its associated effort estimate.

6 - Write the test plan

Use the information collected in the previous steps to create a test plan.

4.8 Cross-Platform Testing

A significant difference between traditional systems and client/server systems is the number of platforms on which they will be deployed. It's entirely possible that a traditional system will run on a single mainframe and one type of user terminal during its entire lifetime. A client/server, in contrast will almost certainly include a number of different types of client workstations. A client side especially undergoes significant changes. During the life of the system, it's almost certain that new client computers or software environments will be introduced.

Including a new type of server computer or client computer in a client/server system requires testing. This testing should closely follow the system testing performed at the end of the development effort. If test scripts were utilized and retained, the impact of cross-platform testing will be minimized. In situations where testing was originally done manually, this testing will be a significant amount of effort. Realistically, this type of platform testing probably won't be done if automated test cases weren't used.

Some test tools have features which specifically address cross-platform testing aspects of client/server systems. QA Partner from Quality Works is one tool which eases the task of testing under multiple platforms. It recognizes over 12 different GUIs and allows the tester to specify which statements within test scripts should be executed under each of them. This allows a single test script to be developed and run on all GUI platforms without further modification. This example is only a single way in which this tool simplifies multiple platform testing.

4.9 Forcing Error Conditions

Is it possible to deliberately cause errors to occur when testing a client/server system? Can this be accomplished without altering the software being tested? If this is done, it allows testers to see how the system handles error situations. A few examples of how this could be accomplished are listed in Table 4.6.

Will these tests prove anything? Will they make the testing process any sounder or more thorough? The answer to both questions is a definite yes. Each of these above situations is very likely to occur at some point during the client/server system's lifetime. Testing in advance how it will react is proactive testing instead of reactive testing.

TABLE 4.6 Forced Errors	Shutting down the database server
	Renaming columns within a table
	Destroying tables in the database
	Dropping database roles
	Revoking grants to objects in the database
	Relocating required DLLs to other subdirectories
	Utilizing all available disk space on the client workstation
	Deliberately locking a frequently accessed table for an extended period of time
	Allocating all memory on the client/workstation to applications other than the one being tested
	Severing network communications between the client machine and the server

One very informative test scenario would combine test scripts with these error conditions listed above. A number of these error conditions could be created and then run as an unattended test of the complete system overnight. The error log in the morning might be interesting.

4.10 Conventions

Before testing the client/server system, it is important to establish some conventions for naming test cases, scripts, etc. The number of tests, test cases, and scripts for a moderately sized client/server system will grow rapidly. Without some scheme for naming and organizing them, it will be almost impossible to keep track of the many objects which accumulate during the testing process.

Naming test scripts in an understandable fashion is important. Although some software platforms allow extended names, the overall naming conventions must be geared to the lowest common denominator. Unfortunately, the eight-character naming limitation of DOS will probably be the limiting factor.

A first step in organizing test objects is to create a number of directories and subdirectories to hold all test objects. The highest level of the directory structure is a directory for the project. Working down the directory tree, the next level would be for major subsystems in the project. Examples might be: Accounts Payable, Invoices, and Orders. Within each subsystem directory are subdirectories for each phase of testing.

These phases are unit testing, integration testing, and system testing. The actual test objects will reside in the test phase subdirectories. Figure 4.3 shows this directory layout in a graphical form. This method of organizing test objects is only one of many configurations. The important thing is not the exact layout, but that some defined method is put into place.

Once a directory structure has been established, conventions for naming files must be defined. The DOS eight-character limitation will be a hindrance, but it can be worked around. The first two characters in the name should identify the subsystem being tested. The third character indicates the testing phase. Characters four through eight are a mnemonic describing the test being performed. The suffix portion of the file name indicates the type of test this is. Figure 4.4 breaks down this suggested naming convention.

Again, this naming convention isn't the only viable possible approach. In many cases a test tool chosen will advise or require that its own naming scheme be employed. What is consequential is that some consistency be defined and enforced when naming objects.

Figure 4.3
Test Object File
Directories

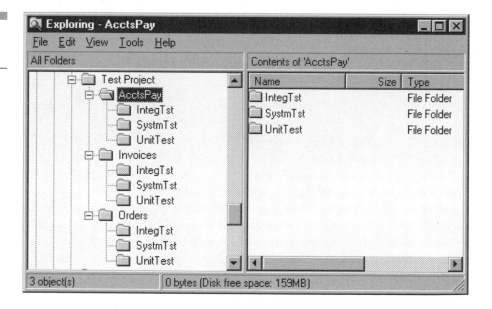

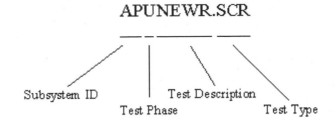

Figure 4.4
Naming Conventions

The naming conventions in this example are:

Subsystem ID is:	AP	- Accounts Payable
Test Phase is:	U	- Unit Testing
Test Description is:	NEWR	- New Record
Test Type is:	SCR	- Test Script

CHAPTER 5

Test Management Tools

This chapter covers both generic test management capabilities and specific features offered by currently available test management products. Mentioning a feature included in a specific test tool is not meant to be an approval of that particular product, nor should this be construed as a statement that other test tools do not include identical or similar capabilities. References to specific products are made only to illustrate the types of functionality that exist in the marketplace.

5.1 What Is Test Management?

Test management involves four main types of activities: test planning, test development, test execution, and error tracking. Each of the four activity types are addressed in the following sections. Test management tool suites generally have the capabilities to address each of these four areas.

5.1.1 Test Planning

Thorough, comprehensive testing does not just happen. Proper testing takes planning and design. The effort that goes into planning for the testing of a client/server system needs to be at the same level as the effort that went into the design of the client/server system.

The issue of when testing efforts must begin is also crucial. If test planning isn't started until all software has been completed, then you're in trouble. If this happens, one of two things will happen. The project completion will be delayed until tests can be designed and executed. A significant amount of momentum will be lost on the project. Personnel who could be performing the testing will be idle until tests have been defined. Eventually the testing effort will kick into gear, but a great deal of time will have been lost.

The other effect of starting test planning too late is even more unpalatable. This option involves either cutting the testing efforts down to fit the available time or skipping the testing altogether. Regrettably, this happens all too often. Think back to projects which you have been involved with. When the schedule started to slip, what were the areas which were most frequently dropped or trimmed? If your experience is anything like mine, the areas neglected were testing, training, and documentation. Taking this path isn't likely to allow a quality client/server system to be delivered to the client.

5.1.1.1 Define Test Subjects.

The first step towards testing a system is to define what components need to be tested. It is an overwhelming task to look at a system and instantly decide how to test it. The system taken as a whole is just too immense to come to grips with immediately. It becomes necessary to decompose the system into smaller, more manageable pieces. By breaking the system down into smaller pieces, it becomes easier to grasp the testing that will be necessary. It's certainly less intimidating to attack the test planning one piece at a time.

A step-by-step approach to the problem also makes it less likely that major areas will be omitted. Take a single area and define the testing that it requires. Review the test plan for flaws and omissions. Any possible improvements? This plan can then become the model for testing the other subsystems. If you have been involved in previous client/server system testing, you can model tests on the knowledge gained from that experience.

A client/server system with a GUI front-end lends itself fairly easy to this decomposition process. The first level of decomposition is to break the system as a whole into functional subsystems. A separate application is developed to implement each subsystem. A test plan for each subsystem needs to be developed.

The next level of decomposition is to break down each application into smaller pieces. Conveniently, the pieces which it can be broken down into are objects defined in the development tool. Development tools deal with windows, functions, etc. Other components at this level that require testing are database type objects. The components in each application that need to be tested are listed in Table 5.1.

Be careful not to carry the decomposition process too far. Don't break the system down into individual controls (e.g., command buttons, text fields, menus, list boxes, radio buttons) at this point in the test definition process. Testing at the control level will be defined later.

TABLE 5.1 Components to Be Tested	
	Windows
	Functions
	Nonvisible Objects
	DataWindows
	Stored Procedures
	Triggers
	Rules

There is a significant amount of functionality within a client/server system that isn't always obvious to the casual observer. Most of this functionality deals with low-level communications which occur between the client computer and the server computer. While tests of these functions could be explicitly created, it will be implicitly tested when higher-level components are tested. For example, testing the login screen of an application will implicitly perform testing of the following functions:

- That the application executable file (*.EXE) invoked is viable.
- Any required initialization (*.INI) files required by the application exist and are accessible.
- A communications protocol stack (e.g., TCP/IP) exists on the client and is properly configured.
- The host address (e.g., IP address) is properly defined on the client workstation.
- The server machine exists, is functional, and is listening.
- Higher-level communications (e.g., Oracle SQL*Net) are functional.
- The database referenced by the application exists and is active.
- The user ID and password entered are valid.
- The application recognizes a successful connection to the database.

Other examples of functionality that aren't always visible are objects which exist at the database level. Stored procedures, triggers, and rules are examples of these types of objects. While these objects need to be thoroughly tested, that testing can occur within the framework of tests being done on other objects. For example, stored procedures are frequently employed to speed up the selection of data from a relational database. By testing the window populated by the stored procedure, the testing of that stored procedure has effectively been done. If rules are employed to enforce data validation, then thorough testing on data input screens tests the rules. Database triggers are frequently used to enforce referential integrity within a system. By testing the windows that enable record creation, the triggers are tested. The only additional concern is to make sure the testing is adequate.

5.1.1.1.1 Tools Which Help Decompose Systems Some test management suites include tools that are substantial aids to the process of defining components to be tested. They help break applications down into smaller pieces. An ability to list all software components in a project in a hierarchical structure is one such capability. This feature displays software modules in a treelike structure and includes the option to display or hide entire branches or levels of components. Icons used to indicate open and closed folders and components within the hierarchy are readily grasped. Specific tests can then be associated with each component. When a software component is modified, test engineers can quickly see what tests need to be rerun.

The advantages of having a tool assist you in this area are twofold. First, having this process automated helps to ensure that you don't overlook any parts. Second, automating the work helps to get test teams over the initial hurdle. Sometimes, getting out of the starting blocks is the most difficult part of the test planning process.

An example of a tool with this capability is the "Import" feature in the "Test Requirements Hierarchy" of SQA Manager. Hierarchies can be imported from PowerBuilder PBLs, ASCII text files, or the outline editor of Microsoft Word. SQA Manager also allows its test requirement hierarchy to be exported to a text file. Staff can modify this file then import it back into the test repository. You must be aware that this activity does not actually create any tests, it just outlines the hierarchy of software components. But as stated earlier, sometimes the biggest hurdle is just getting started. Figures 5.1 and 5.2 demonstrate this SQA Manager capability. Once all the software components that need to be tested have been identified, then tests for each can be defined.

5.1.1.2 Define Test Requirements. Once all of the components that need to be tested have been identified and listed, it's time to get down to business! Each component needs to be closely examined. Tests that

Figure 5.1
SQA Manager Import
Capability

Import			? ✕

Look in: 🗁 Oasis

📁 Dec28
📘 Ancestor.pbl
📘 Oasis.pbl

File name: _____ Open

Files of type: PowerBuilder Files (*.PBL) Cancel

Help

Figure 5.2
SQA Manager Test
Requirements
Hierarchy after
Import

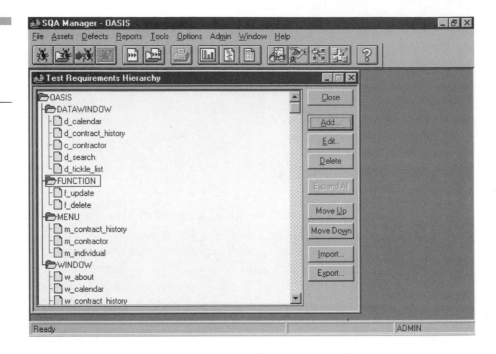

should be applied to it can be laid out. Tests should be designed with the system specifications in mind. Ideally, a copy of the specifications document would be at the test designer's side and open during the test design process. Each test created should verify that a requirement described in the specifications documentation is being met. Most requirements will require more than one test.

Most of the functions outlined in the specifications document are geared towards typical users and the business functions they perform. There will be a set of functions that are more of an administrative nature. Examples of these functions are configuring a printer, adding new users, changing security access for users, setting user preferences, backing up system data, restoring data, deploying the application to a new workstation, etc. While not daily functions, these require just as much testing as the more typical ones.

5.1.1.3 Design Test Steps. While the objects being testing can come in an infinite variety, there are some functional business scenarios which are common to most client/server systems. Certain windows and functions (or minor variations of them) exist in virtually all applications. Tests needed for these objects will be described and the reader can extrapolate for windows and functions not addressed in this book. Some of these commonly occurring windows are listed in Table 5.2

TABLE 5.2

Common
Windows

1) Login Screen

2) Creating a New Database Record

3) Updating an Existing Database Record

4) Deleting a Database Record

5) Find and Display a Specific Record

6) Search Windows

7) Sorting Entries in a DataWindow (Grid)

8) Double Clicking on a Record To "Drill Down"

9) Drop & Drag

10) Report Generation

11) Handling Inactive Terminals

A list of tests that should be run on each of these types of windows is listed in the following sections. This table is meant to be representative but by no means exhaustive. There will almost certainly be local requirements that are not addressed here.

5.1.1.3.1 Login Screen Login screens typically display four controls: entry fields for the user's ID and password, an "OK" command button, and a "Cancel" command button. The expectation is that the user enters his or her login ID and password then clicks the "OK" button. If a mistake was made entering these values, the user is warned and given a chance to correct the values specified. If the user chooses not to log into the application, he or she can click the cancel button. Tests that should be performed on this window include:

Test Description	Expected Result
Click OK button without entering an ID or password	An error message should be displayed
Enter a valid ID and click OK	An error message should be displayed
Enter a valid password and click OK button	An error message should be displayed
Click OK button after entering an invalid ID	An error message should be displayed
Click OK button after entering an invalid password	An error message should be displayed

Test Description	Expected Result
Deliberately enter invalid values several times in a row	An error message should be displayed with each failed login attempt. On many systems, after a configured number of attempts (three is very common) the system terminates itself. An entry in the security log should be created.
Click the Cancel button	Application should terminate
Enter valid values in both fields and click OK button	Successful login
Enter valid values in upper, lower, and mixture of case	Application dependent, but users seem to appreciate systems which accept either case

5.1.1.3.2 Creating a New Record Creating a new record is one of the most fundamental operations which occurs in a client/server system. It can also be among the most complicated. There are a number of steps which can be performed incorrectly by users. The software should be designed to check for these error conditions, but unless testing is done, it is not guaranteed that this important function is correctly executed. Tests that are needed for this area include:

Test Description	Expected Result
Attempt to create a record after entering only part of the required data	User should be warned that all required fields haven't been specified. Ideally, this warning would take place as soon as the required field is tabbed out of.
Attempt to create a record that duplicates an existing record	A new record should not be created. The user should be explicitly informed that no record was created. This requirement can be implemented at the database level. Frequently this is accomplished by creating unique primary keys or indexes.
Enter invalid values into fields. For instance, a character in a numeric field, an integer in a date field, a real value in an integer field, etc.	The user should be warned of the invalid entries. Ideally, this warning would take place as soon as the field loses focus. A less desirable course of action would have the warning appear when the "Create" button is clicked.

Test Description	Expected Result
Attempt to leave the window without saving the new record	User should be warned that he or she is about to lose data. A very clear message should explain what the options are.
Terminate the request to generate a new record	User should be prompted to continue this action. No new record should be created. The application may or may not clear all fields on the window.
Fields which are required should be visibly . differentiated from those which are not required	Attempt to create new records without specifying nonessential fields. This will uncover essential fields which have not been properly identified as being essential.

Many fields have limitations on what their values can be. For example, the state value must be one of the fifty states, dates must be actual dates, ages must be greater than zero and less than 120, etc. Some values are restricted via pick lists, i.e., the user is forced to pick a value instead of entering a value. Other restrictions are enforced via database rules, triggers or code written into the application. All of these data verification requirements must be tested. The need to test requirements applies equally when creating new records and modifying existing records.

Test Description	Expected Result
Attempt to enter any value into a pick list	The application should prevent this from occurring.
Deliberately enter an invalid date into all date fields	The user should be warned of any invalid dates. Ideally, this warning would take place when the field loses focus. A less desirable course of action would have the warning appear when the "Create" or "Update" buttons are clicked.
Deliberately enter invalid values (e.g., 0, −1, etc.) in all numeric fields	The user should be warned of any invalid entries. Ideally, this warning would take place when the field loses focus. A less desirable course of action would have the warning appear when the "Create" or "Update" buttons are clicked.
For fields which are foreign keys, attempt to enter values which do not exist in the foreign table	The user should be warned of any invalid references to foreign keys. Hopefully, the warning presented to the user explains what keys and tables are involved.

A *transaction* is a logical unit of work. This unit must either be processed completely or rejected. It cannot be partially processed. Creating new records in a system frequently involves transactions. One example would be creating a new order. The unit of work might consist of inserting a record into the order table and inserting one or more detail records into the order_details table. Both inserts must be successfully completed to have a valid order.

Tests must be designed, executed, and verified to make certain that transactions are being properly processed. Unfortunately, testing multi-table transactions is more difficult than testing queries that affect only a single table. The tester will need to go through additional gyrations to orchestrate the failure situations which are absolutely necessary to test the system. Some examples of testing situations are described below. Transaction testing for each client/server system tends to be very individualistic because each database is unique. Testing for each system must address its referential relationships. The examples provided here are simply to provide illustrations of the types of testing necessary.

Test Description	Expected Result
Create a record which generates data in more than one table.	Verify that the appropriate rows were inserted into all related tables. This can be done via an ISQL session.
Attempt to create a record which generates data in more than one table, but deliberately cause one of the tables to be locked during this operation. A lock on a table can be created via an ISQL session.	An understandable error message should be displayed. It should explain what happened; most importantly it should inform the user that no data was saved. Verify that no database changes were made via an ISQL session.
If the user has the ability to abort a transaction in progress; initiate such a transaction and abort it before it completes.	An understandable error message should be displayed. It should explain what happened; most importantly it should inform the user that no data was saved. Verify that no database changes were made via an ISQL session

5.1.1.3.3 Updating Existing Records During the normal course of business operations, records get created and subsequently are modified. Individual records may be updated many times during their lifetimes. Each time a change is made to these records, there is the possibility that errors might occur. The first series of tests which must be performed on update windows are all the tests performed on new record windows. These tests were described in Section 5.1.1.3.2. The requirements made of update operations are normally the same as those applied to new records. Some additional tests specific to update operations are suggested here:

Test Description	Expected Result
Attempt to modify the primary key or any part of a multipart key on the update record.	It should not be possible to modify any part of the primary key. An error message should be displayed to the user explaining why the update was rejected.
Attempt to modify a field which is a foreign key to reference a nonexistent row in the foreign table.	It shouldn't be possible to reference a nonexistent row in a foreign table. An error message clearly explaining why the update didn't take place should be displayed.
Modify any field on the update window and attempt to leave the window without saving the changes.	If the user changes any fields on a window and attempts to leave the window, the system should provide a clear warning that data is about to be lost. The message should explain how the data can be saved or abandoned.

5.1.1.3.4 Deleting a Record Frequently, records in client/server systems need to be deleted. This might be because the organization no longer does business with that supplier, an order has been canceled, a warehouse no longer exists, an employee has resigned, etc. Whatever the reason, a record needs to be removed from the system. Deleting records is a serious activity. It has the potential to do an enormous amount of damage to the organization's database. Testing in this area must be exceptionally thorough because of this potential harm. SQL statements that include the command "DELETE" must be tested more intensely than just about anything else in a system.

Test Description	Expected Result
Initiate a record delete request	User should be prompted to confirm that the delete request should be executed.
Back out of the delete request	If the user chooses to back out of a delete request, there should be no database changes. Confirm this via an ISQL session.

Test Description	Expected Result
Initiate a record delete and confirm that the delete should be performed	The record in question and only that record should be gone from the database. Confirm that the record in question has been deleted via an ISQL session.
Initiate a record delete and confirm that only that specific record was deleted.	Before this test begins, obtain a count of rows in the table. Afterwards, confirm that the table contains one fewer rows. This verifies that only the one record in question has been deleted.
Return to the window that allows records to be entered and create a new record with the same primary key as the record just deleted.	This will provide further confirmation that the original record was deleted.

Deleting a record from a given table can have implications beyond that specific table. If another table is related to it via a foreign key relationship, then rows from the second table might also need to be deleted. This concept of verifying that data between multiple tables is properly maintained is called *referential integrity* (RI). Referential integrity can be enforced in a number of ways. Table constraints can be defined, triggers can be used, or it can be enforced with SQL code in the applications themselves.

An example of this situation would probably be of benefit. Table order contains basic information on orders. The customer name, order date, total value of the order, customer address, etc., are contained in this table. A second table, order_details contains details about each order. In this table are the specific items purchased on each order. The item number, per-item cost, number of items purchased, etc., are contained in order_details. Each order will have a single entry in order and one or more rows in order_details. If a customer cancels order number "XYZ," then that row is deleted from table order. At this point all entries in order_details for order number XYZ no longer relate to an order. They have all been orphaned. Since their order has been deleted, all these detail rows must also be deleted.

The best method of handling this is to define table constraints when the database is created. A constraint defines the relationship between tables and what should be done when rows are deleted from the primary table. If the database package being used provides this functionality, then it is a relatively easy way to enforce referential integrity. Unfortunately, not all database systems support table constraints. Another hurdle is that the database designer or database administrator (DBA) must have defined these relationships. If they didn't define these constraints, then alternative methods must be employed.

Creating triggers to enforce referential integrity is an acceptable way of handling the situation. A trigger on the primary table can delete dependent rows in all related tables when a row is deleted from the base table. The biggest advantage of using triggers is that developers and application code can be blissfully ignorant of the action. The downside is that normally only the DBA is authorized to create triggers. If the DBA cannot (or will not) fulfill this obligation, then triggers cannot be used.

The final method of implementing referential integrity is via code written into applications. This also happens to be the worst way to handle referential integrity. There are several reasons why this is considered a poor approach. The code must be duplicated everywhere a delete can be performed. It might need to exist in numerous windows spread throughout several applications. Not only does this create duplicated code, there is also the very likely possibility that it isn't done correctly in every location. Trying to locate the bad or missing delete operation is like finding a needle in a haystack.

Another reason to avoid this approach is that it requires all developers to understand the system's data model. This is not likely to be the case. If a developer doesn't have a thorough understanding of the big picture, then he or she will surely forget to drop rows from related tables during a delete operation. Additional code inspection will then be required to make sure this has been included everywhere it needed to be performed. This results in more work and room for omissions.

Tests must be done which specifically address the referential integrity aspect of delete operations. Each table must be examined to determine if other tables will be affected by delete operations performed on it. The set of tests listed here must be performed for each table that has such relationships.

Test Description	Expected Result
Delete a record from a table which has no related rows	Only the one row from the primary table should have been deleted. No rows from any table should be affected.
Delete a record from a table which has related tables, but no rows in any related table.	The row from the primary table should have been deleted. No rows in related tables should have been deleted. Confirm this via an ISQL session.
Delete a record from a table which has related tables and rows in at least one related table.	The row from the primary table should have been deleted. Any rows in related tables which related to the record should also have been deleted. Confirm this via an ISQL session.

Some systems get a little more complicated in their way of handling deleted records. These systems don't actually delete records when a user requests that a record be deleted. Often what they do is to simply mark the record as having been deleted. Frequently an active_record flag field exists in the table. When a record is to be deleted, the value of this flag is changed from "Active" to "Inactive." The record still exists, but now it won't be picked up or displayed in any window in the client/server system.

The reasons for implementing this deletion technique vary from system to system. Sometimes it is implemented to allow users to change their mind at a later point and shift the record back to an active state. Other times this technique is implemented to support an audit trail. Since records are never physically deleted from the system there is always a complete record of what has happened in the system.

To further complicate matters, some systems implement two levels of deletion. If a record is "deleted," then its flag is simply marked as inactive. At this point the record exists but isn't accessible to users. Later, a high-level user or system administrator can "purge" records from the system. The purge operation actually removes all records marked as inactive from the database. There is no going back after a purge operation. Purged records are gone forever.

The following tests should be performed on systems that have two levels of delete operations.

Test Description	Expected Result
Delete a record from the system.	The active flag should be set to inactive for this record. Verify this via ISQL.
Delete a record from a table which has related rows in another table.	The active flags should be set to inactive for this record and its related rows. Verify this via an ISQL session.
Restore one or more records which have been deleted.	The active flag should be set to active for all affected records and their related rows. Verify this via an ISQL session.
Execute the purge operation after one or more records have been flagged as inactive.	All records marked as inactive should have been physically removed from the database.

5.1.1.3.5 Find/Display Specific Record The most common operation in most computer systems is likely the ability to find and display a single record. This record may be a customer's order, a student's class schedule, an employee's pay history, an inventory list, etc. Many times the user enters a specific key value, such as a customer number, and the record is displayed. Tests that need to be performed on this type of window include the following:

Test Description	Expected Result
No key value is specified and the "Search" button is clicked	A warning message explaining that no key was specified. No data is displayed.
An invalid key value is specified	A warning message explaining that no records matching the key were found. No data is displayed.
A valid key is entered, but the user isn't authorized to view this record. For example, a user may have asked to view his supervisor's salary data	No data is displayed. A warning message may or may not be brought up. Very likely a security violation log entry will be created.
If the keys aren't unique, the user should enter a key value which corresponds to multiple records.	The first record meeting the criteria should be displayed, but a clear indication must inform the user that this is record 1 of x. The user should be able to view successive records by pressing a "Next" button. Preceding records should be accessible via a "Previous" button. When the last record is displayed, the "Next" button should be disabled (grayed-out).

5.1.1.3.6 Search Windows Most GUI applications contain a number of search-type windows. Typically these windows allow the user to enter values into a number of parameter fields. After specifying values and clicking on the "Search" button, all records that meet the entered criteria are selected from the database and displayed to the user in a grid-type control. The user can then examine the returned rows. If the set of rows returned was not what the user meant to see, the parameter values can be modified and another search initiated.

Test Description	Expected Result
Enter a value into each available field and request a search on each individual field.	All rows that contain the specified value in the selected field should be retrieved. The result sets must be corroborated, possibly by examining the database via an SQL session.

Test Description	Expected Result
Repeat the previous test with a variety of values, some of which will return rows and others which won't.	All rows that contain the specified value in the selected field should be retrieved. These rows must be corroborated, possibly by examining the database via an SQL session.
Enter values into two or more fields	All rows which contain the specified value in the selected fields should be retrieved. These rows must be corroborated, possibly by examining the database via an SQL session.
Repeat the previous test with a variety of values, some of which return rows and others which don't	All rows which include the specified value in the selected fields. These rows must be corroborated, possibly by examining the database via an SQL session.
Enter values into fields which are of an invalid type. For instance, a character in a numeric field, an integer in a date field, a real value in an integer field	The user should be warned of the invalid entries. Ideally, this warning would take place as soon as that field loses focus. A less desirable warning would come when the "search" button is clicked.
Click on the "Search" button without specifying any parameters	One of two results could occur. If the select in question could return a very large number of records, the user should be either warned about this or prevented from doing it. If the number of rows isn't excessive, then all rows should be returned.
Some applications allow users to terminate searches if they change their minds about wanting the requested data. Enter some parameters and click Search. Click the button to terminate the search.	The search should be aborted. If this process is going to take any length of time, the user should be informed that the search has been terminated

Some applications allow the user to specify high- and low-limit parameter values. The result set returned includes all rows that fall within that range for the specified parameter. Special testing for this situation must be performed. At a minimum the tests should include:

Test Description	Expected Result
Specify only the high parameter	All records with a value less than or equal to the specified parameter should be returned. An alternative would be to require the user to enter both high and low parameters. This will be system dependent, but it should be documented and consistently applied.

Test Description	Expected Result
Specify only the low parameter	All records with a value greater than or equal to the specified parameter should be returned. An alternative would be to require that the user enter both high and low parameters. This will be system dependent, but it should be documented and consistently applied.
Specify a low value which is greater than the high parameter's value.	Two responses are possible. The user could be warned that an invalid set of parameters has been entered and no search is initiated. The other logical response would be to perform the search exactly as requested. In this case zero records returned. The way this is handled will be system dependent, but it should be documented and consistently applied.

5.1.1.3.7 Sorting Entries in a Datawindow (Grid) Quite often users require the ability to see records sorted in a specific order. The desired order might change from occurrence to occurrence. A common way of handling this is to allow them to call a window and specify the desired sort order. When control is returned to the original screen, the datawindow is sorted in the requested order.

The datawindow containing the records might be reloaded from the database, or the current records might be simply sorted in place. The decision on how this will be handled should be determined by which is more efficient and results in faster response for the user.

Some tests which could be applied to a sort window include the following:

Test Description	Expected Result
User calls the sort window from different windows.	The list of columns displayed corresponds to the columns on the calling window.
User calls the sort window then cancels out.	Control returns to the original window. There has been no change in sort order.
User calls the sort window, but doesn't specify a sort column.	Control returns to the original window. There has been no change in sort order.
User calls the sort window and selects multiple sort columns.	Control returns to the original window. Records are sorted by the columns specified. The first column chosen is the primary sort, second column is secondary sort, etc.

5.1.1.3.8 Double Clicking Row to "Drill Down" After users have retrieved a set of records in a table, they frequently would like to see additional information about one of the records. A common method of implementing this is to allow them to double click on the desired record. This event causes a new window to be displayed with more detailed information on the chosen record. Tests which should be performed to test this capability include:

Test Description	Expected Result
Single click on a row	The row should be highlighted, but nothing more.
Double click on a row	The detail screen should be displayed for the selected row. If this process will take a considerable amount of time, the cursor icon should be changed to indicate this.
Double click on a column header	Nothing should happen.
Double click anywhere else on the window, i.e., anywhere besides the grid being questioned.	Nothing should happen, at least nothing related to testing the drill-down capability.
Double click on a row for which no details exist	The detail screen should be displayed, but it should be devoid of entries.
Highlight multiple rows and double click on one of them.	This capability might not be implemented on all systems. When it has been implemented, the users should be presented with details of the first record. Subsequent records should be accessed by clicking a "Next" button. If not implemented, then details for the double-clicked row should be presented.

5.1.1.3.9 Drop and Drag The ability to drop and drag is available in most GUI interface tools. The drop and drag capability which users are likely to be familiar with is the File Manager in Windows 3.11 and Windows NT. This capability isn't used as widely as it could be, but when it's used, it needs to be well tested. Tests that should be applied include:

Test Description	Expected Result
Attempt to drag an object that isn't draggable	Nothing should happen

Test Description	Expected Result
Drag an object	The mouse icon should change to indicate that a drag operation is underway
Attempt to drop a dragged object onto an object which doesn't recognize drop events	When the dragged object moves over the invalid object the icon should change to inform the user. A common icon used in this situation is a circle with a diagonal line through it.
Drop a dragged object onto an object that does recognize drop events.	This drop should initiate a system event. If the activity will take a measurable amount of time, the mouse cursor should be changed to indicate this. A common icon used in this situation is the hourglass.

5.1.1.3.10 Report Generation   Reports are a part of almost all computer systems. Client/server systems might emphasize a graphical interface, but many users will insist on having the ability to obtain hard copy reports. As long as this necessity exists, there will be reports associated with client/server systems. A test of each and every report needs to be run to assure that each report can be initiated, generates expected output, and contains the data that they should contain. Some tests that verify these requirements are:

Test Description	Expected Result
Generate a report when there is insufficient disk space available	An error message should specify that insufficient disk space was available
Generate a report and assign it a name which is already in use	An error message should specify that the new report will overwrite an existing one
Generate a report and assign it to a subdirectory which doesn't exist.	An error message should specify that the subdirectory doesn't exist. If the capability exists, it should prompt and offer to create the subdirectory.
Generate a report and specify parameter values for it. Follow the guidelines suggested in Section 5.1.1.3.6. This section outlines tests verifying that search parameters are properly validated.	See Section 5.1.1.3.6
Generate a report and direct the output towards each available printer in the system.	Report output should be produced at each printer on the system. Output should be

Test Description	Expected Result
	checked to ensure that the banner information is appropriate.
Generate a report and specify that it be directed to an output file.	Report output should be written to a disk file. This file should be examined to be certain that it's readable and contains the expected output.

5.1.1.3.11 Handling Idle Terminals

Many systems have security requirements which prohibit applications from being up on idle workstations. An idle terminal is one which has not experienced any keyboard or mouse activity for a configurable period of time. Five to fifteen minutes is a common period after which workstations are deemed to be idle. If sensitive data is displayed on a terminal and the user goes to lunch, it constitutes a definite threat to system security.

Most development packages allow applications to recognize an idle terminal situation. Normally a timer is initiated when the application is opened. A time period is specified when the timer is initiated. Each time the mouse is moved or a key is pressed, the timer gets reset to its initial value. If the terminal is idle for the configured period, the timer expires and an event is executed.

5.1.1.3.11.1 Locking Idle Terminals

Once an idle terminal is recognized it must be properly processed. Two methods of handling idle terminals are common. The first approach is to simply display a blank screen when the terminal is deemed to be idle. To regain use of the application, a password must be entered into the terminal. As long as no password is entered, the blank screen stays in place.

One severe disadvantage of this approach is that the client is still connected to the server and its session is still considered to be active. This situation allows the client workstation to continue to tie up resources on the server. One resource which can be tied up is the number of concurrent database sessions. Some database systems are licensed by the number of concurrent user sessions. An idle terminal's open session eats into that number.

The application running on the client workstation might also have an effect on the performance of the database system. The session might be holding locks on database tables or indexes. This can cause performance for other, active users to be degraded. An idle terminal can also impact database log files, snapshots, and recovery capabilities. All told, the effects of an idle terminal are far from benign.

5.1.1.3.11.2 Logging Out Idle Terminals The second technique for handling idle client workstations is to terminate the application. Terminating the application becomes complicated quickly if the user was in the midst of modifying or inserting data. Normally the decision is made to abandon any data that has been entered but not yet saved.

In spite of the complications involved with potentially abandoning changes, logging out inactive terminals has some very positive aspects. By terminating the session, the workstation will have no further effect on the system. All system and database resources are immediately freed. On a system with hundreds of users, this can have a significant effect.

No matter which option is implemented for handling idle terminals, an entry should be inserted into a security log noting that the terminal was idle. Recording each idle terminal situation allows the system administrator to keep track of how frequently this situation occurs. If this becomes a persistent problem, then the handling of it might be escalated from locking out the terminal to logging off the terminal. At a minimum, the need for user training is probably called for.

Testing must be performed to validate that the chosen technique is properly implemented. Tests must be customized, depending on how idle terminals are handled. Some suggested tests are listed here.

Test Description	Expected Result
Allow a terminal to sit idle for the configured idle time period. It should display a password screen.	A password screen should be presented. Enter the appropriate password to resume use of the workstation. A record should be inserted into the security log. Validate that this log entry was created.
Open the application and let the terminal sit idle for the configured idle period.	The application should be terminated. A record should be inserted into the security log. Validate that this log entry was created.
Open the application, select a record, and modify at least one data field. Allow the terminal to sit for the configured idle period.	Modified data should be abandoned. The application should be terminated. A record should be inserted into the security log. Validate that this log entry was created and that the modifications were abandoned.

5.1.2 Test Development

Defining what needs to be tested and the necessary testing requirements are certainly both important activities. When properly done, it can help ensure that the testing process is both thorough and efficient. The next logical step in the testing cycle is to actually develop the tests.

5.1.2.1 Test Creation.   Creating tests for a client/server system is not a quick, easy, or mindless chore. It takes time, hard work, and a great deal of attention to detail. First of all, a tester must have intimate knowledge regarding what the system is required to do. Without understanding the system's functionality, it will be difficult (or impossible) to create tests.

Test creation also takes a mind which can think "outside the box." The tester cannot simply assume that the system being tested works. A tester can take nothing for granted about the software and its correctness. The assumption that everything works as promised must be aggressively challenged.

5.1.2.1.1 Positive Tests   Tests can be considered either positive or negative in nature. A positive test is one that shows that the software performs as documented when the expected input is provided. All the right entries are made in the expected sequences. When the software runs, it should be successful. Complete and accurate records should be created. Reports should come out correctly. Everything which the users want to happen should indeed happen.

5.1.2.1.2 Negative Tests   In contrast, a negative test is one that emphasizes doing things incorrectly and confirming that the system will catch these errors. Invalid values are entered to test the validation and verification software. For example, characters should be entered into a money field, a decimal point can be entered into an integer field, etc. Attempts are made to enter incomplete records to be certain these will not be accepted. Activities are deliberately done in an incorrect manner to see what the system will allow.

Negative testing is an attempt to predict what will be done by your most "challenging" user. Every system has such a user. He or she is the person who either doesn't read the manual or simply chooses to ignore it. Anything which can be done incorrectly will eventually be uncovered by this user. This user probably takes great pride in his or her ability to crash the system. A tester's job is to find all these flaws before this particular user does.

One system I helped to develop had just such a user. While many users are afraid to try something new, Kevin wasn't afraid to try anything. This particular system allowed users to create multiple sessions by opening the application more than once at their workstations. The technique used to uniquely identify user sessions was to create an identifier. This identifier consisted of the terminal ID concatenated with the system time. Unfortunately, the unit of system time chosen was the number of seconds. Kevin succeeded (in true Kevin-style) in opening two sessions before the second value of the system time changed. This caused problems. The system couldn't differentiate between his two sessions and well, let's just say it hosed. This type of user and his propensity to push the system beyond its limits is what a good tester strives to emulate. (Well done, Kevin!)

A good tester must have a demeanor which is simultaneously creative and slightly warped. Questions need to pop into your mind which don't occur to normal users or developers. Many of these questions are essentially "what if" or "can I" scenarios. Examples of this kind of thinking are:

- What would happen if I attempted to drill down on an empty grid?
- What would happen if I imported data twice back to back?
- What would happen if the minimum value is higher than the maximum value?
- What would happen if the system received an entry of two records with the same user ID?
- Can I execute two versions of the application simultaneously on the same workstation?
- Can I log onto two different workstations at the same time?
- What will happen if I try to run more than one report at the same time on the same workstation?

5.1.2.2 Coordinate Tests with Requirements Document.   Designing and creating tests are necessary steps when testing a client/server system. Without these steps, the testing wouldn't get done or at least it wouldn't get done thoroughly and accurately.

From the client's point of view, however, it isn't enough to simply create and successfully execute the tests. The client will demand proof that the functions listed in the specifications have been included in the system and are being adequately tested. This proof can come in the form of a document which maps system requirements with specific tests of those functions. Each system requirement must have all of the tests designed to verify it. A report should be available which lists all the requirements, the tests which support it, and which of those tests have been successfully completed.

5.1.3 Test Execution

The software requirements have been laid out. The tests have been designed. Now comes the easy part, actually running the tests. There are any number of ways to execute the required tests. Some testers do it haphazardly. They jump from one test to another and one area to another. A more disciplined approach is to focus on one area and test it completely before moving onto another area. These testers start slowly and build on each test which has already been executed.

It helps a great deal when testing a system if you always know what the state of the data is at any given time. This is especially true when a relational database is involved. Because of the way the tables are interrelated, this is essential. One way of maintaining control over the database is to always start with a known database. A database can be set to a known state by truncating all the tables and running an import utility to load the database from scratch. Use the tests themselves to add rows to tables, modify rows, and delete rows. If the final tests delete the rows which were added during earlier tests, then the database will end up in its original state.

The idea of using tests to modify the database and later restore it is a great concept. When it works, it makes setting up for the next series of tests much easier. Unfortunately, if any of the tests abort, or if the software malfunctions, the database won't end up in its original state. Early testing efforts are likely to result in a significant number of both aborted tests and software malfunctions. This is a very good impetus for retaining the import files and scripts which were used to populate the database originally.

Another reason for keeping import files and scripts is this retains the ability to create duplicate versions of a database. Having duplicate databases enables multiple teams to perform testing at the same time without impacting each other. This is especially appropriate during the unit testing phase. During this phase it's valuable to allow developers to do whatever they desire to their own copy of the database. Obviously if there are many developers the database each uses might be somewhat smaller than the production database. It might, for instance, contain only tables in the subsystem which they are currently testing.

Modifications allowing the software to access different databases is frequently implemented via entries in an initialization file. Many applications on startup extract the database name from an initialization file. That value is specified when the application connects to the database. Each test team member or group of testers can customize the initialization file on their client workstation to open the database which has been created for them. In this way, they all use reproductions of the same database but don't need to worry about impacting one another.

5.1.3.1 Create Test Sequences.   A test sequence is a collection of tests which are executed together to achieve a specific testing goal. A test sequence might have been designed to prove that the latest version of a subsystem functions correctly. Another goal and test sequence might be to determine if recently added enhancements have introduced errors. Yet another goal might be to verify that the application will function on a new hardware platform. Validating that performance specifications are met might be the goal intended for one last test sequence.

Section 5.1.1.3.2 outlines some tests which are required to test the creation of a new record. A simplified version of these tests will be used in the discussions about test sequencing. A short list of these tests are:

- Attempt to create a record with only part of the necessary data.
- Attempt to create a record which duplicates an existing record.
- Enter values of an invalid type into a field.
- Attempt to leave the window without saving the new record.
- Terminate the request to generate a new record.
- Attempt to create the record without providing data in nonessential fields.

5.1.3.1.1 Why Sequences Are Necessary   A sequence of tests is necessary because the scope of a single test is very limited. An individual test isn't broad enough to prove everything you need. It takes a number of tests to validate that something as simple as a command button functions correctly. By combining numerous tests into a sequence, they are capable of achieving larger goals. The sequence can be given a name to make it easier to identify.

The phrase test sequence isn't the only phrase used to describe this concept. Some test tool products refer to it as a test cycle. Others call it a test procedure. The exact terminology is irrelevant. What is important is the concept that many tests are collected and run together to achieve a larger goal.

Creating the test sequence isn't a task which needs to be started from scratch. The tests, defined in Section 5.1.1.3 for each software component, provide an excellent base for the module's test sequence. At this point the individual tests need to be examined to enable them to function together in a sequence. To function together, the tests probably need to be altered slightly. This allows the sequence to flow from one test to another.

5.1.3.1.2 Test Tools Which Assist in Sequence Creation Many test tools on the market allow testing personnel to define a test sequence and run it unattended. This permits testing staff to execute test sequences without having to continuously monitor them. Test results are automatically written to logs in the test repository or specified subdirectories. The ability to run unattended tests overnight (or over the weekend) enables staff to run test sequences which examine specific subsystems or the entire system. Implementing this technology can significantly improve test productivity.

Each test tool's interface for defining a sequence of tests is slightly different. Figure 5.3 is an example of how SQA Manager's window for defining test sequences is defined.

5.1.3.1.3 Transitions within Sequences Defining the sequence in which tests will run and the transition between tests is extremely important. This sequencing can be done many ways. Defining the sequence is critical when tests are automated. If tests don't flow smoothly and correctly

Figure 5.3
SQA Manager's Test
Sequence Window

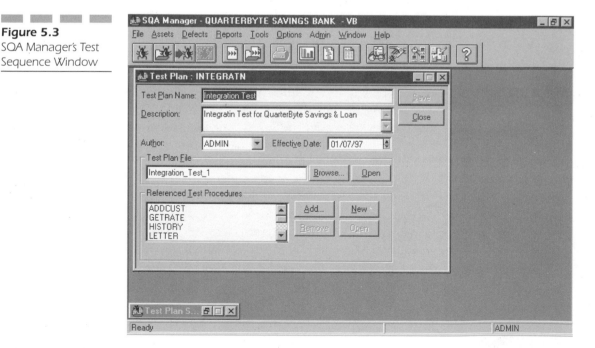

from one test to another, then testing won't be effective. The system can be left in a state which ensuing tests can't recover. If this type of problem occurs, then a sequence of tests which should have run to completion (perhaps overnight) can terminate after only a couple of tests. In the morning the testing staff will be in for a big disappointment. A few nights of this can put a serious crimp in the testing effort progress.

The importance of proper sequencing is pretty obvious for automated testing, but it's also surprisingly important when performing tests manually. If tests don't transition easily from one to another, there can be a considerable amount of time wasted setting up for the second test after the first test completes. When appreciable setup time is required between every pair of tests, the productivity of testing personnel will be severely reduced. Besides the loss of time, the more complicated the testing setup procedures are, the less likely it is that they will be performed accurately and consistently from one test session to another.

5.1.3.1.4 End-To-End Sequencing One method is to have each test pick up where the previous test left off. For example, the first test would test whether an invalid data value could be entered into a field. After an invalid value is entered and the system recognizes it, an error message should be displayed. The test might continue to test a number of other invalid values in the same field. Each invalid attempt provokes an error response from the system. The last value entered into each field would be a valid one. The next test in the sequence would perform similar checking on the next field on the window. The final test would attempt to create a new record. Since the previous tests filled in all fields with acceptable values, the create operation should be successful.

There are advantages and disadvantages with the end-to-end sequencing approach. The advantages are that since tests build on each other, later tests don't have to perform as much setup. The example provided above is trivial, but on a real application the setup steps can be considerable.

The rule in software (and life in general) is each approach has some disadvantages. One disadvantage of end-to-end sequencing is that if one of the intermediate tests fails or is improperly designed, this can prevent subsequent tests from completing successfully. Should one of the validity tests fail for any reason and an invalid value is left in a field, the test to create a record can't possibly pass. The sequence of tests as a whole will be incomplete.

Another disadvantage of end-to-end sequencing is that tests are tied very tightly to previous tests. Since they are so tightly entwined, it becomes difficult to change any individual test and be certain that the changes won't affect other tests. It's equally difficult to add or delete tests in the middle of the sequence when tests are tightly interwoven.

5.1.3.1.5 Baseline Sequencing   Another sequencing technique is to have each individual test begin from a known position (i.e., the baseline). Tests in a sequence aren't relying on previous tests to set things up for them. A baseline-sequenced testing scenario would have the first test in the sequence test the first field with a series of invalid values. Each error response from the system would be acknowledged. When the first test exhausted its attempts on that field, it would clear the field and exit. The next test would perform similar operations on the next field on the window. When all of these tests have completed, the final test would load valid values into each field on the window and attempt to create record operation.

The advantages of this approach are many. First of all, since each test is independent of all other tests, each test can succeed no matter what happened during previous tests. In the above example the create record test wasn't relying on the validity tests to load a valid value into each field. The final test performed those loads itself. It wasn't depending on previous tests to do it.

Since tests are independent of one another, it becomes much easier to modify tests within a sequence. It's also easier to add or delete tests to or from the sequence. The practice of always starting at a known baseline position makes it simpler to concatenate multiple test sequences together to test entire subsystems. Less time will be spent testing the test sequence with this approach.

5.1.3.2 Running Tests, Automated and Manual.   Once the sequence has been defined, it can be used to test the client/server system. The testing can be done manually or via automated test tools. More and more software development shops are finding that automated testing is the only way to achieve the levels of quality they require.

5.1.3.2.1 Manual Testing   If the testing is being performed manually, then the test plan needs to describe each test in the sequence in proper order. When the testing is actually done, the tester will simply turn to the first page of the first test and follow the directions. Any discrepancies from the expected results are noted and documented. When the first test in the sequence is completed, work continues with the second test in the sequence. That particular testing effort is complete when all tests in the sequence have been executed.

Manual testing is fairly straightforward in principal. It becomes very complicated when testing requires any of the following:

- A large number of users on the system simultaneously.
- Extremely precise timing of events.
- Lengthy tests which involve a large number of detailed steps.
- A test needs to be repeated exactly.
- Large quantities of data are being input into the system.

When the testing involves any of the above requirements, human frailties and inaccuracy come into play. Most testers and users make mistakes. These flaws will reduce the validity of system testing.

5.1.3.2.2 Automated Testing   If testing is being done with automated testing tools, the process is somewhat different. Most "automated" testing tools allow the tester to capture all interaction with the application and replay it at a later time. This being the case, running the test sequence the first time is not all that different from testing in a manual environment. The most significant difference is that the tester must remember to turn on the capture capability of the automated test tool. The proper name must also be entered when the capture process is complete. The name under which this test is saved should be clearly stated in the test plan.

Once tests have been manually performed, they can be rerun many times in an automated fashion. The time required to run them subsequent times is only a fraction of the time the original testing tool took. Many tools allow test scripts to be modified and augmented so completely new test scripts can be devised.

5.1.3.3 Analyze Test Results.   Whether tests have been run singly or in a sequence, manually or automated, there is always a common activity after the tests have been completed. The test results must be analyzed. Running all the tests in the world is pointless if the results aren't examined. You must ascertain to be certain that the system being tested performed as required. You have to compare what happened during the test with what you predicted would happen.

The word predicted is the operative word in the previous sentence. For testing to be valid, you must know and document in advance what the output of the test will be. Advice given to new trial lawyers when interrogating witnesses in front of a jury is to never ask a question if you don't know what the answer will be. Testing software should adhere to the same principal. Never execute a test if you don't know what the result should be. If you don't know in advance what the test result will be, then how do you know that they were correct? Follow this guideline and your testing will be successful.

You can't wait until the test is over and then define what the output should be. That isn't rigorous enough. It would be too easy to get sloppy and be influenced by the test results. If your software works correctly, the data is defined, and the test is accurately defined, then your prediction will always come true.

5.1.3.3.1 Analyzing Manual Test Results Tests which are run singly and manually can be analyzed during test execution or immediately afterwards. The test plan for this and every test explicitly lists what constitutes a successful test. If the results deviate from the expected outcome, then the test failed. Actually the test passed, it was the software module being tested which failed. The resulting error must be documented in the error tracking system. The software component will need to be debugged, corrected, and tested all over again.

5.1.3.3.2 Analyzing Automated Test Results Tests which are run as part of a sequence are handled differently, but overall the outcome is the same. The majority of automated testing tools require that each test be run once and its output be captured. This output is called the "baseline." Subsequent executions of the tests can be run automatically. The output of these automated executions is compared against the "baseline" output. The test tool is capable of recognizing differences between the two output streams. If a difference is noted, then the test is considered to have failed.

How do you know that the "baseline" test output is correct? It must be analyzed just like the tests which were run manually. Before relying on this baseline output, it must be examined and compared to the output specified by the test plan. If it isn't what was expected, the baseline output isn't trustworthy. It must be deleted before it causes trouble and confusion. The software module must be debugged, corrected, and retested. Only when the baseline output matches the test plan requirements can it be relied on.

It should be obvious from the above paragraph that automated test tools can't replace the human element in the testing process. Each initial execution of a test must be scrutinized just as closely as it was before test tools were employed. Only after they have passed this initial exam can automated tests be relied on. The productivity improvement promised by automated test tools occurs only when tests are run multiple times. Unfortunately, the drudge work must still be performed at least once.

5.1.4 Error Tracking

The purpose of testing is not to prove that software is error free; it's to prove that errors exist. This being the situation, you should expect errors to occur. When the inevitable happens and errors are found, you will need to be able to track them. Error tracking involves a number of actions. This section defines the actions which need to be taken. Chapter 7 describes tools which are currently available to automate these processes.

5.1.4.1 Record Errors. The first step in error tracking is to record the existence of each error. Errors can be recorded automatically or manually. Many test tool suites integrate their test management tool with their error tracking software. When their comparison tool identifies a failed test, an error record is automatically generated. If the suite either doesn't include an error tracking component or it isn't integrated, then all errors must be recorded manually. It isn't as convenient to record errors manually, but the same ends can be achieved.

5.1.4.2 Identify and Document Errors. Once an error has been discovered and recorded, more information on it needs to be gathered and documented. Details aren't always immediately available, so in many cases it takes some investigation to gather all the necessary details. The old saying "know your enemy" is true when it comes to dealing with errors. If more information is accurately gathered and stored about each error, then less time will be spent performing redundant research on them. Table 5.3 lists some of the basic details which need to be gathered and reported on each error.

Some of the entries in the Table 5.3 are obvious, but others might need some explanation. An explanation for each will be provided in the interests of clarity and completeness.

5.1.4.2.1 ID Number Assigned to Error An ID number must be assigned to this error. Automated tracking systems will frequently assign a unique system-generated ID for each error being logged. This ID will be used to identify this specific error as long as it's tracked in the system. Details on errors must be kept for the life of the project and beyond. There are

TABLE 5.3

Details to Gather
on Every Error

ID number assigned to error

Detailed description of the error

Conditions under which error occurs

The test ID which uncovered the error

Name of person running test

Time and date discovered

Computer on which error occurs (i.e., client or server)

Subsystem in which error occurred

Version or build number of software subsystem

Database on which error was discovered

Component (which window, function, etc.) in which error appeared

Criticality of the error

Priority assigned to fixing this error

Whether the error is readily reproducible

Person assigned to debug and fix the error

Estimated completion date of the fix

Estimate of the time it will take to fix the error

Tests which need to be rerun after the fix is installed

reasons for this. First of all, errors have a nasty habit of reappearing in a system. One cause of this is that the new software wasn't installed correctly or everywhere it needed to be installed.

The other reason for keeping details indefinitely is to assist testers and developers on other, subsequent projects. Errors uncovered during this project might be repeated on other projects. By retaining a history of each error found on all projects, an error knowledge base is constructed. The value of this knowledge base is directly proportional to the number and details of errors which are recorded in it. The greater the detail being kept, the more likely it will shed light on an error later in this project or another project.

5.1.4.2.2 Detailed Description of the Error Without a detailed description of the error, it will be very difficult for other team members to understand the problem. The more details which are included in the description, the better. It would be helpful if the language and terms used to describe errors are consistent throughout the project team.

5.1.4.2.3 Conditions under Which Error Occurs   Some errors occur all the time, e.g., whenever a certain window is opened. Others occur only under certain conditions, e.g., when the window is opened and a certain record is retrieved. The most insidious errors don't appear to have any pattern to them. Again, the more detail which can be provided regarding the conditions under which this error occurs, the easier it will be to track it down.

5.1.4.2.4 Test Which Uncovered the Error   The name or ID of the test which uncovered the error needs to be provided for several reasons. First of all, by knowing which test uncovered the problem, the person assigned to this error will have a very good idea as to what causes the error. Secondly, when the cause of the error has been discovered and fixed, this test, among others, must be rerun to validate that the correction did indeed solve the problem.

5.1.4.2.5 Name of Person Running Test   Whoever is assigned to correct the error will very likely want to contact the person who ran the test which uncovered the problem. There might be questions about exactly how to reproduce the error, what data was used, etc. By including the tester's name, it saves time and effort on the part of the staff member who has to fix it.

This information is also valuable for historical purposes. If records indicate that a single individual discovers an inordinately large percentage of errors, then this person likely has a talent for testing. Project management might want to study her methods in order to get others up to the same level of testing proficiency. Likewise, if an individual doesn't uncover any errors at all, perhaps that person's heart isn't in the testing effort.

5.1.4.2.6 Time and Date Discovered   The time and date are needed to keep accurate statistics on when errors are being discovered and how long it takes to correct them. Without this date, it's impossible to calculate on average of how long it takes to correct errors. Knowing how long on average it takes to correct an error can be used to predict the amount of time and effort until the project is completed.

5.1.4.2.7 Computer on Which Error Occurs (i.e., Client or Server)   The fundamental definition of a client/server system includes a minimum of two computers. It's necessary to identify on which of these computers the error occurred. This information might not be immediately available. There will undoubtedly be instances when it appears that the error is occurring on one computer, when in fact it's on another. Once example would be if incorrect data is populating a data window. At first glance it might be assumed that this error is on the client workstation. If, however, this data window is populated by a stored procedure, then the computer where the error resides would be the database server.

5.1.4.2.8 Subsystem in Which Error Occured   Most software systems, client/server as well as traditional systems, are broken down into subsystems. The developer assigned to fix this problem needs to know what subsystem the error occurred in. This gives at least a broad area in which the search should begin.

5.1.4.2.9 Build or Version Number of Software Subsystem   Client/server systems undergo a large number of versions or builds during their development. The developer tasked with this error needs to know under what build the error occurred. This knowledge is crucial to isolate the problem. Without knowing the build, a considerable amount of time and energy could be wasted chasing after errors which have already been corrected in more recent builds.

5.1.4.2.10 Component in Which the Error Appeared   Besides knowing what subsystem an error occurred in, the developer assigned to fix the problem must be told which specific component displayed the error. In a client/server system with a GUI front-end, the majority of these components will be windows, but some will be in functions, stored procedures, reports, or user objects.

5.1.4.2.11 Criticality of the Error   Not all errors are created equal. Some can stop a system in its tracks. An example of this might be a locking problem occurring when accessing the database. Others corrupt or destroy data. This could occur if SQL statements don't properly define data to be modified or deleted. Others are merely cosmetic problems which don't seriously impact the system. Typographical errors in labels, headers, or on buttons exemplify this type of error.

Each newly discovered error needs to be assigned to a level of criticality. Possible levels are: critical, high, average, cosmetic. Care needs to be taken that assignments are done consistently. Everyone's understanding of what constitutes a critical error should be clear. If this isn't done consistently, then an inordinate amount of time might be spent on a minor flaw.

5.1.4.2.12 Priority Assigned to Fixing This Error Assigning priorities for addressing errors isn't as simple as one might assume. An error of lower priority which occurs frequently might be addressed before a more serious error which occurs very infrequently. Another scenario might have a very visible (i.e., embarrassing) yet cosmetic error being fixed first just so the client isn't constantly reminded of it.

Obviously, the particular priorities used will vary from site to site. In some cases they will be imposed by the choice of test management or error tracking tools chosen. One set of potential priorities are: immediate, high, normal, and as time permits.

5.1.4.2.13 Is the Error Readily Reproducible? A good rule of thumb is that the easier it is to reproduce an error, the easier it will be to fix it. This is because when it's easy to reproduce it, the developer can more easily track it down and correct it. Conversely, the more difficult it is to reproduce an error, the more difficult and time-consuming it will be to correct it. When errors aren't readily reproducible, it's significantly harder to isolate what causes them. Until the cause is found, it can't be fixed.

5.1.4.2.14 Person Assigned to Debug and Fix the Error Someone has to be assigned to the task of debugging and fixing each error. That person is the "owner" of the error until he or she solves it, quits, is transferred, or the assignment is taken away from him or her. Errors which aren't assigned to one, specific individual most likely won't get solved. Unassigned errors tend to fall into the cracks. This isn't to say that the assignee can't confer with other testers or developers to solve the problem, but someone has to have the final responsibility for each and every error.

Project management might have several techniques for deciding who to assign an error to. The simplest method would be to list developers in a queue and assign errors to the next person in the queue. A slightly more sophisticated technique would be to keep track of who has the least number of outstanding errors and assign the next error to that person. Slightly more sophisticated would be to keep track of outstanding errors and the estimated amount of time to fix each of them. A much more sophisticated method would be to keep records on the background and experience level of each developer. When an error occurs it would be assigned to the person with the most experience in that particular area.

5.1.4.2.15 Estimated Completion Date of the Fix   Project management needs to have an estimate of when the error will be fixed. Obviously this is only an estimate, and developers shouldn't be absolutely held to this date. For one thing it's extremely difficult to estimate how hard it will be to find and correct an error. If it were easy to predict the difficulty of fixing the error, then it likely wouldn't have occurred in the first place.

Another reason why estimated fix dates are unreliable is the workload is constantly shifting. The developer might plan to begin work on a particular error, but might get interrupted by an error of higher priority. In essence, this freezes the clock on the first error while the second error is being addressed. The estimate of time spent on the first error might be accurate, but the entire process can be delayed due to a higher-than-anticipated workload.

5.1.4.2.16 Estimate of the Time It Will Take to Fix the Error   This entry is related to the estimated completion date, but it's still a distinct entry. It's an estimate of the amount of time it will take to debug, analyze, and fix the error. This time estimate is independent of the date when the fix will be complete. For example, if the estimated amount of time is 30 hours and work is started on it immediately, then the fix will be available in 30 work hours. If this error is of low priority and work doesn't begin on it for two weeks, then the fix will be available 30 work hours after work on it commences.

5.1.4.2.17 Tests Which Need to Be Rerun after the Fix Is Installed   Once a potential fix for an error is found, it needs to be tested. At first glance one might suppose that the only testing necessary would be to simply run the test which initially uncovered the error. This assumption is dead wrong. First of all, the correction might satisfy the test which discovered it but not satisfy the tests which preceded or followed that test.

Secondly there is the very real possibility that the software change will introduce errors into the system unrelated to the original error that was being addressed. This scenario isn't just idle speculation or academic pondering. It happens all the time in software development. The causes vary, but are primarily due to time and pressure. There isn't enough time to thoroughly investigate the problem or the code in question. Pressure is constantly applied by management or the clients to quickly fix errors and move onto the next problem in the list. When this is the case, developers can inadvertently introduce bigger errors than the one posed by the original problem.

To verify that an error hasn't been introduced into the system, additional testing must be done. This type of testing is called regression testing. The amount of regression testing is highly dependent on the nature of the original error and the amount of code modified by the fix. A purely cosmetic error (e.g., a typo in a label) won't require any testing, while a change to a widely called function (e.g., a stored procedure to retrieve rows) will need to be thoroughly tested. Fortunately, test scripts can be reused to greatly reduce the amount of time and energy spent performing regression testing.

5.1.4.2.18 Summary of Error Details Gathered The exact details to be gathered and stored will be heavily dependent on the error tracking tool being used. Not all tools gather the same details. If there are details about errors which aren't addressed by the test management or error tracking tool being used, your site will need to define for itself what data is to be collected.

Once all required details about the error are gathered and stored in the repository, they need to be relayed to the members of the test team. If the test repository is centrally available, then all authorized team members can access this information online. In this situation an e-mail message can be sent to notify everyone as errors are discovered. If test information isn't being stored in a centrally available location, then team members might have to be informed of newly discovered errors by interoffice mail or reports circulated among the team.

5.1.4.3 Tracking Error Corrections. Tracking errors is essentially following the error to be certain that it's properly handled. Immediately after an error has been documented, it gets assigned to a specific person to be corrected. Project management needs to keep track of all errors to make sure they are being addressed. Tracking errors is primarily a matter of following up to make certain that the assignee corrects the error and distributes the fix.

Once the modified software has been put into place, the component must be retested. In many situations other components rely on the corrected component to work as specified. When this is the case, regression testing must be performed to verify that the fix doesn't adversely affect other components. Regression testing might represent a significant amount of testing activity.

Distributing the correction isn't as simple on client/server systems as it was on traditional systems. The software affected by a single error correction might reside on the database server, an application server, or any number of client machines. The actual software module which was changed could be an executable file, a dynamic link library (DLL), an initialization file, a stored procedure, or a trigger. A complicated problem could involve a combination of different types of files. Each affected module must be distributed to the appropriate machine in a timely manner.

5.1.4.4 Analyzing Errors. It isn't enough to find and correct errors. To improve the software development process, it's necessary to learn something from each error which has been uncovered. This learning process can only occur if records are kept about the errors—details such as which subsystems and modules contained the most errors? Were the errors syntax, logic, or communications? What percentage of the errors were discovered in each phase of testing (unit, integration, system, acceptance)? What type of test is most effective at finding errors? How long does the average correction take to implement? Once a fix is put into place, how many new errors does it create? Only by bringing up and analyzing questions such as these will the software development process improve. To answer these questions, details and statistics on errors must be maintained.

5.2 Generic Capabilities Offered by Test Management Tools

There are a number of test management tools available for testing client/server systems. While most of them offer slightly distinctive functionality, there is a large body of functionality which is common to many tools. The functions which appear in most, if not all, test management tools are described here.

5.2.1 Test Repository

The test assets (test plans, test procedures, test cases, software structure hierarchy, test requirements hierarchy) maintained by the test manager tool should be network based or database resident. The entire testing team as well as developers, users, and project management need quick access to this information. If the repository isn't easily accessible, it will lead to frustration and isolated pockets of out-of-date information.

5.2.1.1 Repository Format. The repository will normally be stored in a collection of files or a database. Typically it will be stored in a database. This is more desirable because a relational database is easier to interface with and maintain than a collection of flat files. Access to a database is fairly easy to control. Read access would likely be given to most of the team and write access to a selected few.

If the repository is kept in a database, the next question to determine is which vendor's database will the test manager support? SQA Manager supports Microsoft Access and Sybase SQL Anywhere. This wrinkle isn't extremely important because the test team will simply be users of this application and database. They won't likely be performing any modifications to it.

5.2.1.2 Multiple Repositories. Can multiple repositories be defined, i.e., one for each project? The alternative would be a single repository maintained with a number of separate projects defined within it. There are advantages and disadvantages to both approaches. The biggest disadvantage of a single repository would be that different projects might negatively impact each other. Performance might degrade if many users from each of several projects continuously access a single repository. Deleting or modifying entries belonging to another project shouldn't occur, but it's certainly a possibility.

A significant advantage of a single repository with multiple projects would be that the project knowledge base would be larger and potentially more valuable. When an error occurs on a new project, the repository could be searched for similar errors. If something resembling that error has already been documented in another project, then it would be advantageous to know about it. The software modified to correct the problem, amount of time it took, who made the fix, etc., would all be very valuable information to know. If all projects were maintained in separate repositories, then it's less likely that this background knowledge would be unveiled.

5.2.1.3 Repository Security. The time and energy spent building your test repository represents a significant investment. The ability to grant different levels of access to users who tap into this valuable commodity would be very desirable. Not all users require or should be granted the same access rights. Some users will need to create and modify data while the needs of others are limited to viewing data.

The ability to grant various levels of access is a desirable capability. It affords a level of protection for your extremely valuable test information. Many test plan managers have a comprehensive list of privileges which can be granted to users. They allow a list of users to be entered and a level of security assigned to each user. Figure 5.4 shows the window in SQA's Manager which allows security rights to be assigned.

Security can be imposed on either a specified project or for the installation as a whole. In SQA Manager, users can't be restricted to a single project. If they are given access to a single project, they can access all projects. It would be very useful to be able to restrict their access to specified projects.

5.2.2 Graphical Representation

Many test planning tools display requirements and other information in a graphical tree structure. This format is immediately familiar to most Windows users. It provides an interface which is extremely readable.

Figure 5.4
Assigning Security in
SQA Manager

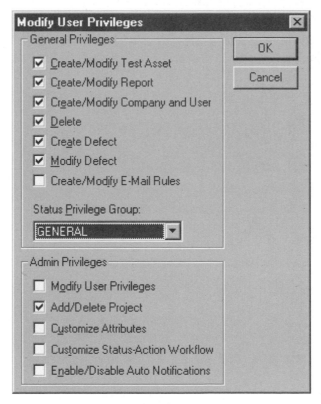

Figure 5.5
Graphical
Representation of
Mercury Interactive's
Test Director

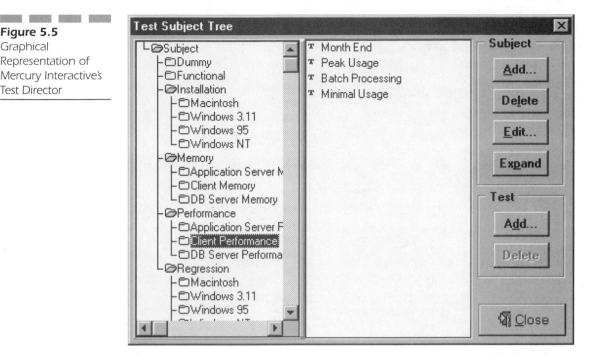

Many tools include this type of representation in their products. Figure 5.5 is the graphical representation used by Mercury Interactive's Test Director to show available tests.

5.2.3 Tool Customization

No two organizations are the same. Each site has its own requirements, its own methods, and its own slightly different vocabulary. A test management tool should recognize local differences and allow local customizations whenever possible. Like many GUI-based applications, test management tools allow users to customize them to varying degrees. When available, this is a very useful capability. Users of management tools vary greatly in their experience and needs. Testers will be entering information about errors. Project management types will be reviewing progress on known errors. User representatives will be looking at the percentage of tests completed. By allowing a degree of customization, these tools can make life easier for this diverse group of users.

Many of the project management tools do provide the capability to do a fair amount of customization. Some common features which can be customized are listed in Table 5.4.

TABLE 5.4

Customizations

Terms

Keywords

Error tracking rules

Reports

Filters

Adding, removing, or arranging buttons on any toolbar

Changing the location and size of any toolbars

Contents of drop-down list boxes

Automatic data refresh

E-mail preferences

Auto save of data when windows are closed

Color and pattern choices for graph reports

Default values when entering records

Pick lists displayed in drop-down list boxes

It isn't worthwhile going into specific details regarding which tool allows what to be customized. As soon as the ink is dry, the data will be obsolete. Products not included in the original edition will be on the market before this book hits the bookstores. The best that can be done in this volume is to alert the reader to the fact that some tools are more customizable than others. Any tools which are being seriously considered for purchase and use should be analyzed for this capability.

5.2.4 Reports

What would a management tool be without a plethora of reports? Reports are an essential method of disseminating information regarding the progress of the testing process. Without a set of precise reports, it would be difficult to communicate testing progress effectively and concisely to management, users, developers, and other interested individuals.

While the format and contents of reports is unique to each test management tool, there are certain types of reports which are included in almost all of test management tools. Many tools offer a set of predefined reports as well as the ability to define customized reports. A brief description of common reports is presented in the following sections. In some cases the reports listed below actually take the form of graphs.

5.2.4.1 Percent of Tests Successfully Run.   A report on this information might include just the statistics of how many tests have been successfully completed. It might list every test and its current status. This type of information will be of great interest to everyone interested in the system being developed. The test team, user representatives, project management, and high-level management will all keep a close eye on this particular report. As this value creeps closer and closer to 100%, expect to produce this particular report more frequently.

5.2.4.2 Description of Errors Discovered.   A report which describes all errors which have been discovered is useful. It allows the test team to get a feel for where problems are cropping up.

5.2.4.3 Status of Outstanding Errors.   A list of all outstanding errors, their priority, estimated completion date, etc., gives the team a quick handle on what is left to be accomplished.

5.2.4.4 Error Distribution.   This report yields an indication of where in the system errors are being found, i.e., which subsystems are incurring the most problems. It allows management to identify situations which result in more, or fewer, errors than normal. Hopefully, this information can be used to improve the software development process for future projects.

5.2.4.5 Defect Age Report.   A report of this type provides information on how old each of the errors, outstanding and corrected, is. It's a handle on how quickly defects are being corrected. It's useful for management to recognize how quickly errors are being fixed after they have been discovered. It provides insight into how tightly resources are being stretched.

5.2.5 Integration between Test Tools

Many of the test plan tools which are available have multiple pieces. Examples of these are test planning tools, capture and replay tools, error-tracking software, and test wizards. Each component covers distinct yet related aspects of the testing process. The more closely these components work together, the easier the tools, as a whole, will be to use.

One example of a tightly integrated product is SQA's Suite. SQA Manager's defect tracking system tracks defects which have been automatically logged by the SQA Test Log Viewer. This takes some of the data entry burden off the testers. Tight integration also limits the likelihood that errors will fall into the "proverbial" cracks.

5.2.6 Filters

Test plan management tools have the potential of displaying large quantities of data to the users. Many such tools allow users to restrict the amount of data being shown by using filters. Examples of how filters are used could include restricting tests being shown to those associated with a specific subsystem. Tests which have not been passed could also be filtered to a display. These two relatively simple examples should give some idea of how filters can allow users to select only the tests they are interested in examining.

In the optimum scenario, the user would be able to create filters, name them, and retrieve them for use at a later time. This ability lets individual users design filters which specifically address their needs. Filters can be extremely convenient time savers and are well worth using.

5.2.7 E-Mail

Corporate America has thoroughly embraced the concept of e-mail. A majority of people wouldn't be able to (or don't think they could) function without the use of their e-mail systems. The first thing most people in our information age do each morning is to check their e-mail. Software developers are no different in this regard.

E-mail is particularly valuable when correspondents are separated by great distance or time. Time in this context refers to the people's time zones or work schedules. While most members of a test team will be in the same time zone, they are not as likely to be working on the same schedule. Testing frequently involves working off shifts. Sometimes this is done to minimize impact on developers. Other times it's necessary because each tester or group of testers requires a dedicated system. No matter what the reason, the outcome is that all testers aren't likely to be working at the same time and place. E-mail is perhaps the only effective means of communicating to the entire test team.

Some test tools have e-mail capabilities built into them. It's possible to generate messages directly out of the tools and attach reports and schedules to these electronic epistles. TestDirector from Mercury Interactive allows bug-related messages (their words, not mine) to be sent to users. Messages about new errors can be directed to TestDirector. These messages can be automatically generated, depending on a number of error related criteria. Examples are if the error priority exceeds a set value or if the error status is a certain value (e.g., Open or Fixed).

SQA Manager is another product which includes embedded e-mail capabilities. Some of the uses of this capability are to automatically e-mail a message to the QA person responsible for testing and validating an error. This can be used when the error's status changes from open to pending validation. Another example is to inform the accountable party when responsibility for repairing a defect changes from one person to another. This capability can go a long way towards avoiding situations where communication between team members falls by the wayside.

5.3 Capabilities Offered by Specific Test Management Tools

Some capabilities of specific test management tools will be discussed here. They are features which aren't generally available across the test tool spectrum. They are being listed in order to provide the reader with a broader background of what is available industrywide.

5.3.1 Cross-Referencing Test Requirements with Test Procedures

The ability to cross-reference test plan requirements with specific tests procedure names has some advantages. First it makes it easier to obtain an overall view of the test plan. It eases the task of keeping track of which requirements have been fulfilled. It also allows test personnel to visually see the tests which must be rerun if a module is modified.

5.3.2 Users from Different Organizations

SQA Manager allows different companies involved in the testing effort to be registered. Examples would be beta test sites, customers, and consultants. This information could be very useful for tracking where and when errors are being discovered.

5.3.3 Customizations to the Repository

Test Director by Mercury Interactive allows tables in its test repository to be modified. Columns can be added to maintain information on details not envisioned in the original design. Adding a column to track the version number of the software being tested would be an example.

CHAPTER 6

Time Lines for Testing a Client/Server System

Testing and debugging a client/server system are necessary evils that can consume up to half of the labor and two-thirds of the schedule. This might not be a very cheery thought to clients and management, but it is reality. No one enjoys devoting such a high percentage of resources to testing, but software which an organization depends upon requires adequate testing.

6.1 When Should the Testing Process Begin?

The correct answer to the question of when the testing process should begin is early, very early. Testing, even when using the best tools that are available, is likely to take significantly longer than original estimates. Unless the planning is begun early in the development project, it can almost be guaranteed that adequate testing will not be achieved.

Escalating numbers of client/server systems being developed today are critical to the success of the organization. Order entry systems, billing systems, government compliance systems, and safety-related systems make up the backbone of many companies. If these crucial systems are not properly tested and debugged, the future of the organization could be placed in jeopardy.

6.1.1 Reasons to Start Testing Immediately

Like anything else, the earlier the testing process is begun, the sooner it will be finished. That's certainly true, but there are a number of other very good reasons for testing early.

6.1.1.1 Less Likely to Impact the Development Schedule. When a system is delivered late or its quality is very low (error-riddled), there are plenty of participants who likely deserve some of the responsibility. Likely it's the QA department who shoulders the majority of the blame. They get targeted primarily for two reasons. First of all, they are tasked with finding errors. Forgotten is the fact that the system was loaded with bugs and QA exorcised a very large percentage of them. The remaining flaws become their burden because they weren't discovered as well.

The second reason that QA is frequently blamed for poor or late systems is that they were the last group to touch it. Testing is normally done at the very tail end of the project. Because the testing group was the last to work on it, somehow all the schedule slippages become their fault. Never mind the fact the product was six months late reaching QA; the late delivery is attributed to them in the minds of a lot of the masses.

The testing phase frequently does take longer than originally scheduled. The reason for this is the system delivered to them was in terrible shape. It should be obvious that there is a correlation between the number of errors in the system and how long it takes to test and debug it. The more errors in a system, the longer it will take to find them, correct them, and retest the system. Had the software quality been originally higher, the testing phase would have been completed sooner.

The preceding paragraphs are a prelude into the assertion that the testing function or testing group already has a marginal reputation. By starting the test planning earlier in the project cycle, testing can be performed more efficiently once the project reaches that state. If this occurs, there will be less ammunition with which to blame QA for being the cause of the product's late delivery or lack of quality.

The concept of starting testing early to avoid delaying the project is especially true for rapid application development (RAD) projects. These projects emphasize close interaction between users and developers to accelerate project development. RAD projects are meant to move quickly. If testing is not started early enough in the development cycle, the project can be nearing completion before a test plan is designed and the testing is begun. In cases such as these, the onus of a late project rightly belongs to the testing department.

6.1.1.2 Errors Found Early Are Easier and Cheaper to Fix. The earlier in a software project that errors are discovered, the less time and money it takes to correct them. Software developers have probably heard this assertion many, many times. Is this statement actually true or is it simply a worn-out cliche that has been handed down from developer to developer?

A hypothetical situation can help answer this question. An Invoice Selection (IS) module in a client/server system has been designed to search database tables and return all invoices which are ready to be paid. The Invoice Selection (IS) module includes an algorithm that identifies the invoices which are to be paid, the window to display them, the ability for the user to remove invoices, and the code to create a text output file.

Output from IS feeds an accounts payable (A/P) subsystem and a general ledger (GL) subsystem. The accounts payable system cuts checks based on the invoices and sends them to the vendors. The general ledger system documents these payments in the organization's general ledger.

It should be obvious that the accounts payable (A/P) and general ledger (GL) systems are highly dependent on Invoice Selection to correctly identify and process invoices. They have both been designed based on assurances that Invoice Selection will function as documented. Both will be designed, coded, and unit tested based on these assurances.

Assume that the design of Invoice Selection includes a fundamental error. There are a number of stages in the project during which this error can be discovered. Table 6.1 lists some of these possible discovery times. There are other potential times, but the ones listed here represent the most likely of them.

The amount of time and effort required to fix this problem will differ drastically depending on when it is discovered. Table 6.2 lists each of these times and a brief description of the amount of effort it will take to correct the design flaw. The later errors are discovered, the more related modules they affect and the more work needs to be undone and redone.

TABLE 6-1

Times When an
Error Can Be
Uncovered

1	During a design check of the Invoice Selection subsystem
2	During a design check of the Accounts Payable subsystem
3	During a design check of the General Ledger subsystem
4	While coding Invoice Selection subsystem
5	While coding the Accounts Payable subsystem
6	While coding the General Ledger system
7	During Invoice Selection unit testing
8	During Accounts Payable unit testing
9	During General Ledger unit testing
10	During Integration Testing
11	During System Testing
12	During Acceptance Testing
13	After Acceptance Testing, but before delivery to the customer
14	After installation on a customer's system

TABLE 6.2

Effects of Errors Uncovered During Each Phase

Time When Error Is Uncovered	Modules Which Will Be Affected	Scope of Changes
Invoice Selection Design check	IS Module. Possibly A/P and GL	Redesign IS. Possibly A/P and GL
A/P Design check	IS and A/P. Possibly GL	Redesign IS and A/P. Possibly GL
GL Design check	IS and GL. Possibly A/P	Redesign IS and GL. Possibly A/P
Coding Invoice Selection	IS Module. Possibly A/P and GL	Redesign and Recode IS. Possibly A/P and GL
A/P Coding	IS and A/P. Possibly GL	Redesign and Recode IS and A/P. Possibly GL
GL Coding	IS and GL. Possibly A/P	Redesign and Recode IS and GL. Possibly A/P
Invoice Selection unit testing	IS Module. Possibly A/P and GL	Redesign, Recode and Retest IS. Possibly A/P & GL
A/P unit testing	IS and A/P. Possibly GL	Redesign, Recode and Retest IS and A/P. Possibly GL
GL unit testing	IS and GL. Possibly A/P	Redesign, Recode and Retest IS and GL. Possibly A/P
Integration Testing	IS Module. Possibly A/P and GL	Redesign, Recode and Retest IS. Possibly A/P & GL
System Testing	IS Module. Possibly A/P and GL	Redesign, Recode and Retest IS and A/P. Possibly GL
Acceptance Testing	IS Module. Possibly A/P and GL	Redesign, Recode and Retest IS and A/P. Possibly GL
After Acceptance Testing	IS Module. Possibly A/P and GL	Redesign, Recode and Retest IS and A/P. Possibly GL
After Installation	IS Module. Possibly A/P and GL	Redesign, Recode and Retest IS and A/P. Possibly GL

As Table 6-2 illustrates, the later in the development process the error is discovered, the more extensive the required changes. Once the module passes to integration testing, the effects on other modules begin to climb. If an error is not found until after the system has been delivered, the costs can be astronomical.

The above scenario involves only three modules. In reality, there are likely to be many more interconnections and dependencies within a client/server system. If a design error is discovered in a module which interfaces with a larger number of subsystems, the effects will be geometrically higher. The scope and amount of effort involved in correcting an error in a more complicated system are significantly higher as well.

6.1.1.3 Flaws in Application Definition or Design Are Exposed Earlier.

A system design can be a beautiful thing—lots of neatly aligned boxes with gracefully drawn lines between them. How could anything so neat and orderly contain an error? Design flaws don't jump off the documents at people. They won't be exposed until someone digs into these diagrams, studies them, and challenges them.

If a design error is found late in the development cycle of a system, several interesting things tend to occur. No one wants to spend the time and energy to completely redesign the system. It involves too much time, effort, and resources to accomplish this. What tends to happen is a Band-Aid correction is applied to the error. The absolutely minimal modifications are made to get around this problem. That may not sound like a bad idea, but what if it has already occurred many times on the system already? The result is that Band-Aids are applied on top of other Band-Aids. Is it realistic to assume that such a system will achieve a high level of reliability or quality? Isn't it more likely that the entire system will be questionable and unreliable?

Flaws that are discovered very early in the project don't have anywhere near the impact that later-appearing errors will have. When discovered prior to the coding and testing phases, the impact of modifying the design is significantly reduced. When changes have less of a disrupting impact on the system (and the schedule), there is a higher likelihood that they will be corrected the way they should be.

6.1.1.4 By Starting Early, It's Less Likely That Testing Will Be Trimmed, Abandoned, etc.

If a project starts falling behind schedule and its costs begin to exceed the budget project, it isn't uncommon for management to go into a panic mode. The first thought tends to be finding what can be pared from the schedule to cut both costs and time of delivery. All too often the area that gets slashed is testing. Two tendencies coincide to make testing a very frequent victim. The first is blind optimism. Management is willing to pretend there is a realistic possibility that no errors will be present in the software. It's the old "if everything goes right" scenario. If everything goes right, then the software won't have any errors and won't need much (any) testing. This is not a practical or realistic likelihood. Anyone with experience on software development projects certainly knows that such optimistic outlooks are never justified.

The second reason why management tends to cut testing is that the testing group doesn't produce anything that is "visible." Other groups produce usable objects, such as windows, reports, subroutines, or manuals. Testing doesn't generate anything that can be touched or pointed to. Its output is much more abstract. Quality isn't immediately visible. When the decision is being made about whether to cut funds for the physical or the abstract, the latter will lose every time.

6.2 Testing Resources

When the testing is just starting to be designed, perhaps the most important action is to lay out what resources are needed to perform a proper job of testing. If adequate resources aren't available and scheduled, there is little hope that the testing will be done correctly and on time.

6.2.1 Resources Required for the Testing Effort

The numbers and types of resources required for the testing effort are quite varied. The most important "resources" are people. Without a skilled, qualified, committed staff, the testing cannot possibly be performed. There is a surprising diversity of the types of people and skills represented in the testing staff. Other resources required during the test phase include computer hardware and other physical equipment. Software and data round out the testing resource requirements.

A construction project or manufacturing process has defined times when each of the many resources being utilized must be available. If the resource isn't obtainable at that time, the process will be delayed or operate at a severely reduced efficiency. Premature arrival of a resource isn't necessarily a good thing. At best it will simply sit idle until it's needed. In the worst case it can congest the working area and reduce the efficiency of all concerned.

The testing effort is no different is this regard. Each resource is needed at its own time. Late arrival of a resource reduces the progress or efficiency of the testing process. Project management must schedule these assets efficiently so they are available when needed and not before.

6.2.1.1 Staff. As stated earlier, the most valuable resource in the testing effort is the staff! Without a qualified, motivated testing staff, the work simply will not be done properly. The operative questions are what types of skills are needed, how large a staff is necessary, and when in the testing cycle is each skill necessary? Table 6.3 is a list of the positions needed when staffing a testing project.

Obviously, the size of the project will affect this list. A very small project that can be tested quickly might be able to get along without an Assistant Test Manager. A significantly sized project will require an assistant test manager and more than one test engineer.

One test tool vendor states that a typical ratio of test staff to development staff is 1 tester to every 2–4 developers. If an organization has no previous experience in this area, it would be safer to staff the testing group at a ratio of 1:2. It comes as no surprise that each organization will vary from the norm. Complete record keeping on the testing efforts will help to generate accurate staffing statistics for future projects.

6.2.1.2 Hardware. Testing certainly cannot be done without the necessary hardware. It's safe to say that without adequate dedicated hardware the testing effort will be stunted. In the past, many projects required testing personnel to work shifts, weekends, and holidays because the only hardware available to test on was the system under development. The plummeting price of computer hardware should eliminate such tales of woe told by the graybeards to today's software newcomers.

6.2.1.2.1 Server(s) All roads lead to the server, and this piece of equipment should be acquired and installed early in the testing hardware buildup. It is usually the most expensive piece of hardware in the client/server system and normally requires the most software to be installed on it. Virtually all client/server systems include a database server and increasingly an application server as well.

TABLE 6.3

Testing Staff
Positions

1. Test Manager

The Test Manager provides the overall direction for the testing effort. His or her responsibilities include participating in the development of the test plan, supervising the test staff, monitoring progress, and reporting the same to upper management.

2. Assistant Test Manager

Everyone needs a replacement and this person serves as the backup for the Test Manager. Although it isn't always considered polite to talk about it, people do get sick, resign, retire, relocate, or even die. This can happen even in the middle of a project. The Assistant Test Manager might be a person who is being groomed to be a Test Manager on the next project.

3. Test Engineer(s)

Test engineers are technically oriented people who worked with the Test Manager developing the test plan. They are charged with actually executing the tests. If a test script needs to be changed, the Test Engineer is the best qualified person to modify these objects. Depending on the size of the system being tested, there may be more than one Test Engineer.

4. Recorder(s)

The recorder keeps track of all the unpopular but necessary paperwork. He or she records the current status of every test and subtest, schedules retests when necessary, produces management reports on their regular schedule, etc. This certainly isn't a glamorous position, but it is absolutely vital.

5. User Witnesses

The client or user community will undoubtedly want to provide their own witnesses during the testing process. These witnesses might be users of the legacy system being replaced, future users of the new system, or experienced consultants engaged for just this task. In some cases the witnesses will participate in the testing effort, while on other projects they will be strictly witnessing the testing activity.

6. Technical Support Personnel (DBA, LAN Administration, or System Administrator)

Problems will invariably be encountered by the test team during the testing process. Many of these will be outside the scope of the applications being tested. Some examples of such difficulties are: communications problems with the LAN, problems accessing files and subdirectories on the server, difficulty obtaining security permission to access database tables, insufficient resources on the server or client machines. Technical support personnel will be needed to help resolve these issues. While people with these skills do not need to be constantly present during the entire testing effort, they should be accessible at all times during the testing endeavor. The testing effort should have sufficient priority to be able to interrupt their day-to-day activities should an emergency arise.

7. Clerical Assistance

The testing activity will produce a myriad of mundane, time-consuming tasks. Examples of these are reproducing reports, hand entering data when required, backing up disk files, etc. These activities are certainly important, but they don't require a tremendously high skill or experience level to perform them. Rather than tie up a technical person doing them, it is preferable to assign them to a clerk.

The database server contains, surprisingly enough, the database. To support this particular piece of software, the server must include a multithreaded operating system. Up until recently UNIX was the overwhelming choice for the operating system. O/S2 and Windows NT are becoming more common choices for operating systems.

The hardware requirements include a fairly fast processor and ample quantities of disk space. The disk space is crucial because databases tend to chew up lots of disk real estate. This is especially applicable when multiple test databases are being supported. RAID (redundant array of inexpensive devices) disk configuration or mirrored drives to allow fault tolerance storage are becoming more commonplace.

A sufficient amount of random access memory (RAM) is also a requirement for the server. Between the needs of the operating system and the database engine, it isn't uncommon for a server to have 96–128MB or more of RAM. Whatever is going to be installed in the production system is what needs to be available for the test platform.

An application server provides a repository for business rules. Such a server exists in a multitiered client/server system. If the client/server being developed has this tier, then the testbed hardware must include such a server.

Server machines require hardware peripherals above and beyond the basic CPU, RAM, monitor, and disk drives. A tape backup is necessary to allow periodic backups to be performed. A CD-ROM device is required because more and more software is deployed on CD-ROMs. Many third-party vendors require or request that the system include a modem and communications software that allows them to monitor their package remotely.

6.2.1.2.2 Client Workstations   Client workstations will be required for testing personnel to execute the test functions. A minimum of one client workstation per tester will be needed. The faster these machines are, the more efficient testers can be during this effort. These test workstations can be the testers' normal computers. Some of the testing, including performance testing, must be done on workstations with a configuration which a typical user will have. A system that mimics the same amount of disk, memory, and speed is essential. This requirement is valuable because it lets the testers get a feel for response times a typical user will experience when using the system. If testers do not have a grasp of performance from a user's viewpoint, then they may be in for a shock when users complain that response time is terrible.

Client/server systems frequently involve connecting a disparate group of client machines. Many times this collection includes computers that were left over from previous systems. This is not a desirable way to assemble a system, but sometimes resource limitations are forced upon the project. If this is going to be the case, the collection of workstations on which the testing is performed must include at least one model of each type of PC the system is to be deployed on. If a certain type of computer absolutely cannot support the client server system, requires nonstandard device drivers or other software, it's much better to know about this up front. Surprises of this variety aren't fun for anyone involved if they come just before the system is scheduled for delivery.

Another type of client computer which deserves mention is the increasingly ubiquitous laptop computer. More and more information workers require a machine that they can utilize either in the office or on the road. A laptop with a docking station is the solution to this growing need. The client/server system must be tested on these portable machines. Two reasons back up this statement. First of all, problems connecting laptops to servers are extremely common. Secondly, if a problem does crop up connecting a laptop to the client/server system, it's a pretty sure bet that the user of the laptop is not a grunt. More likely, it's an executive who has very little patience when you attempt to explain why she cannot access the new system. Again, it's better to uncover problems of this nature long before the users expect to go live on the system.

6.2.1.2.3 Network Hardware The glue that connects client machines with the server is the communications network. Both hardware and software make up the network. When testing a client/server system, it's obligatory to include the same type of network hardware and software in the test environment. Hardware on which tests are exercised is often the same hardware on which the production system will run. When this is the case, there is no need to acquire additional network hardware. Testing needs to be with each type of network device. Depending on the complexity and topology of the system being implemented, the test hardware system can include the following:

- Routers.
- Hubs.
- Bridges.
- Gateways.

6.2.1.2.4 Peripheral Equipment   All computer systems, including client/server systems require peripheral devices. Traditional peripherals include printers, tape drives, modems and plotters. Client/server systems exhibit a mixture of recent and fairly traditional peripheral equipment. Examples of more timely devices are laser printers, bar code readers, scanners, and fax machines.

Prior to testing the subsystems which interface with these peripherals, all of the required hardware must be ordered, received, and installed. Any software that accompanied the equipment must be installed. This may seem obvious, but it's an item which is easily overlooked until testing is about to be performed. When this occurs, it is sure to impact the schedule.

6.2.1.2.5 Specialized Test Equipment   If the client/server system undergoing development involves specialized interfaces with the outside world, the testing phase may require equally specialized test equipment. This will not be the case for the vast majority of client/server development, but it may occur periodically. A primary example of such situations would be the hardware used to interface with real-time data acquisition sensors. Test equipment is used to simulate activity occurring in the external environment.

6.2.1.3 Software.   A collection of computer hardware can be interesting to look at, but it takes software as well to make it a functioning system. The software required in a client/server system will be extremely diverse. Different software fulfills varying requirements and runs on each of the various platforms.

The software will also very likely come from a disturbingly large collection of vendors. This fact is disturbing because software vendors are not usually known for cooperating with each other to solve your problems. Normally problems occurring between products from various vendors elicit a lot of finger-pointing. By purchasing software from this variety of suppliers you become in essence a systems integrator, like it or not.

The following sections describe the software required to build a client/server system. The impact each piece of software has on the effort task will be examined.

6.2.1.3.1 Operating Systems   The operating systems acquired for a client/server system lay the foundation for a significant amount of other software. In most instances, the client and server machines will be running different operating systems. Examples of server-level operating systems include UNIX, Windows NT Server, and O/S2. A multithreaded, robust operating system requires a significant amount of system resources. The amount of memory on a server will likely be 48–64MB (megabytes) and the disk capacity will almost certainly be in the range of 4–10GB (gigabytes).

The capability needed on the server is not necessary or even desirable on all of the client machines. They will more likely be running Microsoft Windows 3.11, Windows 95, or Windows NT Client software. These operating systems adequately fulfill the users' needs, and their resource requirements are much lighter.

Although more and more client/server software products are being expanded to work with multiple operating systems, there are still quite a few that will work with either one or a small repertoire of systems. When choosing the O/S on both the client and server machines, you are affecting your potential choices for development and test tools.

6.2.1.3.2 Test Tool Software Testing software always exists at the client workstation level and frequently is loaded at the server level as well. The software running at the client level can be broken down into several distinctive types. Examples of client-level software includes capture and playback tools, debuggers, error tracking packages, or a test plan management tool.

Server-level testing software is a little less diverse. Often it is on the server to support the testing repository. This enables testing staff across the entire project to access the repository. Other test software on the server is positioned there to enable testing and performance measurement of server-level activity.

6.2.1.3.3 Current Version of System Being Tested The most current version being tested must be installed on the test system. Depending on the architecture, the bulk of the system may reside on the client or the server. The server normally contains the database engine, but some application software is situated on the server as well. The advantage of this is that there is significantly less duplication. This not only saves space, but it also reduces the maintenance effort required to issue new releases. Changed software only needs to be installed on the server instead of on all the client workstations.

Performance and flexibility are two distinct advantages of distributing application software. If the client machine does not have to obtain front-end software from a server, it normally runs faster. By distributing the software, it becomes easier to customize it for different classes of users.

6.2.1.3.4 Communications Software Client/server systems couldn't function without communications software. These products allow the two types of machines to communicate with each other. A couple of these products are Oracle's SQL*Net and TCP/IP stacks, etc. This software normally includes portions loaded at both the server and client workstation levels.

6.2.1.3.5 Other Applications In addition to the client/server software being explicitly tested, there is additional software which will be required by the testing staff. Examples of these types of packages include word processors, e-mail, spreadsheets, and project planners. These aren't explicitly part of the client/server system, but they can add a great deal to the productivity of the testing staff.

6.2.1.4 Staff Training.

Client/server development in general and client/server testing in particular are fairly new in the world of data processing. A great many of the people being drawn into this paradigm are either new to the profession or have migrated from the mainframe environment. Relatively few universities offer degree programs or even specialties in client/server systems. This combination of a new model and people with a fresh background calls for adequate training for all personnel involved.

The training can be formal or informal. It might consist of classes offered by a particular vendor on their particular product. Industry seminars are a common source for classes, as are national or regional user group meetings. The lucky organization will be located near a community college that offers classes in client/server-related topics. The bottom line is that locating a source for training might not be easy, but it's absolutely necessary.

6.2.1.4.1 Testers Trained on Test Tools Testing personnel need to be trained on the tools they will be using to test the system. This training is available exclusively from the vendor. A common practice is to bring in a trainer from the vendor and perform the training in-house. If enough organizations in a geographic region utilize the same test tool, they can cooperate and engage a trainer to educate a common group.

Training on the test tools needs to be done early in the testing schedule. Testing personnel must understand the capabilities and limitations of the product before they design the test plan. If they don't have this knowledge, they will not be able to exploit the tool to its fullest. They might possibly design tests which can't be performed via the tool.

6.2.1.4.2 Users Trained on the System Being Developed Practically all system development projects have users who will require training on the system being developed. Normally this would not come under the auspices of the testing staff, but on a client/server project users are involved earlier and to a higher degree. They are frequently brought into the testing effort to contribute manpower as well as obtain an earlier introduction to the system. If users haven't received adequate training on the new system, they aren't likely to make a positive contribution during the testing phase. In fact, their participation can have a negative effect because they may inundate developers and testers with relatively simple questions.

This acceleration of the training schedule requires that planning and effort be directed towards training earlier than normal. It might require that a training course be based on the system as it exists in its prototype form. The course would later be refined as the system is polished and finalized. This may require a little extra work on the part of the trainers, but the alternative would be that the training is not available early enough to make users productive members of the testing staff.

6.2.1.4.3 Project Management Trained on Project Tracking Tools Many test tool suites include a project planning capability. When this is available, members of the project management team need to be extremely familiar with this tool. If they are not well acquainted with it, then the quality and viability of the project plan will reflect their lack of competence. Such a shortcoming could easily hamper or cripple the testing effort.

Management training on the tool should likely start soon after the test tool is chosen. It is needed early in the time line because these are the tools used to schedule the testing efforts. Training of this nature is available only from the vendor. Since relatively few staff members will undergo this type of training, it's likely that the individuals to be trained will be sent to the vendor's site.

6.2.1.5 Facilities and Infrastructure. The facilities and infrastructure are the bricks and mortar of the effort. They aren't flashy, or high-tech, but try to get your job done without them. Because they aren't often thought about, it becomes easy to overlook their importance. If testing will be done in a new location or the testing group is specifically being formed for this project, make sure appropriate facilities are going to be on hand.

6.2.1.5.1 Cubicles, Desks, and Other Office Equipment It seems pretty obvious that your staff will need a place to sit while they do their jobs. It's surprising how often this necessity is overlooked when a project is gearing up. All too often newcomers on the project are assigned to the project before anyone thinks about where they will sit. A week or two often goes by before they are able to settle down in a desk they can call their own.

Cubicles are the bane of developers' existence. In a cubicle bullpen, there is too much noise, motion, and activity to perform work requiring a high degree of concentration. If at all possible, each member of the test staff should have an office with a door which closes. In this way external noise can be shut out. Office space of this nature may cost a bit more to establish, but will certainly pay for itself in increased productivity.

The typical developer and test staff member don't have enough desk space. They need a lot of surface area to spread out their manuals, documents, listings, and designs. Cramping them into a smaller than necessary area lowers their productivity and enthusiasm.

Phones represent an enigma. Everyone on the test team needs a phone. A speakerphone can be especially convenient. It allows the hands to be free to work the keyboard, open manuals, take notes, etc. Voice mail has become an expected convenience in the modern workplace. The knowledge that your messages are being accurately and consistently received allows test staff to feel comfortable being away from their desks. They also feel more secure in leaving messages for other people, assured that they will be received.

The downside of the telephone is that we have become a slave to it. Too often, workers are deep in creative thought processes when a shrill ringing interrupts. By the time they complete the phone call, they have lost the train of thought and must begin again. All developers and test staff members should be able to turn off the ringers on their phones. Combined with voice mail, this allows them to prevent disturbances yet be assured of receiving important communications.

The above situations occur frequently when consultants are brought onto a project. They show up on Monday morning all set to get to work. There may be no formal procedure for obtaining badges, desks, logon IDs, etc. It may not seem like a lot of time is being wasted, but it adds up to a considerable amount of unproductive time. It would be much more efficient to have all of the above essentials in place before expensive talent comes through the door.

6.2.1.5.2 Networks Client/server systems absolutely depend on the existence of a computer network. Test staff members are equally dependent on the existence and reliability of the local area network. More and more tools and peripherals are connected to the network instead of each staff member's workstation. It is the exception to have a printer connected to one's PC. The norm now is to have a departmental printer connected to the network. Frequently, development tools and suites of desktop applications reside on a server instead of on each individual's workstation.

The advantages of server-based software and peripherals are cost and flexibility. It costs less to have a limited number of printers which every workstation can use. Purchasing fewer server based software licenses costs significantly less than a license for every potential user of the package. This is especially true if the product is something users do not use constantly. It is also easier to maintain a limited number of server based products compared to those distributed to every workstation.

The downside of networks is their reliability or rather lack of reliability. If the server which hosts the development tool or test tool goes down, then productivity will be affected, to put it lightly. If your network isn't absolutely reliable, then placing critically needed tools and databases on it is a high-risk move.

6.2.1.5.2.1 Network Access Limited or prohibited access to the network can be a very frustrating stumbling block. How many developers and testers have had to spin their wheels for the first day or two until the network administration people got around to adding their names to the access list? A common way around this is for someone to lend them their login and password temporarily. Not a good solution. There should be procedures in place to get network logins quickly. In fact, it would be optimal to request the network login in advance. This would enable new staff members to hit the ground running.

Once staff members have network logins, they are all set up for the next stumbling block. Invariably their initial network access doesn't include all the servers, volumes, rights, etc. which they will require. Additional productive time is lost while their network access is corrected. Again, all of the new member's requirements are known in advance, so why not have it set up before they arrive?

6.2.1.5.2.2 Network Disk Space If the test staff is going to rely upon network drives for online storage, then there must be adequate disk space available. There are two aspects to the concept of "adequate disk space." The first part is that disk drives of sufficient size and quantity be available. With the price of online storage spiraling downward, it's hard to justify being miserly with disk drives. It is hard to remain focused and productive when you are constantly worried that your test scripts and logs will be truncated due to a lack of disk space. Time spent searching directories for files which can be deleted isn't very productive.

The second aspect of adequate space is the quota given to testers. Many LAN administrators start users with a fairly restrictive disk quota and only slowly move it up. At times it seems they are playing head games when they grudgingly increase allotments. This type of activity does a lot towards poisoning relations between LAN administrators and the rest of the organization.

On the other hand, users must be realistic about what their true disk storage requirements are. Just because disk space is available doesn't mean it should be wasted. Are test results from six months ago really required online? Couldn't they be safely archived to tape? The test staff must be realistic and responsible when it comes to managing their use of this important and finite resource.

6.2.1.5.2.3 Network Backups and Recovery

If the testing staff is to trust relying upon network-based disk space, they have to be convinced that their files are sufficiently protected. This means that these drives must be backed up regularly. The backup procedures can consist of nightly dumps, periodic full dumps, and daily incremental changes or any other scheme that ensures that files are adequately protected.

Not only must backups be performed regularly, they must also be periodically tested. Tape drives fail, tape cartridges go bad, and procedures can be overlooked. These problems and many others can conspire to render backup tapes worthless. Backups must be checked to ensure that they contain everything they are supposed to and that their contents are still readable. Omitting this testing isn't an oversight; it's criminal. Do not allow a situation such as this to blindside you.

When it comes to network backups, what goes in must come out. Even if the backup procedures are flawless, there can still be confusion when it comes to restoring a file from the backup media. A formalized recovery request process should be instituted. It should inform network users regarding what is being backed up and how long it is retained. A formal method should exist which informs users how to request that a file be restored. The amount of time it takes to restore the file should be documented.

6.2.1.5.3 E-Mail If voice mail has become an expected convenience in the modern workplace then e-mail has become a necessity! Information technology workers unconditionally rely upon this method of communication. Without e-mail, a tremendous amount of additional time would be spent playing phone tag and waiting for intra-office mail.

In addition to being an efficient person-to-person method of communication, e-mail has been integrated into a great number of test tools. This allows team members to be automatically alerted when they are assigned to an error, a test needs to be rerun, a meeting has been postponed, etc. Take away automatically generated e-mail messages, and a lot of communications will not get communicated.

6.2.1.5.4 Meeting/Conference Rooms The need for having a quiet, interruption-free workspace has already been covered. A different kind of workspace is also needed by the test team. This space is in the form of a meeting or conference room. The room must provide a large, quiet space in which the entire team can assemble. Test design sessions, test code reviews, training, and many other activities will take place in these facilities. If an adequate conference room isn't available, these consultations will be forced to occur in someone's cubicle or office. This alternative is never as convenient or productive.

Besides the conference room itself, there are some additional accouterments which are extremely useful. When more than two or three people are using the room it becomes difficult or impossible for everyone to crowd around a normal sized monitor. It's extremely convenient if an overhead projector capable of displaying a computer monitor's screen is provided.

During design sessions, anything that helps get the flow of ideas started can be worth its weight in gold. Once the sessions are underway, thoughts and ideas need to be jotted down quickly or they might be dropped and forgotten. Large white boards are a tool which can be useful to fulfill this need. An easel with a pad on it can work, but is definitely a poor second choice.

6.2.1.6 Data. Data is an often-overlooked resource for the testing effort. Without representative data the testing will not be effective. Test data must include two aspects to be complete. First of all, the test data must exist in sufficient quantity. If only a few rows are generated in each database table, it provides no feel or prediction of what production time performance will be like. Any system will perform well if there are only a handful of rows in its database tables. Without a test database which is roughly the same size as the expected production database, there will be no way to determine what indexes and statistics are needed.

The other aspect of test data that must be addressed is its diversity. There needs to be a diverse collection of records. This is especially true for tables that are associated in a master-detail relationship. Some test instances of a single detail should be provided. Multiple details for other master records also need to be included. When the referential integrity allows it, there should also be master records which have no related details.

6.2.1.6.1 Legacy Data

Data converted from a legacy system provides the most accurate and representative data possible. Since it represents actual records in all their complexity, it provides the best data testbed. Not all client/server systems are replacing an existing system, so legacy data isn't always an option.

The downside to legacy data is that it's always messy and often time-consuming to procure. Frequently, data in legacy systems is in the form of flat files. Flat files normally contain an enormous amount of duplicated and often obsolete data. When this is the situation, a considerable effort is required to convert flat file records into a relational format. Although it's time-consuming and difficult, the data needs to be converted anyway, and doing this in advance allows it to be used in the testing of the system.

6.2.1.6.2 Organization-Specific Test Data

If the client/server system isn't replacing an existing system, then test data must be obtained from another source. One alternate source is to examine transactions, documents, or records currently being produced by the future users of the system. It may take some digging to glean this information, but it will provide accurate, representative test data.

6.2.1.6.3 Computer-Generated Test Data

While accurate, representative test data is needed to thoroughly test the accuracy of the system, a large volume of data is also required. As described above, test data is needed in volume to accurately test and predict system performance. It isn't always practical or efficient to create vast amounts of data by hand. This task needs to be automated. The tools to generate test data can be written in-house, or a third-party tool can be acquired to fulfill this vital requirement.

6.3 What Are the Testing Activities and When Will They Be Performed?

Each type of testing activity must take place in the proper sequence. If it is started too early, there will be a great many delays because the testing activities which should precede it won't have been completed. If it is started too late, then later testing efforts will be delayed. A brief description of the timing of test activities is provided in the following sections.

6.3.1 Unit Testing

Unit testing is performed by developers as they complete the development of individual units of the system. A unit can be a window, a function, a report, or a stored procedure. If problems occur during the unit testing phase, the developer corrects the problem and retests the unit. Once the developer is convinced that the unit is error free, it is turned over to the configuration management team. From that point on, the unit belongs to the project as a whole instead of the individual developer.

6.3.2 Integration Testing

Integration testing is performed to be certain that individual units work with each other smoothly. Potential problems include datatype mismatches, parameter lists which differ, and gaps in processing. If errors are discovered during the integration testing phase, then a formal problem report must be completed. Any changes to the software must go through a configuration management approval process before they can be moved to the repository of software managed by the CM team.

6.3.3 System Testing

As all areas near completion, the task of systemwide testing begins. This effort requires that all modules be unit tested and integration tested. System testing attempts to prove that the entire system is capable of meeting the specifications put forth in the requirements document.

6.3.4 Installation Testing

At some point in time, software needs to be loaded onto both the client machines and the servers. This installation process can be fairly tricky.

6.3.4.1 Installation on a Client Machine. Installation on a client machine is likely to involve creating disk subdirectories, copying files from diskettes onto a hard drive, and modifying system files such as c:\windows\win.ini and c:\autoexec.bat. Icons might also need to be created during the installation process.

To make matters even more troublesome, the person running the installation may have minimal PC skills. Although this person may not be technical, that doesn't stop him or her from attempting to install your product without having read the manual! The installation process needs to be clear enough to be run by a novice.

All-in-all the installation process isn't something you should leave to chance. As this is likely to be the first exposure the user will have with the product, you wouldn't want to do anything which will leave a bad impression. In order to meet all of the conflicting requirements, it will be necessary to test this process mercilessly. The acid test of the process might be to have your most PC illiterate staff member attempt to perform the installation.

6.3.4.2 Installation on a Server. In many ways the installation of software on a server differs from installation on a client machine. The person running the process is likely to be more experienced. He or she is also more likely to have read the instructions. These people have a great deal of respect for the systems they are in charge of and don't want to do anything which might damage them.

Although the person running the installation will be more savvy and more careful, there is still a great deal of risk. Anything which is installed on a server has the potential to do more damage than software installed on a client machine. When signed on as either the root account or the system administrator, a lot of damage can be done very quickly. The bottom line is that installation procedures developed for server-based software need even more testing than client-based installation procedures.

6.3.5 Performance Testing

Conventional wisdom would say that performance testing should take place during or after the system testing. It is true that until this time, complete performance testing cannot be accomplished. However, it's an excellent idea to begin examining performance testing as early as possible. Performance testing can be started during the later stages of unit testing and integration testing—as soon as enough of the system is developed to allow for a meaningful test sequence to be run.

Early examination of system performance has the potential to expose problems earlier than they would otherwise be uncovered. By exposing them earlier, it will be easier and cheaper to correct potentially devastating performance problems.

6.3.6 Phases of Testing Activities

Testing activities can be broken down into distinct activities. Plan, design, develop, execute, and evaluate are representative of these activities. Each of these activities are repeated for every new release or build of the software being tested.

The relative amount of time spent on each of these activities shifts between the early builds and the later builds. Earlier builds tend to include a large amount of new functionality. These new capabilities require that new tests be developed to address them. Most of the testing effort will be directed towards planning, designing, and developing new tests. Less effort will be spent executing and evaluating tests because not as many tests have been created yet.

Builds which occur later in the development of the project incorporate fewer new functions. These builds typically emphasize fine-tuning and correcting errors in existing functions. This activity requires less of an emphasis on planning, designing, and developing new tests. A greater amount of time and effort will be spent executing and evaluating tests. This is because a larger pool of tests exists which needs to be executed and evaluated for each build.

6.4 How Can Testing Time Requirements Be More Accurately Estimated?

Software development in general has not been known for its accurate estimates. It's common knowledge that the majority of projects run over in terms of both schedule and budget. The testing aspect of software development has to take its share of the blame for this problem. There are a number of reasons why it is hard to estimate how long testing will take.

6.4.1 Quality of the Software

Testing is inherently a difficult and time-consuming task. It should be apparent that the more errors in the system being tested, the longer the testing process will take. It's hard to predict how many errors will exist in any piece of software. The number of errors is directly affected by the development tools being used, the experience level of the developers, the quality of the design, the culture of the development organization, and a host of other factors. All of these combine to make an already difficult task even more so.

6.4.1.1 RAD Provides Fewer Written Specifications.   RAD emphasizes iterative development and design. Users and developers jointly frequent the system in an iterative fashion. By and large this means that a detailed requirements specification was probably not written. Without such a document, it makes it very difficult to estimate the testing requirements of the project in advance. The test staff is forced to rely on past experience on projects of similar size and scope. Not a very good measuring tool, to say the least.

6.4.1.2 Little Historical Experience to Rely Upon.   Client/server systems development is an extremely new specialty in a relatively young industry. When compared to building physical structures such as roads, houses, bridges, and skyscrapers, software development is a blip on the time charts. The profession has not matured to the point where a large body of experience has been developed, documented, and studied. Without such a history of knowledge, estimations and predictions are going to be inaccurate.

Sad to say, the future in this area doesn't look as if it is likely to improve. Not nearly enough project teams carry out a post-project analysis. How many projects have you been involved in which made a point to perform such an analysis? A wealth of knowledge and experience is being squandered because as a profession we aren't taking time to analyze our successes or our failures. Some organizations are trying to accomplish this, but as an industry, we have a long way to go until this becomes a standard practice.

6.4.1.3 Integration Testing. A client/server system integrates numerous pieces of software. Some of these pieces are developed in-house, and many are purchased from third parties. Integration testing of any kind is prone to a high degree of unpredictability. Until the pieces are assembled, it's impossible to accurately estimate how much time and effort it is going to take.

6.4.1.4 Greater Reliance on Third-Party Software. Client/server development involves integrating a large number of products from diverse vendors. These vendors and the quality of their products are frequently unknown. Some are built and documented with a high level of quality, but many are not. Documentation is often misleading, inaccurate, and incomplete. When errors are uncovered, not insignificant amounts of time are usually spent determining which particular component is at fault. Once resolved, it can take additional time and effort to get the vendor to acknowledge that its product has an error, let alone address it. Errors located in critical areas can severely impact progress during this period.

6.4.2 Accurate System Requirements Document

The existence of accurate and complete system requirements can make the testing somewhat easier to predict. If the testing staff knows in advance what the system is required to do, they can do better long range planning. There may be additional tools or training which can be obtained that will ease the testing process.

Complete requirement specifications will also be very valuable when resolving disputes with the users. If the specs have left gaps defining what is to be provided or areas are vague then differences in interpretations will invariably occur. When nothing has been firmly documented, the resolution to these arguments will be protracted and leave bitter feelings among testers, developers, and users.

6.4.3 Detailed Decomposition of Requirements

Assume that a detailed requirements specification document was written and reviewed. The next step in the testing process is to decompose those requirements into smaller pieces to assist in designing tests. Small, very focused tests are more effective and reusable than monolithic tests. In order to design tightly focused tests, the specifications must be broken down into equally fine-grained details. If this task isn't properly done, then testing will not be as efficient or complete.

6.4.4 Accurate Historical Statistics from Previous Client/Server Projects

An earlier section stated that the software development industry in general and client/server development in particular don't adequately document their efforts. This is certainly the case. Each project needs to maintain details on both the efforts and outcome of every project. Some historical statistics which would prove valuable are listed in Table 6.4.

6.4.4.1 Correlating Development Effort and Testing Effort. Common sense would lead developers to assume that the more complex the client/server system is, the more time will be spent testing it. This is probably true in a general sense, but what is the exact relationship? Any statistics that help illuminate the relationship between these are worth gathering.

Are certain subsystems of the client/server project more difficult to test than others? Perhaps windows that allow users to generate transactions take inordinately long to test and correct. Since this is how the data gets into the system, it had better function perfectly. The primary effort might be spent on collections of windows which are interrelated, i.e.,

TABLE 6.4

Statistics to Keep on Client/Server Projects

The total number of developers and time each spent on the project

The amount of training / experience of developers

Total number of separate applications developed

Total number of windows (or forms) developed

Number of errors uncovered during each type of testing

Average time spent correcting each error

Total number of tests developed

Number of times each test was executed

Number of tables in the database

Number of rows in each table

point-and-click, drill-down type windows. Upper management tends to use this type of capability more than any other. Are the majority of errors in the area of the user interface? These errors aren't particularly complicated to correct, but are extremely visible to users.

Some parts of the system are always going to be easier to test than others. Test resources should early on be directed towards the most difficult areas. Unless statistics have been maintained on this and earlier projects, there is no way of knowing which errors are which.

Maintaining statistics on client/server projects is an important first step towards documenting the resources it takes to develop and test a client/server system. Granted, this work won't provide significant assistance on your first project, but statistics and estimates will prove to be invaluable for later projects. Documentation of this type needs to be begun sometime, and the sooner it is begun the sooner the rewards can be reaped.

6.5 What If the Testing Effort Falls behind Schedule?

Despite the best efforts of the testing staff it is possible that the testing effort will fall behind schedule. What should be done about it? The first step is to determine whether the test schedule was realistic. Is the testing effort going too slowly, or was it simply an inaccurate estimate of how much testing there was to do and how long it would take? It's hard to tell which is the case on your first project, but after several client/server projects, it should become easier to recognize.

There are a number of ways to react to this unpleasant news. A common initial reaction involves a lot of accusations and finger-pointing. This approach is painful and rarely leads to serious improvement in the situation. Once this stage has been passed, it's time to seriously examine the development and testing activities to see what is going wrong and how it can be corrected.

The number of potential solutions are as varied as the number of potential causes. Each organization and project will solve this problem in its own way. The only solution which is unacceptable is to eliminate the testing effort altogether. Doing this might seem to get the system delivered sooner, but the lack of quality will haunt its developers for a long time to come.

How does a testing project fall behind? One day at a time! Keep this in mind if your testing efforts start to slowly get behind schedule. Once they reach a certain point, it will be almost impossible to catch back up. The time to address a scheduling problem is early on.

6.5.1 Entire Development Effort Is Behind

One explanation of why the testing might be late is if the entire development project is behind schedule. Software that hasn't been delivered cannot be tested. Similarly, if the software was available a month late, it shouldn't be any surprise that the testing is also a month behind schedule.

Since this situation does not represent a shortcoming with the testing effort, there really isn't anything the testing staff can do to correct the problem. Be forewarned, though, that pressure will be placed on everyone in the project to do their part in helping to get back on schedule. You should use this opportunity to reexamine the test schedule to see if there are any ways it can be accelerated. It's better to investigate this possibility before management asks you to do so.

6.5.1.1 Deliver Project in Stages.   One frequent solution to a project that is running late is to deliver it in stages. Core functionality is usually delivered in the initial stage. Later-staged releases include items which, although important, aren't considered critical to the operation of the system. The last releases would involve the least consequential pieces of the system.

The staged delivery solution to the problem has an impact on testing the system. Each individual release will require less testing because it contains less functionality. That's the good news. The bad news is that the overall amount of testing will be greater. The explanation for this is that significantly more regression testing will be required. Before each stage is released, it needs to undergo thorough regression testing to be certain that the new software hasn't introduced new errors into software which previously functioned correctly.

6.5.1.2 Eliminate Functionality.   Another solution to a late project is to eliminate some of the promised functionality in the system. The decision to take this path is made by project management and the client. If this is the direction taken, it has a positive impact on the testing requirements. With less functionality in the system, there is less testing to perform. The testing effort would be trimmed by a percentage that is approximately the same as the amount of functionality eliminated.

6.5.1.3 Revise the Delivery Schedule. Perhaps the most realistic reaction to a late project is to acknowledge the problem. Admit that the project is late and adjust the delivery schedule. This approach doesn't change the software being delivered or the amount of testing which is required. One effect it might have on the testing effort is that team members will be expected to accelerate their efforts to complete the project as soon as possible.

6.5.2 When Just the Testing Effort Is Behind

The previous scenario dealt with the entire software developer effort being behind. It's also possible that just the testing effort is behind schedule. When this is the case, the testing staff will be singled out, scrutinized, and expected to make some improvements. Some of the actions that can be taken are outlined in the following sections.

6.5.2.1 Work Harder. One immediate possibility for adhering to or accelerating the schedule is to force the testing staff to work harder on the project. This solution may or may not be appropriate for each project. The test manager needs to ask some difficult questions. Is the team being efficient? Are they working consistently, or are a lot of breaks being taken? If the project has been going on for a long time, it's natural for people to work at less than full speed the entire time. Just as in a mile-long foot race, testers need to pace themselves. Sometimes people get accustomed (or stuck) in a slower pace. If this is the case, they need to step it up a notch or two.

Is the test team working 40 hours a week? If they are not, then stepping up to this level can provide the immediate equivalent of additional resources. If the team is already working 40 hours a week, is it possible for them to put in overtime? While working large amounts of overtime can be counterproductive in the long run, it can boost production in the short term. This possibility should be well thought out before the team is approached with it. A unilateral decision forcing white collar workers to put in excessive amounts of overtime can have negative repercussions. Productivity can decline, or staff turnover can increase.

Many times the test team is working on more than one development project at any given time. If this is the case, then the amount of time spent on each project needs to be examined. When the testing schedule was drawn up, certain assumptions were undoubtedly made regarding what percentage of time would be devoted to each project. This arrangement must be examined to determine if excessive time was directed toward other projects. In any event, the situation should be examined to see if a higher percentage of time can be applied to the behind-schedule project.

6.5.2.2 Work Smarter. While productivity gains are expected from working harder and longer hours, perhaps the greatest improvements can be achieved by working smarter. To do this, management must examine the team's work habits and patterns to see where efficiencies can be gained. Some areas to explore are listed in the following sections.

6.5.2.2.1 Less Administrative Work Is it possible for the test team to spend less time performing administrative trivia? Tasks such as filling out time cards, attending meetings, responding to irrelevant e-mail, answering the phones for each other, etc., are typical nonproductive activities which testers end up doing every day. Although the individual items seem trivial and harmless, when added up they can constitute a surprisingly large percentage of the work day. Management needs to make a concerted effort to shield testers and developers from tasks of this nature.

6.5.2.2.2 Time Spent Waiting A remarkable amount of time can be wasted waiting for events and other people. Examples of things which testers frequently are forced to wait for include:

- New builds of the software being tested.
- New databases.
- Changes to existing databases.
- New versions of test tools.
- Network access changes.
- Database privileges.

It might be possible to reschedule these events or processes to minimize the time testers spend waiting. For example, attempt to build new releases at night. This would allow testers to access them in the morning. Assign DBA requests by test team members a higher-than-normal priority.

Redirecting resources to areas which cause bottlenecks can increase everyone's productivity. Adding an additional DBA or LAN administrator could allow this type of work to be accomplished quicker. This would improve the efficiently of testers and developers alike.

6.5.2.2.3 Better Tools If the test team isn't utilizing advanced tools, a scheduling crisis might be just the thing to justify acquiring them. Examples of tools that are more efficient include automated test tools, unattended testing, test generation tools, etc. Be warned that when acquiring any tools, there will be an initial decrease in the staff's productivity. This is because it takes time for people to become trained and proficient with new tools. Once they have gotten over this hump, the hoped-for productivity gains should materialize.

6.5.2.3 Adding Resources. One realistic solution to a late project (development or testing) is to add additional resources. Resources can come in the form of personnel, hardware, or software. The particular type of resource which should be added depends on the particular project. The schedule and existing resources should be examined before deciding what should be added to the mix.

6.5.2.3.1 More People If the testing effort is behind schedule simply because testing is taking longer than expected, then adding additional testing personnel might be the solution. If the test plan specified four testers, then bumping that number up by one or two should improve the completion of the testing activity. Adding clerical support could also benefit testing productivity.

Beware of throwing masses of people at a late project. In the classic book *The Mythical Man-Month*, Brookes said adding people to an already late project will only make it later. The reason for this is that new people need to become familiar with the project, the tools, and the environment. While they are coming up on this learning curve, they tend to be a drag on the time of personnel who are already contributing to the project. Additionally, more people on the team guarantees that more time will be spent communicating among team members. Thus, adding people to a late project won't ensure help.

This phenomenon is true for the testing staff as well as for developers, perhaps even more so for testers. Test personnel need to be familiar with a broad spectrum of the client/server system as well as a greater variety of tools. They must be familiar with the types of tests being run, the different databases, etc. The learning curve for testers is usually very steep.

6.5.2.3.2 Include Developers with More Experience An alternative to simply adding warm bodies to the test team would be to be much more selective when choosing the additions. Selecting personnel with previous testing experience, especially with the test tools being used, would flatten out the learning curve. It's a wonderful idea, but people with exactly the desired skill set are few and far between. Looking for experienced people can't hurt, but be realistic in your expectations.

6.5.2.3.3 Hardware On many projects the major bottleneck is the availability of the hardware platform. If only a single test platform is available, then all developers and test personnel must share that resource. People are less than fully productive if they don't have as much access to the machine as they would like. Adding additional hardware can remove this bottleneck. If two test platforms were available, then more time could be allocated to everyone working on the system.

Adding hardware can be accomplished quickly and fairly easily. Other than the initial time and effort to set it up, it has no downside effects. It certainly requires a monetary expenditure, but management must decide if keeping on schedule or getting back on schedule is worth the price of the hardware.

6.5.2.3.4 More or Better Tools If testing isn't being concluded at the scheduled rate, it might be because the tools being used aren't as productive as they were projected to be. Two alternatives to resolve this situation are available. The first would be to learn to more fully utilize the existing tools. It might seem unrealistic to take time at this juncture for training, but that might be just what is necessary. A reasonable amount of time spent on training at this point might increase the staff's productivity enough to get back on schedule.

Another alternative would be to acquire tools that are more productive. The downside to this is that it takes time to investigate which available tools are more productive. Once a new set of tools is decided upon, it will take additional time to acquire them, install them, and be trained on them. In short, changing tools in the middle of the project is a fairly drastic step. It shouldn't be taken without carefully considering the impact it will create.

CHAPTER 7

Handling Software
Errors

The purpose of error testing is to find errors in the system that is being tested. This assertion may come as a shock to some, but it is the cornerstone of software testing. Developers seem to operate under the premise that the purpose of testing is to prove there are no errors. From a personal point of view, this is what they wish to happen. Finding no errors implies they did a good job developing the system. It's no wonder that they subconsciously don't wish to find errors. Finding an error is tangible evidence that their performance was less than perfect.

Project management also seems to operate under a slightly different premise. In many cases their attitude seems to be that testing is simply one of the required steps along the path to deliver a system. If any errors are found, they present potential problems and scheduling concerns. In the best case it will take time and resources to correct the error. The worst-case scenario involving errors would be that the project is postponed or canceled due to the severity of errors.

The purpose of testing is not to prove that software is error free; it's to prove that errors exist. This being the situation, you should expect errors to occur. When the inevitable happens and errors are found, you will need to be able to track them. Error tracking involves a number of actions. This section defines the actions which need to be taken. Chapter 7 describes tools which are currently available to automate these processes.

7.1 Private Versus Public Errors

It would be exceedingly unlikely that a significantly sized client/server system didn't include a fair number of errors during its development cycle. Errors will probably be uncovered during the entire spectrum of testing. Unit testing will find some, integration testing will find others, system and acceptance will uncover yet others. Depending on when the errors are discovered, they are considered to be either "private" or "public" errors.

7.1.1 Private

When a developer writes code (or builds screens), the resulting software component isn't initially accessible to anyone else on the project. In time the developer will release the code to the rest of the development staff, but until he or she has sufficient confidence in the module, it remains personal. Depending on the organization and the individual, this private phase of a component may be short or relatively long.

The transition from a private entity to a public one frequently involves turning the code over to a configuration management (CM) group. In other organizations the code may be given to a librarian. Whatever the name, it is at this point that the code belongs to the development team as a whole instead of solely to the developer. Prior to this point, the developer can make any changes he or she wants to the code without consulting anyone. From this point on the developer no longer has the freedom to modify this code. He or she must go through the change procedures established by the configuration management (CM) group.

Prior to turning the code over to CM, the modules can be thought of as "private." After releasing them, they are considered to be "public" and are open to public scrutiny. A private error is any error which is discovered by a developer before the code is given to CM. The developer can correct these errors as he or she sees fit. No procedures need to be followed when modifying private code to correct private errors.

Developers don't need to document, log, or in any way inform the rest of the team that any private errors occurred. Knowing that their code won't be scrutinized at this early stage allows developers to experiment when developing their modules. This freedom enables them to take chances and learn new techniques. Management shouldn't consider intruding on this freedom. If developers feel pressure or peering eyes, they will tend to take fewer chances, and the art of software development will not advance as quickly.

Because private coding errors are caught very early in the development process, they are the easiest, cheapest and quickest to correct. This is because when a coding error is discovered and corrected, it has absolutely no impact on the rest of the project. Since the code hasn't been released yet, there will be no required changes on other modules. There will be no corrected versions of the module to distribute to the rest of the team. Since errors have such a minimal impact when corrected at this stage, developers should be encouraged to be as thorough as possible in their private testing. Extra time spent doing a thorough job of testing at this stage will save significantly more time and resources later in the project.

7.1.2 Public

In contrast to a private error, a public error is any error found after the module has been released to configuration management. This discovery may be during integration testing, system testing, or acceptance testing. It could be found by another developer, a tester, or a user representative. It conceivably could be discovered by accident by the developer.

No matter who discovers the error or when it is discovered, all public errors must go through a formal error tracking process. Since private errors aren't tracked or documented, all of the error tracking discussed in this chapter refers to public errors. The error-tracking process which public errors undergo is described in the remainder of this chapter.

The statement was made in a previous section that private errors were the easiest and cheapest to correct. This is certainly true. But there are significant differences in the cost of correcting public errors, depending on when they are discovered. Errors found in unit testing are easier to correct than those found in system testing. Similarly, errors found in system testing are easier and cheaper to correct than the ones found in Acceptance Testing.

7.2 Error Tracking

Once a public error has been discovered there are a number of steps which must be taken to properly document it. The steps that are required include:

- Obtain data on the error.
- Assign someone to correct the error.
- Investigate and correct the error.
- Test the correction.
- Distribute the correction.
- Close the error.

The second to last step, "distribute the correction," assumes that the correction successfully passed its tests. If it didn't, then it would need to undergo the "investigation and correction" phase again. Each of the steps in this process are described in the following sections.

7.2.1 Obtain Data on the Error

The first step in error tracking is to record the existence of each error. Errors can be recorded automatically or manually. Many test tool suites integrate their test management tool with their error tracking software. When the comparison tool identifies a failed test, an error record is automatically generated. If the tool suite either doesn't include an error tracking component or it isn't integrated, then errors must be recorded manually. It isn't as convenient to record errors manually, but the same ends are achieved.

Once an error has been discovered and recorded, more information on it needs to be gathered and documented. Details aren't always immediately available, so in many cases it takes some investigation to gather all the necessary details. The old saying "know your enemy" is true when it comes to dealing with errors. If more information is accurately gathered and stored about each error, then less time will be spent performing redundant research on them. Table 7.1 lists some of the basic details which need to be gathered, documented, and reported on each error.

Some of the entries in the following list are obvious, but others might need some explanation. An explanation for each will be provided in the interest of clarity and completeness.

7.2.1.1 ID Number Assigned to Error. A unique ID number must be assigned to each new error. Automated tracking systems will frequently assign a unique system-generated ID for each error being logged. This ID will be used to identify this specific error as long as it is tracked in the system. Details on errors must be kept for the life of the project and beyond. There are reasons for this. First, errors have a nasty habit of reappearing in a system. The cause of this is that the software fix wasn't installed correctly or in every location where it needed to be installed.

The other reason for keeping details indefinitely is to assist testers and developers on subsequent projects. Errors uncovered during this project may be repeated on other projects. By retaining a history of each error found on all projects, an error knowledge base is constructed. The value of this knowledge base is directly proportional to the number of errors and the details on errors which are recorded in it. The greater the detail being kept, the more likely it will shed light on an error later in this project or another project.

TABLE 7.1

Details to Gather
on Every Error

ID number assigned to error

Detailed description of the error

Conditions under which error occurs

Number of occurrences

Symptoms of the error

Test ID which uncovered error

Person running test

Test station ID

Time and date discovered

Computer on which error occurs (i.e., client or server)

Hardware platform

Subsystem in which error occurred

Build number of software

Database on which error was discovered

Component (which window, function, etc.) in which error appeared

Criticality of the error

Priority assigned to fixing this error

Whether the error is readily reproducible

Other

Attached files

7.2.1.2 Detailed Description of the Error. Without a detailed description of the error, it will be very difficult for other team members to understand the problem. The greater the details which are included in the description, the better. It would be helpful if the language and terms used to describe errors are consistently applied by everyone in the project team. This will assist team members in finding similar errors.

7.2.1.3 Conditions under Which Error Occurs. Some errors occur all the time, e.g., whenever a certain window is opened. Others occur only under certain conditions, e.g., when the window is opened and a certain type of record is retrieved. The most insidious errors don't appear to have any pattern to them. Again, the more detail which can be provided regarding the conditions under which this error occurs, the easier it will be to track it down.

7.2.1.4 Number of Occurrences.   An error can occur a single time or many times during the testing which uncovered it. Documenting this tidbit of data will make it easier for the person who will be investigating and ultimately fixing the problem.

7.2.1.5 Symptoms.   Every error has symptoms which accompany it. Because they can provide valuable clues, these symptoms are well worth recording to assist in debugging the error. Possible symptoms include:

- Cosmetic flaw.
- Corruption of data.
- Loss of data.
- Inaccurate documentation.
- Incorrect operation.
- Installation error.
- Absent requirement.
- Performance issue.
- System crash.
- Unexpected response.
- Unfriendly response.

7.2.1.6 Test ID Which Uncovered the Error.   The name or ID of the test which uncovered the error needs to be provided for several reasons. First of all, by knowing which test uncovered the problem, the person assigned to this error will have a very good idea as to what causes the error. Secondly, when the error has been fixed, the same test must be rerun to validate that the correction did indeed solve the problem. Other tests may also be needed as well.

7.2.1.7 Person Running Test.   Whoever is assigned to correct the error will very likely want to know the person who ran the test originally. There may be questions about exactly how to reproduce the error, what data was used, etc. By including the tester's name, it saves time and effort on the part of the staff member assigned to fix it.

This information is also valuable for historical purposes. If records indicate that a single individual discovers an inordinately large percentage of errors, then this person likely has a talent for testing. Project management might want to study his or her methods in order to get others up to the same level of testing proficiency. Likewise, if an individual doesn't uncover any errors at all, then perhaps that person's heart isn't in the testing effort.

7.2.1.8 Test Station ID.   Identifying the test station where the error was discovered will help the assignee when it comes time to rerun the initial tests on the same test station. This should be done whenever possible.

7.2.1.9 Time and Date Discovered.   Certain errors occur only at certain times. A significant number of errors occur when the time or date undergoes a major change. The end of a day is a time when many problems occur. Month-end or year-end closing of an accounting system always brings out errors which couldn't be discovered at any other time.

The time and date are also needed to keep accurate statistics on when errors are being discovered and how long it takes to correct them. Without this date it's impossible to calculate an average of how long it takes to correct errors. Knowing how long on average it takes to correct an error can be used to predict the amount of time and effort needed to complete the project.

7.2.1.10 Computer on Which Error Occurs (i.e., Client or Server). The fundamental definition of a client/server system includes a minimum of two computers. It is necessary to identify on which of these computer platforms the error occurred. This information may not be immediately available. There will undoubtedly be instances when it appears that the error is occurring on one computer, when in fact it is on another. One example would be if incorrect data is populating a data window. At first glance it might be assumed that this error is on the client workstation. If, however, this data window is populated via a stored procedure, then the computer where the error resides would be the database server.

7.2.1.11 Hardware Platform.   This item may at first appear to duplicate the previous section. The distinction is that the system may have been deployed to many different types of client workstations. Examples could be IBM-compatible computers, Apple computers, Sun workstations or X-terminal machines. The particular error being reported may occur on one type of workstation (X-terminal), but not on any of the other hardware platforms.

7.2.1.12 Subsystem in Which Error Occurred. Most software systems, client/server as well as traditional systems, are broken down into subsystems. The developer assigned to fix this problem needs to know what subsystem the error occurred in. This gives at least a broad area in which the search should begin.

7.2.1.13 Build Number. Client/server systems undergo a large number of versions or builds during their development. The developer tasked with this error needs to know under what build the error occurred. This knowledge is crucial when attempting to isolate the problem. Without knowing the build number, a considerable amount of time and energy could be wasted chasing after errors which have already been corrected in more recent builds.

7.2.1.14 Database. The testing process may involve a number of different test databases, each of which may have been built and populated to test one specific aspect of the system. One database may include computer-generated data, while another contains data converted from a legacy system. The error in question may occur only on one type of database. If this information hasn't been documented, the assignee can waste time without being able to reproduce the error.

7.2.1.15 Component (Window, Function, etc.) in Which Error Appeared. Besides knowing what subsystem an error occurred in, the developer assigned to fix the problem must be told which specific component displayed the error. In a client/server system with a GUI front-end, the majority of these components will be windows, but some components will be functions, stored procedures, etc.

7.2.1.16 Criticality of the Error. Not all errors are created equal. Some can stop a system in its tracks while others are merely an annoyance. An example of a very severe error might be a locking problem occurring when accessing the database. Other serious errors corrupt or destroy data. This could occur if SQL statements don't properly specify the data to be modified or deleted. Others are merely cosmetic problems which don't seriously impact the system. Typographical errors in labels, headers, or on buttons exemplify this type of error.

Each newly discovered error needs to be assigned to a level of criticality. Possible levels are: critical, high, average, cosmetic. Care needs to be taken that these assignments are applied consistently. Everyone's understanding of what constitutes a critical error should be clear. If this isn't done consistently, then an inordinate amount of time might be spent correcting a relatively minor flaw.

7.2.1.17 Priority Assigned to Fixing This Error.   Assigning priorities for addressing errors isn't as simple as one might assume. An error of lower priority which occurs frequently may be addressed before a more serious error which occurs very infrequently. Another scenario might have a very visible (i.e., embarrassing) yet cosmetic error being fixed first just so the client isn't constantly reminded of it.

Obviously the particular priorities used will vary from site to site. In some cases they will be imposed by the choice of test management or error tracking tools chosen. One set of potential priorities are: immediate, high, normal, and as time permits.

7.2.1.18 Whether the Error Is Readily Reproducible.   A general rule of thumb when dealing with an error is that the easier it is to reproduce, the easier it will be to fix it. This is because when it's easy to reproduce it, the developer can more easily track it down and correct it. Conversely, the more difficult it is to reproduce an error, the more difficult and time-consuming it will be to correct it. When errors aren't readily reproducible, it is significantly harder to isolate what causes it. Until the cause is found, it can't be fixed.

Whether an error is readily reproducible also has an effect on the amount of testing which must be performed. If an error occurs very regularly, it will be relatively easy to determine that it has been corrected. On the other hand, an error which occurred infrequently will require significantly more testing to be certain that it has been eradicated.

7.2.1.19 Other.   Although every attempt has been made to include all potential meaningful details in this list of details to document on errors, it is almost certain that something will have been overlooked. A free format text field allows a great deal of freedom to include significant information which doesn't fit into any of the preexisting categories.

7.2.1.20 Attached Files.   Describing, understanding, or reproducing the error may be made easier by referencing other files. Examples of such files include screen shots, requirement documents, system documentation, etc. This field allows the names and locations of such documents to be associated with an error.

7.2.2 Tracking Status of Errors

Table 7.1 contains details on errors which are fairly static. There is another collection of data items on errors which is much more dynamic. Many of these data items won't be determined until someone is assigned to the error and begins to investigate it. This data will be frequently updated as the error is investigated and corrected. These details are outlined in Table 7.2 and more fully described in the following sections.

7.2.2.1 Person Assigned to Debug and Fix the Error.   Someone has to be assigned the task of debugging and fixing each error. That person is the "owner" of the error until he or she solves it, quits, is transferred, or the assignment is taken away from him or her. Errors which aren't assigned to a specific individual most likely won't get solved. Unassigned errors tend to fall into the cracks and get forgotten or overlooked. This isn't to say that the assignee can't confer with other testers or developers to solve the problem, but someone has to have the final responsibility for each and every error.

Project management may have several techniques for deciding whom to assign an error to. The simplest method would be to list developers in a queue and assign errors to the next person in the queue. A slightly more sophisticated technique would be to keep track of who has the

TABLE 7.2	Person assigned to debug and fix the error
Dynamics Data on Errors	Severity
	Priority
	Estimated completion date of the fix
	Estimate of the time it will take to fix the error
	Tests which need to be rerun after the fix is installed
	Components affected by the fix
	Current status of the error
	Resolution
	Corrected in build number

least number of outstanding errors and assign the next error to that person. Slightly more sophisticated would be to keep track of outstanding errors and the estimated amount of time to fix each of them. A much more productive method would be to keep records on the background and experience level of each developer. When an error occurs, it would be assigned to the person with the most experience in that particular area.

7.2.2.2 Severity.   The severity of an error reflects the impact that it has on the system and its users. Some suggested levels of severity are listed here:

- Catastrophic. Errors which can potentially cause the destruction of property or cost lives.
- Severe. Errors with the potential to destabilize the system, including the database.
- Damaging. Errors causing erroneous results leading to inadvisable business actions or decisions.
- Performance. Accuracy is not endangered, but system performance is hindered.
- Moderate. Inaccurate output, but not considered exceptionally damaging.
- Convenience. Error doesn't allow the system to be used as conveniently as possible.
- Cosmetic. Buttons or labels with misspelled words, improper capitalization, etc.

7.2.2.3 Priority.   The priority assigned to an error reflects the emphasis which project management is placing on this error. The higher the priority, the more (or higher quality) resources which will be devoted to it. Normally an error's priority is closely associated with its severity. This won't always be the case, though. A cosmetic error which aggravates the senior user representative is likely to be corrected significantly earlier than its severity would indicate. Some potential priorities include:

- Urgent.
- High.
- Normal.
- Low.

7.2.2.4 Estimated Completion Date of the Fix.
Project management needs to have an estimate of when the error will be fixed. Obviously this is only an estimate, and developers shouldn't be absolutely held to this date. It is extremely difficult to estimate how hard it will be to find and correct an error.

Another reason why estimated fix dates are unreliable is that the assignee's workload is likely to be constantly shifting. The assignee may plan to begin work on a particular error, but may get interrupted by an error of higher priority. In essence, this freezes the clock on the first error while the second error is being addressed. The estimate of time actually spent on the first error may be accurate, but the entire process can be delayed due to a higher-than-anticipated workload.

7.2.2.5 Estimate of the Time It Will Take to Fix the Error.
This field is an estimate of the amount of time it will take to debug, analyze, and fix the error. This time estimate is independent of the date when the fix will be complete. For example, if the estimated amount of time is 30 hours and work starts on it immediately, then the fix will be available in 30 work-hours. If this error is of low priority and work doesn't begin on it for two weeks then the fix will be available 30 work-hours after work on it commences.

7.2.2.6 Tests Which Need to Be Rerun after the Fix Is Installed.
Once a potential fix for an error is found, it needs to be tested. At first glance one might suppose that the only testing necessary would be to simply run the test which initially uncovered the error. This assumption is absolutely wrong. First of all, the correction may satisfy the test which discovered it, but not satisfy the tests which preceded or followed that test.

Secondly, there is the very real possibility that the software change will introduce errors into the system unrelated to the original error that was being addressed. This scenario isn't just idle speculation or academic pondering. It happens frequently in software development. The causes vary but are primarily due to time and pressure. There isn't enough time to thoroughly investigate the problem or the code in question. Pressure is constantly applied by management or the clients to quickly fix errors and move onto the next problem in the list. When this is the case, developers can inadvertently introduce bigger errors than the one posed by the original problem.

To verify that an error hasn't been introduced into the system, additional testing must be done. This type of testing is called *regression testing*. The amount of regression testing is highly dependent on the nature of the original error and the amount of code modified by the fix. A purely cosmetic error (e.g., a typo in a label) won't require any testing, while a change to a widely called function (e.g., a stored procedure to retrieve rows) will need to be thoroughly tested. Fortunately, test scripts can be reused to greatly reduce the amount of time and energy spent performing regression testing.

7.2.2.7 Components Affected by the Fix. Every fix which includes changes to software will affect one or more components of the system. All affected components are listed in this area. A cursory examination of the length of this list gives an overview of how complicated the fix is. Errors which affect many components require much more testing than those which changed only a single component.

7.2.2.8 Current Status of the Error. Every new error must be assigned a status. The initial status value will likely be "New." During its lifetime, the status of an error will change many times. This field contains the current status of the error. Maintaining a history of changes in an error's status in a separate table is very desirable. Historical information can be useful when investigating how an error or solution reached its current situation. Possible status values are listed here:

- New. New error, not yet assigned.
- Assigned. Assigned but not yet being worked on.
- Fix in progress. Currently being worked on.
- Reassigned. Error has been assigned to another person.
- Pending retest. Fix is complete, waiting for testing.
- Failed retest. Fix failed the retest.
- Closed. Fix passed test and has been closed.
- Reopened. Error has been reopened.

7.2.2.9 Resolution. Once an error has been repaired, a brief description of the fix should be documented. It is included in the "resolution" field. Since it is likely to be viewed by developers, testers, users, and management, this description shouldn't be overly technical in nature.

7.2.2.10 Corrected in Build Number. After an error has been corrected and passes its retest, it needs to be integrated back into the software being developed. The changed code must be turned over to the configuration management group or its equivalent. Once accepted by CM, it will be included in a future build of the system. This build number needs to be entered into the error tracking system. Documenting the build number will help resolve future problems if the fix proves to be less than flawless.

7.2.2.11 Error Details Summary.   The exact details to be gathered and stored will depend heavily upon the error tracking tool being used. Not all tools gather the same details. If there are details which aren't addressed by the test management or error tracking tool being used, your organization may need to maintain data outside that tool.

7.3 Communications

Once details about the error are gathered and stored in the repository, they need to be relayed to the members of the test team. If the test repository is centrally available, then all authorized team members will be able to access this information online. In this situation an e-mail message can be sent to notify everyone when errors are discovered. If test information isn't being stored in a centrally available location, then team members may have to be informed of newly discovered errors by interoffice mail or reports distributed to the team.

7.3.1 Who Needs to Be Informed of Errors

A number of people associated with the project will need to be informed about errors. While details about errors should never be kept from anyone, different individuals and positions will have a varying level of interest and need to know in regard to error details. Levels of personnel and a brief outline of the amount of detail appropriate for that level is suggested in the following sections.

7.3.1.1 Management.   Management, in general, has minimal interest in the details of errors. Their level of interest is more in the area of statistics and trends. The numbers of errors which have occurred, number of outstanding errors, and errors broken down by severity are the types of information which management will require. Another statistic which management will want to know is the expected completion date for errors.

One exception to management's normal desire for summary information is when an error appears which has the potential to bring the project to a halt. Examples of this might be a major design flaw, crippling performance problems, or a third-party product which proves to be inadequate. Anything which has the capacity to jeopardize the project or the schedule should be brought to management's attention immediately. Failure to do this may have severe ramifications on the project manager's continued service in that capacity.

7.3.1.2 Test Manager. The test manager will need more detail than management. The test manager will most likely be involved in assigning errors, scheduling retesting of errors, and verifying that fixes do what they are supposed to do. These activities require that the test manager has access to virtually all of the details maintained on errors.

7.3.1.3 Person Assigned to Fix the Error. The assignee is one of a few individuals who needs all of the gory details about an error. The greater the detail provided to the assignee the easier it will be to focus in on the error. The assignee will be especially attentive to knowledge on which subsystem the error is in and how it can be reproduced.

7.3.1.4 Developer Who Wrote the Component. Another individual who will have great interest in the error is the original developer of the component where the error was found. This individual's interest should be piqued for a couple of reasons. First of all, the developer might be able assist the person assigned to correct the error. As the person who wrote the code, he or she has a unique insight into how it might be corrected.

The second reason why the developer will be interested is that it might be used as a learning experience. Once the problem has been resolved, the developer might want to examine other modules he or she has written to be certain this problem doesn't exist in other modules. This particular error is one which should be successfully avoided during future development work.

7.3.1.5 User Representative. There may be a number of user representatives involved in this project. If there is more than one user representative, then the particular user associated with this subsystem will be most interested in the error. He or she will want to oversee the error to make certain that it is documented correctly, that the proposed solution is appropriate, and that all of the necessary retesting passes.

High-level user representatives won't want to be swamped with details on specific errors. They will be interested in the same statistics which upper management receives.

7.3.1.6 Remainder of Testing Staff. Testing staff, other than the person who has been assigned to the error, will also want to obtain some details on all errors. Initially the staff will want only high-level details on errors. If they see an error which interests them they must be able to obtain more detailed information on those particular errors. They might have experienced the same problem or one very similar to it. If this is the case, they can provide considerable assistance to the person assigned to fix the error.

7.3.2 When Do They Need to Know?

Just as each position wants to know different levels of detail about an error, each position needs to receive their information in their own time frame. It would be a waste of time and effort to rush information out to someone who doesn't need it immediately.

7.3.2.1 Management Management needs only summary-level data, and this information is needed at periodic intervals. Weekly summaries for management are probably sufficient. Obviously, if a catastrophic error occurs it should be relayed to management as soon as possible.

7.3.2.2 Test Manager. The test manager needs data as quickly as possible. Early notification allows the test manager to more quickly make a decision regarding who will be assigned to correct the error. The earlier this decision is made, the earlier the assignee can begin working on the problem.

Depending on the severity of the error, there may be an impact on the testing schedule. This particular error may prevent or put off other testing which needs to be done. Informing the test manager early allows him or her to ascertain whether some parts of the testing schedule will be impacted and how its impact can be mitigated.

7.3.2.3 Error Assignee. Once the test manager decides who will be assigned to the error, that person should be informed directly. This will allow the assignee to begin work as quickly as possible. Once the assignee has been notified, he or she can review current assignments for potential overload.

7.3.2.4 User Representative.   The user representative will need to be informed about the error reasonably soon. Informing the user representative on a weekly basis should be adequate. In the event of an error which will have a significant impact on the schedule, the user community should be informed as quickly as possible.

7.3.2.5 Developer Who Wrote the Component.   The developer should be informed of the error as soon as reasonably possible. If the developer has an inspiration about the error and how it can be corrected, it makes sense to get this input before the assignee spends a significant amount of time investigating the problem. By informing the developer as early as possible, this input will hopefully save considerable time on the assignee's part.

7.3.3 How Will They Be Informed?

There are a number of different methods by which interested parties can be informed about errors. The technique used for each group relates closely to how much detail they need and how quickly they require the information.

7.3.3.1 E-Mail.   When it's available within the organization, e-mail is the fastest and most reliable method for disseminating information about errors. It allows the communication to be sent out quickly and easily. This method doesn't require the sender and receiver to be at the same place at the same time. It also allows the receiver to review the information at his or her own speed. E-mail allows supporting documents or other information to be attached to the message. Some test management systems are capable of generating e-mail automatically.

E-mail should be used by the test manager to inform the person assigned to correct the error. This method is especially appropriate because the assignee may not be working the same shift as the Test Manager. The component's developer and the remainder of the testing staff should also be informed by e-mail.

7.3.3.2 Interoffice Mail.   If e-mail isn't available within the organization, interoffice mail is the next best method of communicating detailed information about errors. Mailing a copy of the error report has the advantages of providing a high level of detail and not requiring face-to-face meeting.

7.3.3.3 Phone/Voice Mail. Telephone and/or voice mail represents a very poor method of broadcasting information about errors to recipients. The biggest problem with this method is that it is extremely difficult to accurately relay detailed information about errors over the phone. Complex details of this nature are much better transmitted in a written format.

Another problem with using the phone to inform people about errors is that it can be very time intensive. The sender, most likely the test manager, has to repeat essentially the same message to each and every recipient. Besides taking a significant amount of time, it is very unlikely that the exact same message is given to each receiver. Subtle differences can very easily lead to misunderstandings about what is to be done or who is supposed to be doing it.

7.3.3.4 Meetings. Meetings are an appropriate venue for communicating error information to people who require only high-level or summary data. Perfect candidates for this method of communication include upper management and user representatives. A regular meeting, weekly or biweekly, is very appropriate for keeping these individuals informed about the test progress without overwhelming them with details.

One disadvantage with this method is that it requires all participants to be in the same place at the same time. Normally, coordinating attendance at a meeting isn't a problem, but testers and developers are frequently scheduled to work off-shifts. This makes it very difficult for them to attend meetings during "normal" working hours.

7.3.3.5 Reports. Reports are a means of communication which can be used for everyone involved in the testing effort. Upper management and user representatives can be given summary-level reports in conjunction with regular meetings. Staff members can periodically be sent reports listing all of the errors assigned to them. Developers can be sent reports documenting all errors found in their particular software components. The testing staff, as a whole, can be provided with a report summarizing all of the errors uncovered so far and the status of each. By tailoring reports to their intended audience, they can be excellent communications tools.

7.4 Error Correction and Distribution

Distributing error corrections isn't as simple on client/server systems as it was on traditional systems. The software affected by a single error correction might reside on the database server, an application server, or any number of client machines. The actual software module which was changed could be an executable file, a dynamic link library (DLL), an initialization file, a stored procedure, or a trigger. A complicated problem could involve a combination of different types of files. Each affected module must be distributed to the appropriate machine in a timely manner.

7.4.1 What Types of Components Get Corrected and Distributed

When an error is corrected, it can involve a number of different types of software components. The affected pieces must be thoroughly and accurately documented by the person who fixed the problem. Configuration management then combines corrections from many developers and testers to construct a new build. Types of components which will be affected by a change to a client/server system are described in the following sections.

7.4.1.1 Data.   Errors aren't normally corrected by modifying the data, but this happens occasionally. It might be a situation where supporting data isn't included in the database. When data of this type is omitted, it can prevent the relational database from properly joining and returning the expected data. The fix is frequently a script which inserts the needed rows into the affected tables.

7.4.1.2 Database Structure Changes.   Changes to the structure of the database are frequent at the onset of a development project. They tend to taper off as the system matures. Examples of typical database structure changes made as the result of errors discovered during a project are listed in Table 7.3.

Some of the above database changes will have a definite impact on the application and its code. Modifications which add, delete, or rename database objects usually affect software modules. SQL statements which

TABLE 7.3	Adding a new table
Database Structure Changes	Deleting an existing table
	Adding a new view
	Deleting an existing view
	Adding a column to a table
	Deleting a column from a table
	Renaming a column
	Modifying a column, e.g., changing its length or data type
	Adding a primary key to a table
	Modifying a table's primary key
	Defining a foreign reference key in a table
	Adding an index to a table
	Modifying a column to allow it to be NULL
	Extending the database to additional disk devices
	Granting permission to access tables
	Denormalizing a table

reference these objects need to be inspected and potentially updated. Redefining the data type or length of a column will also directly affect software components. Comparisons and conversions will need to be examined and possibly changed. Applications can also be very subtly affected if a column is changed in regards to whether it can contain NULLs or not. SQL statements which previously worked correctly may now return slightly different result sets.

Other database structure changes won't have a direct impact on the software being developed. Examples of these modifications include adding or deleting indexes or extending the database to a new disk device. The database engine makes changes such as these transparent to applications which access the database.

7.4.1.3 Executables.   Executable files are the foundation of most client/server applications. They can reside on either the client machine or on one of the servers. They are frequently initiated when the user clicks on an icon at the client workstation. Changes to these particular components are made quite frequently.

7.4.1.4 DLLs (Dynamic Link Libraries). A *dynamic link library* is a type of file which contains executable code. DLLs can reside at either the client workstation or a server machine. DLLs are loaded into memory on the client machine at run time. DLLs are capable of being used by more than one application at a time. Using DLLs allows the size of executable files to be significantly smaller than would otherwise be possible. The use of DLLs enables only the portions of the application which are currently being used to be loaded into memory. Proper use of DLLs leads to a more efficient use of disk space and memory at the client machine. Virtually all client/server systems being developed will utilize DLLs as a part of their software repertoire.

If the development project has created any DLLs, then undoubtedly the testing process will find errors in at least one of them. New versions of DLLs will need to be distributed to the machines where they have been positioned.

7.4.1.5 Initialization Files. Initialization files normally reside on the client machine and are referenced when an application is invoked. The types of data usually stored in initialization files include user preference information, database connect details, and directory specifications.

Changes to initialization files are not extremely common once they have been established and matured. When these changes do occur, they are difficult to implement because the files normally exist on each client workstation's local drive. The initialization file on each such workstation must be accessed and replaced or modified.

7.4.1.6 Stored Procedures. Stored procedures are collections of SQL statements which are executed as a group. They invariably reside on the database server machine. Stored procedures are used to efficiently perform functions which occur repeatedly within a client/server application. By positioning these statements on the database server, the amount of network traffic can be minimized. Stored procedures usually execute faster than the same SQL statements executed on a client machine because the query plan for a stored procedure only needs to be built once.

Physically modifying stored procedures is relatively easy. This is because they exist in only one place, the database server. Scripts are normally used to document and modify stored procedures, but the code which constitutes a stored procedure can be entered into the database system by hand.

The complication when modifying stored procedures is more of a synchronization concern than a physical access problem. Normally all users must be out of the database to be certain that a stored procedure is properly modified. The other aspect of synchronization is that the stored procedure must be modified in conjunction with components which are calling the new version. If this isn't done properly then unexpected and unpredictable results can occur.

7.4.1.7 Triggers. Triggers are a specialized form of stored procedure. Stored procedures are initiated by specifically invoking them from within applications. Triggers are associated with specific database tables and are executed when certain modifications are made to the specified table. Like stored procedures, triggers reside on the database server. This makes them fairly easy to locate and physically modify. Also like stored procedures, changes to triggers are best done when users aren't accessing the database.

Changes to triggers occur primarily during the initial testing of a client/server system, but potentially can occur at any time during the testing process. The later these changes occur, the more regression testing should be done to ensure that they don't adversely affect existing software.

7.4.2 Where Changes Are Distributed

On a traditional mainframe system, all of the software resided on the mainframe. Terminals didn't have the capability to support any embedded functionality. In contrast to this situation, a client/server allows software components to reside in a number of locations. This contributes to the complications involved when disseminating software changes throughout the system.

7.4.2.1 Database Server. The database server is home to a significant amount of software. The single largest executable on this server is likely to be the relational database engine. While code-level modifications to this component aren't likely, there will be a regular stream of changes from the vendor. Each of these new versions need to be reviewed to determine what impact they might have on the software under development. New versions then need to be tested to be certain that no negative impact will occur by implementing them. Finally, they need to be installed and made available to the test team.

Other components which reside on the server include executable SQL statements. These are in the form of stored procedures and triggers. Access and the permission to change the components needs to be very tightly guarded. Improper or lightly considered changes in this area can impact practically every subsystem in the client/server system.

Changes to the structure of the database must also be made at the database server. Due to the importance and impact of changes to database tables, the ability to make these changes also needs to be tightly controlled. Normally, only the database administrator (DBA) is allowed to make such changes. Having to schedule database changes with the DBA contributes to the complications of distributing changes to client/server software.

7.4.2.2 Application Server.   The application server contains the repository of business logic. This logic might be in the form of remotely called procedures (RPCs). RPCs are functions called by the applications. The applications have no idea how the RPCs are written or where they reside. Using RPCs combines all business logic in a single location. This will have the effect of simplifying the process of distributing software changes.

7.4.2.3 Client Workstations.   The client workstations normally contain a significant percentage of software components in a client/server system. These components include executable files, dynamic link libraries (DLLs), initialization files, and network communications software.

A significant difficulty when distributing software at the client workstation level is that client machines are frequently geographically dispersed. Third-party vendors have developed packages which allow software to be distributed to any number of client workstations and server machines. If your particular client/server system involves widely scattered hardware, the capability in such packages might be worth investigating. The time, energy, and frustration which they save can be potentially significant.

7.4.3 Coordination Between Components.

Perhaps the biggest challenge to face when distributing software changes in a client/server system is the problem of coordinating the changes. Software components between and within different areas can be very tightly interconnected, and changes to them must be carefully synchronized. If changes aren't properly synchronized, the results can be unexpected errors and inconsistencies in the performance of the system. A few examples of possible dependencies requiring coordination are listed in the following.

A window has been modified to use a stored procedure to populate a table. If changes to the stored procedure and window aren't done simultaneously, erroneous data will likely result.

A window or function is enhanced to reference a new database table column. The application will generate an error if the database change isn't implemented at the same time as the software change.

A pick list is added to a window. This object references a new database table. If the pick list change makes it into the latest build but the new table isn't included, the pick list will be empty. Even worse, it will generate errors.

Code to enforce data integrity is moved from an application to a database trigger. If both components aren't changed simultaneously, then either the integrity checks will be performed twice or not at all.

7.4.4 Documenting New Builds

Each new build to be distributed needs to be thoroughly documented. Everyone involved in the development or testing of the client/server system needs to know what changes have been included in each new build. Details which must be recorded for builds include:

- Errors which have been addressed in the release.
- Names of who submitted each fix.
- Components which have been changed, including all:
    - Executable files.
    - DLLs.
    - Initialization files.
    - Stored procedures.
    - Triggers.
    - Rules.
    - Database structure changes.
- Computers where the changes have been made.
- Database(s) where changes have been made.
- Subdirectories where the changes have been made.
- Sizes and last write dates of each changed component,
- Tests which need to be rerun.

7.5 Analyzing Errors

It isn't enough to find and correct errors in the system being tested. Just doing that will get the current project out the door, but it doesn't do anything to improve the next project. To improve the software development process for both the current and future project, it's necessary to learn something from each error which is uncovered. This learning process will be significantly accelerated if records are kept about each error. The details listed in Sections 7.2.1 and 7.2.2 will provide a knowledge base of errors.

When details mentioned above are documented and tracked, it will be possible to begin recognizing trends. Only by examining the error data, posing questions, and analyzing the answers will the software development process in your organization be improved. Trends which will be noticeable include:

■ Were the errors encountered predominately syntax, logic, or communications?

■ What percentage of the errors were discovered in each phase of testing (unit, integration, system, acceptance, post testing)?

■ How much did it cost in time and resources to correct errors found in each phase of testing?

■ What type of test is most effective at finding errors?

■ Which subsystems and modules contained the most errors?

■ How long does the average error correction take to investigate, resolve, and implement?

■ How did the estimates compare to the actual time it took to fix errors?

■ On average, when a fix is put into place, how many new errors are introduced?

■ Are a disproportionately large percentage of errors being generated by a small group of developers? If this is the case, might additional training or unit testing be able to reduce the number of errors?

■ If different tools were used in the development of this system, were a disproportionate number of errors generated in one tool versus the others?

Questions such as those posed above have the capability of improving how your organization develops its systems. The answers will give a great deal of insight into when and where testing resources should be directed. If nothing else, it can help to create more accurate estimates of how long the testing process will take.

7.6 Tools for Tracking Errors

There are quite a few error-tracking packages available in the marketplace. These packages provide a great deal of capability to document and hopefully control errors and changes made to software in a development project. These packages allow details to be entered for each error encountered and monitor who it has been assigned to, current status, expected completion date, and so forth. These packages also include the reports necessary to keep all of the staff up to date on error progress.

A more seamless solution, when available, is when the testing package being used includes an integrated error-tracking capability. The advantage of integrating the error-tracking package and the testing tool is that much of the data entry requirements can be automated. This results in less time and, hopefully, fewer entry errors. Also, less time is spent keying in data which already exists in the computer.

A number of testing tool suites which are marketed for client/server development include an error-tracking feature. Brief descriptions of these packages and their capabilities are included here. Once again, the inclusion or omission of any particular product is not meant to be either an endorsement or negative comment on any particular product.

7.6.1 SQA Manager

SQA Manager from SQA, Inc. is part of the SQA Suite product. SQA Manager includes capabilities for defining test plans, test requirements, software hierarchies, and test procedures. Once the actual testing begins, it includes the ability to track any resulting errors. Entries for new errors can be entered into SQA Manager manually, or they can automatically be entered by the SQA Test Log Viewer. Additional details on each error can be entered into SQA Manager manually.

7.6.1.1 Data Maintained on Errors. As stated in the previous section, errors can be entered into SQA Manager automatically or manually when a test fails. Once entered into the system, there is no distinction between errors entered one way or the other.

The current status of an error is one of the primary pieces of information kept about it. When a test engineer enters a defect into the system, it has a status of "New." Later the QA Administrator will review the entry and determine if it is indeed an error. When this happens, the error status will be changed to "Open," and it will be assigned to a programmer. The assigned programmer will then investigate the error and make code changes to repair it. At this point the error is assigned to a test engineer and its status is changed to "Pending Validation." If the test engineer determines that the error successfully passes testing, its status will be modified to "Closed." At any point in the above process, reports will summarize the state of this and all other errors which have been entered into the system.

Some of the other fields maintained on each error are listed here. In most cases the description of the field coincides very closely with descriptions listed in Sections 7.2.1.1 through 7.2.2.10.

- Description.
- Priority.
- Severity.
- Occurrences.
- Symptoms.
- Resolution.
- Build in which it was found.
- Log ID (of test log) that contains results of test procedure which found the error.
- Test cycle where error was found.
- Hardware platform.
- Operating system.
- Test station ID.
- Reported by name.
- Reported by company.

Figure 7.1 shows one of the SQA Manager screen through which users enter error details.

7.6.1.2 Security Maintaining security is necessary even in a feature such as error tracking. A significant amount of time goes into entering and maintaining information on errors. All of this time and effort could

Figure 7.1
SQA Manager Data
Entry Window

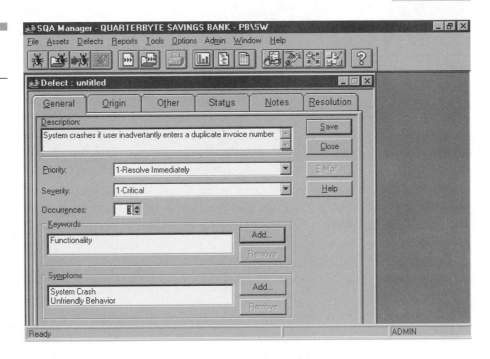

be lost if users were allowed to indiscriminately modify or delete error-tracking information.

Reports that are output from the error-tracking system can attract a high degree of visibility with upper management and user representatives. It is essential that the data which drives these reports not be tampered with. It would be a significant loss of prestige and respect for the QA group if these reports were inaccurate due to irresponsible handling of the error-tracking data.

For the above reasons, it is necessary to have security on an error-tracking subsystem. SQA Manager has met this requirement. When users are registered in SQA Manager, they must be assigned various privileges. The system administrator can assign privileges such that users can accomplish their respective jobs without having the ability to damage error-tracking data. Among the possible privileges are the following:

- Create and modify reports.
- Create defect.
- Modify defect.
- Create and modify e-mail rules.
- Enable/disable automatic notification.
- Customize attributes of SQA Manager.

7.6.1.3 Customizations.   SQA Manager allows the user to customize the product to suit the organization's specific requirements. Customizations can be made to apply to the organization as a whole or only to one particular project. Some of the features which can be set include:

- Labels in defect reporting windows.
- Hardware listed in a drop-down list box.
- Keywords used to describe and group reported errors.
- Operating systems listed in a drop-down list box.
- Priorities assigned to errors.
- Privileges assigned to users within groups.
- Severities assigned to errors.
- Resolutions listed for errors.
- Rules defining the conditions when e-mail is automatically generated.

7.6.1.4 E-Mail.   One of the extremely useful features of SQA Manager is its extensive e-mail capabilities. It allows e-mail messages to be sent to members of the development or testing team automatically when various events occur. In addition to automatic transmission of messages, users can send messages manually at any time from within SQA Manager. Some of the situations which can automatically generate e-mail include:

- When an error is entered into the system.
- When the status of an error is changed.
- If responsibility for an error changes an e-mail, it can be sent to the person currently responsible.
- The software engineer can have a message sent to the appropriate QA test person when the error's status changes to pending validation.

To utilize SQA Manager's e-mail features, the organization must have an MAPI compliant e-mail system and network. If automatic e-mail generation is desired, the SQA Manager administrator must enable this feature. Once enabled it can be used by anyone with access to SQA Manager.

7.6.1.5 Reports and Graphs.   SQA Manager includes a very powerful report writer and graphing engine to help in the analysis of the error data. A number of prewritten reports come with the system. All of these reports can be customized by the users. The following is a summary of the standard reports:

- Defect age. Provides information about the age of outstanding software defects.
- Defect distribution. Lists errors and their distribution amount users, priorities, and statuses.
- Defect trend. Provides information on the progress of defects in the repair/correction cycle.
- Test results progress. A summary of test procedure results over multiple software builds.

A similar collection of standard graphs are included in SQA Manager. The graphs can be modified to display data in various formats. The formats include vertically oriented bar charts, horizontally oriented bar charts, horizontal stacked bar charts, pie charts, and cross tab tables. Graphs can be presented in either a 3-D or 2-D format.

Users also have the option to generate completely new reports based on data kept on errors. The report writer allows users to generate reports without writing any code. Reports are generated via a point-and-click type capability. All reports and graphs can be e-mailed to anyone in the system.

Examples of the standard reports available in SQA Manager are presented in Figures 7.2 and 7.3.

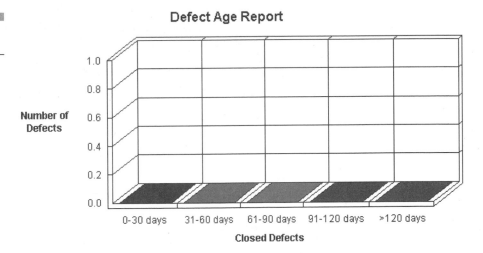

Figure 7.2
Defect Age Report

Figure 7.3
Defect Trend Report

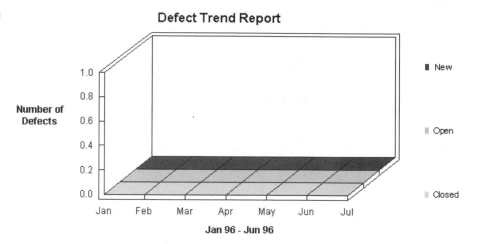

7.6.2 Bug Tracking Mode

Bug Tracking Mode is a capability of TestDirectory from Mercury Interactive. Bug Tracking Mode provides the users with tools to systematically track software errors from initial detection to their resolution. Tables and forms have been designed to help organize large amounts of error-tracking data. New errors can be reported by developers, software testers, or end users during any of the phases in the testing process. Errors can be added manually or semiautomatically via the testing tool in the TestDirectory suite of tools.

7.6.2.1 Data Maintained on Errors. The table which is used to maintain data on software errors is the "Bug" table. The Bug table contains number columns holding information on errors. These columns and a description of each of them are:

- ID#. Record number assigned to each new error.
- To Mail. Field which enables e-mail messages to be sent to users.
- Status. Current status of the error. Available statuses are New, Open, Fixed, and Closed.
- Subject. The application subject in which the error was detected.
- Assigned To. Person responsible for tracking the error.
- Detected By. Person who detected the error.
- Detected in Version. Software version in which error was detected.
- Detection Date. Date when error was detected.

- Test. Name of the test in which error was detected.
- Path. Path of the test in which error was detected.
- Cycle. Cycle of test in which error was detected.
- Run. Name of test run in which error was detected.
- Step. Step in which the error was detected.
- Summary. Short description of the error.
- Project. Project in which the error was detected.
- Severity. Degree to which errors affect the application.
- Priority. When this error will be addressed in relation to other errors.
- Reproducible. Whether error can be reproduced.
- Description. Detailed description of the error.
- Planned Closing Version. Software version in which error is expected to be closed.
- Estimated Fix Time. Estimated time that it will take to fix the error.
- Closed in Version. Software version in which the error was actually closed.
- Actual Fix Time. Actual time it took to fix the error.
- Closing Date. Date that the error was closed.

- R&D Comments. Comments made by members of development team.
- Attachments. Files can be associated with any of the error records in the Bug table.

In addition to maintaining current information on each error, TestDirector provides the capability to capture a history of details on errors. The "History" table maintains the history of all status changes made to a bug. This data can be viewed for one specific error or all errors. The specific fields which will be captured in the history table is configurable by the user. All of the columns described above are potential candidates for historical record keeping.

7.6.2.2 Security. TestDirector recognizes that different types of users exist and each type requires different levels of access to error-tracking data. The different types of users in TestDirector and their access levels are listed below. Table 7.4 documents the error-tracking privileges each user type has.

TABLE 7.4

Error Tracking
Privileges for
Each Group

TDAdmin —	allows full privileges in the database. Should be reserved for a single person.
QATester —	enables users to report new bugs.
Project Manager —	PM can report new bugs, delete bugs, and modify status of a bug.
Developer —	enables users to report new bugs and change a bug's status to Fixed.
Viewer —	read-only privileges.

7.6.2.3 Customizations. One of the customizations available in Test-Director is which data will be maintained on errors in the "History" table. The potential choices include all of the columns maintained in the "Bug" table. The user indicates which columns should be maintained by clicking them in the "Configure bug History" window.

TestDirector also allows error-related field names to be customized at each site. Up to eight user-defined fields can be defined in the error form. These customizations are fairly simple to make.

7.6.2.4 E-Mail. E-mail can be used to send messages directly from Test-Director to users, informing them about changes in the error-tracking system. The changes which generate messages are user configurable and can include any of the columns in the "Bug" table. Details in each mail message include:

- Date and time the error record was modified.
- Name of person who modified the error record.
- Error information currently contained in the error record.

To include users in the e-mail capability, a mailbox must be associated with their names. Users can be configured to receive messages only when certain conditions exist for an error. For example, Robert will only receive messages when the priority of an error is changed to "1." Other users could be sent messages only when the error priority is changed to "2."

E-mail can also be utilized to generate new errors in TestDirector using a utility called the Remote Bug Reporter. This allows users to enter details about an error in a form. The user can then create an error record via e-mail based on these details at a convenient time.

7.6.2.5 Reports and Graphs TestDirector includes a data analysis tool which allows users to create detailed reports and graphs. Reports can be customized at each installation site. The default Bug Tracking Report includes all fields in the Bug table and Bug form. This can be customized by presenting the data in a tabular format and choosing which columns should be included in the custom-built report.

TestDirector also provides the ability to graph data on errors. Graphs can easily be customized by selecting options from a number of list boxes. An example of the Bug Fix Time Graph is illustrated in Figure 7.4. The standard graphs available which deal with Bug Tracking include:

- Bug Tracking Graph. Illustrates the number of errors detected in the database by date.

- Bug Progress Graph. Documents error data according to dates when errors were detected.

- Bug Summary Graph. Illustrates error-tracking data in the database.

- Bug Age Graph. Shows the length of time that errors have been open.

- Bug Fix Time Graph. Graphs a comparison between estimate and actual time to fix errors.

Figure 7.4
Bug Fix Time Graph

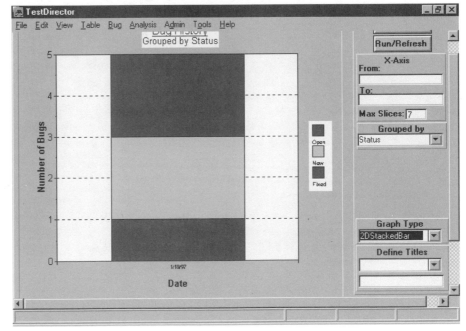

CHAPTER 8

When Is Testing Complete?

All works of humans are imperfect. Client/server computer systems are no exception to this axiom. Testing is an attempt to extricate all of the errors from a computer system. Can any system be tested with all possible test cases? No. Even a relatively simple system will have an infinite number of valid inputs and an equal or larger number of invalid inputs. It isn't humanly possible to perform an absolutely thorough job of testing. Given that all test cases cannot possibly be performed, is it possible to be certain that a system will be completely error-free? Unfortunately, the answer to this question is "no." No computer system can ever be proven to be error-free. The job of the testing staff is to make certain that as many errors as possible, especially the really nasty ones, are discovered and removed.

8.1 How Much Testing Is Necessary?

Everyone would want their computer system to be absolutely perfect and receive the most possible testing, but this isn't economically practical. Not all systems need the same amount or degree of testing. Some need more; some can get by with less. In some cases the cost of the testing could exceed the value of the system being developed. Some variables which determine how much testing is needed are listed in the following sections.

8.1.1 What Is the Purpose of the System?

Differences in the purpose of the system have a tremendous impact on how much testing needs to be performed. Systems which have the potential to cause death or serious injury must be tested to a much more stringent degree than other kinds of systems. The computer system on a Boeing 757 would be tested more thoroughly than a system which computerizes checking out materials from the local public library. A system controlling a pressurized natural gas pipeline must be more trustworthy than a system which doesn't include toxic or explosive materials.

The number of potential users that a system will support has a significant effect on the degree of testing necessary. This requirement is primarily due to the cumulative economic impact a problem will have on the user community. A system which is deployed to thousands of users throughout the world needs to be tested to a greater degree than a system which is installed in-house for three users. The down-time costs for the former system vastly exceed the economic impact of the latter system being unavailable. Besides the opportunity costs incurred while the system is unusable, the costs differ widely on what it costs to distribute any corrections. If serious errors are found within a local system it would cost relatively little to distribute the fix. Deploying and coordinating a fix which must be distributed around the world would entail a significant amount of money and effort.

The value of the information contained in the system must also be taken into consideration. A client/server system which supports a large bank or a Wall Street brokerage house has an extremely high economic content. It should be obvious that such systems need significantly more testing than a computer system which supports a shoe store. Both clients deserve quality, error-free systems, but the impact of the former system crashing greatly outweighs the latter. It wouldn't make economic sense to spend as much time and money testing them both to the same high degree.

8.1.2 Quality of the Software

How good was the software to begin with? A development organization with few or no standards and precious little experience is more likely to produce error-riddled software. Systems developed in a shop which has established standards and a great deal of experience are less likely to be error prone. The amount of testing necessary differs drastically between the two organizations described above.

Unfortunately, organizations which need the most improvement aren't likely to recognize their own shortcomings. The organization which needs a more meticulous testing process is the least likely to have instituted it. In many cases the management doesn't understand the advantages of producing high-quality systems.

8.2 Reliability Metrics

There are several key metrics which can be taken to help determine the reliability of the software being tested. These metrics were developed during projects which developed software for traditional computer systems. The client/server environment has considerably less depth of testing experience than traditional systems do. Each of these metrics are described in the following sections.

8.2.1 Error Density

One measurement of software quality is the number of outstanding errors found per line of code. This value is frequently expressed as errors per thousand delivered lines of source instructions (KDSI) and is referred to as the defect density. The count of lines of code must include code in every event block and function. Code in ancestor modules should also be counted.

8.2.2 Error Discovery Rate

The rate at which errors are being discovered can yield insight into whether the testing phase of a system is close to being finished. Normally the number of errors uncovered during testing starts at a high rate and then subsides as errors are found and corrected. If errors are being found and removed, then eventually the discovery rate drops significantly when fewer errors remain to be found. Eventually this rate will approach zero.

An error discovery threshold can be established below which software can be deployed. The testing manager should fix this threshold prior to the beginning of the project. If it isn't defined in advance, there will be pressure to make the definition "convenient." Read this to be whatever the current error rate is.

If the rate of error discovery isn't dropping or is perhaps even climbing, then system testing is nowhere near complete. If errors are being discovered at a high rate and all tests have been executed, then perhaps more tests should be devised. This could also be a sign that error fixes aren't being made or aren't being distributed.

One tool which can be used to document this tendency is the defect report. When run on a regular basis, this report will clearly document trends in the number of errors being found. While the absolute number of errors being discovered is significant, it's also necessary to track the different kinds of errors which are occurring. A report which lists both quantity and severity could show cosmetic errors that are being found, but serious errors are no longer being discovered.

Obviously, for this report to be useful, the data which is entered into the error-tracking system must be accurate and complete. Entries must be made for all errors. Testers and developers shouldn't be allowed to bypass the system by informally handling errors. It is also incumbent on users to accurately and consistently classify errors. If high-severity errors are being incorrectly classified as cosmetic errors, then the reports will be misleading.

As the rate of finding errors dwindles, the cost of finding each of the last few errors escalates. At this point it doesn't make economic sense to continue testing for most systems. The exceptions to this statement are systems which have the potential for catastrophic results if they malfunction. The control software for a nuclear power plant would be an example of a development project which should continue testing past this point.

8.2.3 Outstanding Errors

Another metric which can help determine whether the system is ready to be released is the number of outstanding errors. Since not all errors have the same impact, they are divided into levels of severity. Before the system is released, the organization's policy might state that there can be no open defects of severity one (highest) or severity two, and fewer than 0.5 total outstanding errors per KDSI.

If test management software is being utilized, it will likely include a report which breaks down errors by severity level. As open errors are fixed and the rate of errors being discovered slows, the numbers will (hopefully) creep downwards to this level. Once testing demonstrates that the software has reached this level, then it is realistic to consider shipping it.

8.2.4 Time Spent Testing

There are a number of estimates of what percentage of time should be spent in each of the phases (analysis, design, coding, testing, maintenance) of a software development project. One estimate is that 30% of the total development time is spent in testing the system. Other sources estimate up to 50% of the total work-hours will be spent on this activity. Every organization's experience will be different. The percentage of time spent testing is driven by a number of factors. A few of them are:

- Experience level of the project team.
- Experience level of the users.
- Hardware platform.
- Quality of the requirements specification.
- Quality of the design document.
- Number of projects the project team has worked on together.
- Development tool being used.
- Quality of test tools being used.
- Amount of hardware available.

Your organization should be documenting how much time is spent in each phase for every project it takes on. As the organization's experience with client/server development increases, these statistics should tend to become more accurate and more consistent. The percentage of time in any given development project should be fairly close to other projects undertaken by the organization, assuming that none of the baseline factors change drastically. If previous data is accurate, then the amount of time spent on the early phases of a project (design) can be used to project how long the later phases (testing) will take.

8.3 Other Testing

The system has made it through the test plan with flying colors. Everything is looking great! The staff is starting to discuss throwing a post-delivery party. Don't send out those invitations just yet. There are several final tests which should be run before burning the system onto the delivery CD-ROMs. If the system hasn't been put through this final battery of tests, then it must pass them before there is serious talk about shipping it out the door.

8.3.1 Endurance Testing

Most developers don't test or run a system continuously for long periods of time. They initiate it, enter a few records, run a few tests, and then exit the application. This isn't the way users normally use a system. They bring it up in the morning and leave it up all day. They use it periodically throughout the day without exiting from the application. If they were permitted to, they would likely leave their workstations running night and day.

Clearly these are vastly different operating environments. Running for extended periods of time has the potential for encountering errors which would never occur during a much shorter time period. Some possible problems which might be uncovered include memory leakage, low disk space, timing problems, overflowing variables, date rollover, and date comparison problems.

Endurance testing must be performed which specifically addresses problems of this type. How long should endurance tests last? The answer to this question is heavily dependent on what the system is designed to do. A bookkeeping system which is used from 8 A.M. till 5 P.M. might be sufficiently endurance tested by running for 24 hours straight. A client/server system which supports medical staff in a hospital has completely different requirements. It must be operational for days on end. Endurance testing for it should be much longer. A client/server system which supports a nuclear power plant has even more strenuous requirements. It, theoretically, would only go down when the plant is taken out of service for maintenance. The endurance test for this should be longer still.

While there may not be one single answer for how long endurance tests should last, there are some durations which seem reasonable. A noncritical system should be tested for at least 100 hours. A life-threatening system should be endurance tested for half again as much, 150 hours. A truly critical system shouldn't have any problem staying up for 10 days or 240 hours.

What should happen during an endurance test? Any computer system is likely to pass an endurance test which consists of simply bringing up the application and leaving it alone. An endurance test should represent the load which will normally be placed on the system. Activity of this nature can be imposed by using tests tools which have been outlined in this book. The activity rate should simulate the daily load peaks which are expected to occur during normal operations.

If at all possible the endurance test should be designed to include the busiest period the system will encounter. An accounting-based system endurance test should include a month-end, end-of-quarter, or year-end situation. A system to support a stock brokerage firm should include endurance testing over the "triple witching hour." An endurance test for an airline ticketing system should include a major holiday, such as Thanksgiving or Christmas.

How many times should an endurance test be run? This question doesn't have a simple answer. One answer which definitely isn't correct is once! A system which passes an endurance test a single time isn't guaranteed to pass it the second time around. Endurance testing should be repeated until it consistently passes the required period of continuous operation.

8.3.2 Memory Testing

Many client/server systems encounter memory-related problems. After such an application has run on a client machine for an extended period of time, memory leakage problems can cause the system to crash. Alternatively, memory problems may be tied to the number of windows (or other objects) opened and closed. In either case, there are occasionally problems related to memory resources on client workstations. Tests aimed specifically at this problem should be performed.

Memory testing can readily be performed at the same time as endurance testing. The basics of this form of testing is to run the application for extended periods of time and periodically determine whether a memory problem exists. If the amount of memory available on the client workstation continuously declines, then a memory problem exists. During the endurance testing, these measurements can be made and documented. Collecting this data could even be included as part of the test scripts run during the endurance tests.

8.3.3 Configuration Testing

The configuration of a system is all the elements which together make up that system. On a client workstation, it would include the make and model of the CPU, the monitor, video card, disk drives, RAM, sound card, operating system, boot settings, software, and other system settings. Each system is likely to be subtly distinct from all other systems. Configuration testing must be performed to verify that the client software will execute successfully on each type of platform it is required to operate on.

Configuration testing needs to be especially vigilant when developers operate under a different configuration than users will use. For example, many developers have 17" monitors on their workstations. If all developers have large monitors, then the applications were likely designed to take advantage of these particular monitors. The forms will be sized large enough to fit the available space. If a user is viewing the system on a 14″ monitor then the application's screens will experience a considerable amount of reduction. This may render the details hard to read. The user may consider the system as a whole to be unusable if he or she can't easily read the screens.

Other configuration aspects which should be considered during configuration testing include:

■ Available memory.

■ Operating system.

■ Number and size of disk drives.

■ CD-ROM drive.

■ Assignment of drives (i.e., is C: always the boot drive? Is E: always the CD-ROM drive?)

■ Parallel ports.

■ Color versus monochrome monitors.

■ Mouse.

■ Modems.

■ Sound cards.

■ External speakers.

■ Video cards.

■ Network cards.

■ Installed communications software (TCP/IP, NetBIOS, IPX/SPX).

■ Operating system differences (e.g. Windows 3.11, Windows 95, Windows NT 3.5, Windows NT 4.0, Macintosh, UNIX, O/S2).

8.3.4 Coverage Testing

Coverage testing refers to the percentage of the source code statements that are executed during the testing process. The ideal situation would be to execute every statement, i.e., 100% coverage. This might not be realistically achievable. There is likely to be code for errors conditions which prove extremely difficult to reach. It may only execute under unusual circumstances.

A more realistic goal for coverage testing might be to execute 80% of all source code and enter 100% of all modules. Given the number of individual source modules in a client/server system, this is a very ambitious goal. Testing needs to be extended until the coverage goal has been reached

How can you determine what percentage of statements and modules were executed? The answer is a coverage analysis test tool. A tool of this kind reports on what instructions have been executed. Coverage test tools add code to an application to document which statements are executed. A suite of tests is executed and the coverage tool tracks which statements in the applications get executed.

8.3.5 Installation Testing

Normally, installing client/server software on the server is fairly straightforward. It is the task of installing software on the client which is more difficult. The primary reason for this is that no two user workstations are identical. Each one will have different hardware components, different software modules, and different boot logic. What works correctly on one workstation may not work properly on another due to differences in DLLs or other files.

Another complicating factor is the skill level of the person doing the installation. If the person installing the software is experienced, then you have a good chance that it will go smoothly. If this job is left up to the user, then be prepared for some difficulties. Instructions will need to be laid out extremely clearly. The terms and phrases should be clear of any hint of jargon, acronyms, and ambiguous words.

The best installation testing is to develop the instructions, assemble the distribution media, and turn them over to someone with minimal computer experience. He or she should attempt to install the system onto a workstation which has never had any of this software loaded onto it. If he or she can't successfully install the software, then rewrite the procedures until the user can do it consistently. Anything less than this method of testing isn't adequate.

8.3.6 Multinational Testing

More and more software products are being marketed internationally. To be accepted in foreign markets, these systems must be enhanced to include the local language. Labels, buttons, reports, column headers, menu items, and error messages must be in the language of the users in the market country. This isn't easy, but it represents one of the costs of marketing in other countries.

The multinational aspects of a client/server system must be tested. This testing is done to assure that the user interface has been accurately and completely translated into other languages. The most obvious aspect to look for is the use of an incorrect language. Flaws in this area might be caused by hard-coding error messages into the application script. It might also be caused by improper translations in table entries.

The lengths of words vary greatly between languages. A button which is adequately sized for an English phrase might need to be lengthened to accommodate the same phrase in German. Buttons, columns, labels, etc., need to be expanded to display the entire text values. If the button is extended too far, it might overlap another control on the window. Menu items which are too long might cause other menu items to be crowded out. Columns headers on reports and windows might also be affected by the length of the titles they contain. Each of these potential trouble spots needs to be checked.

8.3.7 Idiot-Proof Testing

A poster which my wife gave me once displayed a summary of Murphy's Laws as they apply to computers. One of the laws went something like this, "If you develop an idiot-proof system, an ingenious idiot will find a way to crash it." I'm not trying to make any comments about users in this section. It does seem, though, that if it's possible to crash a system through even the most improbable and convoluted series of steps, the sequence of steps will be found.

Many users pride themselves on being able to crash systems. I have spoken with many users who were proud of their reputations as "system busters." Any time the organization wants to find problems in a system, these individuals were asked to test the application.

The system being developed will very likely run into just such a person. Whether it is intentional or just fate, this user will take actions which no one else ever thought to do. Sequences and operations which have never been exercised will be tested by this person. If you don't test these before the system is shipped, he or she will do it for you.

If your organization has a person like this, it might be useful to have him or her log onto the system and attempt to crash it. If the user is able to cause crashes, then you've learned something useful. If the user isn't able to cause the system to hiccup, then consider it a compliment.

8.3.8 Sanity Testing

A sanity check is the last test done. The essence of a sanity check is to rebuild everything from scratch. This ensures that there were no required files which already resided on the system. It makes sure that there aren't any missing files on the distribution media, mismatched libraries, incorrect permissions on files, overlooked bitmaps, or old versions of these files.

It frequently involves rebuilding the software on a newly formatted disk drive or a new computer. The instructions which are being distributed to users should be followed to the letter. At this point those should be absolutely perfect.

In his book *The Soul of a New Machine*, Tracy Kidder describes the project to develop the Data General Eclipse MV/8000 minicomputer. One of the last tests performed on the machine before declaring it to be complete was to play the game "Adventure." This was their version of a sanity check. Developers and testers with significant experience are each likely to have their own version of a sanity test.

8.4 Management Says Testing Is Done

Sometimes the testing staff has very little say about when testing is terminated. Upper management in the organization may make the decision that the system will ship on a certain date, no matter what! This decision may be the result of pressure from clients or economics. If delivery has been promised by a certain date, management might be willing to live with an on-time delivery of less-than-perfect software. When the motivating factor is economic, it might be because cash flow problems demand that the product be delivered to generate income.

When this happens you have little choice but to go along with the directive. At this point the emphasis should be on errors which are relatively high in severity. Cosmetic flaws may be annoying, but don't usually have the potential to do serious damage. Continue testing until it is time to assemble and ship the final build of the system.

Testing Tools

CHAPTER 9

Editors and Debuggers

Text editors and debuggers represent the front line of error-testing tools. They are the tools that developers spend the most time using. Powerful, efficient text editors and debuggers can allow developers to build systems more quickly with fewer errors.

9.1 Editors

At first glance it might seem out of place to discuss editors in a text on testing client/server systems, but there is a good reason for doing so. A significant percentage of errors in computer systems are caused by syntax errors and other errors that are introduced during the coding process. An editor with features that help prevent errors of this nature should be considered an asset in the development and testing effort.

It's easy to overlook the value of a powerful editor. An intuitive, feature-rich WYSIWYG (What You See Is What You Get) editor will cut down on the number of mistakes made while writing code. It will also make the code-writing process faster. This alone will help cut down on the number of errors. Spending less time on the process of manually typing in data will result in less tedium and boredom.

An intelligent editor is a plus during the development phase. It also can be extremely useful during the testing and debugging phase. It's very likely that the person assigned to debug and correct an error was not the original developer. When this is the situation, he or she can use all the help they can get. An intelligent editor can help point out potential problems. It can also help prevent new errors from being inadvertently added to the software component.

9.1.1 Features of Intelligent Editors

Editors included in GUI development environments are becoming more powerful and easier to use. While they each have their own advantages, there are a number of features which are becoming common. These features are described in the followings sections.

9.1.1.1 Color Coded. Color coding is frequently used in an editor to distinguish between various elements in the script being produced. Some of the types of elements that exist are listed here:

■ Script keyword.

■ Script datatype.

■ Integer literal.

■ Float literal.

■ Date literal.

■ Time literal.

■ String literal.

■ Symbol.

■ Invalid text.

■ Identifier.

■ Jump label.

■ Comment.

■ Invalid string.

■ Enumeration.

Visual clues as to the type of each line or word in the script can be extremely useful. It can enable a developer to recognize mistakes and typographical errors in the code immediately. This will result in significantly fewer errors of this type in the final product.

One question to ask about an editor is whether the colors can be customized or even turned off completely. Within a given software development shop, there may be a number of editing tools in use. If they all utilize different colors for a particular element, say a comment, then this will be very confusing to users who develop code on multiple systems. If the colors being used can be customized so they are coordinated between all tools, this would be a great improvement.

9.1.1.2 Insert Closing Statements. A number of statements in development languages involve multiple lines. One element opens the statement and another closes it. Examples of such statements are listed in Table 9.1.

Some editors automatically insert the closing line after the initial statement has been entered. For example, the user enters the line "IF condition = 1 THEN" and presses the Enter key. The editor would automatically generate the associated "END IF" line. This can cut down on the number of errors due to incorrect syntax or typographical errors.

TABLE 9.1

Multiline
Statements

```
IF condition = 1 THEN

        /* Perform logic for condition 1 */

ELSEIF condition = 2 THEN

        /* Perform logic for condition 2 */

ELSE

        /* Perform logic for all other conditions */

END IF


CHOOSE CASE li_value

CASE < 0

        /* Perform logic for li_value < 0 */

CASE = 0

        /* Perform logic for li_value = 0 */

CASE > 0

        /* Perform logic for li_value > 0 */

END CHOOSE


DO WHILE li_value < 20

        /* Statements to be performed */

END LOOP


FOR li_value = 1 TO 25 STEP 1

        /* Statements to be performed */

NEXT
```

9.1.1.3 Automatic Indentation.   A code module that is properly
indented is easier to read and understand. An easily understood module is less able to hide errors among its nooks and crannies. This holds
true whether the developer or someone who is trying to debug the
module is reading it. Normally a developer may think he or she
doesn't need to indent her code. After all, she wrote it so she shouldn't

have any trouble reading or understanding it. Unfortunately, it's a rare individual who can come back to a module six months or a year later and remember exactly what it was supposed to be doing. Indentation helps everyone.

Not every developer will take the time or energy to indent code. This is especially true it they are under a lot of pressure to complete the module. An editor that automatically indents the code while it is being written takes the burden off the developer to perform this valuable but onerous task.

9.1.1.4 Paste Capability.   Almost all editors include the ability to cut and paste text. This is useful, but many script-editing tools have taken the paste capability a step further. A row of paste boxes are positioned at the top of the editor screen. These boxes are list boxes and their contents can be pasted into the text. Standard items that are listed in the paste boxes include: global variables, instance variables, arguments in this function, and objects from the current window. This ability allows the developer to reference these objects quickly and error free.

Another paste capability provided in some editors allows the user to build an SQL statement via a workbench and return it to the script. This workbench allows the user to select the tables referenced in the query. Columns as well as join operations can be specified in this manner. The "where," "group by," "having," and "sort" clauses can also be specified. The workbench tool then assembles the complete SQL statement. While this won't likely be used by experienced developers, it would be extremely beneficial to a less experienced person. Figure 9.1 displays an example of this type of paste capability.

A paste capability similar to the SQL ability which addresses function calls is also available in some development environments. Developers frequently memorize the parameter lists of the more commonly used functions. It would be unusual or impossible for a developer to memorize the names and parameters of all functions available in a system. The ability to paste them in can be advantageously used by beginners and experienced developers alike.

9.1.1.5 Multiple Undo Operations.   The ability to undo editing operations is a great convenience. Being able to undo multiple edit operations is an even greater convenience. This allows the user to cut and paste liberally. If mistakes are made, it's trivial to step backwards and undo recent changes.

Figure 9.1
Paste SQL Statement
from PowerBuilder
5.0 Script Editor

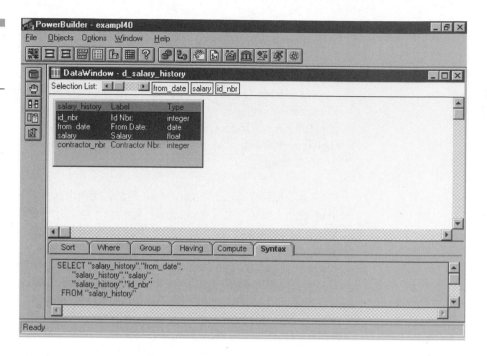

Figure 9.1
Paste SQL Statement
from PowerBuilder
5.0 Script Editor

9.1.1.6 Standardized Keys for Common Functions. When the keys used for standard functions follow general conventions, the developer will make fewer mistakes and generally be less frustrated. Anything that reduces frustration and tedium on the part of the developer has a beneficial effect on the number of errors in a system under development. Some of the more commonly used key combinations and their functions are listed here:

Keys	Function
Ctrl-V	Paste
Ctrl-C	Copy
Ctrl-X	Cut
Ctrl-Z	Undo

9.1.1.7 Find and Browse Features. A find or search function has become standard in most text editors. It can prove to be very useful when searching through a piece of code looking for a particular variable or call to a function. What proves to be especially useful is the ability to browse through many components looking for occurrences of that same variable or function. One example of a browse capability is illustrated in Figure 9.2.

9.1.1.8 Split Screen. A significant difference between client/server GUI development tools and third-generation languages like FORTRAN, COBOL, and C is the length of code modules. In third-generation languages, developers were encouraged to design and develop modules of reasonable length. In GUI tools the developer is almost forced to keep scripts relatively short. This is because event driven programming partitions the logic into much smaller units. A script will be written to execute when a window opens. Another will be written to handle a click event on a button control. The average length is significantly shorter in the client/server GUI world.

As usual, exceptions exist to this general statement. There are some events and functions in a client/server application which can be fairly lengthy. Often, when developing or debugging a module, it is useful to see and compare two segments of the code at the same time. Some editors provide a split-screen feature to allow the user this capability.

Figure 9.2
Visual Basic Script
Editor's Browse
Capability

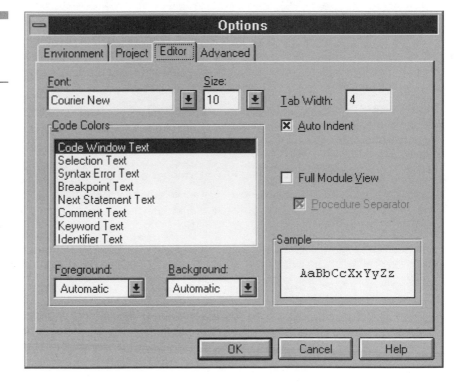

9.1.1.9 Automatic Capitalization of Keywords. A common programming practice is to capitalize all of the keywords of the language being used. Examples of keywords are FOR, BEGIN, END, NEXT, RETURN, DIM, etc. These capitalized words stand out distinctly in the text. This practice makes it easier to recognize keywords and focus on them when it is necessary.

Some editors perform this capitalization automatically. By being done without programmer intervention, it is much more likely that proper, consistent capitalization will be done.

9.1.1.10 Help Capability. When a developer has a question regarding the language being used or the syntax of a particular statement, there is a definite chance that an error will result. If a manual for the development tool is right on hand, it will likely be referenced. If the manual isn't immediately available there is a pretty good chance that the developer will guess how the statement should be written. After all, if he or she guesses wrong about the statement it will be caught during unit testing, won't it?

Many editors come equipped with context-sensitive help. A frequent method of invoking the Help feature is by highlighting the command in question and pressing the F1 key. Sometimes the key pressed is the Shift+F1 or Ctrl+F1 key combinations. Immediately available assistance will drastically cut down on situations where the developer has to rely on hoping or guessing. Less guessing translates into fewer errors in the code.

9.1.2 Examples of Intelligent Editors

The previous sections described some of the capabilities offered by intelligent editors. These features can provide significant assistance in reducing the number of errors in systems as they are being developed. The following sections list some widely used client/server development tools and a brief description of the intelligent features included in each tool's editor.

9.1.2.1 PowerBuilder. The PowerBuilder Script Editor includes a number of the intelligent capabilities described in the above sections. Power-Builder automatically color codes different elements in the scripts. It also allows users to customize colors by setting the font and background color of the script elements from a pull-down window.

9.1.2.1.1 Closing Statements If the user chooses to manually enter a statement block, then the editor will not automatically insert closing statements. The user must enter all of the statements in this case. The user can utilize the paste capability to insert complete statements. This has the effect of entering the closing portion of the statement block.

9.1.2.1.2 Automatic Indentation Automatic indentation is provided in the PowerBuilder editor. Statement blocks that are automatically indented include:

```
IF THEN
IF THEN ELSE
FOR
CHOOSE CASE
DO WHILE
DO UNTIL
DO LOOP WHILE
```

9.1.2.1.3 Paste Functions The ability to paste a number of items into the script being developed is included in PowerBuilder. Some of the items that can be pasted into an event script include:

- Arguments passed to the component.
- Control objects (control buttons, fields, list boxes, radio buttons, etc.) on the window.
- Global variables.
- Instance (local) variables.
- IF THEN statement templates.
- DO LOOP statement templates.
- FOR NEXT statement templates.
- CHOOSE CASE statement templates.

9.1.2.1.4 Undo Operations Multiple undo operations are readily available in the PowerBuilder editor. There does not appear to be a limit to the number of undo operations that can be performed. Once you undo an operation there is no "redo" function which will bring it back.

9.1.2.1.5 Common Keys Keys for common functions follow generally accepted standards. Some of these key assignments are as follows:

Keys	Function
Ctrl-V	Paste
Ctrl-C	Copy
Ctrl-X	Cut
Ctrl-Z	Undo most recent edit operation
F1	Help
Shift-F1	Context-sensitive help

9.1.2.1.6 Find and Browse PowerBuilder includes comprehensive Find and Browse capabilities. Within the script editor, all of the expected find features are included. The ability to browse for a particular text pattern across many components of the application is also available.

9.1.2.1.7 Help PowerBuilder's Help capability is consistently available throughout the entire tool. Pressing the F1 key brings up the generic help capability. To invoke context-sensitive help, the user has to press the Shift+F1 key combination. If the cursor is positioned on a keyword or statement that exists in the help files, that information will be automatically displayed. If the current word doesn't exist, then the help screen will be positioned on the help entry which comes closest to the requested word.

9.1.2.2 Visual Basic. The editor in Visual Basic contains many of the features one expects from an intelligent editor. This editor affords the user a number of configurable features. The intelligent features it offers are described in the following sections.

9.1.2.2.1 Color It colors codes different statements within the script. The user is allowed to set both the background and foreground colors for each element in the script. The screen which lists the types of text and their colors are shown in Figure 9.2. The default color assignments are:

- Key words—blue.
- Comments—green.
- Errors—red.
- Standard code—black.
- Breakpoint text—reverse video black.

9.1.2.2.2 Automatic Indentation   Automatic indentation is performed when the user types in statement blocks that extend across multiple lines. Examples of statements that are automatically indented include:

```
If.. Then .. End If
If.. Then .. ElseIf.. End If
For ... Next
Do While ... Loop
Select Case ... Case ... End Select
Do Until ... Loop
```

9.1.2.2.3 Undo Capability   This editor offers the ability to perform multiple undo operations. An undo is achieved by using the Ctrl-Z key combination or selecting the Edit | Undo Typing menu item.

9.1.2.2.4 Split Screen   A split screen capability is built into Visual Basic's editor. The user can split the current editing screen into two by selecting and pulling down on the upper right-hand corner of the vertical scroll bar. This enables two portions of the current document to be viewed at once. It is especially helpful when a lot of cutting and pasting within the document is being done.

9.1.2.2.5 Automatic Capitilization   The Visual Basic editor automatically capitalizes keywords in the script. The first character of each keyword will be changed to upper case as soon as the editor recognizes it. Consistent capitalization within the program scripts makes it easier for the reader to differentiate which terms are keywords versus those which are user chosen names, etc. A few examples of words that will be capitalized include:

- If
- Then
- ElseIf
- End If
- Dim
- String
- Integer
- Loop
- To

■ False

■ True

■ Step

■ Set

In addition to automatically capitalizing certain words the editor in Visual Basic will insert blank characters in statements to maintain consistent spacing. The purpose of this feature is to make the code easier to read. An example of this activity would be to change the following statement:

```
CurrRow=(CurrRow+1)
```

to

```
CurrRow = (CurrRow + 1)
```

9.1.2.2.6 Required Declaration of Variables   Visual Basic's editor has an option which requires that all variables be declared. This capability is an excellent idea. By requiring the developer to declare all variables, it forces him or her to be a lot more rigorous in coding efforts. This seemingly simple feature can cut down significantly on the number of errors in a system.

9.1.2.2.7 Searching   The Visual Basic edit provides very robust searching capabilities. The user has the choice of searching the current procedure, the current module, or all modules for the entered string. This is extremely useful when you're looking for a string but can't remember what module it is in.

9.1.2.2.8 Help   The Help capability included in Visual Basic's editor is representative of what most help features offer. To invoke context-sensitive help, the user has to press the Shift+F1 key combination. If the cursor is positioned on a keyword or statement that exists in the help files, that information will be automatically displayed. If the current word doesn't exist, then the help screen will be positioned on the help entry that comes closest to the requested word.

9.1.2.3 Microsoft Visual C++.   The editor included with Microsoft's Visual C++ product is an extremely usable and powerful tool. It provides almost all of the "normal" editor functions provided by GUI development tool sets as well as a few additional ones.

9.1.2.3.1 Color Coding Different colors can be specified for various elements of the source scripts. The colors can be chosen by the user from a palette of 16 standard colors. Once colors are assigned to elements, they apply to all source files with the same file extension.

9.1.2.3.2 Indentation Automatic indentation is available in the Visual C++ editor. The auto indent capability can be turned on or off by the user. If it is enabled, each new line in a source file will be indented to match the previous line.

9.1.2.3.3 Undo Multiple Undo actions can be performed in this editor. A Redo command is available to reapply edit actions that have been undone. The number of Undo and Redo actions is determined by the size of the editor's UndoRedoSize buffer. This is a setting that is configurable by the user.

9.1.2.3.4 Cut and Paste The standard cut, copy, and paste operations are available in this editor. Menu items enable the user to specify which of the operations should be performed. The choices include: Cut, Copy, Paste, Delete, Undo, and Redo.

In addition to the usual cut-and-paste methods for copying text, the Visual C++ editor has a mouse-driven method. The user highlights the desired text with the mouse. The selected text is then dragged to the new location and dropped. A pop-up menu will prompt the user to determine if the text should be moved or copied.

9.1.2.3.5 Multiple Source Files This editor allows the user to have multiple source files opened at any given time. Each source file window acts independently of the others. A source file window can be displayed in full screen mode, or it can be split. Splitting an editing window enables the users to view and modify two sections of the file simultaneously.

9.1.2.3.6 Bookmarks Bookmarks are available to mark frequently accessed lines of code in source files. Once a bookmark has been set, menu or keyboard commands can be used to move to it. Bookmarks which are no longer needed can be removed.

Bookmarks are available in two varieties: named and unnamed. Named bookmarks retain both the line number and column position of the cursor when the bookmark was created. Unnamed bookmarks are more temporary. They are deleted when the file containing them is closed or reloaded. Unnamed bookmarks store only the line number, not the column position of the cursor.

9.1.2.3.7 Searching The Visual C++ text editor provides two useful searching methods: full string searching and incremental searching. When full string searching is invoked, the search does not begin until the entire search string has been entered. Under incremental searching, the search is performed as the string is entered.

The ability to find and replace text within a source file is available in the Visual C++ editor. The active window is searched for the string specified by the user. When that string is found, the user is given the option of replacing this occurrence or all occurrences of it.

Search operations can be extended to include multiple files. The user selects the type of files to be searched, e.g., *.C files. The primary directory can be chosen by selecting it from a "Choose Directory" dialog box. Additional subdirectories can also be chosen. Once the setup has been completed, the user initiates the search. All occurrences of the string, including the file name, are listed in an output window. Double clicking on an entry causes that source file to be loaded by the editor.

9.1.2.3.8 Recording Keystrokes If a number of repetitive editing operations must be performed, it would be extremely useful to perform them only once. This would speed the editing operation as well as cut down on errors. The Visual C++ editor provides this ability. It allows the user to record keystrokes, but not mouse movements, which are entered. These keyboard actions can later be repeated at one or more locations in the source file.

9.1.2.4 Oracle Developer/2000. The editor included in Oracle's Developer/2000 has many features which are fairly common, but it also includes a few which aren't seen elsewhere. A short description of its features follows.

9.1.2.4.1 Delete Button This editor has a button used to delete script. The user highlights the desired script and clicks the delete button. The user is then prompted to confirm that the text should be deleted.

9.1.2.4.2 Undo There are two methods of undoing an edit operation in the Developer/2000 editor. A revert button restores the program unit to what it was when the editor was first opened or when the last apply or revert operation occurred. This enables the user to undo a large number of editing steps.

The second method of undoing an edit operation is via the right mouse button. Pressing that button brings up an option box. Undo is the first option on the list. Only the most recent edit operation can be undone.

9.1.2.4.3 Mouse Keys The mouse is used frequently when editing in the Developer/2000 environment. Right clicking the mouse displays an editor-related options box. The user can choose to undo, cut, copy, paste, delete, or select all text.

9.1.2.4.4 Split Screen The Developer/2000 editor does provide a split screen capability. It enables the user to split the editor screen into two panes. The top pane displays source code. The bottom pane displays compilation-related error messages. The user is able to resize these two panes to whatever sizes are desired. This is done by placing the mouse cursor on the split bar, clicking, and holding the mouse button and dragging it up or down.

9.1.2.4.5 Apply Button The apply saves any changes made to the program unit in the editor since it was first opened or since the last apply or revert operation. This button doesn't cause the program unit to be recompiled. After the apply button completes its efforts, the editor remains open.

9.1.2.4.6 Status Bar On the bottom line of the editor is a status bar. This bar displays information about the current state of the program unit. The status bar is divided into two areas, the left and right edges. Information presented in each of these areas is described below.

The left edge of the status bar displays the following messages:

■ Not Modified. No changes have been made to program unit since it was first displayed or last applied.

■ Modified. Changes have been made to the program unit since it was first displayed or last applied.

The right edge of the status bar displays the following messages:

■ Not Compiled. The program unit source text currently displayed has not been compiled.

■ Successfully Compiled. The program unit source text currently displayed compiled with no errors.

■ Compiled with Errors. The program unit source text currently displayed compiled with errors. Errors are displayed in the Compilation messages pane.

9.1.2.4.7 Help Oracle Developer/2000's Help capabilities are fairly standard. It includes the ability to see an overview of the tool's capability. It also provides a search list to allow the user to find a specific piece of information about the product.

9.2 Debuggers

A *debugger* is a tool that enables the user to move through a program in a controlled way. It allows the developer or tester to peer into the internal operations of an application. The purpose of a debugger is to assist the developer in the process of finding code that is causing a particular error.

9.2.1 The Process of Debugging

Debugging is the art or science of being aware of an error and attempting to determine the exact code in the system that causes it. Generally, the sequence is that a test uncovers an error. The error is assigned to someone on the development team to analyze and fix. The process of finding the error is called "debugging." Finding the bug normally constitutes the vast majority of the effort in this activity. Once the error is found, correcting it is frequently relatively easy.

9.2.1.1 Client/Server and Debugging. The move to client/server systems hasn't made the practice of debugging easier. It is more difficult due to several factors. First, code exists on more levels and computers than ever before. In a client/server system, code is located on the client machine, on the server machine, and on an application server if one exists. The code that is causing the error could be located on any of the levels. In a worst-case situation, the error might be caused by interaction between code at multiple levels.

A second reason why client/server systems are difficult to debug is that the code is more fragmented than on traditional systems. Most client/server development tools allow and encourage event-driven programming. End users cause events to occur when they utilize the system. Scripts are written to process each of these events. This plethora of events (and scripts to process them) can make it difficult to trace exactly what happens, exactly when it happens, and in what sequence.

9.2.1.2 The Blind Luck Technique. There are probably as many approaches to the process of debugging as there are people assigned to this type of activity. Some are better and some are worse. The approaches which lean towards brute force are particularly inefficient. One of the worst debugging methods is to start changing code and hope that the problem goes away. Don't laugh! This method sounds like an act of desperation, but it occurs much more frequently than most organizations are willing to admit. If this is the method for finding and correcting errors, then it's extremely likely that new errors will be introduced in the course of fixing the original error. When using this technique, be prepared to deliver a system that is error riddled.

9.2.1.3 Using Print Statements. One of the more simplistic approaches to debugging is to scatter print statements (or their equivalent) throughout the application or at least the portion of the application where the error is suspected. Each print statement uniquely identifies itself and lists pertinent variables. By observing the print messages that are output and the variables being printed, the programmer can see what is going on inside the application. Like the previous approach, this technique isn't state of the art, but it happens more than most developers will admit.

The primary drawback to this approach is that it isn't very efficient. It takes a long time to include the print statements, recompile the application, and execute it. Once this has been done, the program must be stepped through to where the print statements are. If there are a lot of print statements, or they are in a lengthy loop, it can take a long time to get past them to the point where the error is suspected to be. Sometimes, output from the print statements can be redirected to a file. This can speed up the process considerably.

If the error isn't located during the first iteration (and it seldom is), then the entire process must be repeated. Current print statements need to be removed, new ones added, or additional variables need to be included in the current print statements. With the new debug statements in place, the application is recompiled, executed, and stepped through to where the new print statements have been positioned.

One last caveat when using this technique is that the programmer must remember to remove all of the print statements. While leaving in some of the debug print statements isn't usually fatal, it can be extremely embarrassing explaining what they mean and why they were left in to the user community or the testing team.

9.2.1.4 Using a Debugging Tool. A debugger is a tool that enables the user to move through a program in a controlled way. The tester can specify that execution will stop on a particular source code statement. Execution can also be stopped on a statement when certain conditions exist, e.g., a variable is negative. By adroit use of a debugging tool, the user can dig deep into a program to find errors. A debugger's capabilities are a great tool for helping to trace the thread of execution from one event script to the next.

There are a number of great advantages to using a debugger over techniques mentioned in earlier sections. Utilizing a debugger is generally faster than any of the other methods. It isn't necessary to add print statements and later modify them. The tester is also able to specify exactly where in the source code execution should stop. If this doesn't turn out to be the correct point, then it doesn't take long to modify the location and rerun the application.

Debuggers don't require any modifications to the source code. There is no necessity to modify source code and recompile the application. For a sizable application, this can be a tremendous time saver. Eliminating source code changes also removes the embarrassing possibility of leaving debug print statements behind when the testing is complete.

Most of the client/server development tools include a debugger in their functionality. Since the capability is already provided, there is no time or expense necessary to acquire this test capability.

9.2.2 Common Features of Debuggers

Each client/server development tool offers slightly different wrinkles on the debugger features. Each suite tries to differentiate itself from the competition and stresses what it feels is most important. Nevertheless, there are a number of features that are common to many of them. The following sections describe some of the generally offered capabilities.

9.2.2.1 Setting Breakpoints. The term *breakpoint* refers to a specific line of code in the application at which execution will stop, i.e., break. Breakpoints are frequently set by entering the debugger and double-clicking on the desired line of source code. Another method of specifying the breakpoint is to right-click the mouse on the desired source statement. The statement at that point will display some indication that it is a breakpoint. It might be displayed in reverse video or present a special symbol in the left-hand margin.

Most debuggers allow the tester to define a large, if not unlimited, number of breakpoints. While this is a very generous offering, it can lead to sloppy testing practices. If an excessive number of breakpoints are being set, then you most likely have not analyzed the error and the code enough to be setting any breakpoints. Spend more time studying the application and the code before jumping into the debugger.

9.2.2.2 Clearing Breakpoints. Once an error is solved, it is desirable to remove all breakpoints. If this isn't done, the user or testing staff will be impacted by the debugger if they happen to hit a breakpoint in the application. While the test staff will understand what is happening, the users will be extremely confused. For developer-client relationships, it's important to clear all breakpoints before you release any code modules.

Fortunately, most debuggers allow the tester the ability to remove all breakpoints at one time. This is a quick and easy way to make sure debugging statements don't remain.

9.2.2.3 Single-Step Execution. A breakpoint has been set and the application executes to that point. Where does the tester go from here? A common capacity of debuggers is the ability to single step through the application. By clicking a function key, the next source statement will be executed. By continuously clicking this key, the tester can progress through the application one statement at a time.

By single stepping through the application, it's possible to find out exactly what is going on inside it. This won't be a fast way to debug, but it is certainly thorough.

9.2.2.4 Step-over Procedure. Sometimes when debugging an application there is code that isn't necessary to investigate. A procedure or module might be called which has nothing to do with the error in question. When this is the case, it would be a waste of time and effort to step through the procedure. Some debuggers allow an entire procedure to be avoided by "stepping over" it. The debugger stops execution on the instruction following the return from the procedure in question. This capability can save a significant amount of time during the debugging process.

9.2.2.5 Run to Cursor. Setting breakpoints is convenient, but they can accumulate and be hard to sort through. Single stepping is thorough, but stepping through a loop that executes a great number of times can be tedious. Isn't there some combination of these two techniques? The answer to this plea is, "yes." Some debuggers include a "run to cursor" capability. The tester simply clicks on the desired source statement and presses the appropriate function key. Application execution will continue until it reaches the designated statement. This ability mimics the flexibility of setting a breakpoint without the burden of cluttering up the debugging session with too many of them.

9.2.2.6 Run to Completion.　When the test session is complete, the tester has a couple of choices for terminating it. Debug sessions can be terminated. This immediately kills the application. Another choice is to run to completion. This ability allows the application to run without regard to any breakpoint statements. It's useful when the tester wants the application to complete normally. This might be desired because the database needs to be updated, committed, or disconnected.

9.2.2.7 Examining Variable.　Once the execution of the program has been halted at a breakpoint, the user can poke around in the internals of the program. Most debuggers allow the user to specify a variable and examine its contents. This is an extremely useful feature! It enables the tester to really understand what has happened in the application and what is likely to happen in the future.

Many debuggers allow the tester to set up a "watch list." This is a list of variables whose contents are displayed in a separate window. If a few variables are going to be examined often, it makes sense to put them in this list and continuously observe their contents.

9.2.2.8 Setting Variables.　Another extremely valuable function is the ability to modify the contents of a variable. For example, the tester might recognize that a certain variable has been loaded with an incorrect value. He knows that this value will cause an undesired logic path to be taken. Rather than kill the session and modify the code, the tester can load a more desirable value into the variable. This permits the session to continue productively.

9.2.2.9 Modifying Code from within the Debugger.　Some debuggers allow source code to be modified from within the debugger. This is sort of a mixed blessing. While the source code can indeed be modified, the changes normally do not take effect until the current debugging session is completed and a new one is initiated. The primary advantage of changing code while in a debugging session is to avoid forgetting to do it later. The tester is looking right at the code and knows what needs be modified. Implementing the modifications immediately is safer and more certain than doing it at a later time.

9.2.3 Examples of Debugger in Development Tools

As implied earlier, each development environment offers slightly different wrinkles on the debugger capabilities. The debuggers of some of the major client/server development tools will be briefly described in the following sections. This information is not intended to be an exhaustive manual on these tools. It is designed to be an introduction to the unique features of each product. For more complete information, the reader should obtain a copy of the user guide for the desired tool and its debugger.

9.2.3.1 PowerBuilder. The debugger in PowerBuilder is fairly representative of the debugger offered in most client/server GUI development environments. Like most debuggers, it stops execution just before it hits a statement containing a breakpoint (stop). This enables the tester to look at (and change) the values of variables in the statement about to be executed.

9.2.3.1.1 Breakpoints Adding a breakpoint in the PowerBuilder debugger is simply a matter of pointing and clicking. To add a breakpoint, use the Select Script dialog box to specify the script containing the line where you wish to stop execution. Double-click each line in which a breakpoint should be inserted. A stop sign will be displayed at the start of each line that has a breakpoint. Figure 9.3 shows a breakpoint set on a line of code in a PowerBuilder script.

PowerBuilder's debugger only allows breakpoints on lines that contain an executable statement. Breakpoints cannot be defined on lines that contain variable-declarations, comment lines, or blank lines. To remove a stop, double-click the line containing the stop.

One caution that PowerBuilder mentions is that the user should not set a stop in the Activate or GetFocus events. The process of going to and returning from the Debug window can cause recursive triggering of the events. This will have the effect of hanging the debug session in an endless loop.

One convenient feature is that breakpoints are maintained across debug sessions. When you close Debug, PowerBuilder stores the breakpoint information as Stop variables in the Debug section of PB.INI. The next time this application is debugged, whether in the current PowerBuilder session or another one, the breakpoints will be used.

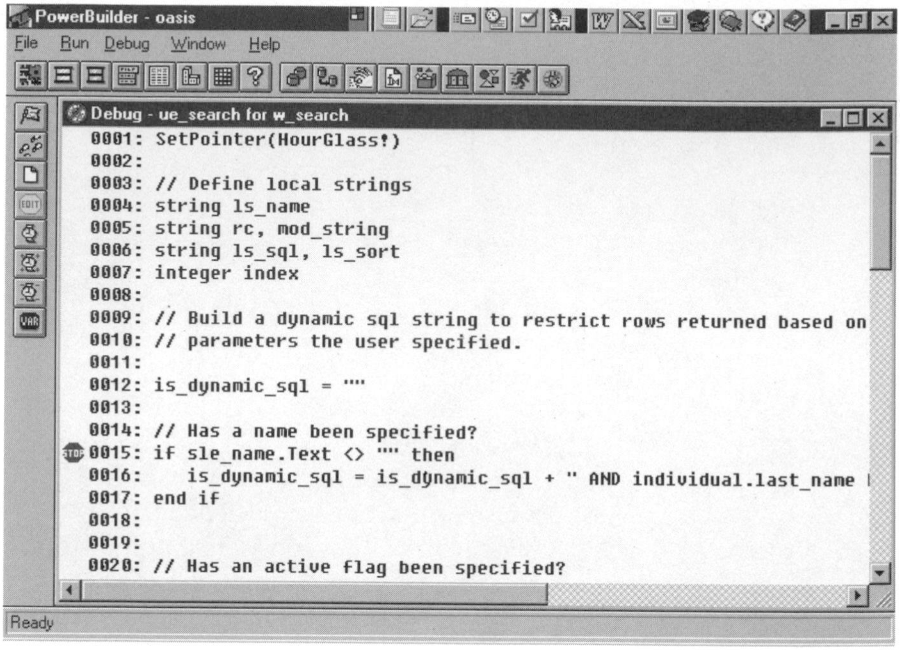

Figure 9.3

Setting a Breakpoint
in PowerBuilder

```
PowerBuilder - oasis
File   Run  Debug   Window    Help

Debug - ue_search for w_search
0001: SetPointer(HourGlass!)
0002:
0003: // Define local strings
0004: string ls_name
0005: string rc, mod_string
0006: string ls_sql, ls_sort
0007: integer index
0008:
0009: // Build a dynamic sql string to restrict rows returned based on
0010: // parameters the user specified.
0011:
0012: is_dynamic_sql = ""
0013:
0014: // Has a name been specified?
0015: if sle_name.Text <> "" then
0016:    is_dynamic_sql = is_dynamic_sql + " AND individual.last_name
0017: end if
0018:
0019:
0020: // Has an active flag been specified?

Ready
```

A window in the debugger, The Edit Stops dialog box lists all breakpoints currently defined (Fig. 9.4). The following information is presented on each break:

- The state of the breakpoint (enabled or disabled).
- The name of the object that contains the breakpoint (a window, menu, user object, global function, or the application object).
- The name of the control, menu object, or user object whose script contains the breakpoint.
- The name of the event with the breakpoint.
- The number of the line in the script at which the breakpoint is set.

9.2.3.1.2 Disabling Breakpoints This debugger allows breakpoints to be disabled without deleting them. PowerBuilder will not stop execution at disabled breakpoints. Later you can enable the breakpoint again. Being able to disable breakpoints without actually deleting them can be a significant time saver. If a complex set of breakpoints has been defined, it might take quite a while to restore them. Instead of deleting and rebuilding them each time, they can simply be disabled.

9.2.3.1.3 Stepping Through the Application Once execution of an application is stopped at a breakpoint, it is very easy to step through the application one statement at a time. To execute the next statement and stop, click the Step button. Debug executes the current line, then stops and returns you to the Debug window. This process can be repeated as many times as desired. This feature is especially useful when the tester has very little idea where the problem is occurring.

To continue execution, click the Continue button. The application continues until the next breakpoint is encountered. If you want to continue running the application without stopping at any breakpoints, then they can all be disabled prior to clicking the Continue button.

When Debug encounters a breakpoint, it suspends the application before executing the statement with the breakpoint. The Debug window is displayed at this time. The statement that will be executed next is highlighted. At this point, the state of the application can be examined. Some of the points that can be examined include:

- Display objects and their properties in the current application.
- Display the current values of the global, shared, instance, and local variables.
- Change the value of any variables.
- Select the variables to be included in the watch list.

Figure 9.4
PowerBuilder Edit
Stops Dialog Box

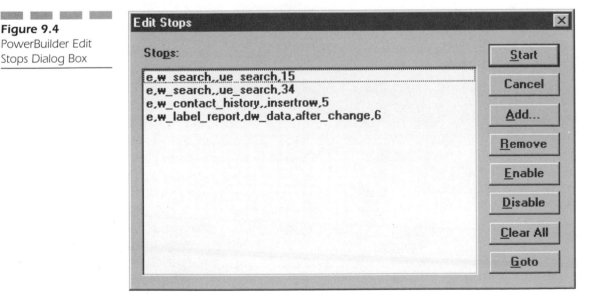

- Edit the breakpoints.
- Print variables and watch variables lists.

9.2.3.1.4 Displaying Variables   To display the current values of variables, click the Show Variables button in the Painter Bar. Another method of displaying variables' values is to select Debug | Variables Window from the menu bar. At this point the Variables window is displayed. Steps to display the variables whose values you want to see are as follows.

To examine	Perform these steps
Global variables	Double-click the Global button. PowerBuilder displays all global variables defined for the application and lists all objects (such as windows) that are open.
Shared variables	Double-click the Shared button. PowerBuilder displays all objects that have been opened so far. Click an object to see its shared variables.
Variables that are local to the current script or function.	Double-click the Local button
Instance variables of an object	Locate the variable in the object itself.

String variables can become quite lengthy. When examining long strings, the Debug window displays the first 128 characters of the variable's value. To inspect a value that exceeds 128 characters, double-click the variable. You can scroll through the variable's complete contents in the resulting window.

9.2.3.1.5 The Watch List   PowerBuilder allows the tester to create a list of variables that is displayed at all times during the debug session. This is called the Watch List. Any number and type of variables can be included in the Watch List. Obviously, if the Watch List contains a long list of variables it will be difficult to keep an eye on all of them. As the application precedes, PowerBuilder displays these variables in a Watch window and updates their values in real time. Figure 9.5 shows the Watch window.

The lists of variables and watch variables can be printed. To print them on the default printer, select File | Printer. To direct output to a different printer, select File | Printer Setup on the menu bar before printing.

PowerBuilder registers the variables selected as watch variables in the Debug section of its initialization file (PB.INI). The next time the

Figure 9.5
PowerBuilder Watch
Window

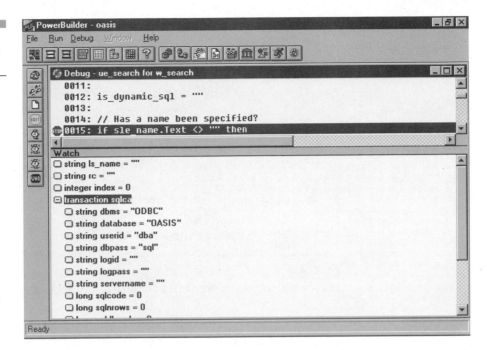

Figure 9.5
PowerBuilder Watch
Window

debugger is used, whether in the same PowerBuilder session or another one, the same list of watch variables will be restored.

9.2.3.1.6 Modifying Code from the Debugger If an error in a script or function is found while using the debugger, it can be corrected. To fix a problem:

- Terminate the application. This returns you to the Debug window.
- Close the Debug window by selecting File | Close from the menu bar.
- Open the appropriate Painter (editor) and modify the script to fix the error.

Caution: Be sure to close the Debug window before making any changes to your application.

Check the fix by running the application in debug mode. Click the Debug button in the tool bar and then click the Start button. All breakpoints and watch variables previously set are still defined.

9.2.3.2 Visual Basic Debugger. Breakpoints in the Visual Basic debugger function much like their counterparts in other debuggers. Execution is stopped just before execution of a specific line of code.

9.2.3.2.1 Setting Breakpoints To set or reset a breakpoint, the user positions the cursor on the desired line of code and chooses Run | Toggle Breakpoint. Two other methods of defining a breakpoint are to click the Toggle Breakpoint button on the toolbar or press the F9 function key. All statements that have been defined as breakpoints are highlighted in bold and displayed in a user-defined color in the Code window.

An alternative to defining a statement as a breakpoint is to insert a Stop statement in the script. When Visual Basic encounters a Stop statement it halts execution and switches to break mode as is done with a breakpoint. There are a number of significant differences between a Stop statement and a breakpoint. Stop statements persist if the current session is exited and later restarted. Breakpoints don't persist in this manner across sessions. Stop statements also remain in the executable and act like End statements when an executable (.EXE) file is created. Breakpoints aren't included in executables.

9.2.3.2.2 Stepping Through the Procedure The Visual Basic debugger allows the tester to execute code one statement at a time. This is invoked by calling the "Step Into" menu item or toolbar button. If it isn't desirable to "Step Into" a procedure, then the "Step Over" command should be used. This acts just like the "Step Into," except control won't go into procedures.

9.2.3.2.3 Step to Cursor If the tester wants to completely skip a large block of code the "Step To Cursor" option can be used. The first step is to place the cursor where the next stop is desired. Select menu option Run | Step To Cursor or press the CTRL+F8 keys. The application will stop just prior to executing the line on which the cursor is located.

9.2.3.2.4 Tool Bar Buttons Visual Basic provides several buttons on its tool bar to ease the use of its debugger. These buttons are:

- Breakpoint. Defines a line in the Code window as a breakpoint.
- Instant Watch. Displays the current value of an expression when the application is stopped.
- Calls. When the application is stopped, a dialog box is displayed which shows all procedures that have been called but not yet run to completion.

- Step Into. Executes next executable line of the application, including called procedures.

- Step Over. Executes next executable line of the application without going into a procedure.

9.2.3.2.5 Calls Dialog Box There are frequent instances in client/server systems where one procedure calls a second procedure. Within the second procedure a third procedure is invoked. This nesting of procedures can go on indefinitely. Situations of this nature can be very difficult to debug. Visual Basic provides tools to help in these situations. The "Calls" dialog box displays a list of all procedures that were called but haven't yet finished executing.

The Calls Dialog Box feature (Fig. 9.6) is especially useful when diagnosing recursion problems. If an application is improperly written, a situation may occur where one procedure calls a second. The second procedure then turns around and calls the first. This condition is referred to as recursion. If recursion continues indefinitely, it can utilize all of the memory in the stack. The result will be an "Out of Space" error. This box allows the tester to determine which procedures have been called and by whom. If a recursion situation is occurring, the Calls Dialog Box makes it easy to recognize.

9.2.3.2.6 Watch List A list of variables or expressions to be watched can be defined in Visual Basic. These expressions are listed in the Watch pane of the Debug windows. Each time the application is in break mode, these expressions and their current values are displayed.

In addition to observing the value of variables in the Watch list, these values can be used to control the debugger. The tester can use a watch

Figure 9.6
Visual Basic's Calls
Dialog Box

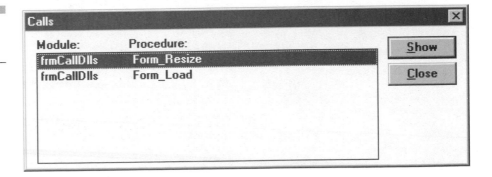

expression to break the application when a variable reaches a specified value. The application can also be stopped when a flag in a procedure changes value. Using the watch variables in this way relieves the tester from tediously stepping through loops until the variable under observation reaches a specific value.

9.2.3.2.7 Correcting Errors   Visual Basic allows some run-time errors to be corrected from within its debugger. After correcting the error, the application continues execution. Examples of the errors that can be corrected include misspelled variable names, mismatched properties, and properties applied to the wrong type of object. To correct errors of this type, simply enter the correction and choose Continue from the Run menu item.

Other error types require that the application be restarted before changes can be put into effect. Examples of this type of error include changing variable declarations, adding new variables, or adding new procedures. When a restart is required, Visual Basic will ask if you want to restart the application.

9.2.3.3 Microsoft Visual C++ Debugger.   As a programming language, C++ allows the developer to work at a lower level than tools such as PowerBuilder, Visual Basic, and Developer/2000. It should come as no surprise that the debugger that accompanies Visual C++ also provides significantly more functionality than other debuggers. It enables the user to examine the executing program at a much lower level than possible with most debuggers.

9.2.3.3.1 Debugging Windows   A number of windows exist to display debugging information. Each window contains specialized debugging information about the program being examined. A right mouse click on any of these windows displays a pop-up menu listing commonly used commands for that window. Table 9.2 lists these debugger windows and outlines the information they display.

Several debuggers' windows use spreadsheet fields as their interface with the users. Like standard spreadsheet implementations, the user can resize columns by dragging the divider between them. Data within and between debugger windows can be moved by either the cut-and-paste or drop-and-drag methods.

9.2.3.3.2 Breakpoints   As in other debuggers, breakpoints instruct the Visual C++ debugger when execution of a program should be interrupt-

Window	Information Displayed
Call Stack	The stack of all function calls that have not returned.
Disassembly	Assembly language derived by disassembling the program's compiled code.
Memory	Current memory contents.
Output	Information about the build process. This includes any compiler or linker errors.
Registers	The contents of general-purpose and CPU status registers.
Variables	Details about the variables used in recently executed statements.
Watch	A list of values and expressions on the watch list.

TABLE 9.2

Debugger
Windows

ed. When the program is halted at a breakpoint, the state of the program can be examined. Several distinct types of breakpoints are supported by this debugger. Each type is described in the following sections.

Location breakpoints halt the debugger at a specific line of code. Other places where a location breakpoint can be defined include the following: at a label, at the beginning statement of a function, or at a specified memory address.

A variable or expression can have a data breakpoint assigned to it. A data breakpoint interrupts program execution when the value of a variable or expression changes or when the value becomes true. An example would be to create a breakpoint if and when variable "salary" is assigned a value greater than 100,000.00. Breakpoints can also be triggered when the value at a specific memory address changes.

Message breakpoints can be set to occur when a message is received by an export Windows function. The user can select to break on either a specific message or on any message from a designated class of messages.

Conditional breakpoints are a form of location breakpoints that interrupt execution only if a specified condition is met. The condition involved could be when the value of a variable or expression changes. It could also be when the value of a Boolean expression is false. An option that is available for conditional breakpoints is the ability to skip the breakpoint for a specified number of times. One usage of this feature would be if an error only occurs after a loop executes "x" number of times. Set the number of times it should be skipped to "x-1" and run the program.

It must be possible to see what source code statements have breakpoints associated with them. The Visual C++ debugger uses a set of characters in the left margin to denote this. A red dot in the left margin indicates that a source statement is a breakpoint. A disabled breakpoint has a hollow red circle in the left margin. Lines with statements can have multiple breakpoints. If a line contains more than one breakpoint, and some of them are disabled while others are enabled, a gray dot is displayed in the left margin.

9.2.3.3.3 Controlling Program Execution Within the debugger there are a number of commands that the user can execute to control execution within the program. Each of these commands and the action that they cause is listed in Table 9.3.

9.2.3.3.4 Viewing and Modifying Variables and Expressions When execution of a program is halted at a breakpoint, there is a wealth of information available to the user. Any variable and expression in the source code can be examined. By simply placing the cursor over a variable (or expression) a Data Tips pop-up information box is displayed. This box will display the current value of the object in question.

Variables and expressions can be placed in the Quick Watch list. The Quick Watch displays the current value of one variable or expression at a time. Structures, objects, and arrays are valid candidates to be placed in

TABLE 9.3

Debug Program
Execution
Commands

Command	Action Which Will Be Taken
Go	Execution begins at the current statement and continues until either a breakpoint is encountered or until the program exits.
Restart	Reloads the current program and begins execution at the first statement of the program. Contents of variables are flushed, but breakpoints and watch expressions are maintained.
Stop Debugging	Terminates the debug session.
Break	Halts the program at its present location.
Step Into	Single steps through statements in the program. If a function call is encountered, the debugger will execute statements in it.
Step Over	Single steps through statements in the program. If a function call is encountered, it is executed without the debugger displaying it.
Step Out	Executes the remainder of code in a function call and stops on the first instruction which follows the function.
Run to Cursor	Executes the program until the statement where the cursor is located is reached. This statement replaces the need to create and delete a temporary cursor.

the Quick Watch list. The value of the variable contained in this watch can be modified by the user.

If the current values of multiple variables are desired, the Watch Window should be used. This window allows a number of variables to be listed and their values displayed. Objects contained in the Watch Window can also have their values modified.

9.2.3.3.5 Other Debugging Windows The Visual C++ Debugger contains a number of other debugging-related windows that aren't available in most debuggers. The windows present a level of details which development packages such as PowerBuilder, Visual Basic, and Developer/2000 do not generally provide. A brief summary of these windows is provided here.

9.2.3.3.5.1 Call Stack Window The Call Stack Window displays the stack of currently active function calls. As each function is called, details about it are pushed onto the top of the stack. When the function completes and returns control to the caller, its entry is popped off the stack.

9.2.3.3.5.2 Registers Window The Registers window displays the contents of the CPU registers, floating-point stack, and flags. Users can modify the value in any register or flag while a program is being debugged. A certain amount of caution should be exercised when registers are modified. The EIP and EBP registers in particular can impact program execution.

9.2.3.3.5.3 Memory Window The Memory window enables the users to view memory contents beginning at any specified address. Any memory location in the program's address space can be examined by using the scroll bars in the Memory window. The default display format is decimal (base 10), but the user can change the display to hexadecimal (base 16).

9.2.3.3.5.4 Disassembly Window The Disassembly window displays disassembled code along with source-code annotations and symbols. This window can switch between displaying source code and disassembled code. When in disassembled mode, all location references are to the lines of disassembled code, not source lines.

9.2.3.3.6 Additional Visual C++ Debugger Features Some additional features available in the Visual C++ debugger are described here. These capabilities and techniques aren't available in debuggers that accompany higher-level, GUI products.

9.2.3.3.6.1 Just-in-Time Debugging The Visual C++ debugger is used to debug a program in the development environment. Once the program is compiled and linked into an executable file, the debugger is no longer available. However, there are situations when the features of a debugger would be useful to analyze problems with an executable program. Just-in-Time debugging allows debugging to be performed outside of the development environment. To enable this feature, the Just-in-Time debugging option must be set prior to executing the program.

9.2.3.3.6.2 Debugging OLE Applications An Object Linking and Embedding (OLE) application is one application that can control another application's objects. An example would be if a C++ program could launch Excel, create, modify, and print a spreadsheet without leaving the original application. The interactions and potential complications between the two applications mount rapidly. Debugging a problem in such an environment would be difficult, to say the least.

The Microsoft Developer Studio debugger has support for debugging OLE client and server applications. When the initial application launches the OLE remote procedure call (RPC), a second instance of the debugger is initiated. This instance of the debugger interacts with the OLE server. All normal debugging facilities are available in this copy of the debugger.

9.2.3.3.6.3 Remote Debugging Many times it is almost impossible to use a single computer monitor to follow both the program being debugged and information from the debugger. The program being debugged might take control of the monitor to display graphics information. The problem might be a window-activation problem. Both of these situations would preclude the use of a single monitor for both purposes.

One solution to debugging problems such as these would be to use separate computers for the application and the debugger. Microsoft Developer Studio refers to this as "remote application debugging." It is enabled by placing a small debug monitor program on the target computer, e.g., the one running the application. The debugger is initiated on a second machine, called the remote computer. The host computer communicates with the remote computer through a serial or network connection. Debug commands are sent back and forth across this communications link.

9.2.3.3.6.4 Debugging Multithreaded Applications The Microsoft Developer Studio, of which Visual C++ debugger is a part, allows developers to construct multithreaded applications. A thread is a path of execution within a process. Each thread is capable of performing one function at a time. Multiple threads can be used to handle background or maintenance tasks that don't require the user's focus. Another use of multiple threads is to handle asynchronous processes.

The Threads Dialog box in the debugger lists all threads that exist in the application. By selecting a thread from this list, the user can test, suspend, or resume any of the existing threads. Via this functionality, multithreaded applications can successfully be debugged.

9.2.3.3.6.5 Debugging Optimized Code In order to generate more optimized code, compilers frequently reposition or reorganize code. The optimize might, for example, recognize that a variable is being set to a literal value inside a loop. By relocating this assignment statement outside the loop, the program can be made more efficient. A single example like this doesn't sound like much of an improvement, but if this is repeated many times, the cumulative effect can be considerable.

One downside to the optimization process is that the developer isn't certain exactly what the optimized code will look like. The source code statements are no longer an accurate road map to what the compiled and linked version of the code looks like. One technique that can be employed to assist in debugging optimized code in Visual C++ is to use the /Zi compiler option. This outputs a maximum amount of symbolic information from the compiler about the program. Another technique is to make greater use of the Disassembly and Register windows.

9.2.3.4 Oracle Developer/2000 Debugger. Oracle Developer/2000's Debugger includes a few additional features which aren't typical of GUI development tools. Features standard in most other development tools are included and are fairly complete.

9.2.3.4.1 Creating Breakpoints Like most debuggers, this one allows the tester to create breakpoints. Execution is suspended just before reaching the line on which the breakpoint is specified. Once execution is halted the Debugger's features can be used to inspect or modify the state of the program.

When a debug action is created, the breakpoint or debug trigger must be attached to a program unit source line that is an executable statement. Source statements are considered executable if they contain one or more statements for which the PL/SQL compiler generates code. For example, source lines containing assignment statements and procedure calls are executable. Code lines that contain comments, blank lines, declarations, or the NULL statement are not executable.

9.2.3.4.2 Debugger Panes The Developer/2000 Debugger window includes four main elements or panes: The Debugger menu and toolbar, the Source Pane, the Navigator pane, and the Interpreter pane.

9.2.3.4.2.1 Debugger Menu and Toolbar The first element consists of the Debugger Menu and Debugger Toolbar. The menu includes items that allow the tester to display each of the other panes. Other menu items allow the tester to initiate most Debugger functions. Some of the functions that can be initiated are:

- Display the Breakpoint Dialog Box. From this dialog box, breakpoints can be created.
- Display the Trigger Dialog Box from which debug triggers can be created.
- Execute the STEP command to step a specified number of instructions through the application.
- The Reset command returns control to an outer debug level without continuing execution in the current debug level.
- The Log command saves a transcript of Debugger input and output to a specified file.
- Disable the selected breakpoint.
- Enable the selected breakpoint.

The Debugger Toolbar includes icons for the following functions:

- Step Into. Directs the debugger to step into subprogram calls.
- Step Over. Prevents the debugger from stepping into subprograms
- Step Out. Resumes execution until the current subprogram has returned.
- Go. Resume program execution until the currently executing thread terminates or is interrupted by a debug action.
- Reset. Returns control to an outer debug level without continuing execution in the current debug level.
- Close. Runs the chosen form.

9.2.3.4.2.2 Source Pane The second pane of the Debugger is the Source pane. This element displays a read-only copy of the program unit currently selected in the Navigator pane. The Source pane contains line numbers along the left-hand margin which correspond to the line numbers of the displayed program unit.

9.2.3.4.2.3 Navigator Pane The Navigator pane is the third pane in the Debugger. It displays a hierarchical list of program units, attached libraries, debug actions, the stack, built-in subprogram packages, database objects, modules, global variables, system variables, and command line parameters. From the Navigator the tester can examine and alter system variables, global variables, and item values.

9.2.3.4.2.4 Interpreter Pane The final element of the debugger is the Interpreter pane. It provides a command line interface, allowing the tester to enter PL/SQL constructs and debugger commands. Commands can be entered and executed immediately against the database.

9.2.3.4.3 Debug Actions When a debug action is created, it is automatically assigned a unique numeric ID. While debugging, each debug action can be referred to by this ID. This ID allows users to browse, display, or modify a specific debug action via Oracle Forms debug commands.

9.2.3.4.3.1 Browsing Debug Actions The tester can display detailed information about one or more debug actions, including its ID, source location, and whether or not it is enabled. The source line to which a debug action is attached can also be displayed in the Source pane. Browsing debug actions is performed in the Navigator. The tester accomplishes this by expanding the Debug Actions node. The Navigator displays a list of the debug actions associated with the current form.

9.2.3.4.3.2 Disabling, Enabling, and Removing Debug Actions Specific debug actions can be temporarily disabled through the Navigator pane. This feature allows the tester to keep debug actions defined during the debug session but avoid stopping them temporarily. They can later be enabled. Debug actions can also be permanently deleted via the Navigator or Interpreter panes.

The current execution location specifies the next PL/SQL source line that will be executed. This is frequently referred to as the program counter, or PC. When the Debugger gains control of a program (e.g., when a breakpoint is encountered or via a step operation), the Source pane in the Debugger lists the source line associated with the current execution location.

9.2.3.4.3.3 Creating Debug Triggers Debug Triggers are a debugging function that aren't offered by any other debuggers. This allows the tester to create a trigger by associating a block of PL/SQL code with a specific source line within the program unit, trigger, or menu item command. When the source line is reached, the debug trigger executes.

9.2.3.4.3.4 Creating Persistent Debug Actions Debug actions created within the Debugger are not saved across debug sessions. Each time the tester starts a new debug session, all desired debug actions must be rebuilt. One technique for reusing breakpoints from session to session is to create them at design time. This can be accomplished by calling the BREAK built-in subprogram within the desired code. The BREAK built-in subprogram provides the same functionality as a breakpoint created within the Debugger.

The above method can also be used to create conditional breakpoints in a code module. This can be done by adding conditional logic when using the BREAK command. One example of this technique is:

```
IF :employee.sal > 7500 THEN
   Break;
END IF;
```

9.2.3.4.3.5 Examining the Stack The Debugger provided by Developer/2000 is unusual among GUI development tools in that it includes the capability to examine the stack. The stack represents the chain of subprogram calls starting from the initial entry point down to the currently executing subprogram. For example, if Procedure X calls Procedure Y which in turn calls Procedure Z, and a statement in Procedure Z is currently executing, the current call chain would appear as shown below:
Stack:

```
(0) X (Procedure Body) Line 13
(1) Y (Procedure Body) Line 32
(2) Z (Procedure Body) Line 15
```

Each procedure call is represented on the stack by a frame. A frame contains information about the corresponding procedure call—its name, local variable values, actual parameter values, and the next statement to be executed.

Oracle Forms follows the standard debugging convention of a downward growing stack. Newly entered subprograms are added to the bottom of the stack. In this manner, the earliest frame, which corresponds to the initial program entry point, sits on the top of the stack. The most recent frame, associated with the most deeply nested subprogram call, is at the bottom of the stack.

9.2.4 Shortcomings of Debuggers

Debuggers are very powerful tools for finding errors in application software. Like any tool there are situations where they are very useful and other situations where they are not quite as effective. Some of the conditions under which debuggers are not as effective are outlined in the following sections.

9.2.4.1 Timing.
Certain kinds of errors only occur under certain timing and sequence conditions. An example would be if the error only occurs if a particular sequence of user steps occur within a relatively small timing window. Errors of this kind are extremely hard to find, isolate, and reproduce. This causes them to be one of the more difficult classes of errors to debug.

Debuggers are particularly ill-suited to errors of this nature. The introduction of breakpoints into an application has a dramatic effect on the flow and timing of its execution. Previously, the timing of the application was controlled by the data and speed of the processor. Once breakpoint statements are inserted, the timing is dictated by the tester's thought time. Insertion of even a single breakpoint will very likely eliminate the possibility of discovering a timing-related problem.

9.2.4.2 Multiple Users.
In many, many cases a client/server system will execute flawlessly when only a single user is accessing it, but fall to pieces when a large number of users access it simultaneously. If all testing is done with only a single user, comprehensive testing has yet to be accomplished. Numerous problems won't manifest themselves until multiple users are accessing the system. Since the production environment of the system must support a number of users, the testing must include an emphasis on this factor.

The types of stresses that are introduced by multiple users are many. The most obvious ones are performance and resource utilization. Inadequate performance isn't usually a problem on a system with a single user. The CPU, disk drives, memory, and all other resources are able to be dedicated to that one user. Adding additional users results in these resources being divided among the various users. Not all systems handle multiple resource requests as efficiently as necessary.

A debugger is not as effective solving a performance problem because its use has the effect of slowing resource demands down to a fraction of what is normal. The debugger slows application execution down to the speed at which the tester can read and respond to the system. Human response time is an eternity compared to the time it takes the system to process resource requests. Consequently, if a debugger is used to analyze a resource or performance type problem, it frequently isn't possible to reproduce it.

9.2.4.3 Locks.   The majority of relational database management systems use a complex system of locks to allocate and protect system resources. Locks are used to allocate memory, buffers, data pages, and database tables to one specific user. The concept behind locks is that a requesting application is granted the sole use of a resource until that process voluntarily yields it. If a significant percentage of these resources are tied up for extensive periods of time, system performance degrades.

It has already been stated that human response time is extremely slow compared to an application's normal execution. An application that is being run via the debugger will almost certainly hold locks and resources for time periods much greater than normal. When this is the case, the normal locking and resource allocation scenarios are thrown out the window. It won't be possible to simulate a "normal" locking environment when the debugger is being utilized.

9.2.4.4 Deadlocks.   A deadlock is a situation where one process has one resource and wishes to obtain a second resource. At the same time another process has control of the second resource and wants access to the first. Since neither process is willing to give up the resource, they have until after they get the other resource, they become deadlocked. Relational database engines can recognize this situation and rectify it by killing one of the two processes. If an application has been properly designed with this problem in mind, deadlock situations are fairly rare.

When a debugger is being used by a tester, timing windows in which resources are kept locked widen considerably. Widening these windows can have the potential to make deadlocks much more common than would otherwise occur. When it comes to deadlocks and other locking problems, use of a debugger can tend to create problems instead of helping to solve them.

9.2.4.5 Stored Procedures.   Stored procedures are blocks of SQL code that execute at the server level. An application at the client machine level invokes a stored procedure by referencing it by name. In some cases one or more parameters may be passed by the calling process to the stored procedure. Some relational database engines allow result sets to be returned by a stored procedure to the caller, e.g., Sybase. Other database systems allow only a single value to be returned, e.g., Oracle.

A debugger resides and executes exclusively on the client machine. It isn't capable of executing, viewing, or controlling code on any other machine in a client/server system. With this limitation in mind, it should be obvious that if an error exists in a stored procedure, then a debugger at the client machine won't be able to analyze it. The closest it can come to helping with this problem is allowing the tester to view the value or result set returned by the stored procedure.

9.2.4.6 Remote Procedure Calls (RPC).   Remote procedure calls are similar to a stored procedure in that they constitute a block of executable code that resides on another computer. RPCs frequently reside on and execute on an application server. They are frequently utilized to enforce business rules. Since the debugger executes on the client machine, it cannot provide any insight into the internal workings of RPCs executing on other computers.

9.2.4.7 Third-Party Software.   Third-party software components are a common building block used when building a client/server system. These components may reside on and execute on just about any machine in the system. A frequent format of third-party software is a dynamic link library (DLL). Most debuggers provided by GUI tool sets are unable to create breakpoints in DLLs or other external modules. Without the ability to do this, the debugger is of little use in analyzing what transpires within such external components.

9.3 Other Tools Which Can Be Used for Debugging

The purpose of a debugger is to allow the developer or tester to "get inside" a program. By enabling the user to stop the program and view its registers and variables, the user can determine what is going wrong in the program. While a debugger can be an extremely useful tool, it isn't the only one available that gives an insight into what the program is doing. The following sections describe other tools which can be used to test and debug client/server systems.

9.3.1 Profilers

A *profiler* is an analysis tool used to examine the run-time behavior of programs. The information returned from a profiling tool can be used to determine which sections of a program are being executed more than others. This information can be used to determine what parts of the program will yield the greatest benefits when the program is tuned or optimized. If a module is only executed once a day, there won't be much benefit achieved by improving its efficiency. On the other hand, a module that executes once a second would be a worthy target of optimization.

While a profiler is not a debugging tool per se, it can be used to determine if parts of an application are executing more frequently than expected. For example, the developer expects that a certain module should be executed relatively infrequently. The profiler's output might make it evident that the module is being executed repeatedly. This information should cause the developer to investigate why it is being exercised more frequently than had been expected. The cause might be a logic error, a design problem, or a user training deficiency. In any event, the system should be investigated to determine what is occurring. This would be especially pertinent if the code in question was a large consumer of system resources.

One example of a profiler is the one included in Microsoft's Developer Studio. This profiler allows profiling to be done at the function or line level. Function-level profiling monitors the number of times a function was called and the amount of time that was spent in the function. It also provides a list of which functions were called as well as those which weren't called. Function-level profiling is faster than line profiling because it gathers less information.

Line profiling documents the number of times each line is executed (hit). It provides information on which lines were executed and those which weren't. While it is extremely useful, this type of profiling slows system performance down considerably. Performance is degraded drastically because the profiler inserts a debugging breakpoint for every line of source code in the module(s) being profiled. Line profiling also gathers and stores a significant amount of data. Consequently, this particular feature should not be overused. The best technique is to identify a narrow segment of the system and perform line profiling on only that code.

Whenever possible the scope of profiling should be limited to as few modules as possible. Only the modules under investigation should be profiled. This will reduce the amount of data generated as well as the execution time required to profile the application.

9.3.2 SQL Analyzers

One of the trickiest aspects of a client/server system is writing and testing the SQL statements that query the database. The amount of SQL code written for most systems does not usually represent a high proportion of the number of lines of code developed, but its impact is extremely far-reaching. For a number of reasons, SQL code can be difficult to thoroughly test.

A number of third-party tools are available that allow SQL queries to be trapped or traced, tuned, and corrected.

Some of the functions that are promised by tools of this nature include:

- Graphs which document the system requirements of trapped SQL statements.
- A display of SQL statements and pertinent details about them which have been trapped.
- Reports on disk I/O activity broken down by table spaces, database files, and database tables.
- A graph of the most resource-intensive SQL statements.
- Assistance tuning resource-hogging SQL statements.
- The ability to collect SQL statistics over an extended period of time.
- Expert advice on indices and their usage in the database.
- I/O bottleneck resolution.

Some of these third-party tools are equally effective on systems for which no source code is available. This is particularly advantageous when testing and deploying a third-party application. Frequently, systems that are either shrink-wrapped or "off the shelf" allow very little insight into their internal workings. The ability to analyze the efficiency of its SQL code allows the tester to present the vendor with specific comments instead of vague statements like "the system runs too slowly."

One drawback to tools of this nature is that they are generally specific to a single relational database vendor's product. If the client/server system being tested includes multiple vendors' databases, then a tool that addresses only a single vendor's product will be less than satisfactory.

9.3.3 Spy++, A Utility to Graphically View System Information

Spy++ is a Microsoft Win32-based tool that provides a detailed, graphical view of the processes, windows, window messages, and threads in the system. This information can be used to help resolve problems in client/server systems. The types of windows and information that are provided by SPY++ are described in the following paragraphs.

The first view Spy++ provides is a list of all windows and controls in the system. The windows lists are presented in a hierarchical, graphical format. By clicking on a special icon, that entry will be expanded to display other windows that are children of the first window. Details provided for each window include the class name and title. Additional information can be obtained about each window by double-clicking on it. A few of these additional details for each window include:

- Window caption. Text in the window caption field.
- Window handle. Unique identifying ID for this window.
- Window Style. Window style codes.
- Owner window. Handle ID of this window's owner window.
- Next window. Handle of the next sibling window in the same Z-order sequence.
- Process ID. ID of process that owns the thread which created this window.

The Processes view is the next type of information that can be accessed via Spy++. Microsoft Windows products are able to support multiple processes. Each of these processes can have one or more threads. Each thread can have one or more top-level windows associated with it. The Processes view window presents a graphical representation of all processes, threads, and windows currently running in the system. Details on each process include the following:

- Process ID. Unique ID of the process.
- Module name. Name of the module.
- Base priority. Current Base priority of the process.
- Threads. Count of threads currently active under this process.

The Threads view is a listing of all threads in the system. It also displays the windows associated with each thread. Some of the property details that are displayed for each Thread include:

- Module name. Name of the module.
- Thread ID. Unique ID of the thread.
- Process ID. Unique ID of the process.

- Current priority. Current dynamic priority of the thread.
- Base priority. Current Base priority of the process.

Each window in the system has associated with it a stream of messages. The Messages View window allows the user to view this message stream. Details which appear in this window include:

- Window handle. Unique ID of the window.
- Nesting level. Depth of nesting at which this message appeared.
- Message. Number, status, and name of windows messages.
- lResult. Value of the lResult parameter.
- wParam. Value of the wParam parameter.
- lParam. Value of the lParam parameter.

9.3.4 ODBC SQL Driver Trace

Many client/server systems use an ODBC interface to connect the client-based front-end interface with a relational database running on the server machine. The ODBC Driver Manager Trace function records information about ODBC API calls made by a front-end (e.g. PowerBuilder, Visual Basic), and an ODBC data source. This information is written to a log file. Information available through this log file can help to:

- Identify and resolve problems connecting with the database via ODBC.
- Understand what the user interface on the client machine is doing internally.
- Provide useful information should a call to a vendor prove to be necessary.

Like many other utilities that gather information on client/server systems and communications, there are two caveats that should be kept in mind. First, executing a system with the trace feature on will have a definite impact on performance. Second, a significant amount of data can be output to the log file. It's best to turn tracing on only when it is needed and turn it back off as soon as possible. Otherwise, applications will likely run noticeably slower and disk space can become much scarcer.

CHAPTER 10

Capture/Playback Test Tools

Capture/playback test tools represent the first level of automated testing. They can be used in a large number of testing situations to automate testing. Although they don't obviate the need for user involvement in the testing process, they represent a significant improvement over completely manual testing.

10.1 Capture/Playback Fundamentals

The fundamental concept of capture/replay testing products is that the test tool captures all user interactions with the application and database server. This includes keystrokes, mouse movement, menu selections, drag-and-drop operations, and button clicks. Responses which the user sees, i.e., windows changing, drop-down list boxes appearing, messages returned, and dialogue windows displayed are recognized and captured. All activity is stored in the form of a test script. At a later time when the script is replayed, the test tool initiates the same actions which were originally performed by the user. The expectation is that since input is the same, the system will respond in exactly the same way both times. Responses which occur during the testing phase are compared with those which occurred during the original cycle. Differences in responses are documented by the testing software. This enables the tester to determine if new or different errors have been introduced into the software.

Test tools typically require that a "capture" program be initiated and then the tester simply steps through the functions of the application. SQA Robot, a product by SQA, Inc., has an intuitive interface. The tester initiates SQA Robot, sets the desired recording options, names the output file (or accepts the system-generated name), and starts recording. The user can pause or terminate recording at any time. When the user is satisfied with the test procedure, then he or she simply needs to stop recording.

While recording with a capture/playback tool, the tester frequently has the option of inserting objects into the test script being generated. Some of the objects which can be added to a test procedure include the following:

■ Testcases. Capture specific conditions, states, or values during test procedure recording and store the data as the expected baseline for the application under test.

- Wait states. Provide a way to synchronize test procedure playback with the application under test. Setting wait states lets the tester define specific conditions for which the test procedure waits before continuing with subsequent test actions. Several of the many examples of such conditions are waiting until a specified file exists, waiting until the contents of two specified files match, and waiting until a selected window exactly matches the recorded window image.

- Timers. Allow the insertion of start and stop time commands to record the duration of events in a test procedure, such as database or network access.

- Insert calls to existing test procedures or other applications.

Capture/playback test tools are extremely well suited for GUI client/server systems. Tools of this nature aren't retread versions of character-oriented testing tools. They have been developed specifically for testing GUI, client/server systems. Some of their characteristics which enable them to work so well with GUI systems are described in the following sections.

10.1.1 Graphical Interfaces

One of the primary advantages of client/server systems is that their graphical nature allows users to be more productive. There's no reason why similar gains in productivity can't be experienced by application testers. Most current test tool sets are highly graphical. Test execution is activated by pointing and clicking icons in the test product's graphical interface. Test tools are replete with menus, toolbars, drop and drag, multidocument interfaces (MDI), drop down list boxes and other GUI features. These graphical interfaces allow testing personnel to be more productive.

10.1.2 Easy to Use

Test tools which are easier to use can be utilized by less technically proficient personnel. A graphical interface eliminates the necessity to memorize obscure codes, commands, and key combinations. Easy-to-use tools enable end users to become more heavily involved in the testing process. Greater end-user involvement has two major advantages. First, it allows them to get their hands on the system earlier. This will let them find errors sooner and give them a greater sense of ownership. Secondly, having the end users perform more of the testing has the effect of freeing up developers for fixing errors or completing the development work. Almost all of the new generation of tools are sufficiently friendly to allow application users to work with them with a minimal amount of training.

10.1.3 Capable of Testing Multiple Hardware and Software Platforms

One major way in which client/server systems differ drastically from traditional, mainframe systems is in the diversity of hardware and software involved. Software for a mainframe system had to work with one CPU, one operating system, and one type of dumb terminal. Client/server systems, in contrast, must function in a heterogeneous world. The database server might be a Sun UNIX box running Sybase or Oracle as the database engine. An application server might be a Windows NT system. The client machines will most likely be a hodgepodge of different makes and models of workstations. To make matters worse, the client workstation will probably be running a medley of operating systems. There will almost certainly be Windows 3.11 systems on some of the client machines. Likely there will also be client workstations which are operating under Windows for WorkGroups, Windows 95, Windows NT Workstation, X-terminals, and OS/2. All of these environments must be tested. To be effective, the capture/playback should be able to function on most (if not all) of them.

10.1.4 GUI Objects Are Recognized and Handled

GUI development packages build applications from objects. Examples of objects are windows, data windows, menus, toolbars, check boxes, drop-down list boxes, and buttons. To be an effective test tool, it must be capable of handling objects and not be mislead by minor changes in appearance or position.

The new generation of test tools was designed to handle object-oriented development packages. SQA Robot by SQA, Inc., for example, recognizes standard Windows objects such as CheckBoxes, RadioButtons, PushButtons, ComboBoxes, ListBoxes, and EditBoxes. SQA Robot even handles environment-specific objects such PowerBuilder DataWindows, Visual Basic Custom Controls (VBXs), and SQLWindows Table Windows. If objects in the user interface change locations, tests will pass because SQA Robot scripts are not location dependent. In addition, scripts require no maintenance as applications undergo cosmetic changes to the graphical user interface (GUI).

10.1.5 Unattended Testing

Unattended testing is the ability for a testing staff member to initiate a test session and be able to walk away from the testing station. The test tool is able to continue running the session by replaying one or more test scripts. The concept of unattended testing also implies that the test tool will be able to handle unforeseen circumstances gracefully. The optimum method of dealing with an unforeseen situation would be to document it in a log and bypass it. This allows the tester to determine later what happened, but in the meantime the tests could continue on.

Unattended running of test scripts is provided by many test tool packages. AutoTester Client/Server by AutoTester, Inc. stores test results in a database for a complete history of errors and an audit trail of what has, and has not, been tested. It also includes sophisticated automatic recovery capabilities that allow true unattended testing to be accomplished. Automatic recovery scenarios handle unexpected conditions as they occur, so that testing can continue without operator intervention. Tests can be run unattended at night, extending the amount of testing which can be accomplished each day.

10.1.6 Comparison Tools

As tests are being played back, the responses (e.g., text fields, list boxes, radio buttons, etc.) are compared to a baseline which was captured when the test originally ran. If the test program observes a difference between the original responses and the current responses, then the test is declared a failure. The failure will be logged so the testing staff can investigate it once the entire test operation has completed. The logging function becomes increasingly important as the number of tests within a test cycle increases. If the testing cycle includes hundreds or thousands of individual tests, then a test log allows the testing staff to quickly recognize the tests which have failed.

The specific differences which caused the test to be declared a failure may not be immediately obvious. It might be that one row differs in a grid or table with a large number of rows. It might be a difference in a graphical object being displayed. The difference could be as subtle as a command button being disabled. No matter what the difference was, the tester must be able to detect it before she can investigate the problem. Time spent searching for the cause of the test failure represents time which could have been spent solving the error.

Most capture/playback tools provide a set of utilities which allow the tester to compare baseline results with the test results which were declared a failure. These capabilities frequently include one or more tools for specific types of comparisons. A text comparison tool is fairly standard. The text comparison tool addresses differences in purely textual data areas such as menus, list boxes, text entry fields, etc. A tool to compare bitmaps is also fairly common. This tool compares the visual appearance of large areas of windows.

10.2 When to Use Capture/Playback Test Tools

While capture/playback test tools are extremely useful and productive, they aren't a panacea to all testing problems and scenarios. There are some testing situations when they are more appropriately used than others. What phases of testing are capture/playback tools especially useful for? Each of the major testing phases and the applicability of capture/playback tools are discussed in the following sections.

10.2.1 Unit Testing

Unit testing is a fairly rough-and-tumble operation. If the system is being developed under a RAD paradigm, things might still be in a state of flux when unit testing begins. The application, specifically the interface, is still subject to change during this time period.

Unit testing is normally left to the individual developer to perform. Tests are designed, run, and interpreted by the developer. Since the system will likely change, it won't be guaranteed that tests designed during this phase will be meaningful during later testing phases. This being the case, the time required to capture test steps may not be worth the investment.

When all of the previous items are taken into consideration, it shouldn't be a surprise that the use of a capture/playback tool might not be appropriate for unit testing. The biggest reason is that these tools weren't designed to make the first testing cycle easier. They were developed to make later test cycles faster and more reproducible. Since unit testing doesn't emphasize running the same tests multiple times, there is little to no efficiency gained by using these tools at this time.

10.2.2 Integration Testing

Integration marks a point at which the design and testing of a system start to mature. While errors are still being found, the number of changes hopefully are significantly fewer than during the unit testing stage. Tests which are used during this phase have reached a level of maturity where they won't be changing so frequently.

Integration testing also is something of a watershed when performing the same tests many times. A suite of tests will be defined for integration testing. The tests will be run. If the software being integrated fails the tests, then it will be handed back to the developers to be corrected. When they have finished making their changes, the same suite of integration tests will be performed. If certain parts of the software fail during the second iteration of testing, then the developers are again handed the software to be corrected. This cycle of testing/failing/fixing may be repeated many times.

The need to repeat tests until the software passes fits in perfectly with the abilities of capture/playback test tools. Capture/playback tools make it easy to repeat tests over and over again. Each repetition of the tests can be performed with minimal effort and guaranteed accuracy.

10.2.3 System Testing

System testing takes advantage of another strong point of capture/playback testing tools. Its strength is that tests are reproduced accurately each time the test is run. By the time a client/server system enters the system testing phase, the system and the tests have firmed up considerably. Fewer changes to the tests means less time spent recreating or modifying test scripts. This translates into even greater re-use of scripts and higher efficiency.

The tests which are performed during system testing can be based heavily upon the tests designed for the integration testing. Since capture/playback tools have a great deal of accuracy when rerunning tests, preexisting test scripts can be used and trusted.

10.2.4 Regression Testing

If there is one phase of client/server testing in which capture/playback test tools can have the biggest potential impact, it would be regression testing. When done correctly, manually performing regression testing on any computer system requires an incredible amount of time, effort, and resources. Client/server systems are no exception to this statement. Adequately regression testing a system requires that virtually every test performed to date be repeated. Each test result must be compared to the expected result, and any deviations need to be documented.

Deviations need to be investigated to determine why they occurred. The deviation may be explained away as the result of a system enhancement or correction. Frequently, though, the deviation is the direct result of an error which has been introduced into the system. Virtually every change in a client/server system has the potential to cause errors in far-removed parts of the system. Regression testing is intended to catch errors of this nature in client/server systems.

Regression testing needs to be performed under a surprisingly broad variety of situations. Some of the circumstances which necessitate regression testing include:

- New builds of the client/server system being developed.
- New releases of the operating system on the client or server platforms.
- Updates to the communications software which ties clients and servers together.
- New versions of the database management system.
- Updates to the development tool being used.

Because regression testing represents such a large commitment of time and resources, as a rule, it isn't done frequently enough or thoroughly enough. Most development shops either ignore regression testing completely or skimp on the regression testing which is performed. The existence of a capture/playback tool and a complete set of test scripts can make this type of testing much, much easier. These tools minimize the amount of manual testing which must be done. If regression testing is easier to do, then there's a significantly greater chance that it will be done.

10.3 Tips for Developing Test Scripts

Good tests scripts don't just appear; they have to be designed. The quality of tests can be improved if consistent design steps are followed. Some tips for designing consistent, good test scripts are listed in the following sections.

10.3.1 Testing a Single Function

One of the fundamental design principles of structured programming is that each module should fulfill only a single function. No module should be designed to perform multiple differing functions. One of the primary reasons for this is modularity. If a component performs a number of functions, it isn't as likely to be re-used because not many situations will arise which call for exactly those functions. If, on the other hand, the component focuses on a single function, it can be called to perform that function from many other modules.

Another reason against having a module performing multiple functions is complexity. Modules which are forced to address different functions quickly become very complex. The code in a complex module gets messy fast. Frequently modules of this nature have multiple entry points or multiple exit points. Another complication is that one or more flags are frequently used. These flags dictate which processing should be performed. Errors are more likely to occur in modules with complex code. If the module later has to be modified (was there ever a module which didn't need to be modified?) it will be more difficult to maintain than a simpler module.

Test scripts should be designed under the same principles. No test script should be designed to test more than a single function. By sticking to testing a single function, the test can be focused. It will also have only two possible outcomes: either the test failed or it passed. If a script tests two functions, there can be four outcomes; functions A and B both passed, A passed and B failed, A failed and B passed, and both A and B failed. Handling four possible outcomes is significantly more difficult than handling only two.

Short, focused test scripts are easier to maintain than long, rambling scripts. A short script with an error would be easier to understand and modify than a script which attempts to test many functions.

Sometimes changes do occur in the user interface of an application. The change might represent an enhancement or just an alteration in user desires. Any change will require one or more test scripts to be rerun or modified to adapt. If a given script tests a number of items in an application, then that script will need to be altered if any of the many items change. It would be much easier to identify and modify one short test script to address a single change.

10.3.2 Consistent Steps in Test Scripts

Each individual test script should have certain identifiable steps. These steps are as follows:

1. Move the application from an initial, known window to the window which is to be tested.
2. Test the application's function and compare it to the baseline state.
3. Return the application to its original window.

By following the above conceptual steps, the following advantages are achieved:

1. Testcases are independent; they shouldn't rely on preceding tests running or passing.
2. Testcases can be strung together in any order.

10.3.3 Each Test Is Amenable to Building Larger Scripts

Many test tools allow individual test scripts to be combined to build a larger test plan. The user defines which test should be performed first, which should go second, etc. A number of tests can be grouped together to test a subsystem. All of the subsystem tests can be concatenated to define the complete system test.

The first tip was that each test performs a single test. The second tip was that each test script should expect to start and conclude at a known window. If these two suggestions are followed, it makes it easier for each individual test to be part of a larger test script. If each test script doesn't begin and end at a known place, then it will be much more difficult to combine them into a larger test plan.

10.3.4 Start Early

Building test scripts can be started in the early stages of development. User interface objects such as menus and dialog boxes are usually built fairly early in the project and don't undergo much change. Test scripts for objects such as these can be done during initial testing efforts. If these test scripts follow the suggestions that tests begin and end at a known place in the application, then they can easily be combined with other scripts to build comprehensive test procedures.

10.3.5 Minimize Other Activity on the Client Machine

During the period when a test is being recorded, other applications and activity on the client machine should be minimized. This will help assure that replay operations won't be confused or distracted by interrupts caused by other applications. The exception to this would be if the test is specifically attempting to stress the client machine. In this case it would be beneficial to run as many other applications as feasible.

10.3.6 Naming Conventions

By the time the testing of the system is complete, there will be a large number of test scripts, error logs, and other objects produced by the testing activities. A standardized naming convention needs to be established and adhered to. This might include standardizing names and suffixes for all files. Directory structures also need to have naming conventions applied to them. If no conventions exist or if existing conventions are not enforced, it will be difficult (or impossible) to find any particular test object.

10.3.7 Use Complete Path Specifications

Whenever a file, executable, script, etc., is referred to, use the complete path specification. The compete path specification would include the drive letter and all subdirectories. Doing this will help cut down on referring to incorrect files or old files.

10.3.8 Use Mouse Clicks Instead of the Tab Key

During test capture operations, it is better to use mouse clicks to position the cursor instead of the Tab key. Using the Tab key assumes that the Tab order hasn't changed within the application window. While this assumption is probably correct, it isn't guaranteed to be so.

10.4 Drawbacks of Capture/Playback Test Tools

As useful as capture/playback test tools are, they don't (yet) remove the human factor from testing. A human being still has to develop tests, correctly execute them (at least once), and capture them in a script. If this isn't done, then replay tools can't be utilized.

10.4.1 Garbage In–Garbage Out

Like many other areas of computer testing, capture/playback tools are affected by the "garbage in–garbage out" rule. The use of a capture/playback tool doesn't automatically improve the quality of the tests being run. It merely allows them to be run faster. If the tests developed are neither thorough nor correct, then running them faster won't contribute to the improvement of a system's quality.

10.4.2 Test Object Management

Once test scripts have been correctly built, they must be properly managed. They need to be documented to detail what system functions they address. They also need to be stored in such a manner that they can be found and re-used when needed. If the testing staff doesn't know what tests have been developed or what aspect of the system each one addresses, then they won't be of much use.

10.4.3 Test Output Must Be Examined

The output from playback sessions must be meticulously examined. These tools frequently allow test scripts to continue running after an error has been encountered. The error is simply documented and testing continues. Just because the test script completes is no guarantee that the test was performed successfully. If the final display makes it look like the test was successful, it becomes easy to forget about checking the error logs. If error output logs aren't checked after each test script runs, then no one will know the system includes errors until customers start reporting problems.

10.5 Specific Tools

A number of capture/playback tools are available on the market. Some of these tools are part of suites, while others address only the capture/playback test niche. Several tools and their capabilities are discussed here. This section is not meant to be a complete list of tools which are available, nor is it meant to be a thorough review or analysis of each tool's capability. Once again, the mention or absence of a tool here is not meant to be either an endorsement or a rebuke of a tool.

10.5.1 SQA's Robot

SQA Robot is one component in the SQA Suite. This set of tools is an integrated product suite for automating the testing of client/server applications developed for the Microsoft Windows environment. SQA combines client/server testing tools, project management tools, and a formal methodology for testing enterprise-level client/server applications.

10.5.1.1 Platforms.   SQA Robot runs on the following operating systems:

- Windows 3.1.
- Windows 95.
- Windows NT.

Tests recorded on a 32-bit application can also be played back on a 16-bit version of the same application. Similarly, tests recorded on the 16-bit version of an application can also be used on a 32-bit version of the application. This capability will be greatly appreciated by an organization which supports both 16- and 32-bit platforms. It can also be comforting knowledge to an organization which intends to migrate from 16- to 32-bit platforms in the future and would like to be able to use existing test scripts to validate the new platform.

10.5.1.2 Repository.   SQA Suite and SQA Robot maintain the information they require and generate in a database repository. When SQA Suite is installed, the option is given to utilize either a Sybase or Microsoft Access database as the repository. This repository is available to any member of the testing staff.

SQA Robot arranges testing information on a project basis. Inside SQA Robot, multiple projects can be defined and relevant information on each project is stored in the repository. Information maintained on each project include test procedures, testcases, and defect information. Complex systems being testing can be partitioned and stored as multiple smaller projects.

10.5.1.3 Language.   The default scripting language used by SQA Robot is SQABasic. This language is completely compatible with Microsoft's Visual Basic language. The other alternative language is Visual Basic itself. By utilizing a standard language for its script, SQA Robot doesn't require testing personnel to learn and become fluent with yet another language. Figure 10.1 provides an example of SQA Basic code.

Commands in SQA Robot test procedures can be grouped into four types. These types are:

- Control flow commands. These commands define the beginning and end of SQA Robot scripts. They also mark the begin and end

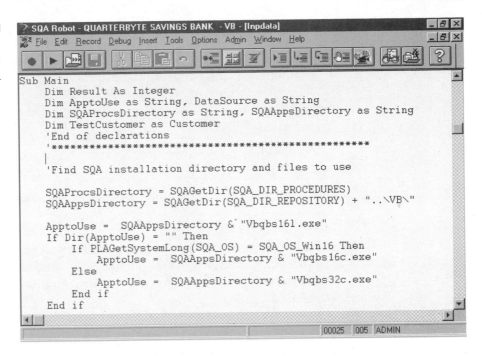

Figure 10.1
Example of SQA Basic
Code

```
Sub Main
    Dim Result As Integer
    Dim ApptoUse as String, DataSource as String
    Dim SQAProcsDirectory as String, SQAAppsDirectory as String
    Dim TestCustomer as Customer
    'End of declarations
    '******************************************************

    'Find SQA installation directory and files to use

    SQAProcsDirectory = SQAGetDir(SQA_DIR_PROCEDURES)
    SQAAppsDirectory = SQAGetDir(SQA_DIR_REPOSITORY) + "..\VB\"

    ApptoUse =  SQAAppsDirectory & "Vbqbs161.exe"
    If Dir(ApptoUse) = "" Then
        If PLAGetSystemLong(SQA_OS) = SQA_OS_Win16 Then
            ApptoUse =  SQAAppsDirectory & "Vbqbs16c.exe"
        Else
            ApptoUse =  SQAAppsDirectory & "Vbqbs32c.exe"
        End if
    End if
```

of commands which save or restore windows. The final tasks control flow commands perform are the initialization and termination of test procedures playback operations. Examples of control flow commands include:

- InitPlay. Initializes playback of a test procedure script.
- EndPlay. Designates the end of a test procedure playback operation.
- EndSaveWindowPositions. Ends scripts commands which save positions of window restorations.
- StartSaveWindowPositions. Begins script commands which save window positions.

- User action commands. These commands correspond to user actions or activities which occur in the application during recording. Examples of user action commands include:

  - AnimateControl. Initiates action of an animation object.
  - CheckBox. Initiates action on a check box.
  - Desktop. Initiates a Windows desktop action.
  - InputKeys. Forwards keystrokes to the active window.

- MenuSelect. Performs a menu selection operation.

- Testcase commands. Compares state of objects from baseline data with status of object during the playback operation. If the value or state of the objects are the same, the testcase passes. If the value or state of the objects differ, the testcase fails. Examples of testcase commands include:

  - CheckBoxTC. Testcase of a check box.
  - ComboBoxTC. Testcase of a combo box.
  - ListViewTC. Testcase of a list view.
  - SpinControlTC. Testcase of a spin control.

- Utility commands. Utility commands set wait times, call other test procedures, start and stop times, and start other applications. They are also used to direct output to test logs. Examples of utility commands include:

  - CallProcedure. Invokes another test procedure.
  - StartTimer. Starts a timer and outputs a message to the test log.
  - StopTimer. Stops the specified time and outputs elapsed time to the test log.
  - WriteLogMessage. Writes a message to the test log.

10.5.1.4 Help Facility. Online help is available at all times inside SQA Robot. Help can be invoked by pressing the F1 function key, selecting the Help menu item, or clicking the Help button on the toolbar. Once inside the Help facility, the user can choose from Help contents or SQABasic language commands.

Four toolbars providing buttons for frequently used menu commands are available in SQA Robot. Active buttons are displayed in color, while inactive buttons are grayed out. Tool tips for each button are displayed when the cursor pauses over a toolbar button. All four toolbars can be floating, resized, and customized. Users are also allowed to create their own custom toolbars. Table 10.1 provides a list of the capabilities of each of the standard toolbars.

10.5.1.5 Test Scripts. SQA Robot records test procedures in the repository. A test procedure is a sequence of steps or user actions required to execute one or more testcases. When a test procedure is recorded by SQA

Robot, a test script is being generated which tracks each action included in the test. The test procedure becomes the baseline of expected behavior. In the future when the test script is replayed, the results will be compared to results recorded in this test procedure. Any differences in the results will be recorded as a possible failure of the software.

Recording a test in SQA Robot is relatively uncomplicated. The steps which are required are listed in Table 10.2.

■ Testcases. A testcase captures and records data on the state of an object in the application being tested. Testcases are inserted into the script so the baseline state of the object can be recorded and compared with the state of the same object when the test script is replayed. During playback the baseline data is compared with the test results obtained during the replay. If a difference is detected, the testcase fails. Examples of objects which testcases can be based on include:

■ Data entry fields.
■ The Clipboard.
■ Data windows.
■ File comparison.
■ File existence.
■ List boxes.
■ Menus.
■ Software module in memory.
■ Object properties.
■ Data in OCXs/VBXs.
■ Table objects.

TABLE 10.1 SQA Robot Toolbar Definitions	Standard toolbar	Allows users to record, play back, edit, and debug test scripts, insert new recorded actions into existing scripts, start other SQA Suite applications, and invoke the online help facility.
	Record toolbar	Enables the user to pause, stop, view the SQA Robot main window, and display the Insert toolbar during recording operations.
	Insert toolbar	Allows a number of types of insert operations to be performed. Test cases, wait states, and comments can be inserted into the test procedure script during a recording session.
	Debug toolbar	Assists the user when a recorded test procedure is being edited or debugged. It includes buttons for debugging and editing scripts, starting other SQA Suite applications, and starting online help.

TABLE 10.2

Steps to Capture
an SQA Robot Test

1. Start the application and position it at the desired position (window, form, etc.)

2. Initiate SQA Robot.

3. Choose File-> Record Test Procedure to display the Record Test Procedure dialog box

4. Enter the name of the test procedure being created by either typing it or selecting it from a list

5. Begin testing by clicking the OK button

6. Step through the application by using it as a user would. All activity at this point is being recorded.

7. The capture process can be paused by clicking the Pause toolbar button.

8. Recording can be resumed by clicking the Pause button a second time. For continuity, the application being tested should be in the same state when recording is resumed.

- Active windows.

- Bitmap comparisons.

- Wait states. Wait states provide a mechanism for synchronizing test procedures with the application being tested. When the test is being played back, each script command will wait for up to 20 seconds for the application to respond. If the application requires additional time for a response to occur, then a wait state should be inserted. Examples of such events are for the database to respond, disk files to be created, or a modem to connect. Wait states allow the test script to pause until these events occur before continuing with subsequent test actions.

- Timers. The tester can insert timer commands into test procedures. Timer commands can be used to record the duration of system activities. Examples of activities which might be timed include database access operations, network access functions, and disk I/O operations. One useful application of timers is to time how long it takes to complete a series of standard user operations. This test script can then be run on a number of user machines which have different hardware configurations to determine how the client hardware affects performance. Timer values recorded during the test script playback are displayed in the SQA Test Log Viewer. Multiple timers can be created during a test script. Timers are allowed to overlap, i.e., timer01 can be running when timer02 is started.

- Comments. At any time during the testing operation, the tester is free to pause the test and insert comments into the test procedure.

These comments will appear in the test script with an apostrophe in the first column.

■ Calls to other test scripts. Calls to other test scripts can be included in any test script. This would enable one test to chain another to it.

■ Application calls. An application can be invoked from within a test procedure. This would enable a second application to be started without requiring any intervention on the part of testers.

The process of recording test procedures creates a test script. This script is an ASCII file and it resides in the \Repository\Project\PROCS directory. SQA Robot begins each test script with a two-line comment listing the time and date that the script was created and the name of the test procedure. As mentioned earlier, the language used to produce test scripts is either SQABasic or Visual Basic.

10.5.1.6 Playing Back Test Scripts.   After a test script has been created with SQA Robot, it must be played back to be of any use. There are two types of test procedure playbacks. The first should occur immediately after the script has been created. This playback is performed to validate that the script has been successfully captured. The other type of playback is to actually test the application. Both types of playback operations are initiated in the same way. The steps to perform an SQA Robot playback are listed in Table 10.3.

TABLE 10.3 Steps to Replay an SQA Robot Test	1. Return the client machine environment to the same state it was in when the test script was captured. This means that the same applications should be running, windows be open, etc. The application being tested also needs to be in the same state as when the script was originally created.
	2. Decide what the SQA Robot options setting will be. These options determine how SQA Robot will handle inexact matches, what will be logged, what recovery actions will be taken, and how unexpected windows will be handled.
	3. Initiate playback of the test procedure. SQA Robot allows a test procedure to be initiated by simply selecting the File	Playback Test Procedure menu item. A dialog box allows a choice of which test procedure will be initiated.
	4. View the results to determine whether the test passed or failed. This can be done by utilizing the SQA Test Log Viewer. It displays pass/fail results for test procedures. If the test failed, determine whether it's because an error occurred or the application has undergone a change.
	5. If the problem was caused by an error, then generate a defect entry in SQA's "correct the error."
	6. If the application has changed, then run SQA Robot in capture mode to update this particular test's baseline.

10.5.1.7 Handling Unexpected Windows. A client machine on a client/server system doesn't exist in a vacuum. It will undoubtedly be connected to the server via a LAN. There most likely are users and processes on the LAN which have nothing to do with the client/server system being developed and tested. Sometimes during the testing process, unwanted messages or other activity generated by other users or processes will appear on the client machine while tests are being performed. Examples of such intrusions include e-mail messages, network error announcements, messages from the LAN administrator asking people to log off, warnings that network disk drivers are full, etc.

If these messages appear during the recording of a test procedure, the result is a minor inconvenience. The test will simply need to be rerecorded over again from the beginning. If, however, an unexpected message appears during an unattended test playback session, it can represent a much bigger problem. If the test tool being used doesn't recognize that this message is an extraneous event, it could abort or mislead the test session. If the test session is a regression test which is running all night, then the repercussions can be severe. The test staff will be disappointed to see that the regression testing didn't run to completion during the night.

SQA Robot has the capability to recognize and recover from unexpected windows. The user sets options to predetermine how unexpected windows will be handled. Choices for dealing with these occurrences include the following:

- Capture Screen Image. Directs SQA Robot to capture a bitmap image of the unexpected window's screen. When a test script is being run unattended, this will allow the tester to view the screen at a later time.

- Send Key. A keystroke which will be sent to the unexpected window. The default value is the Escape key, but any alphabetic key or the Enter key can be selected.

- Select Pushbutton With Focus. SQA Robot will click the push button which has focus.

- Send WM_CLOSE to Window. SQA Robot sends a Windows WM_CLOSE message to the unexpected window. This is the functional equivalent of clicking the Windows Close button.

The three previous options are attempts to deal with the unexpected window. If the unexpected window cannot be removed, the user has several other options. These options include:

■ Continue Running Test Procedure. SQA Robot will continue running the test procedure at the script command which follows the command which caused the unexpected window to appear. This option may cause repeated script failures to occur.

■ Skip Current Test Procedure. Halt playback of the current test procedure. If this test procedure was called from within another procedure then playback will continue in the calling procedure.

■ Abort Playback. Test procedures are halted completely.

10.5.1.8 Error Recovery. SQA Robot offers the test staff a number of options to dictate how it will handle error situations during playback. Examples of errors which can occur include script command failures during playback, testcase failures during playback, and general protection faults (GPFs) during playback. Choices include:

■ Continue Execution. Test procedure continues playing back. Failure incident is recorded in test log.

■ Skip Current Procedure. Current test procedure terminates. If the current procedure was called from another test procedure, then playback resumes in the calling procedure.

■ Abort Playback. All playback activity halts completely.

The users also have the option of capturing certain system data if a GPF occurs during playback. GPF information is saved in a log file. Figure 10.2 displays the error recovery information which can be captured and logged. Details which the user can choose to capture include:

■ Stack Trace. Contents of the stack for noncurrent tasks.

■ Module and Class Lists. Module and class list information will be captured.

■ Heap and Memory Statistics. System heap and memory manager information for 16-bit applications will be retained.

■ Heap Dump. Contents of the system heap will be captured for 16-bit applications.

■ Notify Script. Control will be released to the currently executing test procedure.

10.5.1.9 Comparison Tools. SQA Robot includes a test log viewer and three specific comparison tools for assisting the testing staff. These help

Figure 10.2
Error Recovery
Options

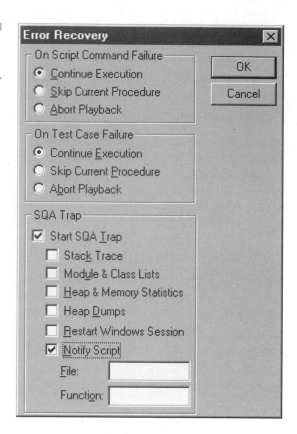

determine the cause of a test failure. SQA refers to these tools as comparators. Scanning through the test log viewer allows the tester to quickly identify tests which have failed. Double-clicking on a failed test entry will automatically activate the appropriate test comparison tool.

The three comparator tools included in the SQA Suite product are the Image Comparator, the Object Properties Comparator and the Text Comparator. Each of these tools can be invoked from the test log viewer, SQA Manager, SQA Robot, SQA LoadTest, or the Windows desktop. SQA LoadTest is a component which will be introduced in Chapter 11.

10.5.1.9.1 Image Comparator The purpose of the SQA Image Comparator is to view and compare bitmap images generated by SQA Robot. These images were captured because a test SQA Robot that was running failed. A number of differences might cause such a failure, among them:

- Fields which no longer appear on a window.
- Changes in labels on a window.

■ Differences in the font used.

■ Color changes for labels, windows, fields, etc.

■ Differing values in list boxes, text fields, etc.

■ Radio buttons with different selections.

By using the capabilities of the image comparator, the testing staff can quickly and easily identify differences between the baseline or master image and the image of the test which failed. Table 10.4 lists some of the methods by which the image comparator enables the tester to recognize differences between images.

TABLE 10.4

Image Comparator Functions

Function	Description
Display Summary Information	Displays summary information about the current master and failed image files.
Locate First Difference	Locates the first difference between the images and zooms in on that area.
Locate All Differences	Displays an inverted box around all differences between the windows.
View Master Image	Displays the master image of the current test case.
View Failed Image	Displays the failed image of the current test case.
Blink	Toggles between the master image and the failed image. This allows the tester to visually compare them.
Overlapped	Overlaps both images. The areas where differences occur will be quite noticeable.
View Masks	Masked areas on an image can be defined during the test definition. Each mask will be highlighted by an inverted color rectangle.
Zoom	Small details of an image can be zoomed in on.
Actual Size	Returns a zoomed image to its original size.
View Oldest Failed Image	If more than one failed image for this test has been captured, then display the oldest failed image.
View Previous Failed Image	If more than one failed image for this test has been captured, then display the previous failed image.
View Next Failed Image	If more than one failed image for this test has been captured, then display the next failed image.
View Newest Failed Image	If more than one failed image for this test has been captured, then display the newest failed image.

10.5.1.9.2 Object Properties Comparator When a test procedure is created with SQA Robot, a test can be inserted to capture the properties of standard windows objects. This capability is referred to as an Object Properties testcase. An example of the types of objects which might be captured include labels, command buttons, combination boxes, edit boxes, radio buttons, etc. Specialized support is provided for a number of environment-specific objects such as PowerBuilder DataWindows, SQLWindows, Table Windows, Centura Table Windows, Visual Basic objects, VBXs, and OCXs. The properties which are captured and can be compared include whether the object is visible, enabled, blinking, or colored. Its current position can also be captured. Property information is written and maintained in a disk file. Figure 10.3 displays an example of the Object Properties Comparator.

When tests are replayed later, the test might fail because an object has changed. The Object Properties Comparator allows the tester to view and compare the properties of the object in the initial test and the later test. Table 10.5 describes the capabilities the Object Properties Comparator provides to help determine what object difference caused the test to fail.

10.5.1.9.3 Text Comparator The SQA Text Comparator allows the tester to view and compare text-type data which has been captured during test playback operations. SQA Robot testcases can capture data from the following sources:

Figure 10.3
Object Properties
Comparator

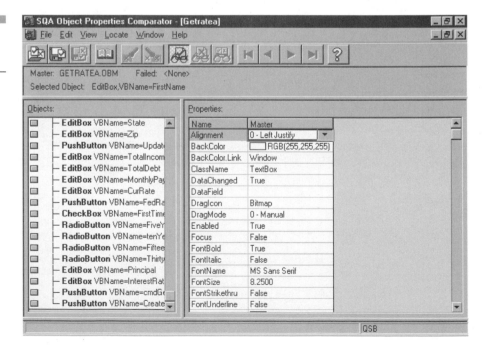

Function	Description
Display Summary Information	A summary of information about the current master and failed data files is displayed.
Locate First Failure	Locate the first difference between the two test cases.
Locate Next Failure	Locate the next difference between the two test cases.
View Master	Display the master data file for the current test case.
View Failed	Display the failed data file for the current test case.
View Master and Failed	Display the master data and failed data files side by side.
View Oldest Failed File	Displays the oldest failed data file for the current test.
View Previous Failed File	Displays the next oldest failed data file for the current test.
View Next Failed File	Displays the next newest failed data file for the current test.
View Newest Failed File	Displays the newest failed data file for the current test.

- Clipboard.
- DataWindows.
- List boxes.
- Menus.
- OCXs and VBXs.
- Table Windows.

Alphanumeric data is obtained during the baseline testcases and is stored in a master data file. When the test is subsequently repeated, the new data is captured in related data files. The Test Comparator allows the testing staff to compare data captured in the baseline test with data captured from later executions of the test procedure. Table 10.6 describes the capabilities the Text Comparator provides to help determine what text values caused the test to fail.

10.5.2 Mercury Interactive's WinRunner

WinRunner is Mercury Interactive's automated test tool for Microsoft Windows-based applications. It works with other tools in Mercury Interactive's TestSuite to provide an integrated solution for testing client/server systems. WinRunner enables the entire testing process, from test

TABLE 10.6

Text Comparator
Functions

Function	Description
Display Summary Information	A summary of information about the current master and failed text data files is displayed.
Locate First Failure	Locate the first difference between the two test cases.
Locate Next Failure	Locate the next difference between the two test cases.
View Master	Display master data file for current test case.
View Failed	Display failed data file for current test case.
View Side-By-Side	Display the master data and failed data side by side.
View Top-To-Bottom	Display master data and failed data top-to-bottom.
View Oldest Failed File	Displays the oldest failed data file for the current test.
View Previous Failed File	Displays the next oldest failed data file for the current test.
View Next Failed File	Displays the next newest failed data file for the current test.
View Newest Failed File	Displays the newest failed data file for the current test.

development to execution to be automated. The test scripts created with this tool are reusable and adaptable.

10.5.2.1 Platforms. WinRunner runs on the following operating systems:

- Windows 3.1.
- Windows 95.
- Windows NT.

10.5.2.2 Repository. The repository used by WinRunner is based upon a relational database. The same database repository is used for all tools in the Mercury Interactive TestSuite. Users of any of these tools can be assigned access rights to this database, ranging from read-only to full read/write/update privileges.

10.5.2.3 Language. WinRunner generates its test scripts in a language called Test Script Language (TSL). TSL is a "C"-like language. The scripts generated by WinRunner can be further enhanced via manual programming. A visual programming tool provided by Mercury Interactive can be used to add functions to recorded test scripts.

10.5.2.4 Help Facility. The Help facility in WinRunner is more than adequate. It provides the ability to view contents, take a quick tour of the tool, or view sample test scripts. Its Help facility is based on Microsoft Windows Help 4.00. WinRunner also provides an online documentation capability. All of the documentation can be viewed online using Acrobat Reader.

10.5.2.5 Test Scripts. Creating test scripts with WinRunner is accomplished by recording interactions with GUI objects in the application under test. Two modes of recording tests are available. The Context Sensitive mode records actions performed in the application being tested in terms of the GUI objects selected (e.g., windows, buttons, drop-down lists, etc.). The physical location of the object on the screen is ignored. The second mode of recording is the Analog mode. When this mode of recording is chosen, the exact coordinates of objects and mouse movements are recorded. An example of a situation when the Analog mode of recording would be appropriate is when testing a drawing application.

WinRunner builds a series of "maps" of the application being tested. These maps are called "GUI maps," and they contain details on the objects contained within each window in a client/server application. GUI maps can be built by the tester manually stepping through an application or by using a wizard (Run Wizard). The recommendation is to use the wizard for all but the most trivial applications. Run Wizard is discussed in more detail in Chapter 11.

Checkpoints within a WinRunner script allow a comparison to be made between the current behavior of the application to its behavior during baseline execution. If a checkpoint indicates that the values aren't the same, then the test has failed. Discrepancies are captured and saved as verification results. These results can be viewed in the Report form.

Three types of checkpoints can be added to a test script. A description of each type of checkpoint follows:

1. GUI checkpoints which compare information about GUI objects. An example of a GUI checkpoint would be to verify that a particular menu item is enabled during both the baseline test and the current test.

2. Bitmap checkpoints take a snapshot of a window (or portion of a window) and compare it with a similar snapshot from the baseline test run.

3. Text checkpoints compare text in GUI objects (e.g., data entry fields) and bitmaps with similar text values from the baseline test run.

WinRunner includes a method for handling timing problems which can occur during testing. The tester can create synchronization points in a test. A synchronization point directs WinRunner to suspend test execution until the application being tested is ready to continue. Synchronization points can be based on delaying until windows or portions of a windows pass a bitmap comparison.

Synchronization points can also be created by manually adding code to the test script. For example, suppose a test should be delayed until a button becomes enabled before clicking it. A statement which calls function button_wait_info could be used to wait until the button is enabled. Other script statements can be used to synchronize testing based on similar events.

10.5.2.6 Playing Back Test Scripts.   WinRunner is able to run tests in three different modes—Verify, Debug, and Update. Each of these modes is used in different phases of the testing process. The Verify mode is used to test applications. When in Verify mode, WinRunner compares the current applications to the baseline or expected responses. Discrepancies are captured and saved as verification results.

Debug mode enables the tester to identify bugs in test scripts. Discrepancies between expected and actual results are stored in a debug directory. When in debug mode, there are several debugging facilities which can be used. Breakpoints can be used to pause test execution at predefined points. A Watch List is available to monitor test script variables during execution. Step commands allow the tester to proceed through a test script a single statement at a time.

Update mode is used to revise the expected results of a test script. It enables the tester to create a new baseline, and this becomes the point of reference against which later Verify tests are compared.

Multiple sets of expected results can be created from a given test. An example of when this might be useful would be if an accounting report or window was being tested. The output would be different depending on whether the current date was the first day of the month, the fifteenth day of the month, or the last day of the month. Three different sets of output results could be created, one for each of the above examples.

10.5.2.7 Handling Unexpected Windows.   WinRunner provides an exception handling capability during test runs. This allows WinRunner to detect and recover from unexpected events. The capabilities in Win-Runner are broken down into four general types of unexpected events. The types of exceptions are:

- Popup exceptions.
- TSL exceptions.
- Object exceptions.
- Unrecoverable application errors.

An example of a popup exception which might occur during a test is if a report is supposed to be printed but the printer is offline or out of paper. When this occurs, a popup window will be displayed on the client machine informing the user. The application and testing will be suspended until a button (OK, Retry, Cancel, etc.) is clicked. Unfortunately, if an unattended test is being run, the suspension will continue until the next morning. A Popup exception can be defined to handle a situation like this. A handler function can be called which will perform predefined responses to each unexpected popup.

TSLs enable the detection of specific error codes returned during test execution. If an application being tested crashes, TSL exception can instruct WinRunner to recover the test execution. This can be done by exiting the current test, rerunning the application being tested, and continuing with the next test in the batch process.

Object exceptions enable the tester to recognize and react to changes in GUI objects in the tested application. An example is the color of a text field. If the on-hand quantity of a certain product exceeds the reorder quantity, then the color of the value will be green. If the quantity falls below the reorder quantity, then the value's color will turn to red. An object exception can be used to detect the difference in color and call a handler to order additional supplies of the product. The handling of unrecoverable errors is covered in Section 10.5.2.8, Error Recovery.

10.5.2.8 Error Recovery. Unrecoverable application errors (UAE) can occur during the course of testing an application. Two examples of unrecoverable application errors are an attempt to divide by zero and attempting to use an unallocated pointer. When events such as these occur, the Windows environment will respond with an unrecoverable application error. During normal operations the user would be prompted to either ignore the error or abort the application. During testing the UAE_set_trap function can be used to control how WinRunner handles a UAE. The available choices are to ignore the error, terminate the application, terminate the application and restart Windows, or reboot the computer.

10.5.2.9 Comparison Tools. The checkpoints which can be added to WinRunner test scripts can be used to determine if changes have occurred since the baseline test was captured. Checkpoints can be used to compare a number of different aspects of the GUI application. The ability to compare GUI Objects, bitmaps, and text fields is explicitly provided by WinRunner.

10.5.2.9.1 Bitmap Comparisons When WinRunner tests are being created, the tester is able to select objects, windows, or specific areas on a screen. The tester can define any rectangular area on the screen and have it captured as a bitmap. The selected area can be any size; it can be isolated to a single window, or it may include parts of contiguous windows. These areas will be captured and stored as bitmaps when the test script is executed.

Multiple versions of each bitmap will be created and saved. The first version of the bitmap is captured when the baseline test is run. It is referred to as the expected bitmap value. Bitmaps which are captured during replays of the testing are called the current actual bitmaps. WinRunner generates a third bitmap which represents the difference between the expected and actual bitmaps. This information can be used to identify the differences between the baseline test and later tests.

10.5.2.9.2 Gui Object Comparisons Test scripts can include GUI checkpoints to compare the behavior of GUI objects during testing. Examples of GUI objects which can be captured and compared include windows, command buttons, menus, list boxes, radio buttons, labels, and edit checks. GUI object comparisons are the ability to compare properties of a GUI object. Some of the properties which can be compared are listed here. Not all properties apply to every type of GUI object.

- X. X coordinate of top left corner of the object.
- Y. Y coordinate of top left corner of the object.
- Width. Pixel width of the object.
- Height. Pixel height of the object.
- Select. Whether object has been selected.
- Enabled. Whether object is currently enabled.

- Focus. Will keyboard input be directed to this object?
- Content. Contents of the object.
- Items Count. Number of objects listed in the object.
- State. State of the object (on/off).

10.5.2.9.3 Text Comparisons A text comparison allows a test script to compare text in a GUI object or in any area of an application's windows. When the test script is being created, a call to a function-to-read text is made. The specific area where the text is to be captured from is either learned automatically by WinRunner or is indicated by pointing to it during the test creation. Once text has been captured, it can be compared via a function called compare_text.

10.5.2.10 Other Features. WinRunner provides tailored support for a number of common development environments. These environments include PowerBuilder, SQLWindows and Visual Basic. Specialized support for the specialized objects provided by WinRunner are described in Table 10.7.

WinRunner includes the capability of executing a group of tests in an unattended manner. To accomplish this, a batch test is defined. The batch test is simply a test script which contains statements calling other test scripts. When the batch test run has completed, the events that occurred during the process can be viewed. If a single test called from within the batch test failed, then the entire test is marked as a failure.

10.5.3 Segue's QA Partner

QA Partner is an automated testing solution which allows the user to create unattended, reusable, cross-platform tests. QA Partner's tests allow a development shop to re-use tests across releases, platforms, and networks. Another tool in Seque's Quality Works tool suite is QA Planner. QA Planner integrates test planning and management with QA Partner's capabilities.

10.5.3.1 Platforms. QA Partner runs on a large number of operating systems. This breadth can prove valuable to a company which has or is planning to deploy their applications on a number of platforms. A list of the major platforms which QA Partner supports includes:

- Windows 3.1.
- Windows 95.

TABLE 10.7

Specialized Object
Support

Environment	Special Object	Description of Object and Specialized Support
PowerBuilder	DataWindows	PowerBuilder DataWindows automates the interface between a data source and users. DataWindows presents, updates, prints, and manipulates data with a minimal amount of programming. WinRunner recognizes DataWindows and can access data displayed within them.
PowerBuilder	DropDown lists	DropDown list boxes allow the programmer to provide users with a pick list from which to choose a value.
Visual Basic	Grid Controls	Grid controls enable developers to display data in a row and column format. WinRunner can capture the values in grids and compare them with values at the time the test is rerun. Comparisons can view the contents of grids as text or number. Text comparisons can be case sensitive or insensitive. Number data comparisons can be either exact matches or compared against a numeric range.
Visual Basic	Custom Controls	Every Visual Basic control has attributes or properties. Examples of some properties include the current value, color, whether the control is visible, whether the object is enabled, the position of the control, etc. WinRunner allows the tester to access and compare these values for all types of controls, including custom controls.
SQL Windows	Table Windows	A table window displays data from a database in a list, table, or other format. WinRunner allows testing to be performed on how applications process this data.

- Windows NT.
- OSF/Motif.
- Macintosh.
- Sun O/S.
- Sun Solaris.
- HP-UX.
- AIX.
- VMS.
- OS/2.

10.5.3.2 Repository. The repository used by QA Partner is a relational database. The same database repository is used for all tools in the Quality

Works suite. Users of any of these tools can be assigned access rights to this database, ranging from read-only to full read/write/update privileges.

10.5.3.3 Language. The language used in QA Partner scripts is called 4Test. 4Test was designed specifically for the needs of quality assurance professionals. Its features can be broken down into three basic types of functionality:

A library of object-oriented classes and methods which specify the way a testcase interacts with an application's GUI objects. Each kind of GUI object has an associated class defined in 4Test. Methods are defined to handle each action which can be performed on objects of each class type. Classes provided in the library include TextField, CheckBox, Any-Win, AgentClass, and ChildWin.

Some of the methods provided are Accept method, which closes a dialogue box and accepts the values specified in it. A Dismiss method closes a dialogue box without accepting its values. TextField classes have a number of methods available, including IsBold, IsItalic, SetText, Clear Text, GetText, and VerifyValue.

Statements, operators, and data types are used to add logic and structure to a testcase. Examples of statements include a while statement, a switch (CASE) statement, and a "for" statement, which is much like the for statement in C. Data types include char, int, short, long, unsigned char, unsigned int, float, and double.

A library of built-in functions is available to support common tasks. Some of these operations include numeric operations like maximum value, minimum value, square root calculation, and an absolute value function. File manipulation operations such as file open, file close, read a value, and write a value are provided. String operations include trim white space from a string, return a substring from within another string and find a substring within a string.

10.5.3.4 Help Facility. The help facilities within QA Partner are quite usable. The menu items under "Help" include an overview, a library browser, and online books. The library browser provides an easy-to-use tab-formatted window which lists the methods and properties for all classes. The browser also includes a one-line description of all functions and their calling parameters.

10.5.3.5 Test Scripts. In QA Partner, the first step in automating tests is to create a testplan. Testplans are structured as a hierarchical outline of the test. They contain descriptions of individual tests and groups of tests. Testplans also contain statements linking test descriptions in the plan to testcases. Testcases are 4Test routines which actually perform the testing work. The contents of a testplan are displayed in Figure 10.4.

QA Planner is a tool in the Quality Works suite which allows client/server system tests to be designed and managed. It presents a test plans in a hierarchical fashion. An application can have one or more groups of tests associated with it. Within each group description are one or more test descriptions. Each test description is associated with a single test script. Figure 10.5 shows a QA Planner outline.

The first step toward creating a test script in QA Partner is to open the Record Testcase dialog window. This window allows the tester to name the testcase, start recording the testcase, and paste the completed testcase to the script file. Recording the testcase requires that both QA Partner and the application be open. Recording is started by clicking the "Start Recording" button. All mouse movements and keystrokes are recorded until the "Paste to Editor" button is clicked. Once the test script has been saved in a file, the tester can view it and edit it. This can be used to delete script entries for any inadvertent mouse or keyboard activity which might have been recorded.

The recording activity simply records actions. It doesn't include any verification operations. While the recording is being performed, the tester can insert verification actions at any time. To record a verification

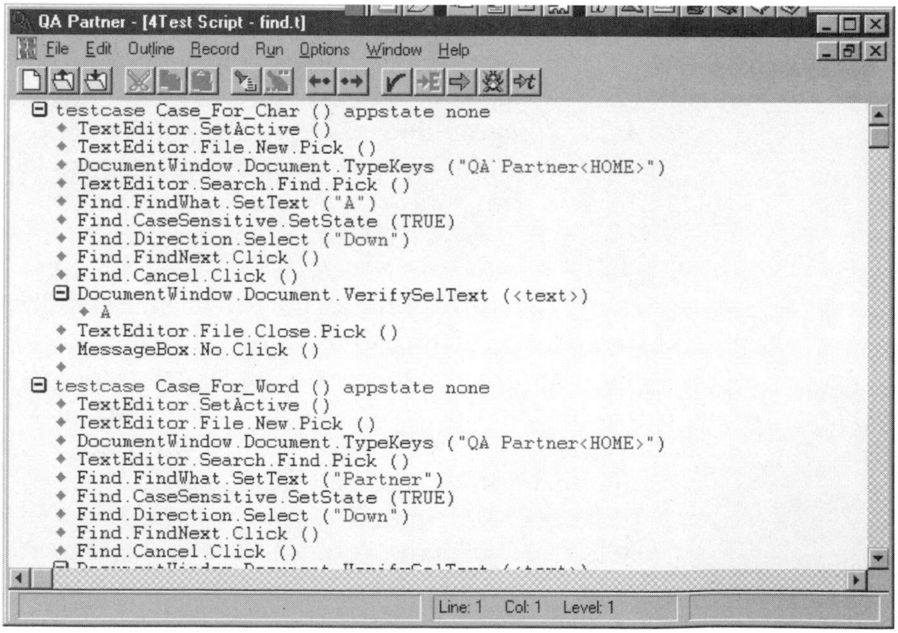

Figure 10.4

Contents of a QA Partner Testplan

```
QA Partner - [4Test Script - find.t]
File  Edit  Outline  Record  Run  Options  Window  Help

testcase Case_For_Char () appstate none
    TextEditor.SetActive ()
    TextEditor.File.New.Pick ()
    DocumentWindow.Document.TypeKeys ("QA Partner<HOME>")
    TextEditor.Search.Find.Pick ()
    Find.FindWhat.SetText ("A")
    Find.CaseSensitive.SetState (TRUE)
    Find.Direction.Select ("Down")
    Find.FindNext.Click ()
    Find.Cancel.Click ()
    DocumentWindow.Document.VerifySelText (<text>)
        A
    TextEditor.File.Close.Pick ()
    MessageBox.No.Click ()

testcase Case_For_Word () appstate none
    TextEditor.SetActive ()
    TextEditor.File.New.Pick ()
    DocumentWindow.Document.TypeKeys ("QA Partner<HOME>")
    TextEditor.Search.Find.Pick ()
    Find.FindWhat.SetText ("Partner")
    Find.CaseSensitive.SetState (TRUE)
    Find.Direction.Select ("Down")
    Find.FindNext.Click ()
    Find.Cancel.Click ()

Line: 1   Col: 1   Level: 1
```

Figure 10.5
QA Planner Outline

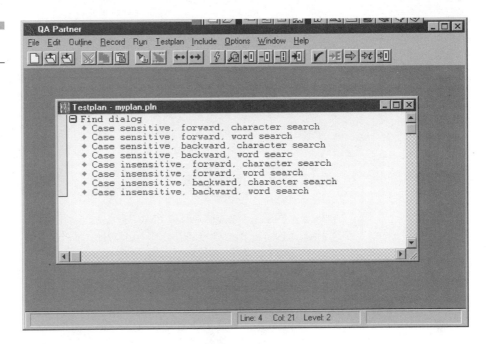

Figure 10.5
QA Planner Outline

of the application's state, the tester presses the Ctrl+Alt keys. This action opens the Verify Window dialog. Within this dialog window the tester can specify verifications which should be performed. When either the OK or Cancel buttons are pressed, focus returns to the running application and recording continues.

10.5.3.6 Playing Back Test Scripts. Once testcases have been recorded, they can be either played back individually or in groups. Individual testcases can be grouped together into a suite file. To play back a testcase or group of testcases, the application being tested and QA Partner must both be running. Within QA Partner the desired script or suite needs to be the active window. To initiate testing, the tester selects the Run | Run menu item. All recorded steps are performed within the application being tested.

At the end of the script, QA Partner opens a results window which displays the outcome of the testing. The results window provides details on how many tests passed, how many failed, starting and elapsed time, total number of errors, and the overall success or failure of the testplan. A brief error description is provided for each failed test. Error descriptions also include an icon which is a link to a tool which provides more details on exactly what differed between the baseline data and the current test run. Depending on the kind of error, this icon may lead to the

Difference Viewer or the Bitmap Tool. Figure 10.6 is an example of the QA Partner results window.

When a test is replayed, the recorded steps flash by very quickly. To the human eye, they tend to be little more than a blur. This condition is normally OK for replay activity. Occasionally the tester might want the tests to run at a slower pace so the steps can be more easily viewed. QA Partner provides a timing panel which allows the tester to force delays after both mouse movements and keyboard operations. This can be used to slow down test replays to a point where they are observable. No changes are required to any test scripts for this timing change.

10.5.3.7 Error Recovery. QA Partner includes a recovery system to ensure that error situations which occur during testing are properly handled. This makes running unattended tests more likely to be successful and therefore more productive. The core of QA Partner's recovery system is the ability to restore applications to their base state. The base state of an application is typically defined as one in which the application is running, it's not minimized, the main window is open, and all other types of windows (message boxes, prompts, dialogs) are closed.

While the default base state is to have only the main window open, the tester can specify that other windows are to be left open. This allows

Figure 10.6
Results Window

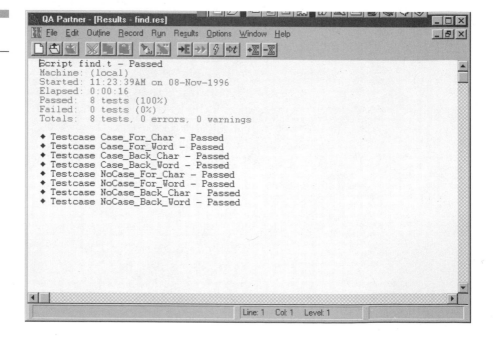

the recovery system to successfully handle applications which require other windows to be open. If there is other behavior which should be added to an application's base state, there is a method in QA Partner which allows it to be recorded and applied to the application.

The recovery system is able to restore applications to their base state at any time during testcase execution. Prior to the first line of a testcase running, the recovery system restores applications to their base states. This is intended to ease recovery from unexpected errors which might occur between testcases. If an application error occurs during a testcase, the recovery system terminates the test, logs the error, and restores the application before the next testcase is initiated. Once a testcase completes, there is the chance that the application won't be able to clean up after itself. If this occurs, the recovery system restores application before beginning the next testcase.

10.5.3.8 Comparison Tools. QA Partner provides two tools for comparing differences in test results. The first, the Bitmap Tool, compares bitmaps. The second, the Difference Viewer, displays differences for nonbitmap objects. Each of these tools will be explained in the following two sections.

10.5.3.8.1 Bitmap Tool The QA Partner Bitmap Tool is used to compare bitmaps captured during tests. To compare images, one bitmap must be designated as the baseline value and the second as the result. The comparison commands which can be performed include the ability to show, zoom, scan, and produce comparison statistics. The commands are described below:

- Show. Displays areas of discrepancies in a Differences window.
- Zoom. Displays an expanded view of a selected area in the baseline, result, and difference windows.
- Scan. Allows the zoom operation to automatically display differences one after another.
- Comparison statistics. Creates statistics on the differences between baseline and result bitmaps. These statistics include the differences in the width, height, color format, number of pixels, and number and percentage of differences between the two bitmaps.

10.5.3.8.2 Difference Viewer When a test has failed for a reason other than a difference in a bitmap, the tool provided by QA Partner is the

Difference Viewer. This tool displays two windows side by side. The left pane contains the expected values and the right pane holds actual values. QA Partner highlights all occurrences where the values differ.

When inspecting the results of the Difference Viewer, it might be the case that the Actual values are correct and the expected values are incorrect. This might be the case when an application is modified. The original baseline is out of date. The Difference Viewer allows you to update the expected values with the more accurate results. This is done by selecting the Results | Update Expected Values menu item.

10.5.3.9 Other Features.   QA Partner has provided a technique which separates the physical implementation of application logic from test logic. This is achieved by declaring application objects and creating a unique "tag" for each of them. These tags are maintained in a window declaration. Throughout the test script, the windows declaration acts like a translation table between the physical name for objects and how they are referred to within test scripts.

For example, assume that a menu item name "Edit" existed on a window. The name of this object within the application might be "mnuEdit." Within tests scripts it might be desirable to refer to this object as simply "Edit." Window declaration will allow it to be referenced in this manner.

Using declarations provides a great deal of flexibility in testing. Renaming an object in an application would normally require that all test scripts be rerun or rebuilt. Within QA Partner the use of windows declarations would only require that one line in the declarations module be edited. This is especially valuable when supporting multiple platform deployment of applications.

10.5.4 AutoTester

AutoTester from AutoTester, Inc. can be used to automate all levels and types of testing. Modular, reusable test scripts can be created which can be shared between unit testing, integration testing, system testing, and regression testing. AutoTester allows tests to be created without the need to write any code or scripts manually. All testing can be done in a GUI, point-and-click mode.

10.5.4.1 Platforms.   AutoTester runs on the following operating systems:

- Windows 3.1.
- Windows 95.

- Windows NT.
- OS/2.
- UNIX.

10.5.4.2 Language. The language used by AutoTester is a proprietary language. When viewed through the Outline Panel (described in Section 10.5.4.4), the tester sees a column of descriptions and another column of commands. This makes the script easier to read than if it were composed entirely of commands.

10.5.4.3 Help Facility. The help facility included in AutoTester is quite adequate. It is based on Microsoft Windows Help. The details and quantity of information presented is both clear and adequate.

10.5.4.4 Test Scripts. AutoTester creates and runs tests within the context of an "outline." An outline is a test script which contains the commands used to drive the test as well as documentation to explain how the test works. A typical outline contains statements to perform some or most of the following functions:

1. Read test data from a disk file.
2. Emulate users by interacting with the application being tested through the mouse and keyboard.
3. Captures application response and compares them with the expected response. The expected response can be obtained from a data file.
4. Control logic flow within the outline via comparison statements.
5. Output test results and reports to a disk file.
6. Read and/or write test data to a comma-delimited ASCII file.

The Outliner Panel is used to create and view outlines. This facility is displayed in Figure 10.7. The left-hand portion of the Outliner Panel contains comments about the test script. Comments in test scripts must be written and included by the person creating the test. The actual commands are listed in the right-hand part of the panel. Commands are captured by executing the application being tested and walking through its functions.

When recording an application's test outline, it is necessary to include verification checks to make certain the values displayed during playback match values captured during baseline testing. AutoTester

Figure 10.7
AutoTester Outliner
Panel

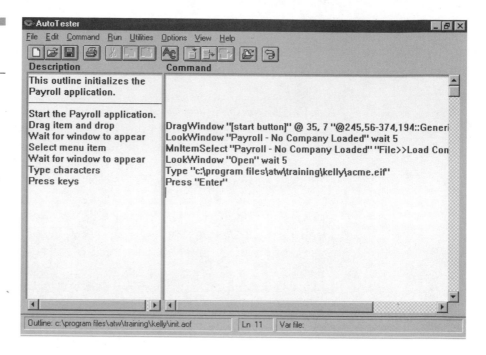

Figure 10.7
AutoTester Outliner
Panel

includes a verify command which allows these verifications to be performed. The verify menu item prompts the tester to select the type of window or control which is to be tested. When the type is selected, a verification dialog box appears and requests more specifics about what aspects of the window or control should be verified. If the control being verified is a menu, the following information can be specified:

- Menu path. Complete menu path name as it appears in the application, e.g., File | Save As.

- Include submenus. All submenus will also be verified.

- Enabled only. Causes only the enabled menu items to be verified.

- Disabled only. Causes only the disabled menu items to be verified.

- Checked only. Causes only the checked menu items to be verified.

- Unchecked only. Causes only the unchecked menu items to be verified.

- Include mnemonics. Causes only menu items which include a "&" character to be verified.

- Include accelerators. Accelerator keys as well as menu items will be verified.

10.5.4.5 Playing Back Test Scripts. When playing back a test script in AutoTester, the user has control of where the script will begin executing. Execution can begin at the top of the test script or at the line on which the cursor is located. Breakpoints can be defined at lines in the test script. When execution reaches a breakpoint, it pauses until another Run command occurs. A continue option allows execution to proceed from the current point until either the end of the test script or the next breakpoint. Execution can also be restricted to a single command line by selecting the "Step" option.

Other outlines can be called from within an outline by using either of two commands. The first method is the "Call" command. When a call statement is encountered, the outline specified will be executed. Control is returned to the original outline test script when a "Resume" statement is encountered. The second method of invoking another outline is to use the "Chain" command. This command permanently transfers control to the second outline. Control doesn't return to the original outline when the second one completes. Both of the commands allow a command line other than the first line in the outline to be specified and have control begin at that line.

While playing back test scripts, AutoTester provides the ability to report on the results of tests played back. Results can be logged to a temporary file, a permanent file, or not logged at all. All commands can be logged or only the ones which failed can be logged. AutoTester can log bitmaps of all windows which come up during testing or only those windows which are up when a command fails. The Logging option of AutoTester is where the user indicates what should be logged. The Playback Options window is displayed in Figure 10.8.

Results from an outline execution are viewed in the Results Viewer. This viewer allows the tester to view all aspects of a test execution. Test logs, host logs, and error log reports can be generated from this window. The Results Viewer also allows the tester to transfer results data and test data between various components in AutoTester (e.g., Bitmap Viewer, Variable Panel, etc.).

10.5.4.6 Error Recovery. AutoTester provides four methods of dealing with system errors. The Options window allows the tester to select which method will be used. Occurrences of system errors will be logged in the "Critical Error Log." The location and name of the critical error log can be entered on the Options window. Some examples of what constitutes a system error include:

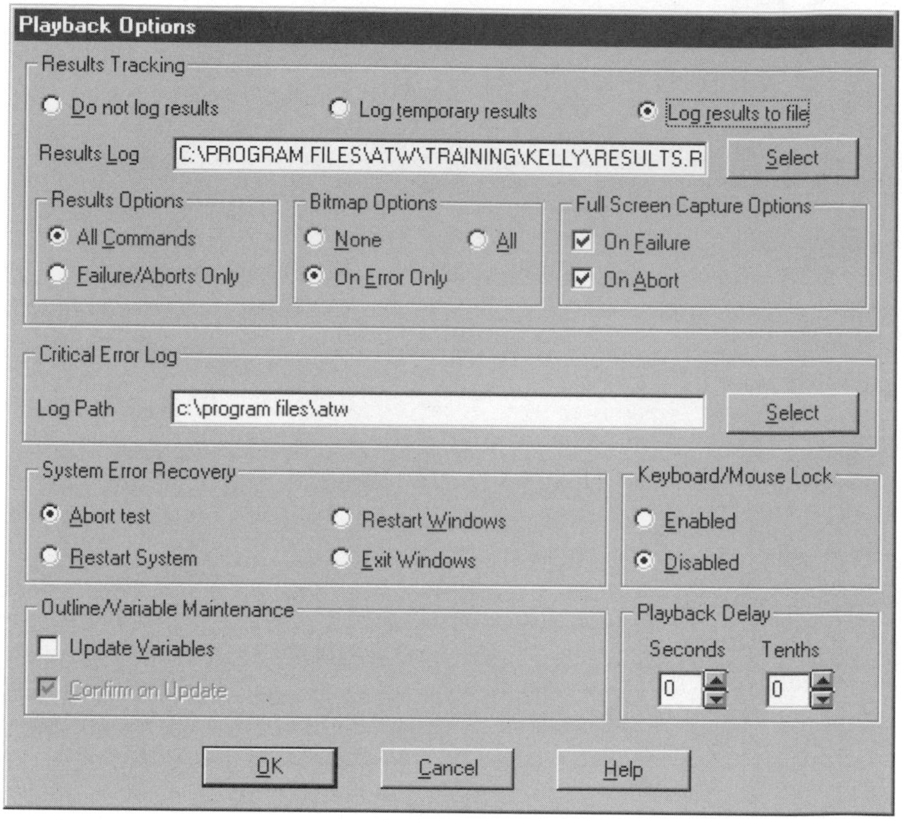

Figure 10.8
AutoTester Playback
Options Window

- DOS text file access errors.
- Memory error while attempting to allocate memory.
- Macro play error when playing a macro.
- Outline file access error when accessing an outline.
- Outline command error when executing an outline command.
- Outline command logic error when there is an error in an outline's command logic.
- Variable file access error when accessing a variable file.

The choices of dealing with a system error are

1. Abort the outline test if a system error occurs. If the system is still functional after the error occurs, the Outliner will show the line which was being executed when the system error occurred. When this information is provided, it is easier to determine the cause of the error.

2. Restart the system after a systems error occurs. This option initiates a warm boot of the system if a system error occurs. Further tests won't be corrupted after a system restart.

3. Exit and restart Windows after a system error occurs. Performing a restart of Windows can be a very reliable method of being sure further tests won't be corrupted. The system won't reboot, so network and other connections remain intact over the restart.

4. Exit Windows if a system error occurs. Windows will be shut down and the system will be left at the DOS prompt.

10.6 Picking a Capture/Playback Tool

Selecting and implementing a capture/playback tool is a very large investment. The initial cost of the tool denotes just a fraction of the time and money which will be invested in the tools. Time and resources will be spent installing the product, training staff to use the product, and developing test scripts with the product. The tool selected must be one which fits in well with the organization and its needs. Selecting an inappropriate package would set back the testing effort significantly.

There are a number of questions to ask before choosing a capture/playback tool. Some of them will be easily answered, but others will require significant amounts of research before they can be properly responded to. The list of questions which follows represents just the start of what should be asked before a tool is chosen.

10.6.1 What Is the Targeted Hardware Environment?

What hardware has your organization deployed its client/server applications on? Examples of hardware platforms would include Intel-based PCs, X-terminals, Sun workstations, other UNIX workstations, and Macintosh computers. Are additional platforms being considered for deployment in the near future? Any capture/playback tool being seriously considered has to operate on all of the platforms currently deployed to, as well as the ones involved in future expansion plans.

10.6.2 What Is the Targeted Software Environment?

What software operating systems are being utilized by workstations in the organization? Some examples are Windows 3.11, Windows 95, Windows NT, UNIX, OS/2, and Macintosh. Any tool under consideration should work under all of your platforms. If a given tool only works with some of these software environments, then you will be faced with two choices. The first would be to use multiple test tools. This will entail extra tools, costs, and training. Think long and hard before opening this can of worms. The second choice would be to perform testing on only some of your platforms. This choice is definitely unacceptable because it won't provide a consistent, error-free system.

10.6.3 Development Environment

What development package(s) are being used? Some widely used development packages are Visual Basic, C++, PowerBuilder, and Oracle Developer/2000. Each of these languages has capabilities which are specific to that tool. For example, PowerBuilder has created datawindows to make application development faster and easier. Do the capture/playback tools being considered include extensions to handle specific capabilities of your development tools? If not, then it will be much more difficult and time-consuming to test these capabilities.

10.6.4 What Is the Scripting Language Like?

Testers will be spending a lot of time writing or examining the script generated by the capture/playback tool. This is true even for those tools which claim that no programming is required. Script languages generally fall into two camps. Either they are open or proprietary. Open languages are identical or very similar to standardized languages used in software development. The two most frequently used open scripting languages are based upon C and Visual Basic. Proprietary languages, by comparison, aren't similar to any standard language.

While it isn't necessarily hard to learn a proprietary language, it represents an additional learning curve which must be battled before testers become proficient with a test tool. All things being equal, it would be better to select a tool which uses a script language similar to something your testers and developers are already familiar with.

10.6.5 E-Mail

Is the product e-mail enabled? Can reports, errors, data, scripts, etc., be transmitted to other team members via e-mail? Can the tool automatically mail out information of this type? This becomes extremely important if your testing staff is large or decentralized (time wise or geographically).

10.6.6 Are All the Bells and Whistles Necessary?

Realistically, what features on a testing tool are really needed? Does your organization want or need a complete test tool suite or just a tool to capture and replay tests? If you don't anticipate utilizing the entire suite, then perhaps you're better off without it.

10.6.7 Network Considerations

Does your organization routinely deploy software on a network accessible drive or on users' local drives? There are a number of advantages to positioning software on the network. It's easier to maintain software which exists in a single location. Licensing costs can be substantially less to buy a single network copy instead of a number of individual copies. If users access the tool infrequently, it doesn't always make sense to install it on their local drive. Can the capture/playback tool being considered be installed on a network drive and used by multiple users via the network?

10.6.8 Technical Expertise Required

Some tools emphasize that they can be successfully used without writing any code. Others imply that tweaking their test scripts is desirable, even advisable. What is the technical level of your testing staff? If they don't want to write scripts manually, then a tool which doesn't require this to be done will be more acceptable.

10.6.9 Training

No matter what the vendor states, a certain amount of training is necessary to successfully use a testing tool. The training can consist of a well-written tutorial, a videotape, CD-ROM based CBT package, a class at the vendor's site, or in-house training. The particular type of training necessary will depend on your budget, what the vendor makes available, and the complexity of the testing package.

10.6.10 Tool Sophistication

One of the major differences between tools is how they handle cosmetic differences which might occur between test executions. Examples of such cosmetic differences include when a control is moved slightly from its original position, reordering items in a menu, and resizing a list box. If the tool isn't able to distinguish between cosmetic changes and significant changes, then its test scripts will be almost worthless. Every minor change to a window or control will require that the test baseline be rebuilt. If this happens, then the concept of re-using test scripts can be tossed out the window.

Most capture/playback tools claim that their product is capable of recognizing and ignoring cosmetic changes of this nature. Each package handles these differently, but the emphasis is on being able to handle GUI controls as objects instead of bitmaps. Before choosing a tool make sure that the vendor's method for handling this situation is well explained and that you're comfortable with the vendor's claims.

11

Stress Test and Load Test Tools

It is easy for the distinctions between stress testing and load testing to become blurred. While these two types of testing are closely related, there are very clear distinctions between them. The most significant difference between these types of testing is what is expected to be gained from each. Stress testing is an attempt to push the system so hard that it breaks. The part of the system which malfunctioned is investigated to see how it can be corrected or improved upon. Load testing loads the system with activity which simulates legitimate user activity. The statistics which result from load testing are then used to predict what performance and response time users will see. Both forms of testing need to be done on client/server systems before the system can be shipped.

Because the objectives for stress testing and load testing are different, the tests they run will be subtly different. Many capture/playback test scripts include user "think" time in them. This is the time delay during which users examine the information returned to them from the database. For most users and applications, these delays can represent a significant percentage of time. Load testing would want to include these delays in the test because they reflect authentic user behavior. Stress testing, on the other hand, would want to exorcise these delays. This form of testing isn't attempting to mimic user behavior. It wants to exercise the system to the fullest extent possible. Including delays in the test scripts detracts from the amount of stress that tests put on the system.

Using tools to perform stress testing and load testing are absolutely mandatory on a client/server system. It isn't practical for people to generate the load these types of testing require. Proper stress testing and load testing resembles a ballet or other well-choreographed dance. Test activities must be performed right on queue and do exactly what they were scripted to do. There is little tolerance for a test which is initiated late. There is even less tolerance for typing or entry mistakes, which human beings are so prone to do. The timing and consistency required to properly perform these types of tests can only be achieved through automated techniques.

Another reason why stress testing and load testing should be automated is the costs involved. It involves a lot of time and planning to design and perform this testing. When people are assigned to participate in stress or load testing, there will be a quantitative dollar cost and loss of productivity as each of the tests are performed. Scripting out the role each person performs and instructing him or her how and when to perform the part takes time. Stress and load testing can be quite lengthy. People involved in this testing aren't able to perform other assignments.

Proper stress testing and load testing normally include tests of extended duration. Both stress testing and load testing need to include tests which exceed 24 hours in duration. Performing a script which lays out exactly what buttons to push, keys to enter, pick lists to view, etc., gets to be extremely boring. During tests of this length, it is very difficult for the test staff to maintain their peak interest and efficiency. Bored staff members aren't likely to run the tests exactly as scripted. Nor will they notice subtle differences between expected and actual test results.

Additionally, stress testing and load testing will need to be performed numerous times. Using people to carry out repeated testing is neither repeatable nor cost-effective. There is no guarantee that test staff will manage to do exactly the same steps at the same relative time. If two activities which are scripted to begin at the exact same time don't meet this requirement, this execution of the test isn't comparable to previous test runs.

If people are utilized during each test effort, then significant personnel costs are incurred each time testing is done. Assume that a test requires 12 individuals to run it and lasts 24 hours. Both of these estimates are on the low side, plus they don't include the time necessary for setup and training. If the cost for test staff is $40 per hour, then the total cost to run this test is $11,520 ($12 \times 24 \times 40$) per iteration of the test. How many times will a test like this need to be performed during the development of the system?

If automated testing is employed, then personnel costs incurred while testing is performed will be significantly lower. The initial costs of developing test scripts will be the same with or without automated testing. By using automated test tools, the most significant personnel costs will be incurred in executing the applications and capturing test scripts. Once these test scripts have been generated, the tests can be replayed with a minimal amount of effort. Depending on the specific tool being used, it might take only a few mouse clicks to initiate a 24-hour test. Compare this with the 288 work-hours required to perform the testing manually, as in the cited example.

The work-hour cost estimate to run a 24-hour test was previously estimated at $11,520. How many more times would this series of tests be performed if it cost only $40 for executions other than the first one? What if the test could be kicked off every Friday evening as the testing staff was heading out the door? How much value would there be if this test ran for 60+ hours every weekend? Would this catch a few additional errors or bottlenecks? Automated testing can make this scenario possible.

Another advantage of automated test products is the analysis tools which generally accompany them. Unexpected results are logged. Screen images can also be saved. When the test has been completed, there is normally a single window which indicates whether or not any errors occurred. When tests are performed manually, error detection relies on the alertness of each testing participant. If an error or difference is noticed, then it will be documented manually. Compiling errors and differences documented by all participants would require additional time and effort.

11.1 Stress Testing

Stress testing verifies a system's response to bursts of activity. The amount of activity that the system must be able to handle should be detailed in the systems specifications document. Stress testing is an attempt to cause the system to fail at that level of activity or lower. For example, the specifications may state that the system must be able to support 100 concurrent users on the system. Stress testing should concentrate on how the system handles approximately 100 users. Testing with 50 users won't prove anything because it isn't a severe enough trial. Testing with 200 users might be entertaining, but it doesn't prove anything because the system isn't required to handle that number of users.

Stress testing determines if the system will break down or otherwise malfunction when it is being overloaded. The failure may come during a high-volume scenario (i.e., a large number of transactions over a long period of time) or high-stress conditions (i.e., exceeding the maximum load at a given time). Proper stress testing must produce both of these situations. If and when failures occur, then the cause of the problems must be uncovered and corrected. The corrected software must then be subjected to stress testing once again.

Any failures occurring during stress testing are likely to have been caused by the system running out of resources. During unit testing and integration testing, there is little or no emphasis on emphasizing this aspect of the system. Stress testing must be specifically designed to cause these low-resource situations to occur. Examples of system resources which frequently become exhausted include:

- Memory.
- Disk space.

- CPU time.
- Database locks.
- Semaphores.
- Printers.
- Swap space.
- Heap memory.
- Stack memory.
- Network bandwidth.
- TCP/IP addresses.

Failure can occur on any of the machines in the client/server system. Stress-related failures can also occur in any software in the system. Running out of memory can occur on a client machine as well as a server. While the server will likely contain more memory and better memory management software, it has a larger number of processes attempting to allocate the available memory. CPU resource problems are just as likely to represent a problem on a client machine as on a server. Again, the server will have greater CPU resources (e.g., faster CPU, possibly multiple CPUs), but it will have more processes making requests of those resources.

Obviously, some problems can only occur on certain machines. A problem with database locks can't happen on a client machine. It can only occur on the database server which employs these locks. Although this particular resource exists at the database server level, the problem is caused by activity generated at the client level.

Besides resource failures, there are a number of other classes of problems which stress testing will uncover. These problems aren't likely to appear during normal systems operations. It's only during an extremely high activity level that they tend to occur. Descriptions of some of these problems are listed in the following sections.

1. Interrupt problems. An interrupt occurs when the CPU is currently handling one process but is required to respond to an external signal. This signal might be the I/O handler returning a requested data block, or it might be an interrupt caused by a user pressing a key. No matter what the source of the interrupt, the system must stop what it's doing to decide how to handle this new request. Problems will occur in systems when interrupts aren't properly handled. A lightly loaded system isn't likely to exhibit interrupt-related problems. They are much more likely to occur when the system is heavily loaded.

2. Database deadlocks. A deadlock occurs when two (or more) processes each have one database resource (e.g., a table or a data page) and require another resource to complete their processing. Neither is willing to free the resource(s) they have until they obtain the coveted resource and complete their transaction. If each process has a resource that the other process requires, neither will be able to acquire the resources needed to complete their own transactions. A deadlock can't occur when a single process is being tested. They occur more frequently as database activity increases.

3. Pointer problems. An application that has errors in its usage of pointers might reference or modify memory which hasn't been allocated to it. When relatively few other processes are running, there is a higher likelihood that this indiscretion will go undiscovered. If many other processes are active, altering random memory is more likely to be discovered. Usually this discovery comes about when the victim process aborts.

4. Memory leakage. A memory leakage occurs when a particular piece of code allocates (requests) memory and doesn't properly deallocate (return) it. Memory that isn't returned to the available pool of memory can't be reused. If this situation continues, it can reach a point where inadequate memory is left to satisfy requests. The developer may not be directly responsible for this problem. The software at fault can quite likely be embedded within the development tool itself. Very small amounts of memory lost during each leak might not be noticed until after many occurrences of the leak. This is much more likely to be detected if a stress testing tool repeats the activity many times. When short, simple tests are run and the system is rebooted, the leakage isn't likely to be noticed.

11.2 Load Testing

One of the definitions in the *Random House Webster's College Dictionary, 1992 Edition* for the word "load" is: "the amount of work assigned to or to be done by a person, team, department, machine or mechanical system." Given this definition, load testing measures the amount of work a computer system can do. Of great interest to users is the number of transactions (orders, reservations, invoices, etc.) which can be processed by the system. Of even greater interest is the response performance users will see while the system is performing various transaction levels. A system which slows to a crawl when heavily loaded is likely to frustrate users. If performance degradation is serious enough, users may refuse to use the system!

Load testing simulates user activity and allows the testing staff to analyze its effect on the client/server system. The number of users simulated must represent a realistic user load. Proper load testing can be used to predict whether a system will perform at an acceptable level once it is deployed. Problems can be uncovered in the development cycle instead of after deployment. The goal is that these problems will be discovered early enough in the development cycle so that corrections won't be too difficult or expensive to implement.

System response time can be measured while the load testing is being performed. Measurements can be taken as the load is periodically increased. This information can paint a fairly clear picture of how far the system can be stretched before it breaks. Bottlenecks can be identified, addressed, and corrected. Load testing can then determine what the new limits of the system are.

Load testing can also be very profitably used after a system has been deployed and becomes operational. Suppose a system was designed to support a certain number of users, say 100. After the system is in production for six months, it is so successful that other departments clamor to get access to it. It might be necessary to allow an additional 50 users to access the system. Will the system, as it currently exists, be able to support this extra load?

One method of resolving this question would be to simply add these users to the system. Acquire the required client workstations, train the users, purchase the additional licenses, deploy the applications to the new users' desktops, and hope for the best. Unfortunately, with this approach if the answer is negative, performance for the existing users (as well as the newcomers) will suffer. Neither the current users nor the new users will be happy with the system. This approach will also be costly and time-consuming. Time, effort, and money will be spent before assurances are available that the expansion will be successful.

A better solution to this situation would be to simulate the load that the extra 50 users will place on the system. Run a series of load tests on the system and measure the response times. Modify the load tests to reflect additional users and measure the new response times. Is the response time with new users acceptable? If this test demonstrates that performance will degrade to an unacceptable level, then this knowledge was gained cheaply. If the tests indicate that the system will be able to support additional users, then deploy it to them immediately. In either event, the knowledge was obtained without significant expenditures or time, effort, or money.

If load testing indicates the system can't support additional users, then there are at least three courses of action which can be taken. The first choice would be to add resources such as more memory, additional CPU processors, more disk drives, or disk controllers to the system. Once resources have been added, the same schedule of load tests should be repeated. Response times of the system with the additional resources should be compared with the original observations. Additional resources might enable the system to support the desired number of users.

The second choice would be to identify system bottlenecks and tweak them in an attempt to improve overall performance. Identify the portions of software which impose the greatest load on the system and undertake to improve them. One viable improvement would be to add or improve indexes on database tables. Moving resource-intensive SQL statements to stored procedures can significantly improve efficiency for those queries. Resource-intensive code can be improved. Batch processing can be examined for efficiency, or jobs can be better scheduled. After these improvements have been implemented, then rerun load testing to determine if a measurable improvement has occurred. If the current bottlenecks can be resolved by making improvements, then the system might be able to support new users. Even if new users can't be accommodated, the performance for existing users will likely have been improved.

The final alternative would be to abandon expansion plans on the current system. This would be the action advised if testing indicates that additional resources won't improve system performance. It could be the case that only a major overhaul of the system would allow an expansion of the user base. No matter which path is taken, the use of load testing can help it to be decided without impacting the current users.

11.3 When to Perform Stress Testing and Load Testing

Stress testing and load testing should be performed as early as possible. The earlier this testing is done, the sooner any potential alarms will be raised. By identifying and addressing potential problems earlier, it will be much easier and cheaper to correct them. Errors which heavily impact system performance aren't usually cosmetic errors. They frequently indicate an underlying system design flaw in either the database or the applications. Identifying and correcting design errors of this nature is easier the earlier they are identified.

There are additional advantages to performing stress and load testing as early as possible.

1. It might be that the system can't possibly meet performance specifications requirements. No reasonable amount of tweaking or hardware additions would be enough to get performance up to snuff. If load testing is done early, then this situation will be uncovered. Knowing about this can make it easier for contingency plans to be laid.

2. The earlier that stress and load testing are started, the more times they can be repeated. No matter how tightly designed, coded, and timed, each testing effort will be slightly different than all others. Each slightly different set of tests and conditions has the potential to uncover different errors. The more often stress testing is done, the more errors it can uncover.

3. Stress and load testing can be a part of the regression testing performed after each system build. Regression testing determines if errors have been inadvertently included in new releases. Including a dash of load testing into the regression testing can make sure that performance hasn't degraded from one build to the next.

Unfortunately, the phrase "as soon as possible" is fairly ambiguous. It can mean vastly different things to different people. Perhaps a better description of when to perform this testing would be as soon as enough pieces are in place to allow viable testing to occur. The following sections describe the pieces which must exist to allow productive testing to occur.

11.3.1 Hardware

Prior to performing any form of testing, the hardware must be installed and operational. The database server must exist before any application can access the database. Should this client/server system include a third tier, then the application server at that level must be functional. One or more client machines must be up and running. The exact number will depend on the test tools which are being used. Section 11.5 discusses approaches to testing which require the use of differing numbers of client workstations.

11.3.2 Network

The network is the glue which holds client/server systems together. A network that isn't in place and reliable isn't ready to have tests of any kind run. It would be pointless if not impossible. Stress testing and load testing are particularly susceptible to problems which might exist in the network. Statistics gathered by load testing will be badly skewed if there are network bottlenecks or errors. Stress testing on an unreliable network will choke and die due to network-related problems long before other problems affect the system. It's realistic to say that stress and load testing shouldn't take place until the network is in place, reliable, and performing well.

11.3.3 Applications

Applications are the focus of both stress testing and load testing. Both testing activities seek to uncover problems or gather data by emulating users and how they exercise applications. If these applications haven't been written yet, then there won't be much to test.

The above paragraph shouldn't be taken to mean that an application must be 100 percent complete before it can be stress or load tested. This is far from the truth. Useful testing can be performed as soon as the core functionality of the applications is complete. Core functionality can be defined as the ability to insert records, update records, produce major reports, or search for specific data. Operations of this type will comprise the bulk of activity in stress and load testing. Meaningful stress tests aren't likely to concentrate on whether or not a particular pick list has been implemented.

Some of the secondary functionality of a client/server system may never be tested by stress and load testing. Exercising the Help capabilities of a system wouldn't be an effective target of stress testing. An unlikely target for load testing would be the steps necessary to deploy and install the system. Each of these aspects of the system needs thorough testing, but neither stress testing nor load testing should be concerned with them.

11.3.4 Tests Must Exist

Once the core functionality of applications has been written, the next requirement of stress testing and load testing is that the tests must have been designed. Most methods of implementing stress and load testing rely upon test scripts which have been designed and written for other testing areas. The test scripts developed for integration testing and system testing are frequently the sources for stress- and load-testing activities. There is no advantage to reinventing the wheel when it comes to testing. The wheel may need to be altered slightly, but for the most part, these tests can be used "as is."

Re-using test scripts yields a tremendous performance gain. Separate tests don't need to be designed, written, or debugged. However, in order for test scripts to be re-used they must be well designed, well documented, and well catalogued. Stress and load testing can't use a test script which isn't focused, can't be understood, or can't be found. All of the stress-testing and load-testing tools described in Section 11.7 use scripts which could have been built for earlier phases of testing.

11.3.5 Test Databases

A realistic test database must be created before stress testing or load testing can be performed. This is especially true for load testing because it involves keeping more statistics and records than does stress testing. A database must be realistic in both the number of rows and the diversity of data within those rows. If the production database is projected to have 10 million rows in an orders table, then a test database with 1,000-row orders table can't be considered representative. If the production orders table has a uniform distribution of 25 different types of orders within it, then a test orders table with only one or two order types isn't comparable. Is the database realistic in both of these aspects? If not, then the statistics gathered by testing aren't likely to be comparable to what the users will experience.

It is advisable to create and maintain separate databases for testing purposes? If a consistent database is used for testing, then performance differences can be attributed to other differences. These changes might be changes in system load, available resources, or differences in the software. Running tests against dissimilar databases each time load testing is performed would probably yield vastly different statistics. At best the results would be questionable and at worst they would be extremely misleading. Decisions based on shaky statistics are highly questionable.

For comparable statistics, a test database must be virtually identical at the beginning of each testing effort. Tables in the database must have the same number of rows for each test. The tables need to be located on the same disk drives. The same primary keys and indexes must exist on tables for each test. Internal database statistics should be updated just before each test begins. One way to meet these requirements is to rebuild or restore the database before each test cycle. The major tables, i.e., tables which undergo changes, should be truncated and reloaded from scratch. Bulk load capabilities are available in most commercial database packages. If scripts are built to perform the database rebuild, it doesn't need to be manually intensive or time-consuming. It could be run the night before tests are scheduled.

An alternative to restoring the test database before each testing operation would be to have concluding queries in the test scripts that restore the database to its original state. Records which have been deleted during the initial testing steps would be inserted by the final steps. Records which were added would be deleted. Updates to records can be cleared away by means of a second update statement. If the tests are designed in this manner, a number of advantages will be experienced. There won't be a need to perform database restoration between tests. The tests will likely represent a diversity of database operations. The only maintenance step between tests would be to update database statistics.

NOTE. The pessimist within me screams that a method to recreate the test database from scratch must exist. It would be called upon in case the system or test scripts crash during testing. If such a crash were to happen, the restoration portion of the test would likely not have been exercised. The database is in an unstable, unpredictable state at this point. A rebuild from scratch would be necessary. The means to rebuild it from scratch should be in place even if the database normally is restored during the testing. If this procedure isn't in place, then testing will be stymied until the procedure has been developed.

Another method for restoring test databases would be to utilize the replicating feature of the database engine. Obviously, this suggestion is only feasible if the database system being used supports database replication. The general idea would be to maintain a control copy of the test database on the same database server or on another database server. After the testing has concluded, invoke the replication capability with the control database as the source. This would restore the test database to its original state.

11.4 Debugging Errors Uncovered by Stress Testing

Errors which are uncovered by stress testing have to be debugged differently than those which normal testing discovers. An error uncovered by normal testing (e.g., unit testing, integration testing) is much easier to confirm. Repeating the test, either manually or via a test script, will almost always exhibit the same error situation. An error which is reproducible is generally easier to hunt down and correct. It's also easier to demonstrate that a reproducible error has been corrected. An error which occurred consistently before a fix that is no longer occurring can be assumed to be fixed with a fairly high degree of certainty.

Unfortunately, the above generalizations are not the case with stress-related errors. These problems frequently are only exposed under very specific conditions. The condition might be that a certain threshold of activity exists on the system, e.g., a high rate of disk activity or many transactions being processed. It might be when two processes are attempting to access the same database table or data page as in a deadlock error. Stress errors might exhibit themselves only when a certain amount (or less) of memory or disk space remains available. Reproducing these conditions can be difficult and time-consuming.

It shouldn't come as a surprise if some errors which are turned up never occur again. They can be caused by a unique set of conditions within the client/server system which rarely occur. The situations which create them aren't stumbled upon again during subsequent testing. If the system has been stress tested beyond what users are likely to impose, then errors of this nature may never occur in production.

11.5 Hardware versus Software Tools

There are a number of tools available which help to perform stress testing and load testing. These tools all allow the testing staff to generate a certain level of system activity with minimal manual intervention. Most tools of this nature utilize capture/playback techniques described in Chapter 9. Background activity is generated by replaying test scripts of user interaction with the system captured earlier. This background activity is what enables stress testing and load testing to be effective. Additional test scripts can be executed if a higher level of activity is desired.

11.5.1 Hardware-Intensive Tools

Two general techniques exist for generating the background system activity needed for stress testing and load testing. The first technique employs multiple client workstations to impose load. A test script is initiated from each client workstation. The application being exercised on each client machine interacts with the network and database just as if a user were sitting at the machine moving the mouse and pressing keys on the keyboard.

Test tools frequently utilize agent software at each client workstation to allow centralized initiation of all stress and load testing. One workstation acts as a controlling or master station. It communicates via the network with the agents situated on each client workstation. The master station directs each client machine as to what test script should be executed. Test results are posted back to the repository, and the agent executes the next test script that the master station instructs it to perform.

Test tools which are hardware intensive have a number of distinct advantages and disadvantages. The most obvious disadvantage is that the testing is limited to the number of client machines which are available. If only five suitable client machines are available, then that is the maximum number of test scripts which can be run. If testing is being done early in the development cycle, this shortage of hardware may represent a real stumbling block to thorough and adequate testing.

Another disadvantage of this approach to stress testing is simple logistics. Software needs to be loaded onto each test client machine. Depending on the amount of disk space required, this might be a significant problem. Before each testing effort begins, the test staff must make certain that all the client workstations (which are to be used) are turned on, communicating with the network, and don't have any other software running.

There are some definite advantages to utilizing multiple client machines. The client machines being employed can be selected to accurately represent the diversity of actual users' hardware. Different makes and models of computers are by no means equivalent. Some problems will occur on only specific types of machines. Involving a variety of hardware platforms in the testing from the beginning will identify problems of this nature very early in the testing process.

Some test tool suites require that a minimal amount of software be loaded onto client machines. If the test scripts themselves reside in the repository, then only the agent software will need to be loaded onto client machines. This agent program can be fairly easily deployed to client machines. Loading the agent software onto the client machine is the only time that the computer needs to be physically touched. All subsequent interactions with the client workstation are done via the network.

11.5.2 Software-Intensive Tools

The alternative to using a number of client machines to generate system activity is to have a single computer simulate the actions of many client workstations. A number of testing tools take this approach. These packages initiate multiple application sessions with the client/server system. The test software running on a single computer keeps track of each of these sessions or threads. Each thread represents user actions from a single capture/playback session. When the server responds, the test software recognizes the specific thread involved and transmits the next activity from its test script.

The most obvious advantage of this implementation is that a single test computer is able to simulate the activity of a number of client machines. Stress testing and load testing can be accomplished prior to the acquisition of computers which will be deployed to the system's user population. The maximum number of sessions which can be simulated depend on the capacity of the computer and the specific software test package being used.

When one testing machine is used to simulate multiple client machines, less distribution of software is required. Less management overhead is certainly an advantage of this approach.

11.6 Guidelines for Selecting an Automated Test Tool

Each automated testing tools has its own collection of features and requirements. This section includes a compilation of some of these features. Some of the more common or particularly useful features are listed and described. While no single tool can be expected to include all of these features, it is useful to be aware of what's available. This knowledge enables comparisons between tools being considered with industry standards.

This section also includes a number of questions which need to be asked before selecting an automated test tool. Each tool is different. They offer different capabilities and require different software and hardware before they can be installed and utilized. Choosing an incorrect tool will certainly result in a less-than-optimal testing environment. It's possible that a poor tool choice will result in no automated test tool being used whatsoever.

11.6.1 Environment

The first group of questions which must be asked relate to the environment in which the automated tool will be functioning. What LANs can the test tool operate on? Some common possibilities include Banyan Vines, Novell Netware, IBM Token Ring Network, or 3COM. Another very important consideration is what network transport protocols will the tool work with. Some of the more common protocols in the client/server world are TCP/IP, NetBIOS/NetBEUI, and IPX/SPX. If a tool being considered won't work on your LAN or with your protocol, it must be removed from consideration.

What operating systems the tool is able to work under is the next question to ascertain. What types of operating systems must be running on the client machines versus the server machine? Some of the more common operating systems include Windows 3.1, Window 95, Windows NT, UNIX, OS/2, and Macintosh. If your client/server system includes more than one operating system at the client level, then the tool selected should be capable of functioning under each of them. Being forced to purchase, learn, and use more than one tool isn't necessary or productive.

Suppose multiple platforms are supported. Can test scripts developed on one platform be used on another? Is there any conversion which must be done? The productivity which will be gained by being able to port tests directly from one platform to another shouldn't be minimized! The ability to port test scripts between platforms should be kept in mind if the number of platforms supported ever expands.

11.6.2 Configuration

The next group of questions deals with how tests are configured or distributed between client workstations. The most fundamental question in this area is whether the tool can use a single client machine to simulate the activity of multiple users. If the answer to this question is no, then the stress and load generated is limited to what can be produced by the number of machines physically available. For some development shops, this limitation won't be a problem. For others, it will represent a significant hurdle.

If the tool being considered can simulate multiple clients on a single client machine, the question must be asked "how many?" How many clients can be simulated on a single workstation? How many workstations are allowed? Using these figures, do you have workstations available to generate the desired amount of load? If not, then you must acquire additional test machines, select a different tool, or be satisfied with the amount of load you can generate.

If multiple client workstations will be required, what software must be installed on each machine? Is an agent program the only software which needs to be distributed? Do test scripts get distributed, or are they resident in a central repository? If the list of software is lengthy, then the time and resources required to install and maintain the test machines must be factored into your test schedules.

The last question in this area is how many client machines can a master workstation control? Will this number allow you to generate the amount of load necessary? Suppose the client/server system being developed is projected to support 1,000 users. If the test tool can only control 10 test client machines, this won't enable a representative load to be generated. Another automated tool must be considered.

11.6.3 Test Script Generation and Usage

The third area of questions which needs to be examined deals with test scripts. The most important topic in this area is how are test scripts generated? The least desirable answer to the question is that they must be written manually. You need to think long and hard before purchasing a tool which requires test scripts to be manually written. They will take a lot of time and effort to produce, document, and test. Additionally, it won't be possible to utilize users in the script creation process if scripts must be manually written.

Using a capture tool is a much better solution. Tools which aren't part of a suite frequently include capture tools much like those discussed in Chapter 10. These tools allow the tester to produce a test script by executing an application and capturing its interaction with the server. Tools of this nature are significantly easier to use. They enable users to assist in the generation of test scripts.

Perhaps the best technique for generating test scripts is to re-use scripts which have already been built. If the automated test tool is part of a tool suite, it might be able to re-use scripts which have already been generated. Test scripts which were built for unit testing, integration testing, or system testing might be easily adapted and put to use during stress testing and load testing.

There will come a point in time when you will need to closely examine test scripts. There might a question about what the test actually does or how may times it does it. An error might be occurring and it becomes necessary to see what statements cause the error to occur. It might be desirable to expand a script to do more things or do the same things more times. No matter what the impetus, it will be necessary to peer into test scripts at some point in time. How easy are the test scripts to read and modify? Are they written in a "standard" language (such as Visual Basic or C), or is the language proprietary? Do they automatically include documentation? Can comments be added to a script by the test staff? The scripting language of any tool being considered should be inspected. This may not be a point which weighs heavily in the final decision, but it should be taken into consideration.

11.6.4 Test Script Usage

Looking past the question of how test scripts are generated, the next logical questions are what can the scripts do and how are they used? Do scripts merely capture user interactions with an application? Can scripts be written which have nothing to do with the GUI interface? Such scripts could be used to generate a baseline load of activity. Are there additional functions within the script language which can be called?

One question concerning how scripts are used is how closely they mimic actual user activity. Do test scripts include user "think" time? Think time represents the time it takes users to examine and react to data returned by the system. In most cases the majority of time during a user session could be attributed to this time. Stress testing would like to remove these delays from test scripts. Load testing would be more representative of actual user usage if pauses are left in. Is it possible to have it both ways? Can delays be removed? How easily?

An earlier chapter exhorted the reader to generate short, focused test scripts. Numerous advantages were attributed to this practice. If the reader followed this advice, can these diminutive, focused scripts be used by the automated test tool? The basic question here is whether multiple test scripts can be tied together to create longer tests? If this isn't possible, either new test scripts must be created or a great deal of time will be spent cutting and pasting all the short scripts into fewer, longer ones.

One of the promised advantages of automated test tools is that they can be run unattended. This allows testing to continue after the test staff has left for the night or turned their collective attention elsewhere. Do the tools being considered allow unattended testing? If discrepancies between expected results and actual results occur, are they properly documented? If unexpected situations occur, are they logged and the tests continued? A tool which doesn't properly and thoroughly address unattended testing shouldn't be seriously considered.

There are certain aspects of testing, especially stress testing, which require a certain amount of synchronization. The requirement might be that "x" number of processes attempt to read from the database. It might be that multiple processes attempt to access the same table. No matter what the circumstance, the question will be whether or not the automated test tool can allow testing staff to control events to this level. Can the activity of multiple users (or virtual users) be synchronized to maximize the load imposed on the system? How is this done? Does it require a great deal of programming? Can existing scripts be modified to include this condition? Stress testing will definitely require this, so make sure that tools being considered include this capability.

11.6.5 Analysis

Once a stress test or load test has been performed, the results need to be analyzed and published. Facilities within test tools can make this particular phase of the testing process easy or difficult. If the tool doesn't include a facility for analysis and reporting, then data will need to be extracted and exported to a different tool which does include this functionality. The task of extracting, massaging, and importing data is always significantly more effort and trouble than originally anticipated. Reporting and graphing capabilities that are built into the tool will make the process quicker, easier, and more accurate. The troublesome steps required to move data around won't be necessary.

The following sections include some questions which should be asked about a test tool regarding its report and analysis capabilities. It's better to ask the questions before choosing a tool than to overlook the importance of this crucial piece of the testing effort.

One of the most fundamental questions is, "What statistics can be captured by the tool during test sessions?" Examples of data which prove to be useful are response times for database operations, network delays, number of failed tests, and number of tests which pass. The more information the tool gathers, the more informative the tests can be. If very little data is captured, then reports and graphs won't have much they can report on.

The next logical question to ask is what standard reports, charts, and graphs come with the package? Is this repertoire adequate? Can the existing reports be customized, i.e., can different data be substituted for the current set of data? Is it possible for the report to encompass only a specified date or time range?

Can completely new reports be developed? How flexible and easy to use is the reporting tool? New reports aren't possible without data on which to base them. Is the amount and type of data maintained by the test tool well documented.

In many cases poor performance of a particular function can be directly attributed to one specific SQL query. Does the test tool allow specific SQL statements to be isolated and captured? Once the statement is isolated, does the test tool provide any facilities for tuning or optimizing SQL statements? If the answer to the last question is no, you should check the relational database package for this capability.

What error information is being logged, and is it included in any of the standard reports? Are errors encountered by any of the individual test sessions logged? What exactly is retained when an error occurs? Is a description of the problem stored? Are text fields which didn't match retained? Will bitmap images which don't exactly match the baseline test data be logged?

Does the tool monitor system resource usage on the database server? Examples would be memory utilization, disk I/O, disk utilization, CPU idle time, or number of active processes. This information would be valuable during load testing. If system utilization versus the number of users could be charted, it could help to predict the maximum number of users the system could support.

Does the tool monitor network communication activity? Some of the data that would be valuable includes the number of packets being sent, size of packets, delay for packets, etc. This information would help analyze both stress-testing and load-testing situations.

11.7 Specific Tools

Most of the load-testing tools which are available are part of tool test suites. Several tools and their features are discussed here. This section is not meant to be a complete list of tools which are available, nor is it meant to be a thorough review or analysis of each tool's capability. It simply is a discussion of some of the significant facilities of tools which are designed to perform stress testing and load testing on client/server systems. Once again, the mention or absence of a tool here is not meant to be either an endorsement or a rebuke of a tool.

11.7.1 SQA LoadTest

LoadTest is part of SQA Suite from SQA, Inc. It provides a single point of control for multiuser testing, stress testing, load testing client/server systems. LoadTest can ensure that a client/server application is production capable before it is deployed to the user community.

LoadTest is fully integrated with all SQA Suite products. Test procedures or scripts generated with SQA Robot are used to generate the application activity and load in LoadTest. The scripts can be used to perform cross-Windows testing. The test procedures recorded for a 16-bit application by SQA Robot can be used to test a 32-bit version of the same application. Tests originally recorded by a 32-bit application can also be used to test a 16-bit version of the application. This seamless usage of test procedures can be very valuable if the environment being deployed includes a mixture of machines. If can also be useful when a client/server system is being migrated to more recent versions of the Windows operating systems.

11.7.1.1 Operating Environment. The operating systems which LoadTest is capable of running on is limited to the Microsoft Windows environments. It will run on Windows 3.1, Windows 95, and Windows NT. SQA LoadTest will function on network transport protocols TCP/IP, IPX/SPX, and NetBIOS.

The fundamental unit when testing with SQA LoadTest is called a *test schedule*. Test schedules define a set of tests which are to be executed on one or more test stations. A test schedule can run any test procedure or start any executable program simultaneously on multiple test stations. Each specific test in a test schedule is referred to as a test entry.

In the LoadTest view of the client/server world, there are three types of computers. The first type is the Master Test Station. This computer is the controlling computer, and there is only a single instance of this type. SQA LoadTest runs on this machine and from it directs other machines to initiate tests. Other software which runs on the Master Test Station includes a network analyzer utility and a tool to graphically display performance data.

The second type of computer from the LoadTest viewpoint is the Agent Test Station. There can be one or more machines of this type. Test procedures actually execute on the Agent Test Stations. A software agent runs on each Agent Test Station. This agent communicates with the Master Test Station to be informed what test procedure should be run and when. During and after test script execution, statistical information is passed back to the Master Test Station.

The third and final computer that LoadTest deals with is the Network Server. The Network Server contains the SQA Repository. Test schedules and test procedures reside in this repository. The repository is also where statistics gathered by test procedures and LoadTest are maintained. Other data stored in the repository includes defect reports and test logs.

11.7.1.2 Installing and Starting Agent Processes. Before a test schedule can be run on SQA Agent, each agent test station must be installed and started. When SQA Suite is initially installed, the SQA Agent program and setup files are loaded in the network-common SQA directory. The agent software must be installed once on each computer prior to using it in the role of a test station. To install this module on each test station, perform the following steps:

1. Power up each test station and start Windows.

2. Perform either of the following:

Choose Start->Run from the Windows Task bar.

Choose File|Run from Program Manager's menu.

3. Enter the network drive into the dialog box.

4. Provide the information requested in the following dialog boxes.

Once the agent software has been installed on each test station, it must be activated prior to running SQA LoadTest. An automatic method of doing this is to place the agent software in the workstation's StartUp folder. The alternative is to initiate the program manually on the agent test station. This is accomplished by double-clicking the SQA

Figure 11.1
Adding a Test
Procedure to a
Test Station

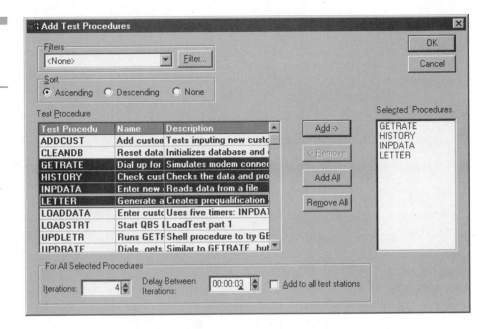

Agent icon or choosing Start->Programs->SQA Suite->SQA Agent. The automatic method is easier, but might not be desired if the test workstation is used for other purposes a good deal of the time.

11.7.1.3 Creating Test Schedules. Test schedules are created without any programming in LoadTest. They are built via a series of windows using a point-and-click approach. Before any test schedules can be defined, agent test stations must be registered with LoadTest. This is accomplished by simply adding the name of the test station to a window which currently lists defined test stations. Any test schedule can now include those test stations in its testing.

After a test schedule has been created and test stations have been defined, test procedures need to be added to the test schedule. To assign test procedures to a station, highlight the station and select menu item Edit|Add Test Procedures. The window exhibited in Figure 11.1 will be displayed. This window allows any number of test procedures to be assigned to the test station by simply clicking them. These steps are repeated to assign test procedures to all stations.

The "Add Test Procedures" windows has more functionality than just what the name implies. It allows the tester to specify the number of times a test procedure should be iterated. A delay between iterations can also be designated on this window. Being able to repeat a test procedure indefinitely provides a method for placing an ongoing load on both that workstation and the system. This method of repeating tests and creating system activity is an easy and intuitive interface.

Figure 11.2 represents a completed test schedule. It has specified four distinct workstations and one general queue. Test procedures assigned to "Any Station" will be run on the next available workstation. To run this test schedule, all the tester has to do is to click the "Run Test Schedule" toolbar icon or select menu item Run|Run Test Schedule. An alternative to starting the test schedule immediately is to use a timed start and stop facility within LoadTest. The tests can be scheduled to start at a specified time (e.g., 10:00 P.M.) and stop at another time (e.g., 7:30 A.M.). This could be used to minimize the impact testing has on other system or network activity.

As the test schedule progresses, agents on each test workstation report their status back to the Master Test Station. When the test schedule has completed, the tester will be shown a window summarizing the results of each procedure. Tests which have failed are highlighted in red. A status message box provides details on the cause of the failure. Test failures can be evaluated in greater detail using one of the SQA Comparator tools. These tools are described in Chapter 10.

Figure 11.2
A LoadTest Test
Schedule

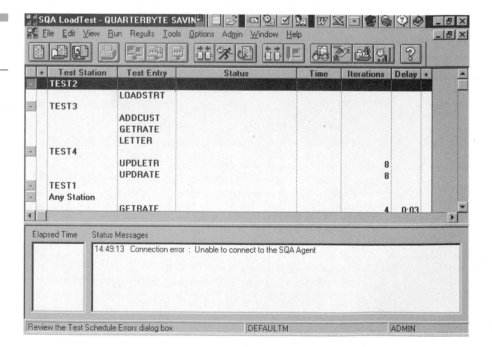

The user interface presented by LoadTest is both flexible and utilitarian. Its toolbar includes icons for every major function the tool allows. The column width of all columns can be adjusted to allow the user to display more columns of greater interest and less of other columns. Columns can also be minimized to remove them completely from sight. Test Stations can have all of their test procedures displayed, or they can be minimized. In almost all cases, a minimized row or column is represented by a plus sign ("+"). Settings which have been specified are saved when a test schedule is saved. The next time that test schedule is opened, the settings are restored.

11.7.1.4 Scheduling Test Procedures. SQA LoadTest provides a great deal of flexibility concerning the agent test station that test procedures are run on and when they are initiated. Test procedures can be scheduled to run on a specific agent test station, or they can be placed in a general queue and run on the next available test station. Each of these approaches has advantages and uses. If the testing being done is attempting to simulate multiuser interactions, then procedures would probably be scheduled to run on specific test stations. This would ensure that the procedures run simultaneously. This would test the client/server system's ability to deal with multiple, concurrent users.

If the testing being performed is load testing or functionality testing, then it may not be crucial that certain test procedures execute at the same time. For testing of this nature, it would be acceptable to queue all test procedures to the next available agent test station. This is accomplished by assigning a test procedure assignee to "Any Station." As each test station completes its current test procedure, it will execute the next test procedure assigned to "Any Station." This will guarantee that all test stations and the system stay busy until the assignment queue empties.

Placing test procedures in the "Any Station" queue has an additional benefit. If a test procedure is assigned to a specific test workstation, it cannot run anywhere else. If a workstation crashes with a hardware error or network error, then any test procedures assigned to it won't run. If all test procedures are assigned to Any Station, then as long as a single workstation remains functional, all test procedures will be run on it. This creates a reliable, fault-tolerant environment for running extended test schedules.

When tests are assigned to specific test workstations, they will run in a specified sequence on that machine. Another technique which Load-Test provides for controlling when tests are scheduled is the ability to synchronize tests via a dependency. One or more test procedures can be defined to be dependent on another procedure. The dependent procedures won't begin execution until the defined procedure has completed. By synchronizing procedures via a dependency, the testing staff can control the timing of tests so they all access the database simultaneously.

Test procedures can also be forced to delay before they begin execution. They can be required to delay for a set period of time after other procedures. They can be forced to pause a specified number of minutes and seconds before running.

11.7.1.5 Error Recovery. Before running a test schedule, it is advisable to direct LoadTest how to handle errors. If an unexpected error occurs during an unattended testing, it would be desirable for LoadTest to attempt to continue the test in spite of the error. The choices which are available allow the test staff to terminate the test schedule or continue it after an error occurs. Figure 11.3 displays the available choices for dealing with errors.

11.7.1.6 Unexpected Windows. Running a test on a network can result in unpredictable windows being displayed on the test station's terminal. An example of such an unexpected window would be a mes-

Figure 11.3
SQA LoadTest Error
Recovery

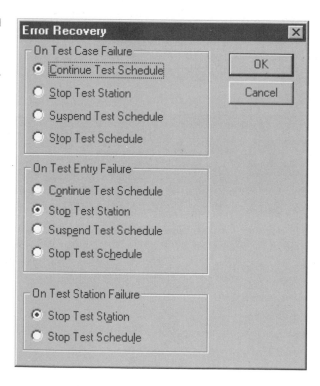

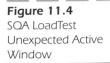

Figure 11.4
SQA LoadTest
Unexpected Active
Window

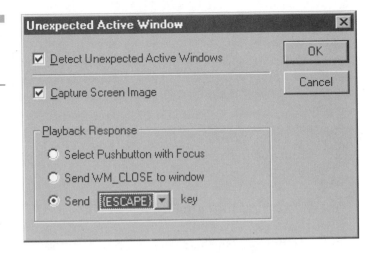

sage from the LAN Administrator. SQA LoadTest provides several alternatives for dealing with this situation. The product can be directed to capture a screen image of the window. It can also be instructed to attempt actions which might make the unexpected window go away. These actions include selecting the control button which has focus, sending a WM_CLOSE message to the window, or sending any selected key code to the window. It is hoped that the action chosen will close the unexpected window and allow the test schedule to continue undisturbed. Figure 11.4 displays the window and choices to be taken for unexpected active windows.

11.7.1.7 Execution Statistics. Once a test schedule has completed, a great deal of information becomes available in the test log. This can include timing information. StartTimer and StopTimer commands can be included in the test procedure to determine how long specific actions within the application take. This capability might be used to track how long database transactions take. Insert transactions, update transactions, select transactions, and report queries are just some of the types of transactions which can be timed using these statements. Timer information is available in the "History" section of the main test schedule window as well as in the test log.

SQA LoadTest can accumulate performance information across multiple runs of test schedules. This accumulation of data can help determine whether the performance of an application is speeding up, slowing down, or remaining constant. During performance tuning, this type of data-gathering capability will prove to be invaluable. Run the test schedule, modify the system, rerun the test schedule, and compare the performance statistics. The test schedule can include multiple workstations, dozens of test procedures, and hundreds of iterations to assure that it is representative of production-level usage of the system. An improvement in system performance means keep the changes; otherwise, back them out.

11.7.1.8 Reports and Graphs. LoadTest provides windows for viewing the results of test schedules as well as a number of reports and graphs. Two windows which display information on test schedule runs are the Execution Summary Report and the Execution Detail Report. The summary report displays a high-level overview of the test schedule run. It lists the begin time and completion time of the test. Other information presented includes the number of test stations and the test stations which stopped. It also lists the number of test procedures which passed, failed, and stopped.

The Execution Detail Report, as one might expect, provides more details about the test schedule run. It lists the names of all stations, each test procedure which ran on that station, the number of iterations, and the elapsed execution times (average, minimum and maximum) for each test procedure. If timers were defined in a test procedure, elapsed time data for them is presented as well.

LoadTest includes a collection of 14 predefined graphs to display information about test schedule runs. The names and a short description of these graphs is presented in Table 11.1.

11.7.1.9 Network Analyzer Utility. SQA LoadTest includes a utility to help test network configuration parameters. The SQA Network Analyzer tests to verify that the chosen network transport protocol and configuration parameters are appropriate. The Analyzer performs the following tasks:

- Verifies that the chosen network protocol can be accessed by SQA LoadTest.

- Performs a ping operation to confirm communications between the Master Test Station and all Agent Test Stations.

- Allows network protocol settings to be modified.

- Displays information about the network configuration, e.g., IP address, Winsock32 location.

TABLE 11.1

LoadTest's
Predefined
Graphs

Name of Graph	Description of Graph
Elapsed Times of Timers over Relative Start	Actual elapsed time for each instance of a timer across all stations.
Elapsed Times by Relative Start Time	Actual elapsed time for each instance of a test procedure or timer across all stations.
Elapsed Times by Test Procedures/ Timers over Test Schedule Runs	Displays variance in response time among test schedule runs. Differences might be due to time of day, database used, network loading, etc.
Elapsed Times by Test Procedures/ Timers over Test Stations	Variance of response time across all test stations. Can be used to compare performance between different hardware platforms.
Elapsed Times by Test Procedures/ Timers over Test Station	Performance of test procedures and timers on each test station. Can help determine how test stations impact duration of procedures or timers.
Elapsed Times by Test Procedures/Timers	The best, worst, and average times for each test procedure/time.
Elapsed Times by Test Station over Test Procedures/Timers	Displays the time of each test procedure and timer broken down by workstation.
Elapsed times by Timers over Test Station	Graphs the speed of each test timer by test station.
Performance under Load over Test Procedure	Charts the effect that increasing system load has on elapsed time of each test procedure broken down by station.
Performance under Load Timer	Graphs how increasing system load affects the elapsed time of each timer on every test station.
Server Throughput	Shows response time of the average transaction per second over the number of clients for each procedure and time.
Transactions by Test Procedures/Timers over Test Schedule Run	Graphs the variance in the transaction rates between different test schedule runs.
Transactions per Second	Charts the number of transactions per second.
Transactions per Second over Timer	Displays the number of timer transactions which complete each second.

11.7.2 Mercury Interactive's LoadRunner

Mercury Interactive's TestSuite product includes a tool designed to generate system load. LoadRunner allows the testing staff to simulate multiple users accessing a client/server concurrently. It allows heavy user load to be simulated and the resulting system performance to be accurately measured. This information allows developers to understand and predict system behavior.

LoadRunner runs on both PC and UNIX platforms. UNIX-supported platforms include Solaris, SunOS, HP-UX, and IBM AIX. Windows-supported platforms are Windows 3.1, Windows 95, and Windows NT. Windows machines must have the following system configurations:

- CPU—IBM PC or compatible 386/25.
- Memory.—Minimum of 8MB; 16MB is recommended.
- Disk Space 15—17MB of free disk space.

The only communications protocol supported by LoadRunner is TCP/IP.

Using LoadRunner to simulate system use involves creating scenarios. Each scenario defines the events that are designed to occur during a test session. Parameters which can be defined in a scenario include the number of users being simulated, the actions performed by each simulated user, and the workstation each scenario will execute on. Each simulated user in a scenario is referred to as a virtual user or a Vuser. A scenario can simulate the activity of tens, hundreds, or thousands of Vusers (virtual users). Multiple Vusers can be programmed to run simultaneously on a single workstation. A Vuser script is defined for each Vuser. Figure 11.5 displays the window in which Vusers are defined.

These scripts, or programs, can include statements to measure and record system response time and performance. They might, for example, include statements to measure the time it takes to create a new record, update existing records, search a table, etc. After the tests have been completed, this information can be used to produce performance analysis reports and graphs.

Load on the system can be peaked by having multiple Vusers perform the same function at the same time. This coordination of activity is referred to as rendezvous points. As each Vuser reaches a rendezvous point in its script, it is paused until all specified Vusers reach the same point. Once they are all ready, they are all released to execute the next command in their own scripts. An example of when this capability might

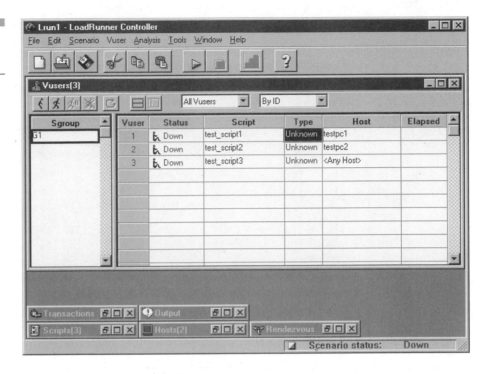

Figure 11.5
Virtual User (Vuser)
Control Window

be used could be when testing an order entry system. In this situation a rendezvous point could be defined which would cause several hundred DB Vusers to create new orders at the same time. This would test the client/server system's ability to handle a large amount of simultaneous user requests.

LoadRunner supports two types of Vusers on PCs. The first is referred to as a DB Vuser (database virtual user). This type of user doesn't rely upon software on a client machine. It interacts directly with the system database server through API calls. Scripts for DB Vusers (database virtual users) are C programs which submit requests directly to the server. Scripts for DB Vusers can be programmed in C using a provided template as a guide. Scripts can also be generated with Mercury Interactive's Virtual User Generator. Multiple DB Vusers can run on a single PC. The number of DB Vusers is limited only by the machine's resources. LoadRunner can run hundreds of simulated DB Vusers in parallel on one or several machines distributed across the network, creating a high level of system activity.

The second type of Vuser provided by LoadRunner is called a GUI Vuser. This type of virtual user simulates a single user logged into a GUI application running on a client workstation. The script submits

Figure 11.6
LoadRunner Hosts

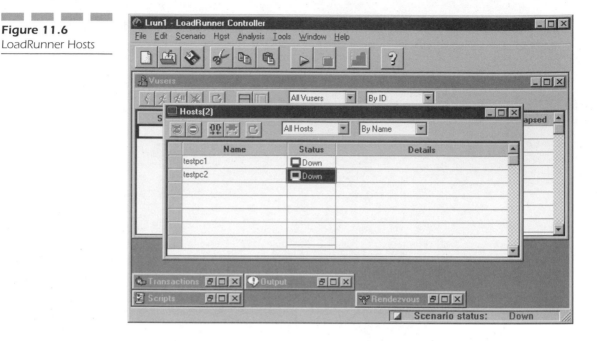

input to and receives output from client/server software running on the client machine. The application in turn makes requests of the server to obtain data from the database. GUI Vuser scripts can be produced with Mercury Interactive's GUI testing tools. These tools include WinRunner for MS Windows-based applications and XRunner for X Windows-based applications.

The method of developing and running scenarios in LoadRunner is through a program called the Controller. This application can be run on any PC connected to the network. It allows the test staff to initiate scenarios on any workstations networkwide. Status of ongoing tests can be viewed via the Controller. After a scenario has completed, the results can be analyzed through the Controller's performance analysis of graphs and reports.

Each workstation involved in the testing is referred to as a host. An agent application must be deployed to all hosts prior to any LoadRunner testing. When the scenario is run, the agent is launched. The agent facilitates communications between the host machine and the Controller. The Controller tells the agent which Vuser scripts should be run, paused, and terminated. The agent returns status information on each Vuser back to the Controller. Figure 11.6 is a screen shot of the window which provides details on hosts defined in LoadRunner.

Each host machine is limited to running a single GUI Vuser. Each host can run multiple DB Vuser sessions. Hosts can be configured to run both types of Vusers at the same time.

LoadRunner allows scenarios to be administered through the Controller, or they can be run unattended. During manual control, the test stall can initiate specific scenarios or Vusers. Both of these testing objects can be paused, restarted, or killed at any time.

The current status of all Vusers is available in the Vuser window of the Controller. The statuses which Vuser sessions can be operating in are listed in Table 11.2

As the scenario is running, agents on the hosts and Vusers are passing error and notification messages to the Controller. These messages can be viewed in the Output Window. The details which are available for each error include:

- Time the message arrived at the Controller.

- Type of message.

TABLE 11.2

Vuser Statuses

Status	Description
DOWN	The Vuser is in its starting state.
WAITING	The Vuser is waiting to run. The Vuser will run when conditions proscribed in its scheduling attributes are met.
PENDING	The Vuser is ready to be loaded and is waiting for an available host.
LOADING	The Vuser is being loaded.
READY	The Vuser is ready to run.
RUNNING	The Vuser is running. The Vuser script is being performed on a host.
PAUSED	The Vuser has stopped running and is waiting for the signal to resume.
RENDEZVOUS	The Vuser has arrived at a rendezvous point and is waiting to be released by LoadRunner.
EXITING	The Vuser has finished running or has been killed.
DONE.PASSED	The Vuser has finished running. The script passed.
DONE.FAILED	The Vuser has finished running. The script failed.
ERROR	A problem occurred with the Vuser. Check the Status field on the Vuser form for a complete explanation of the error.
ABORTED	The Vuser stopped when the Abort command was invoked.

- The Vuser's host machine.
- ID of the Vuser session which sent the message.
- Path of the Vuser test script which encountered the error.
- Message text.

Performance data is collected by LoadRunner during each scenario run. One type of performance data gathered is the time the server takes to respond to requests and tasks submitted by Vusers. Scripts can include begin and end points which mark activities that should be measured. This information can be viewed and analyzed as either reports or graphs from within Controller. LoadRunner provides a number of standard reports and graphs which can be used to view and analyze scenario-related information. Table 11.3 summarizes these reports and graphs.

Graphs default to displaying information gathered for the entire time period the scenario ran. The graph can be enlarged to display just a portion of the scenario. For example, a scenario might have run for thirty minutes. If the performance degraded during the last five minutes of the test then the user might be interested in seeing greater detail for just that period. The desired section of the graph can enlarge by highlighting it and selecting the View|Zoom In menu option.

Other capabilities of performance information include the ability to modify the scale of the x-axis to make the information easier to view and analyze. Performance data can also be exported to spreadsheets or statistical analysis packages. LoadRunner converts the graph data into text (.txt) files. Reports can be exported into a number of different file formats, including comma-separated values.

11.7.3 Segue's QA Partner: Distributed

QA Partner:Distributed allows client/server applications to be testing in a networked environment. Test scripts that were written to verify functional capability of applications can be readily re-used for stress and load testing. If desired, individual scripts can be edited to increase the particular areas of activity imposed by that script on the system. QA Partner:Distributed specifically addresses the needs of concurrent testing, stress testing, and load testing.

QA Partner:Distributed provides support for a wide variety of platforms and network protocols. The operating systems which it will run under include Windows 3.1, Windows 3.11, Windows 95, Windows NT,

TABLE 11.3	Running Vusers	Graphs the number of active Vusers per second of the scenario run.
LoadRunner's Standard Reports and Graphs	Transaction Performance	Graphs the average time the server took to perform transactions during the scenario run.
	Successful Transactions per Second	Graphs the number of completed, successful transactions performed each second during the scenario run.
	Failed Transactions per Second	Graphs the number of completed, unsuccessful transactions performed each second during the scenario run.
	Transaction Performance Summary	Graphs minimum, maximum, and average performance time for all scenarios in the scenario run.
	Transaction Performance Summary by Vuser	Graphs the time taken to perform transactions by individual Vuser.
	Performance Under Load	Graphs transaction performance time based on the number of active Vusers during the scenario run.
	Transaction Distribution	Graphs distribution of the time taken to perform a transaction.
	Scenario Execution	Reports major events which occurred during the scenario run.
	Transaction Performance Summary	Reports a summary of all transactions executed during the scenario.
	Transaction Performance by Vuser	A report which summarizes, by Vuser, all transactions which executed during the scenario.
	Detailed Vuser	Lists transaction details by Vuser.
	Performance Under Load	Reports on the performance time for transactions based on the number of active Vusers during the scenario run.
	Failed Transactions Report	Lists the number of completed, unsuccessful transactions performed during each second of the scenario run.
	Failed Vuser Report	Lists the number of Vusers which were in states ERROR, ABORTED, or DONE.FAILED during the scenario execution.

OS/2, SunOS, Solaris, HP-UX, AIX, Ultrix, VMS, SCO, and IRIX. The three network protocols which it functions on are TCP/IP, NetBIOS/NetBEUI, and IPX/SPX. Not all of these protocols are supported on every operating system platform. Table 11.4 provides a cross-reference of which protocols can be used on what platforms.

If multiple machines are being used during QA Partner:Distributed testing, then all of them must use the same communications protocol to communicate with each other. The only protocol supported on UNIX machines is TCP/IP. If the client machines being tested in the system include a mixture of PC-based machines and UNIX-based machines, then TCP/IP must be the protocol and all client machines must be capable of supporting it.

The features of QA Partner:Distributed which help to rigorously test client/server applications include the following:

1. It can provide automatic control of multiple applications.

2. Specific tests can be executed on particular machines in a multimachine test environment.

3. Applications can be tested concurrently by multiple threaded test sessions.

TABLE 11.4

Platform Protocol Cross-Reference

Platform	TCP/IP	NetBIOS/NetBEUI	IPX/SPX
Windows 3.1	x	x	
Windows 3.11	x	x	x
Windows 95	x	x	
Windows NT	x	x	
OS/2		x	
SunOS	x		
Solaris	x		
HP-UX	x		
AIX	x		
Ultrix	x		
VMS	x		
SCO	x		
IRIX	x		

4. Results can be reported broken down by individual threads.

5. Testing can be performed across networks using a number of protocols.

6. Direct database access is available from within test scripts.

QA DBTester is a facility which allows test scripts to connect directly to the database server. This capability is significantly different from QA Partner's focus of driving GUI application by capturing and replaying scripts. The ability to interact directly with the database using DBTester provides the testing staff with a great deal of power and flexibility. This tool might be used for the following purposes:

1. Perform administrative functions on the database which aren't available from the GUI application.

2. Build or reset the database to a known position prior to the beginning of a test sequence.

3. Verify application test results in the database independently of the application being tested.

4. Select test data from the database which will be used as input later in the test script.

5. Maintain a historical record of test results, performance data, or error-tracking information.

6. Loop through database access operations designed to load the server.

Test scripts must be edited to include additional information when testing in a multimachine environment. The types of information which must be manually specified include:

1. Which test machine each script has been designated to run on.

2. Synchronization of operations between multiple test machines.

3. Access of global variables which can be used to coordinate systemwide testing.

There are two distinct software components involved in a QA Partner:Distributed test environment. The first type is QA Partner's host software which is used to develop, edit, compile, run, and debug 4Test scripts and test plans. This computer on which this software executes is referred to as the host machine or QA Partner machine. There can only be a single host machine during a QA Partner:Distributed test session.

The other type of software component performs a translation of 4Test script statements into GUI-specific commands. It acts as an agent to drive and monitor the client/server GUI application being tested. This type of software can run on any number of remote machines in the networked environment. These systems are referred to as target machines. If desired, both the host machine software and the target machine software can operate on a single computer. This would enable local testing to be performed before the network is ready.

Tests are initiated and controlled by the QA Partner machine. It transmits to target machines the scripts which are to be executed from the target computer. Results of these tests are communicated back to the QA Partner machine.

Test result reports produced by QA Partner:Distributed allow the testing staff to view data in a number of different formats. Each format presents the data sorted in a different manner. The available formats are:

- Elapsed time. Results are sorted for all threads and target machines by the order in which events occurred. This gives an overview of what the load on the server was for any particular time period.

- Machine. Results for all threads are sorted by target machine. The secondary sort is the order in which events occurred. This presents the view of what the system response was for tests run on each machine.

- Thread. Results are sorted by thread and then by the order in which events occurred.

CHAPTER **12**

Wizards

12.1 What Is a Wizard?

The definition of exactly what constitutes a wizard is as varied as the wizards which exist. Essentially, a wizard is a tool which advises or leads the user through a process. Many times the wizard will do a significant portion of the grunt work once the user has outlined what he or she wants to be done. This is especially true when what the user wants to do is a fairly standard activity.

A number of wizards have been included in recent releases of shrink-wrapped software. Microsoft Access, for examples, contains wizards that will create databases, tables, queries, reports, forms, and charts. Microsoft Word includes wizards which answer questions, create tables, and provide tips to the user. Visual Basic 4.0 from Microsoft includes a setup wizard to create distribution and setup diskettes for Visual Basic applications. PowerBuilder 5.0 provides wizards to help the developer create charts.

Given that wizards have become fairly common in other areas, it shouldn't be a surprise that they are being included in testing software. Currently only a few test tool packages include wizards. The trend will almost certainly be towards widened availability and increased functionality of wizards.

12.2 Realistic Limitations

A wizard, no matter what the application, is simply a helpful tool. It might make suggestions, provide information, or guide its users through a multistep process. Wizards can't think. They don't read minds or perform tasks by themselves. A wizard can be extremely helpful, but it can't design forms, create databases, or write test scripts by itself.

If the user doesn't know what to test or how to test, then the wizard won't be of much use. The resulting tests will still be incomplete, inadequate, or misdirected. The only significant difference will be that tests built with a wizard may have been completed a little faster than without it. Experienced developers will realize the limitations of wizards and use them accordingly.

One of the most common capabilities of testing wizards is to produce basic test scripts. Their vendors claim that the wizards can grind out a significant portion of the scripts needed. This allows testing staff to concentrate on the more difficult testing situations.

12.3 Mercury Interactive

Mercury Interactive's Test Suite product includes a number of wizards. Each of these will be briefly described in the following sections.

12.3.1 RapidTest Plan Wizard

RapidTest Plan Wizard assists the tester through the initial stages of test planning. Assistance in the form of a wizard at this point can provide much-needed guidance to someone who is new to the job of testing. The Plan Wizard can help categorize the system being tested according to major categories or subjects. The default test subjects or areas which Plan Wizard provides are:

- Cross platform.
- Functional.
- Help.
- Installation.
- Memory.
- Regression.
- Performance.
- Permissions.

The tester is able to easily add additional subjects to this standard list. Examples of additional subject areas which might be added to the standard list include: stored procedure testing, concurrent usage testing, transactions testing, and data entry validity testing. The list of additional subjects is only limited by the complexity of the system being tested. Figure 12.1 displays the Plan Wizard window which allows subjects to be selected.

Once the major subject areas have been laid out, tests within each subject will be planned. Test designers at this point are left on their own to a large degree. Tests which need to be designed are highly individualistic to each client/server system. The wizard can't predict or generate the tests which are necessary for each test area. Figure 12.2 is an example of the hierarchical display of tests defined for each subject.

The last step of Plan Wizard is to convert the subjects and tests into TestDirector's standard format. From this point on, Plan Wizard's involvement

Figure 12.1
Plan Wizard Subject
Choices

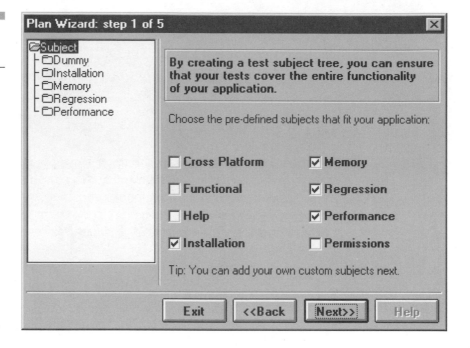

ends. The test plan from this point forward is accessed via Mercury Interactive's TestDirector product. Tests defined within TestDirector can be documented, executed, maintained, and tracked. Figure 12.3 displays the window which the tester uses to interact with TestDirector.

12.3.2 RapidTest Script Wizard

The Test Wizard guides you step-by-step as it walks through your application and learns its objects and windows. By recognizing the objects within an application, the wizard can create test scripts which check for standard test items. To thoroughly test the system, the test staff will need to create additional, more detailed tests.

Once the Wizard completes "walking" through your application, it provides you with automated tests you can run immediately. The advantages of using Script Wizard to automate parts of your tests is twofold. First, having much of the testing automated gets the novice up and running quickly. Many times it's difficult to get started because an inexperienced tester feels overwhelmed. Jump-starting the process enables the staff to begin with a quick and easy success. A boost in confidence never hurt a testing effort.

The second advantage of Script Wizard automating the standard tests is that it cuts down on the dull and repetitive (but necessary) work. No one enjoys creating almost identical tests for each of the many, perhaps hundreds, of similar objects within a system. Eventually, this type of work becomes mind-numbing and opens the door to oversights, omissions, and errors. By automating a significant amount of the repetitive work, the testing staff can be freed to concentrate on the more difficult tests.

The first step when using RapidTest Script wizard is to open and identify the initial window of the application which is to be tested. Once the application has been identified to Script Wizard, then the tester has the opportunity to indicate what type of tests the wizard should produce. Figure 12.4 displays the choices from which the tester can choose. These choices are:

- GUI Regression Test. Performs a comparison of GUI features between a baseline and later versions.

- Bitmap Regression Test. Performs a bitmap comparison between a baseline versus later versions.

- User Interface Test. Checks for adherence to Microsoft Windows User Interface conventions.

- Test Template. Builds a test script template.

Figure 12.2
Plan Wizard Display of Tests Defined Thus Far

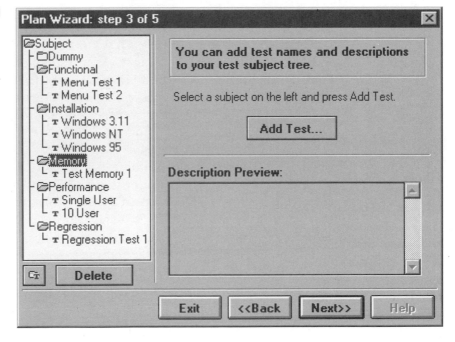

Figure 12.3
TestDirector's Test
Plan Window

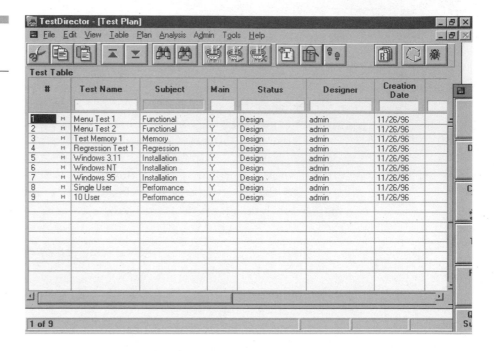

In order to effectively create test scripts Script Wizard must "learn" about all the objects in the application's User Interface. The first step towards accomplishing this is to open every window and dialog box in the application. Once the windows have been opened, then Script Wizard locates all of the objects in each windows.

To thoroughly navigate within the application, Script Wizard needs to identify and activate all controls which navigate from one window to another. Examples of these types of controls are menu items and command buttons. If any other of these controls are omitted, then the test script produced won't be complete. Windows and their tests will be missing.

Some conventions exist to clue users that certain controls will bring up another window. Script Wizard will prompt the tester to determine what characters and symbols are used in the application and to follow these conventions. The two sets of symbols presented as a default are a pair of greater than symbols (">>") and ellipses ("..."). An application convention for a "Next" type button might be to have a trailing ">>" symbol. The Microsoft User Interface standard is to include ellipses on all menu items which bring up another window. If the application being tested uses symbols besides these, they should be included with the default symbols. Armed with this knowledge, Script Wizard is able to recognize controls which are used to move the application to other windows.

Script Wizard is able to set the learning flow into two different modes. The "express" mode will step through each window and control in the application using WinRunner defaults. This mode runs significantly faster and is simpler to use. It doesn't allow the user to customize scripts as they are being generated.

The comprehensive, or advanced, learning mode pauses after each window and dialog box is brought up. This interlude allows the tester to insert customized information into the test script. The test staff can use this capability to include comments into scripts that make them easier to understand, enhance, and debug.

As Script Wizard begins the processing of each window and dialog box, the tester is presented with a list of objects and controls it recognizes. These controls are broken down into two types: those objects which open other windows and those which don't open windows. The accuracy and completeness of this information is crucial for the wizard to be able to find all windows in the application.

Figure 12.5 displays this window for a demo application. If the application being tested doesn't have conventions for controls which bring up other windows, then Script Wizard likely won't recognize all of these controls. A certain amount of manual intervention will be required here. The tester needs to scan the "B" list to look for controls (which do

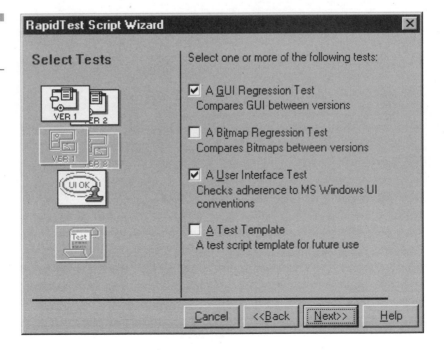

Figure 12.4
Available Test Types
in Script Wizard

open windows) which Script Wizard didn't identify. These controls can be moved to the "A" ("Go To") list by selecting them and clicking the "Move" button. This step, although dull, is extremely important. If "Go To" controls aren't completely identified, then parts of the application won't be tested.

During its processing of controls for each window, Script Wizard brings up the window and highlights every control on it. Even controls such as labels, lines, and boxes will be highlighted. Script Wizard will highlight each of them in order to "learn" the application. As each object is highlighted, an entry for that object is created in the test script being generated. This process moves along quickly, but an application with a large number of windows and objects will take several minutes to be completely learned.

The complexity of the test scripts generated are controlled by the choices which were made earlier. The window displayed in Figure 12.4 allows the tester to determine what type of tests would be created. Details on each of these choices is presented in the following sections.

The least complex test script available is a test script template. This test includes simply a call to each of the windows in the application. Table 12.1 contains the script generated for a demo application when the template selection was made. The first statement in this script obtains a

Figure 12.5
Objects Script Wizard Recognizes on a Window

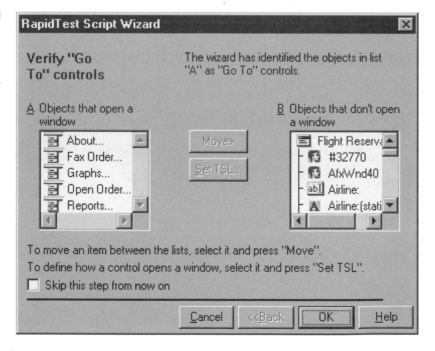

TABLE 12.1	
Test Script Template	

```
time_out=getvar("timeout")
win_open("Flight Reservation",time_out);
            #Enter code for window "Flight Reservation" here
    win_open("About Flight Reservation System",time_out);
            #Enter code for window "About Flight Reservation System" here
    win_close ("About Flight Reservation System");

    win_open("Graphics Server",time_out);
            #Enter code for window "Graphics Server" here
    win_close("Graphics Server");

    win_open("Open Order",time_out);
            #Enter code for window "Open Order" here
    win_close("Open Order");

    win_open("report - Notepad",time_out);
            #Enter code for window "report - Notepad" here
        win_open("Find",time_out);
                #Enter code for window "Find" here
        win_close("Find");

    win_open("Open", time_out);
                    #Enter code for window "Open" here
    win_close ("Open");

    win_open("Page Setup",time_out);
        #Enter code for window "Page Setup" here
        win_open("Page Setup_1",time_out);
                #Enter code for window "Page Setup_1" here
        win_close("Page Setup_1");
    win_close("Page Setup");

            win_open("Save As",time_out);
                    #Enter code for window "Save As" here
            win_close("Save As");

    win_close("report - Notepad");
win_close("Flight Reservation",time_out);
```

timeout value. The remainder of the code simply opens and closes all of the windows in the application. The usefulness of this is that the wizard can generate it quickly and thoroughly. No windows in the application will be overlooked.

One of the aspects of a client/server system which needs to be examined is whether it adheres to standards. One set of standards which can be checked is in the area of the user interface. Script wizard allows the tester to generate test scripts to validate this facet of the system. These scripts can be generated with virtually no user direction. If the system being testing has no standards in this area, then this capability won't be required or appreciated. If such standards

TABLE 12.2

User Interface
Adherence Test
Script

```
load("chkui",1,1);
load_os_api();
time_out=getvar("timeout");

###Use the list of checks below to define the UI checks you want the test to perform.
###Define a check as "TRUE" if you want it to be included.

lbl_chk=TRUE;                          #checks capital letter of labels on controls.
ok_can_chk=TRUE;                       #checks existence of OK/Cancel buttons.
sys_chk=TRUE;                          #checks existence of system menu.
text_chk=TRUE;                         #checks if all text of controls is visible.
overlap_chk=FALSE;                     #checks that controls do not overlap.
align_chk=FALSE;                       #checks alignment of controls.

configure_chkui(lbl_chk,ok_can_chk,sys_chk,text_chk,overlap_chk,align_chk);
win_open("Flight Reservation",time_out);
        check_ui("Flight Reservation");
        win_open("About Flight Reservation System",time_out);
                check_ui("About Flight Reservation System");
        win_close("About Flight Reservation System");
        win_open("Graphics Server",time_out);
                check_ui("Graphics Server");
        set_window ("Graph", 10);
        menu_select_item ("sys_Close Alt+F4");

        win_open("Open Order",time_out);
                check_ui("Open Order");
        win_close("Open Order");
        win_open("report - Notepad",time_out);
                check_ui("report - Notepad");
                win_open("Find",time_out);
                        check_ui("Find");
                win_close("Find");
                win_open("Open",time_out);
                        check_ui("Open");
                win_close("Open");
                win_open("Page Setup",time_out);
                        check_ui("Page Setup");
                        win_open("Page Setup_1",time_out);
                                check_ui("Page Setup_1");
                        win_close("Page Setup_1");
                win_close("Page Setup");
                win_open("Save As",time_out);
                        check_ui("Save As");
                win_close("Save As");
        win_close("report - Notepad");
```

have been installed then utilizing an automated tool to validate them is extremely efficient. Table 12.2 shows the script generated to determine if an application adheres to the Microsoft standards.

The GUI Regression Test creates a test script which captures the basic GUI interface of the client/server application. All windows are stepped through and captured. When a comparison test is run later the screens at that time are compared with the baseline versions. This type of testing should be a fundamental part of the client/server system testing regimen. Table 12.3 contains an example of the script generated by this facet of Script Wizard.

When the test is later run, any differences between the baseline version and the later version will be detected. These differences can be displayed as they are encountered, or viewing them can be delayed until the entire test script has been completed.

The final choice of test scripts which can be produced is one which compares the look of each window in the application. Each window is captured as a bitmap file. When the test is later replayed, it will compare the original bitmap file with the current bitmap image of each window. Any differences are reported by the test tool. Table 12.4 is the test script generated to perform a bitmap test for the demonstration application.

An earlier section made the statement that wizards of any type are no substitute for human action. Script Wizard is able to generate test scripts which check for the existence of GUI objects. It can test to determine if some of the significant attributes of GUI objects have changed. This testing is absolutely necessary for a client/server GUI system. A tool which automates it will prove to be extremely useful.

The test scripts produced don't begin to test an application's functionality. The application used in the examples for WinRunner's wizards has a number of data entry fields and functions. None of the tests produced by the wizards tested data entry into these fields. None of the tests checked whether transaction processing functioned correctly. None of the tests checked whether concurrent usage of this application by multiple users resulted in problems.

In summary, the test scripts produced by these specific wizards are extremely valuable. Intelligent use of these wizards can help jump-start a testing effort. They can be extremely productive. But the bottom line is that they are no substitute for a human being creating tests which check the functionality of the application.

12.3.3 RapidTest Cycle Wizard

In the parlance used by Mercury Interactive, a test cycle is a group of tests which are run to achieve a testing goal. A test cycle might be composed to test a new build of the system. It might test existing software on a new hardware platform. A test cycle might be designed to

TABLE 12.3

GUI Regression
Test Script

```
time_out=getvar("timeout");
set_window("Flight Reservation",time_out);
        win check_gui("Flight Reservation", "list1.ckl", "gui1", 1);
set_window("Flight Reservation",time_out);
        menu_select_item("About...");
        set_window("About Flight Reservation System",time_out);
                win_check_gui("About Flight Reservation System", "list2.ckl", "gui2", 1);
        win_close("About Flight Reservation System");
set_window("Flight Reservation",time_out);
        menu_select_item("Graphs...");
        set_window("Graphics Server",time_out);
                win check_gui("Graphics Server", "list3.ckl", "gui3", 1);
        win _ close("Graphics Server");
set_window("Flight Reservation",time_Out);
        menu_select_item("Open Order...");
        set_window("Open Order",time_out);
                win_check_gui("Open Order", "list4.ckl", "gui4", 1);
        win_close("Open Order");
set_window("Flight Reservation",time_Out);
        menu_select_item("Reports...");
        set_window("report - Notepad",time_out);
                win_check_gui("report - Notepad", "list5.ckl", "gui5", 1);
        set_window("report - Notepad",time_out);
                menu _ select_item("Find...");
                set_window("Find",time_out);
                        win_check_gui("Find", "list6.ckl", "gui6", 1);
                win_close("Find");
        set_window("report - Notepad",time_out);
                menu_select_item("Open ...");
                set_window("Open",time_out);
                        win_check_gui("Open", "list7.ckl", "gui7", 1);
                win_close("Open");
        set_window("report - Notepad",time_out);
                menu_select_item("Page Setup...");
                set_window("Page Setup",time_out);
                        win_check_gui("Page Setup", "list8.ckl", gui8, 1);
                set_window("Page Setup",time_out);
                        button_press("Printer...");
                        set_window("Page Setup_1",time_out);
                                win check gui("Page Setup_1", "list9.ckl", "gui9", 1);
                        win_close("Page Setup_1");
                win_close("Page Setup");
        set_window("report - Notepad",time_out);
                menu_select_item("Save As...");
                set_window("Save As",time_out);
                        win_check_gui("Save As", "list10.ckl", "gui10", 1);
                win_close("Save As");
        win_close("report - Notepad");
```

TABLE 12.4

Bitmap Regression
Test Script

```
time_out=getvar("timeout");
set_window("Flight Reservation",time_out);
        win_check_bitmap("Flight Reservation", "Img1", 1);
set_window("Flight Reservation",time_out);
        menu_select_item("About...");
        set_window("About Flight Reservation System",time_out);
                win_check_bitmap("About Flight Reservation System", "Img2", 1);
        win_close("About Flight Reservation System");
set_window("Flight Reservation",time_out);
        menu_select_item("Graphs...");
        set_Window("Graphics Server",time_out);
                win_close("Graphics Server");
```

test performance of a system after changes have been made. The possible objectives of a test cycle are as varied as the client/server system itself.

RapidTest Cycle Wizard is a wizard of a different color. It doesn't build test scripts. What it does is to provide assistance in putting test scripts together into a comprehensive test cycle. Once the test cycle has been created, Cycle Wizard can be employed to initiate the test cycle.

Cycle Wizard allows the tester to build upon test outlines which have been built with Plan Wizard. When Cycle Wizard is initiated, it prompts the tester to select a test database. If an existing database is specified, then the subjects and tests defined in that database are listed. Figure 12.6 presents a test database and its subjects and tests.

Tests can be added to the current test cycle by highlighting them in the left part of the windows and dragging them to a table on the right part of the screen. As many or as few tests can be added to the cycle as desired. Cycle Wizard allows the tester to easily create a large number of test cycles, each of which can focus on a particular testing objective.

It is a very good idea for the testing staff to enter general information on all test cycles which are created. Examples of the types of information these should include are: the cycle name, open date, close date, current status, and a description. As more test cycles are defined, it becomes more difficult to locate specific ones with this information being defined. Figure 12.7 displays the window which allows background information on test cycles to be entered.

Once all tests for the test cycle have been defined, Cycle Wizard creates an entry in TestDirector. The need to use Cycle Wizard for this particular test cycle has ended. From this point on the tester will interact with TestDirector to initiate the test cycle and analyze its results.

Figure 12.6
Contents of an
existing Test
Database Viewed
Through Cycle
Wizard

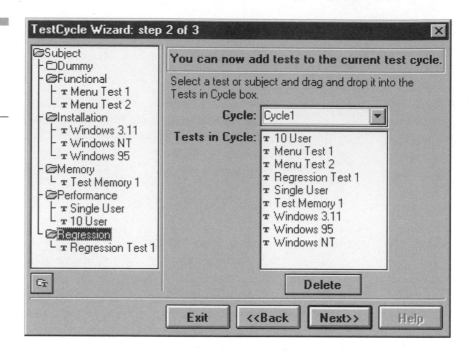

It should be fairly obvious by now that the tools in Mercury Interactive's tools suite are designed to complement each other. They will be particularly effective when they are used in conjunction. The Test Plan Wizard is used to lay out the broad outline of testing. Script Wizard is then used to generate automated test scripts which test GUI objects in the application. Cycle Wizard assists the testing staff in creating groups of tests used to check specific objectives. Test cycles built with the Cycle Wizard are initiated via TestDirector. The wizards provided within this test suite don't need to be used, but they provide a great deal of direction and assistance.

12.4 Segue's GO!

GO! is a product in Segue's Quality Works suite which will automatically test client/server system software. It generates scripts and test plans to perform much of the essential but routine test cases. Tests created by GO! are reusable by other testing tools in the Quality Works suite.

12.4.1 Testing Phases

Segue cleaves the set of all client/server system testing into three phases. The first phase is operability testing. Operability testing is done to verify that the basic functionality of the system exists. The focus of this testing includes:

1. Verify that user interface (UI) controls are present and conform with standards and specifications.
2. Validate that UI controls are properly initialized.
3. Confirm that the tab sequence is correct.
4. Verify that UI controls support speed keys, i.e., keys which are underlined on UI controls.

The second phase of testing is functionality testing. Functionality testing verifies that a single user can successfully use the application to perform documented activities. This phase of testing is roughly equivalent to the description of Unit Testing described earlier in this book. Descriptions of tests performed during this phase include:

1. Verify that application algorithms produce correct results and the UI controls display these values.
2. Monitor and observe UI control changes which should occur.
3. Check that database connections and queries function correctly.
4. Confirm that DDE and OLE processes function when called.
5. Verify processes initiated by the application become active as appropriate.

Figure 12.7
Test Cycle General
Information

Edit Cycle	⊠
Cycle:	Cycle1	OK
Open Date:	12/1/96	Cancel
Close Date:		
Status:	In Progress	
Description:	Integration Test for Demo Application	
☐ Copy data from Cycle:	Cycle1	

The third and final phase of testing defined by Segue is distributed client/server testing. This validates that the client/server system functions correctly when multiple users access the system simultaneously. The definition for System Testing earlier in this book corresponds roughly with Segue's description of phase three testing. Tests which should be performed in this phase include:

1. Confirm that multiple users can concurrently use the system, database, etc.

2. Monitor system performance as increasing levels of load are imposed on the system.

3. Verify that events which trigger other events function correctly.

12.4.2 Test Phases Where GO! Is Applicable

Segue's wizard, GO!, doesn't pretend to automate testing for all three phases. Segue recognizes that testing during the second phase is heavily dependent on knowledge about the functionality of the client/server system and its individual application(s). It isn't possible for an automatic tool or wizard to include this type of information. Only a human tester, relying on the system specifications, can provide test cases which adequately test the functionality of the system.

The third phase of testing can use some of the scripts created for phase two. Executing these scripts to sufficiently exercise the system can't be accomplished by GO! either. Adequately testing the distributed nature of a client/server system requires in-depth knowledge of the applications, database, network, and a number of other topics.

GO! addresses the testing done during just the first phase of testing. This testing could certainly be performed manually, but it is monotonous work. It would be easy for the testing staff to overlook some of the aspects of the UI which must be tested. Automating the UI portion of the testing reduces the amount of effort by a significant amount while reducing the dull, repetitive work which the staff must perform.

12.4.3 Using GO!

Developing a test script using GO! is pretty intuitive. The steps to create a series of UI tests on a Text Editor type application are listed in Table 12.5. Exposing each window in the application to GO! is

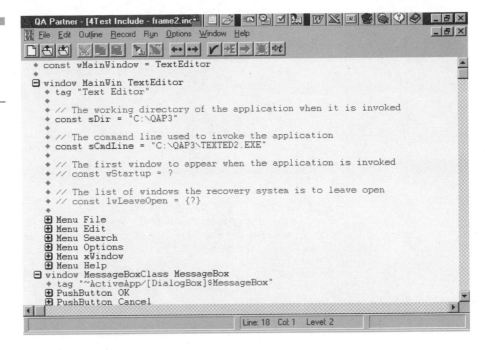

required. Fortunately the steps which must be repeated for each window are easily performed and can be done very quickly.

Steps 1 through 10 in Table 12.5 create statements to check a single window or dialog box. Steps 3 through 10 have to be repeated to capture details on every window and dialog box in the application.

Once the test script has been captured, it must be tested. GO! can be directed to execute the script by selecting the Run|GO! menu option. GO! will open the window(s) declared in the test frame. Any errors will be logged in a results file.

Figure 12.9 is an example of the script created to invoke a single window.

12.5 Questions to Ask Before Acquiring a Wizard

Wizards come in a variety of shapes and sizes. Some are more automated than others. Wizards address a wide range of what they will test. Some require a great deal of hands-on interaction and others require very little. A number of questions should be asked before acquiring a wizard. The following sections bring up a number of topics which should be considered when choosing a wizard.

TABLE 12.5

Steps to Create Test
Scripts with GO!

1) A Test Frame must be created for each application to be tested. The steps to create the test frame are to select File|New within QA Partner, click the Test Frame radio button.

2) At this point a list of all currently running applications will be presented. Select the application for which GO! is to create test scripts. GO! will generate a description of the application's main window. This description includes the menu tree.

3) QA Partner now must be exposed to and capture details on each window and dialog box in the application. To capture these descriptions, bring up the first window to be learned and select menu item Record|Window Declarations in QA Partner.

4) Position the mouse cursor on the title bar of the current window and press the CTRL-ALT keys.

5) Click on the *Paste To Editor* button. This will add declaration statements for this window to the test frame. Close both the window and the QA Partner *Record Window Declarations* dialog box. Figure 12.8 displays how QA Partner appears once declaration statements have been created for the first window in the application.

6) Now QA Partner must be taught how to invoke this window or dialog box. Select menu item Record|Method in QA Partner.

7) When the *Record Method* window comes up, select an appropriate value for drop-down list box *Method Name* and click the *Start Recording button*. Focus will automatically be returned to the application being tested.

8) Perform the steps required to bring up the window or dialog box. This might be clicking a button or selecting a menu item. Each of these steps are recorded by GO! and written to the test script.

9) Terminate recording by clicking the *Done* button on the *Record Status* window.

10) Click the *Paste To Editor* button back on the *Record Method* Window.

Many of these questions will sound familiar to readers. Some of them are very similar to questions that need to be considered when selecting an automated test tool. The reason for the similarity is that most, if not all, wizards are associated with or very similar to the automated test tools already discussed.

12.5.1 What Testing Aspects Does the Wizard Automate?

For the most part, wizards focus on testing user interface controls. These controls and their properties are fairly consistent and predictable. This consistency makes it easier for wizards to process them.

Does the wizard being considered automate the type of testing you are planning to do? Some wizards focus heavily on determining if an application's user interface is compatible with published standards. If your shop doesn't adhere to these standards, then a wizard which focuses on this type of testing wouldn't be too valuable.

12.5.2 Is It Part of a Suite?

Almost all wizards are a single component offered as part of a suite of test tools. Generally, these wizards are tightly integrated with the rest of the suite components. The value of the wizard by itself is insignificant. If your shop isn't considering a particular testing suite, then the wizard component shouldn't be considered by itself. The test scripts output by the wizard will be useless outside of that particular testing environment.

12.5.3 Does the Wizard Run on Multiple Platforms?

This same question was posed for automated testing tools. It is just as appropriate to ask it about wizards. If the tool runs on only a single

Figure 12.9
GO! Script to Invoke
a Window

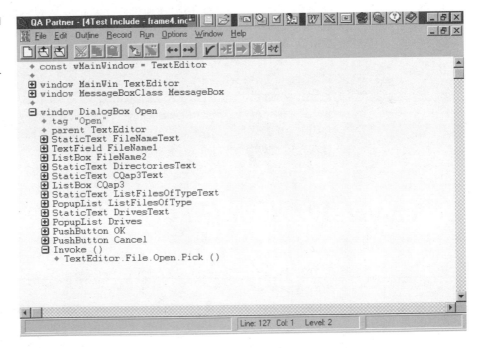

platform and your enterprise encompasses multiple platforms, it might not be appropriate.

12.5.4 What Level of Skill Is Required?

While wizards promise to perform a significant amount of the testing automatically, they still require a fairly high level of understanding. In fact, the skill required to set them up and run them might be higher than other test tools. Does the testing staff possess this level of skill? If they don't possess it, can they acquire it? Is management prepared to invest in the effort needed to research and acquire the proper tool, set up the tool, and train its users? If the answer to any of these questions is no, then successful use of this tool is doubtful.

12.5.5 Are the Test Scripts Produced Re-usable and Editable?

One thing that can be said about client/server systems that is certain to be true is that they are always changing. The user interface changes constantly as users make their wishes (demands) known. The hardware which client software runs on is frequently upgraded. The operating system and other related software on both server and client machines is upgraded.

Test scripts produced by the wizard must be able to cope in the changing environment. Tests should be able to run on multiple platforms with little or no modification. Modifications to enhance or augment test scripts should be easy to implement. Test scripts should be usable in multiple testing situations, including unit testing, integration testing, system testing, and regression testing.

12.6 Summary

While wizards vary in their approaches, thoroughness, and usability, there are a few statements about them which apply to them all. They offer the testing staff a number of efficiencies and advantages. For certain types of tests, they can save an appreciable amount of time. Some literature provided by vendors claims that their products allow tests to be developed at a minimum six times faster than the same tests produced manually. While the exact savings may not be that precise, these types of tools are certainly efficient and productive.

The area where they are of the most value is doing the required standard tests. An automated tool which produces tests of this type will save a significant amount of time. Basic testing of the user interface certainly fits this description.

A wizard will also commit fewer omissions than a human being while producing tests which are very repetitive in nature. People tend to get bored and make mistakes when performing monotonous, boring testing. If tools can automate the mundane tests, then the testing staff can concentrate on tests which require more ingenuity and experience.

A wizard that has been well designed and is easy to use can be a substantial help in minimizing regenerating testing after nominal changes to the application. In some cases the wizard is simply executed again. Other wizards require that test scripts be edited. Since applications undergo frequent changes, a wizard which easily adapts to application modifications will prove to be priceless.

Perhaps the biggest area where wizards help is that they can get the testing effort jump started. Testing the user interface, while not exciting or particularly challenging, must be done. A client/server system with a large number of windows and controls will require a fairly large number of tests for the UI alone. Being able to automate this step can allow the test team to produce a significant percentage of their test scripts very quickly. This can prove to be a great confidence booster for the team.

Don't make the mistake of being deluded by marketing hype; wizards don't completely automate all of the testing. They can be of great value, but a human being needs to set up the process, oversee tests being developed, and check the output. Wizards are far from testing systems all by themselves.

Overlooked Aspects of Client/Server Testing

CHAPTER 13

SQL Testing
and Databases

When testing client/server systems, there frequently is not any testing performed which specifically addresses the database and the statements that access it. If any testing is directed towards these areas, it is incidental testing that results from testing the front-end user interface. The database and data manipulation statements accessing it require focused testing. Without an explicit effort to test this area of the system, you can't be certain that major problems aren't lurking about the system.

13.1 Testing SQL

Virtually every client/server system uses the structured query language (SQL) to access relational databases. The SQL language combined with a relational database might represent the ultimate example of a two-edged sword. SQL enables the user to access and manipulate an incredible amount of data with a few fairly straightforward statements. A single query is able to select, massage, group, and summarize millions of rows of data in a database. It allows the developer to quickly and with relative ease develop statements which return data for display in windows and reports. A single statement can also modify a single, numerous, or all the rows in a database table. If triggers or dependencies have been defined, one update statement has the potential to affect many other tables in the database.

All of this potential power is accompanied by a price tag that isn't always recognized or understood. The potential exists for some mammoth blunders to be made when using SQL to access a relational database. Poorly written and tested statements can easily return incorrect data from a query. Decisions based on this data should be subject to question. Insufficiently tested SQL statements can have a significantly adverse effect on system performance as well. A badly coded SQL statement can be amazingly less efficient than one that has been well thought out and designed.

13.1.1 SQL Pitfalls

There are a number of areas related to SQL that should be explicitly examined. These areas have an enormous potential to impact performance or accuracy. A brief description of some potential pitfalls is outlined in the following sections.

13.1.1.1 Query Statements.

SQL select statements are deceptively easy to write. A "select" here, list one or more tables in the "from" section, a couple of "where" clauses and, viola, results are returned to the developer. Like most instances of things being too good to be true, this applies to SQL programming. Select statements need to be examined in detail to make certain they are returning the desired rows, no more and no less.

One area that should always be examined closely is the practice of properly identifying columns in select statements. If multiple tables are being referenced in a query, there is the possibility that one or more columns in these tables will have the same name. When this is the case, these column references cannot be allowed to be ambiguous. The developer must specify the table when referencing an ambiguous column. Good programming practice would dictate that the developer always identify the table for all columns in every SQL statement. Correlation names (also known as aliases) can be used to minimize the amount of extra typing required.

A potentially explosive problem related to this situation is when tables are altered to add columns. The SQL statement as originally written might work successfully. However, when one or more of the tables are changed six months down the road, the statement may no longer function. The problem might be that the statement originally left out table specifications because no ambiguous columns existed at that time. Later the same query will abort because more than one table has a column by the same name. A desk check should examine all SQL code to make certain all columns include table references.

Another practice that could incur future problems is using a "select*" statement. SQL certainly makes it convenient to select all columns from a table by using the "star" notation. When being introduced to SQL, many examples in primer-level books emphasis this practice. Unfortunately, if the table is later modified to include additional columns, this convenience will probably cause problems. The result set will include additional column(s) after the table is modified. The best practice is to specify all columns by name even if it means additional typing.

13.1.1.2 Modify Statements.

SQL statements that modify the database can be even more dangerous than query statements. This list of statements includes insert, delete, update, drop table, and truncate table. A single SQL statement has the potential to wipe out or incorrectly alter vast amounts of data. Each statement that has the capability to modify the database must be thoroughly tested to obtain a high level of confidence in it.

Most SQL books provide examples that are pretty vanilla. One typical example used to demonstrate how an update statement works involves giving everyone in the employee table a 10% raise. The code to accomplish this task is:

```
UPDATE employee SET emp_salary = emp_salary * 1.1
```

While this example certainly is accurate, it's pretty simplistic. In the real world, most update statements don't update the entire table. Update operations are normally much more selective. They frequently update a single row. Sometimes, though, they need to modify rows in table A which exist in another table (B). This type of update is extremely powerful but equally dangerous. A poorly written statement or incorrect data in table B will cause the wrong statements to be updated.

Any statements which delete rows from tables or deletes tables themselves should be confirmed with users prior to being performed. The user should be informed in no uncertain terms of the action that is about to be taken. Normally this is done with a dialogue box or a popup window. The popup window which presents this information should also include two clearly labeled buttons. One should continue the operation in question and the other should allow the user to cancel the operation. Testing should verify that the correct action is taken when each of the buttons is clicked.

13.1.1.3 Table Joins.   Table joins present a huge opportunity for errors to creep into SQL statements. Improper joins made in the where clause of SQL statements create the possibility for data to appear multiple times or not at all. If the developer writing the code does not completely understand the relationships between tables being joined, it's a disaster waiting to happen. A statement which doesn't correctly include all the required join conditions will return incorrect results.

Developers might attempt to join tables that have no business being joined. They both might have one or more identically named columns, but these columns and tables may have absolutely nothing to do with each other. Section 13.3 explains how a data dictionary can help prevent problems of this nature.

The warnings about incorrectly joining tables are especially applicable when aggregate functions are being used. Because these functions don't present individual data rows, it is easier for a reasonable looking but erroneous result to be accepted. Section 13.1.1.9 addresses the problems and testing of aggregate functions in SQL statements.

13.1.1.4 Outer Joins. Outer join conditions often produce invalid result sets. A description of an outer join condition will probably be more enlightening initially than a textbook definition. Assume there are two database tables: account and transaction. The columns in these tables are listed in Table 13.1. The current contents of these two tables are listed in Table 13.2

A report is desired to list all of the account numbers, name of account holders, and the number of outstanding transactions. One SQL statement that would returns this information is:

```
SELECT a.acct_number, a.acct_name, COUNT(t.acct_number)
FROM account a, transaction t
WHERE a.acct_number = t.acct_number
GROUP BY a.acct_number, a.acct_name
```

The result set returned by the above statement is:

```
acct_number acct_name COUNT(t.acct_number)
100123789 Smith, Homer 3
100632942 Green, Estes 7
```

Even the most casual observer should notice that one of the three accounts in the account table hasn't been included in the report. The expectation was probably that this account number and name would be listed with a count of zero. This is not what happens in the SQL real world. This is because Ms. Quisling didn't have any rows in the transaction table. Without rows in both tables, the join between the two tables won't include her in the result set. This situation is referred to as an outer join problem.

13.1.1.5 Outer Join Extensions. Some RDBMS have the capability to specify that result sets should include all rows with an entry in either of the tables being joined. The syntax of specifying that the statement

TABLE 13.1

Account Table and Transaction Table Definitions

Account	Transaction
acct_number	acct_number
acct_name	trans_date
acct_address	trans_amount
credit_rating	merchant_id
current_balance	
date_opened	

TABLE 13.2

Account Table and
Transaction Table
Contents

Account Table Contents

Acct_number	Acct_name	Acct_address	Credit_rating	Current_balance	Date_opened
100123789	Smith, Homer	123 Anywhere St.	A	1023	1/1/95
100234678	Quisling, Ima	45 Tattle Tale Lane	D	5500.32	1/1/96
100632942	Green, Estes	89 Mountain View	B	300.1	6/6/95

Transaction Table Contents

Acct_number	Trans_date	Tran_amount	Merch_id
100123789	1/3/97	45.23	654322
100123789	1/14/97	434.77	724136
100123789	1/28/97	12.45	912345
100632942	1/3/97	66.78	123546
100632942	1/13/97	1000.54	913247
100632942	1/19/97	65.98	613245
100632942	1/19/97	9.57	720987
100632942	1/19/97	298.99	654322
100632942	1/28/97	25.35	720987
100632942	1/31/97	65.45	981254

should include the outer join data isn't standard across the industry. Each vendor that provides this capability has its own syntax, notation, etc. One method of denoting an outer join is to include a plus sign ("+") in the table declaration. The position of the plus sign indicates which table constitutes the "outer" table. The following SQL statement is the same as the previous statement, except that it specifies that an outer join should be used.

```
SELECT a.acct_number, a.acct_name, COUNT(t.acct_number)
FROM account+ a, transaction t
WHERE a.acct_number = t.acct_number
GROUP BY a.acct_number, a.acct_name
```

The result set returned by the above statement is:

acct_number	acct_name	COUNT(t.acct_number)
100123789	Smith, Homer	3
100632942	Green, Estes	7
100234678	Quisling, Ima	(NULL)

The results returned include an entry for the account which has no entries in the transaction table. The value supplied for the third column is the NULL value. Since there is no value for this column the database engine needed to provide something. Some RDBMS systems will allow the programmer to specify a value which can be substituted for a NULL value. Other systems can only return a NULL value in this situation. Both the development staff and the testing staff need to be aware of the specifics for the database system being tested.

13.1.1.6 Cartesian Products. SQL statements with incorrect or incomplete "where" clauses often cause a Cartesian product to result. This also happens if tables are being joined which have no logical relation with each other. A Cartesian product is a situation where every column in every table is joined together and returned. This represents probably the worst-case scenario of table join problems. The number of rows being returned is equal to the number of rows in the first table times the number of rows in the second table. If additional tables are involved, then their rows' counts are included in the product. Tables with tens of thousands of rows are common. It isn't uncommon for tables to contain close to a million rows. A query that creates a Cartesian product can easily return hundreds of thousand or millions of rows.

Drawing on the tables described in Section 13.1.1.4, the following select statement creates a Cartesian product. The intent of the select statement was to display all account numbers and the transactions associated with them. However, the where clause that specifies that "a.acct_number = t.acct_number" has been omitted. The result will be a Cartesian product.

```
SELECT a.acct_number, a.acct_name, t.trans_date, t.tran_amount
FROM account a, transaction t
```

The Cartesian product returned by the above statement is presented in Table 13.3. Instead of returning the ten rows it should produce, the result includes thirty rows. By comparing these rows with those in Table 13.2, it's obvious that transactions have been associated with accounts they shouldn't be. One account had no related rows in the transaction table, but the results show that it had the same ten transactions as the other two accounts. This example presents a Cartesian product created by two extremely simple, small tables. The effects would be devastating if each of the tables had hundreds, thousands, or even millions of rows.

When aggregate functions are used in select statements, they have the potential to hide or disguise the creation of Cartesian products. This is because individual rows aren't being displayed. The aggregate might be processing a number of values and returning just the sum or average as a result. Without extensive testing or familiarity with the test database it would be easy to miss errors in these aggregate results.

One characteristic of Cartesian products which is likely to be noticed immediately is that performance will get bad very quickly. Instead of selecting and returning a reasonable number of rows, the load will be much heavier. The database engine will grind away to produce a result set much larger than expected. Once the database has processed the query, then the network will be heavily loaded as all those rows are returned to the client machine which requested it.

Obviously no developer would intentionally write an SQL statement which produces a Cartesian. How, then, do they get into systems? One answer is simply inadequate testing. If the developer doesn't examine his or her queries closely (and the results even more closely), then this problem can inadvertently occur.

A situation which can contribute to select statements generating Cartesian products is an inadequately sized and distributed database. If database tables used for testing have relatively very few records, such as the account and transaction tables used in the above examples, a Cartesian product can occur and be easily missed. Getting back 30 rows instead of 10 is a mistake

TABLE 13.3

Cartesian Product
Result Set

Acct_number	Acct_name	Trans_Date	Trans_Amount
100123789	Smith, Homer	1/3/97	45.23
100123789	Smith, Homer	1/14/97	434.77
100123789	Smith, Homer	1/28/97	12.45
100123789	Smith, Homer	1/3/97	66.78
100123789	Smith, Homer	1/13/97	1000.54
100123789	Smith, Homer	1/19/97	65.98
100123789	Smith, Homer	1/19/97	9.57
100123789	Smith, Homer	1/19/97	298.99
100123789	Smith, Homer	1/28/97	25.35
100123789	Smith, Homer	1/31/97	65.45
100234678	Quisling, Ima	1/3/97	45.23
100234678	Quisling, Ima	1/14/97	434.77
100234678	Quisling, Ima	1/28/97	12.45
100234678	Quisling, Ima	1/3/97	66.78
100234678	Quisling, Ima	1/13/97	1000.54
100234678	Quisling, Ima	1/19/97	65.98
100234678	Quisling, Ima	1/19/97	9.57
100234678	Quisling, lma	1/19/97	298.99
100234678	Quisling, Ima	1/31/97	25.35
100234678	Quisling, lma	1/31/97	65.45
100632942	Green, Estes	1/3/97	45.23
100632942	Green, Estes	1/14/97	434.77
100632942	Green, Estes	1/28/97	12.45
100632942	Green, Estes	1/3/97	66.78
100632942	Green, Estes	1/13/97	1000.54
100632942	Green, Estes	1/19/97	65.98
100632942	Green, Estes	1/19/97	9.57
100632942	Green, Estes	1/19/97	298.99
100632942	Green, Estes	1/28/97	25.35
100632942	Green, Estes	1/31/97	65.45

which could be overlooked. If the test database included production-sized tables, it would be very difficult if not impossible to miss a Cartesian product being returned. It would be difficult to overlook getting back a million rows instead of the 100 rows which had been expected. If nothing else, the impact on performance should warn the developer or tester that something is seriously amiss with the query being tested.

13.1.1.7 Dates and Time.   Dates are an especially tricky area to program and test because each RDBMS handles date and time values in its own way. There are not yet any industrywide standards on how this type of data is handled, processed, or stored. Until standards are created and implemented across the industry, then date and time processing will continue to be difficult and error intensive.

Each RDBMS seems to use a different internal format and reference point to maintain its dates. Most store their date values as the number of seconds since a reference point. The reference point on which dates are based range from 12/30/1899 to 1/1/1900 to 1/1/1970.

There is no standard for the ranges of valid date values or the amount of storage space that dates will occupy. Eight bytes is fairly typical, but storage requirements of four, seven, and twelve bytes exist. Some systems include normal and small date formats. The small date formats have a more restricted date range that they can hold. Small date formats frequently don't maintain time to the second granularity. Minutes are the finest unit of measurement offered by small date formats.

Some database systems include a time value in their date data field. Other databases maintain time in a field which is separate from the date field. While neither approach is "better" than another, the inconsistency makes it difficult to transport data and test scripts from one system to another.

The formats which database systems expect date values to be presented in varies drastically. Some database systems are extremely flexible, while others are fairly rigid. The delimiters which can be used to separate dates vary as well. Date values being input might need to be formatted in an "MM/DD/YY" format. Other systems may require that dates be specified in a format of "JAN/01/96." Other systems will take dates in practically any format.

Functions to compare dates, calculate differences between dates, and convert dates to and from text are all extensions to the standard SQL statements. This all but guarantees that no two database systems will have the same functions. Migrating date processing and test scripts from one platform to another is a tedious and manually intensive process.

13.1.1.8 Transaction Processing.

Transactions have already been defined to be a logical and indivisible unit of work. Transaction processing is too important to be left to chance or random testing. This logic must be explicitly tested. Improper handling of transaction processing can result in data being lost or corrupted and/or tables being locked for extended periods of time.

One of the classic examples of a transaction comes from the world of finance. The example is a banking customer wishing to transfer funds (i.e., $100.00) from a savings account to a checking account at the same bank. The transaction consists of two separate steps. The first step is to perform an update statement which subtracts the funds from the savings account. The second step is to update the database to add the funds to the checking account. This transfer of funds between accounts must be handled as a single activity. Either both steps succeed or both steps fail. Transaction processing won't allow one step to succeed and the other to fail. If the step fails, then the database engine will back out the first step so the database is left in its original state.

Defining exactly what constitutes a transaction is the first step in testing transaction processing. In the client/server system being developed, a transaction might involve simultaneously creating entries in more than one table. It might require that values in multiple tables be updated simultaneously. Whatever the requirements, the first step is to determine and define what exactly constitutes a transaction. This step should be performed during the design phase. This would allow the developers to write code to properly handle transactions. If it wasn't done at that time, then it must be done before testing begins.

The second step towards testing transaction processing is to code the SQL statements that actually perform the database manipulations required by the transaction. If the code has already been written, then these statements need to be identified. A single SQL statement is by default a transaction, so what needs to be identified is multiple SQL statements; these statements are required to process a unit of work. It's especially important to identify the first and the last statements which constitute a transaction.

Step three involves examining the code between the first and last statements of the transaction to make sure it includes as little processing as possible. The objective is to minimize the code within a transaction to the absolute minimum. The reason for this is twofold. First of all, reducing the number of statements in the transaction block reduces the amount of time it takes to complete the transaction and commit it.

Secondly, by minimizing the time that transaction requires to be processed, you reduce the impact on other users attempting to access the same tables. The tables will be released as quickly as possible.

What needs to be especially protected against is the possibility for the system to allow transactions to be extended indefinitely. One way this might occur is if there is the possibility of user think time allowed to occur during a transaction. If the transaction begins when the user selects data and ends when the user saves the data, then the transaction would continue while the user examines the data. It might even be open while the user goes to lunch!

The danger of allowing a transaction to stay open indefinitely is that the database engine is holding locks on the affected tables during this entire process. If the locks are being held, there is the definite possibility that other users will be denied the ability to access the tables in question. If these tables are crucial to the client/server system, then the entire system can very easily grind to a halt.

The proper duration for a transaction should be limited to the code within a single event. It might be all contained within the "click" event of a "Save" command button. Once the user clicks the "Save" button the transaction begins, is processed, and is committed. When transactions are designed this way, there is very little possibility that they will be held open for extended periods of time.

Identifying to the database engine what constitutes a transaction is step four in this process. Most database systems require transaction processing to be bound by "begin transaction" and "commit transaction" statements. The database engine recognizes that all query statements within the begin and commit block need to be handled as a single transaction. The exact syntax differs among different database vendors. In some systems there is no explicit begin statement. All queries which have occurred since the most recent commit statement constitute the current transaction. Consult the documentation provided by your database vendor.

The final step of dealing with transaction processing is to actually test the transactions. Once they have been identified, it is time to try to force transactions to malfunction. The methods of doing this are as varied as the transactions themselves.

One test would be to force processing to terminate in the middle of a transaction action. This could be done by powering down the terminal. A less drastic method would be to insert code which causes the application to terminate. Another approach would be to have another process obtain a lock on a resource the transaction requires. Deliberately causing a database deadlock would also create a good testing situation. Once the transaction has been halted or terminated, it is necessary to examine the state of the database tables involved. They should be in the same state as they were prior to the transaction being started. The database engine should have rolled back any transactions which terminated in the middle of their processing.

13.1.1.9 Aggregate Functions. Aggregate functions (also referred to as set functions) operate on a collection of values in a single column of a table. They summarize data based on a group of rows from the database. Aggregate functions also return a single value instead of a result set which could include many, many rows. Aggregate functions aren't standardized. Each database vendor provides its own set of aggregates, although some of the common functions are available from almost every vendor. Examples of some commonly available aggregate functions include count, count unique, sum, sum unique, average, average unique, min, and max. Table 13.4 contains descriptions of these aggregate functions:

SQL statements which include aggregate functions are susceptible to errors. The reason is that it isn't immediately obvious whether an aggregate statement is returning the correct results or not. Since individual

	Function Name and Parameter	Description of Function
TABLE 13.4 Descriptions of Aggregate Functions	AVG (column name)	Returns the arithmetic mean of the column specified for the group of rows.
	AVG (DISTINCT column name)	Returns the arithmetic mean of distinct values for the specified column for the group of rows.
	COUNT(*)	Returns the number of rows in the group.
	COUNT(DISTINCT column name)	Returns the count of unique values in the specified column for the group of rows.
	MAX(column name)	Returns the maximum value of the specified column for the group of rows.
	MIN(column name)	Returns the minimum value of the specified column for the group of rows.
	SUM(column name)	Returns the sum of the specified column for the group of rows.
	SUM (DISTINCT column name)	Returns the sum of the unique values of the specified column for the group of rows.

rows aren't displayed, it can be difficult to determine what rows are included in the aggregate calculation.

One method of testing the accuracy of a statement is to remove the aggregate call and examine the rows which are returned. Seeing the individual rows frequently enables the tester to determine whether the set of data is what should be expected. It also allows the tester to make the calculations manually to compare them with what the aggregate returns.

An example of this technique is provided which references the account and transaction tables. Suppose the user wants a report which counts the transactions on a day-by-day basis. The statement to provide this information is:

```
SELECT trans_date, COUNT(*)
FROM transaction
GROUP BY trans_date
ORDER BY trans_date
```

The results from the previous query are:

trans_date	Count(*)
1997-01-02	1
1997-01-03	2
1997-01-13	1
1997-01-14	1
1997-01-19	3
1997-01-28	1
1997-01-31	2

How does the tester know that this result set is correct? If the number of rows in the two tables are fairly limited, then it should not be hard to check. Modify the query to remove the aggregate function and the "group by" clause and rerun the statement. Columns acct_number and tran_amount have been added to the select list. This is to make it easier to recognize the different transactions. The result query statement would be:

```
SELECT trans_date, acct_number, tran_amount
FROM transaction
ORDER BY trans_date
```

The results from this query are:

trans_date	acct_number	tran_amount
1997-01-02	100632942	(NULL)
1997-01-03	100123789	45.23
1997-01-03	100632942	66.78
1997-01-13	100632942	1000.54
1997-01-14	100123789	434.77
1997-01-19	100632942	65.98
1997-01-19	100632492	9.57
1997-01-19	100632942	298.99
1997-01-28	100123789	12.45
1997-01-31	100632942	25.35
1997-01-31	100632942	65.45

The COUNT values returned by the SQL query can be verified by examining this result set and counting the number of transactions which occurred on each of the dates. To be effective, the test data must include dates on which zero, one, and more than one transaction occurred. If the test includes this diversity of data, then comparing the results of these two query statements should adequately test the aggregate call.

SQL statements containing other aggregate functions can be tested in the same manner. Assume a report in the client/server system required that the sum of transactions be displayed for each account. The SQL statement and the results would be:

```
SELECT acct_number, SUM(tran_amount)
FROM transaction
GROUP BY acct_number
ORDER BY acct_number
```

acct_number	SUM(tran_amount)
100123789	492.45
100632942	1532.66

To test this query you would modify the query to select accounts and transaction amounts and order them by account number. This would allow the tester to verify the SUM aggregate by calculating the sum manually. Test data in the transaction table should include accounts with zero, one, and more records. The test SQL statement and results would be as follows:

```
SELECT acct_number, tran_amount
FROM transaction
ORDER BY acct_number
```

acct_number	tran_amount
100123789	45.23
100123789	434.77
100123789	12.45
100632942	66.78
100632942	1000.54
100632942	65.98
100632942	9.57
100632942	298.99
100632942	25.35
100632942	65.45

The technique of verifying the results returned by an aggregate by rewriting the SQL query to remove it can be used to test about any query. Some will be more complicated and require a little more ingenuity. Another important requirement to test aggregates is to have a set of test data which is comprehensive. The topic of test databases is covered in Section 13.1.1.14.

13.1.1.10 String Manipulation. String manipulation is not particularly developer friendly within most RDBMS packages. No two systems provide the same string related capabilities. Most of the functions offered are fairly basic, but function calls can be combined to achieve more complex manipulations. Some of the functions which are available in many RDBMS packages are listed in Table 13.5

The functions listed in Table 13.5 could be used to separate values from within a single string field. In the account table the acct_name

TABLE 13.5

String Manipulation Functions

ASCII(string)	Returns the ASCII code value of the first character in string.
Char(integer)	Returns the ASCII character which the integer value represents.
Left(string, count)	Returns the leftmost "count" characters from string.
Lower(string)	Converts the characters in the expression to lowercase.
Locate(str1, str2, start)	Locates the first instance of str2 within str1. If a start value is provided then the search starts at that address.
Ltrim(string)	Returns the string with leading blanks removed.
Right(string, count)	Returns the right-most "count" characters from string.
Rtrim(string)	Returns the string with trailing blanks removed.
Substr(str1, start, length)	Returns a substring from str1 beginning at position "start" for "length" characters.
Trim(string)	Returns the string with leading and trailing blanks removed.
Upper(string)	Converts the characters in the expression to uppercase.

column contains both the last name and the first name. These two values can be extracted separately by employing a combination of string functions. The select query to accomplish this is as follows:

```
SELECT acct_number, LastName = LEFT(acct_name, LOCATE(acct_name,
',')-1 ),
  FirstName = RIGHT(acct_name, LENGTH(acct_name)-LOCATE(acct_name,
','))
FROM account
ORDER BY LastName
```

The result set returned by this query is:

acct_number	LastName	FirstName
100632942	Green	Estes
100234678	Quisling	Ima
100123789	Smith	Homer

When testing string functions of any kind, the most important consideration is to make sure that the data is varied enough. If the test is performed on a very limited sample of data, the query will probably work correctly. If the production data contains more diverse data or bad data, the query results may not come out so cleanly.

The example query provided above assumes that the name value will always contain a comma separating the last name from the first name. What if the comma wasn't there? What if two commas were somehow included? What would the result set look like then? The only way to determine this is to test for it. If a row didn't contain a comma, the result would be:

acct_number	LastName	FirstName
123456789		Nocomma Joe
100632942	Green	Estes
100234678	Quisling	Ima
100123789	Smith	Homer

If a row existed with two commas in the acct_name field, the results of the above query would be:

acct_number	LastName	FirstName
100632942	Green	Estes
100234678	Quisling	Ima
100123789	Smith	Homer
123456789	Twocomma	,Joe

It should be obvious that neither of these result sets is probably what was expected. All query statements which include string functions must be tested thoroughly. Data validity can have a potentially devastating impact on query results. This is especially true if string manipulation is used.

Many database systems allow string functions to be used in both the select list and in where clauses. Care must be exercised if a function is used in the where portion of an SQL statement. The following query demonstrates a statement with such a where clause. The reason for this caution is that the use of a function in a where clause will likely force the database engine to perform a complete table scan of the table being searched. Indexes won't be used when developing the plan for this query. While this won't be a significant impact when selecting from a test table with a few dozen entries, it can cripple a system which has hundreds of thousands of rows in production tables.

```
SELECT acct_number, acct_name, acct_address
FROM account
WHERE RIGHT(acct_address, 3) = 'St.'
```

The result set returned by this statement is:

acct_number	acct_name	acct_address
100123789	Smith, Homer	123 Anywhere St.

The need to use extreme measures such as string functions in a where clause might indicate improper database design. The account table in the examples is a good example. It is extremely unlikely that a table in a production database would contain an entire name. Normally the last name is held in one column, the first name in another column, and the initial in its own columns. If SQL statements include string functions in the where clause, that might indicate that columns have included data which should be divided into separate fields.

13.1.1.11 Infrequently Used SQL Functions. There are several other SQL functions that bear close testing. One reason for this is because they are less frequently used, and therefore developers are less adept with them. Partly it is because they have the potential to impact performance. A list of these functions, what they do, and why they bear watching is included in the following sections.

13.1.1.11.1 Outer Joins When two tables are joined, the normal result set returned includes only data from rows which exist in both tables. Suppose, for example, the join is on the account and transaction tables. A normal join, also called an inner join, won't return data about accounts which don't have rows in the transaction table.

There are times when it is desirable for a query to return all records from the tables, whether they have rows in both tables or not. Referring to the above example, a report may need to list all accounts and a count of their transactions. Accounts should be returned whether they have records in the transaction table or not. This is referred to as an outer join.

Developers don't normally deal with outer joins. When an SQL query with an outer join is written, it should be rigorously tested. It would be very easy for the developer to make a mistake in the statement.

13.1.1.11.2 Union Operator   A union statement allows the results of multiple select statements to be combined into a single, larger result set. Union statements are fairly uncommon, and developers should be aware when writing them. One tricky aspect of union statements is when the user wants the result set to eliminate duplicate rows. When this is desired, the "union all" statement should be used.

13.1.1.11.3 Distinct   When an SQL select statement is coded, it can easily return duplicate rows. Adding the word "distinct" to the select statement will eliminate duplicate rows. There are two potential dangers when this is done. The first problem is that eliminating duplicate rows can take significantly longer to process. The second problem is that in many cases the duplicate being returned actually represents an error in the SQL statement.

Use of the distinct clause should be reserved for situations where it is truly needed. Developers should also examine the statement to make sure that they aren't masking a problem.

13.1.1.11.4 Having   A select statement restricts rows being returned to those which meet any "where" clause in the SQL statement. In a similar manner, a "having" clause also restricts the rows being returned. Having clauses are used when the select statement involves an aggregate function and a "group by" clause. Many developers aren't very experienced with this statement. Any selects which include them should be tested to make sure the correct result set is being returned.

13.1.1.11.5 Subqueries   A subquery is a select statement embedded within another select statement. The inner select returns a single value. A subselect is frequently used in a where clause to restrict the rows being returned. An example of a subquery is provided in the following SQL statement. This statement returns the set of all transactions which involve an amount greater than the average transaction.

```
SELECT *
FROM transactions WHERE transaction_amount >=
(SELECT AVG(transaction_amount) FROM transactions);
```

Subqueries have a fair amount of risk. A poorly written subquery can be extremely inefficient. Statements of this type can be difficult to write correctly. It can be quite easy to unknowingly accept incorrect results from such a statement.

13.1.1.11.6 Update Update statements are risky primarily because they change data. Any query which modifies data is hazardous. The run-of-the-mill update statement is fairly straightforward. Update statements can become more complicated. A second table can be referenced in an update statement. This is the point at which this type of statement starts to get risky. The following SQL statement updates the balance column in the account table with the sum the account's transaction balances.

```
UPDATE account
SET balance = SUM(transaction_amount)
FROM transaction
WHERE account.account_no = transaction.account_no
```

The danger here is that the column can be updated with the wrong value. If the where clause in this example were omitted, each row in the account table would have a balance equal to the sum of all transactions.

13.1.1.12 NULLs. The concept of NULL values and whether they should be allowed in a database has been the topic of many papers, articles, letters, and rebuttals. The subject has become a wedge between many of the notable players in the relational database field. This book is not intending to join that fray. The reality is that all relational database systems allow NULL values. Whether this is right or wrong, good or bad is immaterial. NULLs exist in databases, and their existence requires that client/server systems be capable of handling them. Testing must be designed to verify that NULLs are being handled properly.

13.1.1.12.1 Effects of NULLS on Aggregates NULLs complicate the writing and testing of SQL statements significantly. There are a number of justifications for this statement. The first explanation is that aggregates don't handle NULL values well. Some examples of how NULLs complicate aggregate functions are described. To make matters worse, there is no guarantee that aggregate functions from different database vendors handle NULL values in the same manner. All query statements which include an aggregate function should be closely examined to determine how NULL values could conceivably affect their processing.

13.1.1.12.2 Comparing NULL Values The second major way in which NULL values complicate SQL queries is the way NULLs are handled in comparison operations. The following SQL statement is intended to select all rows which have a transaction value less than or equal to $10.00:

```
SELECT acct_number
FROM transaction
WHERE tran_amount <= 10.00
```

Suppose that a number of transactions had NULL values in their tran_amount fields. Would these rows be included in this result set? Should they be? Most relational systems will not include a NULL value within the result set returned by the above statement. This example is fairly trivial, but the effects of NULL values can have a significant impact on SQL queries. This is especially true if the developers of a client/server system aren't aware of how the RDBMS system will handle NULL values.

The above statement could be rewritten as shown below. A where clause to explicitly test for the NULL condition has been added to the query. It will then return rows with a transaction amount of NULL. Unfortunately, there is a very strong likelihood that developers won't consistently include the second comparison clause. If this isn't done uniformly within the client/server system's logic, then a significant amount of time will be required to find and correct such omissions.

```
SELECT acct_number
FROM transaction
WHERE tran_amount <= 10.00
OR tran_amount IS NULL
```

13.1.1.12.3 NULL Values Returned by Functions   Many functions called from SQL statements have the potential to return NULL values. Aggregate functions in particular will return a NULL value for a query which contains no rows. The following select statements are examples of queries which return NULL values:

```
SELECT AVG(tran_amount)
FROM transaction
WHERE tran_amount > 10000

AVG(tran_amount)
(NULL)

SELECT SUM(tran_amount)
FROM transaction
WHERE merchant_id = 'bad merchant'

SUM(tran_amount)
(NULL)
```

Aggregates aren't the only functions which have the potential to return NULL values. Most arithmetic-type functions will return a NULL if the field or column being referenced contains a NULL value. String functions, such as LOCATE, can return NULL values.

The return values from all functions which can possibly return a NULL must be checked for this prospect. A variable which is set to NULL can't be compared to anything but a NULL value. For example, assume that the following SQL statement returns a NULL value. If avg_salary is later included in a comparison statement, the result will be negative no matter what the comparison. Avg_salary isn't zero, it isn't greater than zero, and it isn't less than zero. It's NULL. The only comparison that will result in a TRUE value is when it is compared to NULL. The possibility that such variables can be assigned NULL values must be checked after each function call.

```
SELECT :avg_salary = AVG(salary)
FROM PAYROLL
WHERE dept = 'Training'
```

13.1.1.12.4 MINIMIZING NULLS' EFFECTS ON TESTING How can the impact of NULL values on testing be minimized? First of all, the database design must determine whether NULLs will be allowed in each column in the database. This information should be published in the system's data dictionary. Most database systems will not allow NULL values in fields that are part of a table's primary keys. It's also not advisable to allow nulls in fields upon which indexes are based.

Finally, NULLs shouldn't be permitted in fields which are likely to be the object of either aggregates or where clauses. This can be enforced by declaring the column to be NOT NULL when the table is created. If the database system doesn't provide this capability, then the only alternative would be to include a test for NULLs in the validity checking at the user interface level. Adhering to these suggestions will help to minimize the impact of NULL values on system testing.

13.1.1.13 RDBMS SQL Extensions. Many industry pundits are predicting that relational database systems are quickly becoming a commodity product. As more and more standards are agreed upon, the vendors have less freedom in their RDBMS package design. As this process continues, then the developer becomes hard pressed to recognize the differences between two vendors' offering. In an effort to differentiate themselves from increasingly standardized packages vendors offer extensions to the standard relational database system capabilities.

Some examples of these extensions include:

- Date function calls.
- String functions.
- Unique data types.
- User-defined data types.
- Bitwise operators.
- Large text field support.
- BLOB (binary large object) support.
- Multimedia object support.
- Updates of rows in views.
- Temporary tables and other database objects.
- Control over indexes.
- Ability to insert data from one table into itself.

The standard vendor claim is that RDBMS extensions allow them to offer their clients the best possible database package. A discriminating buyer might wonder if there is a more insidious reason for including extensions. Using nonstandard extensions has the effect of locking clients into a database package. Capabilities within systems become dependent upon these extensions. As this occurs, it makes switching to a different system that much more difficult, time-consuming, and expensive. Keep this in mind when deciding whether to use nonstandard SQL functions.

The decision whether to take advantage of RDBMS extensions must be made on a project or organizationwide basis. Leaving a decision of this nature up to individuals is courting disaster.

How do extensions affect the testing process?

1. Consistent usage of extensions must be checked.
2. Complicated queries must be tested.
3. Scripts which test extensions cannot be used on other platforms.

13.1.1.14 Return Codes. I don't know if the majority of developers are optimists, lazy, or a combination of the two. No matter what the explanation, as a rule their code frequently doesn't check the return codes returned by database calls. Code after every database query needs to check the SQL return code. This code indicates whether the query completed successfully. Some of the codes are dependent on the RDBMS package, but many of them have been standardized industrywide. These codes provide extremely valuable information about the success (or lack of success) of the SQL statement, but they are worthless if they aren't checked and acted upon.

Some examples of codes that might be returned by the database engine include:

- Database engine not running.
- Deadlock detected.
- Dynamic memory exhausted.
- Invalid data conversion.
- Invalid operation on joined table.
- Error writing to log file.
- Communications error.
- Invalid user or password.
- Not connected to SQL database.
- Primary key for table xxx is not unique.
- Operation successful.
- Row not found.
- Too many connections to the database.
- Value truncated.

The method to detect an SQL-related error is different in each development environment, but they are all somewhat similar. A PowerBuilder-based example of checking for an error would be:

```
CONNECT;
If SQLCA.SQLCode = -1 Then
        MessageBox("SQL error " + String(SQLCA.SQLDBCode),
SQLCA.SQLErrText)
End If
```

Some errors will be obvious to the user. For example, if data isn't being displayed, the user will figure out that something has gone wrong. Other situations, like inserts and updates, might not be obvious to the user. If the user isn't informed that an error has occurred, then it would be reasonable for him or her to assume that the operation was successful. Action must be taken when an error code is returned by the database engine.

The action which should be taken upon error detection depends heavily on the type of error and the function which the user was attempting to perform. When feasible, the application should attempt to perform the same operation again. If the operation isn't successful after a configurable number of attempts, the system should escalate to the next level of processing. This would be to inform the user that a problem has occurred and instruct them what their options are. Options might include retrying the operation again or refreshing the data. In extreme circumstances, users might be instructed to call a support person to assist with a problem.

If possible, all logic which handles error returns should be included in a subroutine or other separate object. There are many advantages to modularizing this function. The first is that it doesn't leave this important logic to each individual developer. Writing it correctly once and simply calling this code after each SQL statement is much more efficient. It also makes correcting the code easier and faster if it resides in a single module. The alternative would be to make changes in hundreds of places throughout the application. This can create a regression testing nightmare.

Actually, creating all of the potential error return codes might prove to be impractical. This means that some logic might not be testable before that particular error occurs. Desk checking of code should include scrutinizing the error-handling code after each SQL query.

13.1.1.15 Data.   SQL statements rely heavily on accurate, complete data. If the data is questionable, then the results will be questionable. What constitutes questionable data? Rows with a significant number of NULL values are suspect. At some point test cases or users are going to refer to this data and it won't be there.

Duplicate rows present another type of data quality problem. Like the arguments which surround NULL values, the question of whether duplicate rows should be allowed in databases crops up. One camp argues that a relational database shouldn't allow duplicate rows. They would allege that the need for duplicate rows represents a flaw in the database design.

No matter which position ultimately wins out, developers and testers need to make a decision about duplicate rows. Should they be allowed? If not, how can they be prevented? What are the implications on queries, reports, and testing?

The concept of referential integrity means that data in one table refers to data in other tables. If values in one table refer to rows in other tables which don't exist, then the data's integrity is poor. An example can be made from the account and transaction tables introduced earlier. A row in the transaction table might contain a reference to account number "xyz." If there is no account "xyz" in the account table, this presents a referential integrity problem.

13.1.1.15.1 Imported Data
Bad data can come about in at least two ways. Inaccurate or incomplete data can be loaded into the system. Data is only as clean and reliable as the source of the data enables it to be. Many times the source of data is a feed from another system, a conversion from a legacy system, or an import from a flat file. These sources should be examined closely to be certain they contain "clean" data. Are the records complete? Is referential integrity valid? Are there duplicate rows? Other systems, particularly those which are flat-file based, aren't as stringent as relational databases on these topics.

A co-worker recently asked me to look at an SQL statement she was working on. She had added an "order by" clause to a query and had experienced unexpected results. She said the query was now returning each row two times instead of just once. This had not been happening prior to including the "order by" she claimed. Her query joined three tables. Tables A and B had a one-to-many relationship based on a bank number. Tables B and C had a one-to-many relationship based on a client account number. She couldn't understand how simply reordering the rows could cause each row to appear twice. I told her it wasn't possible for the "order by" clause to do this, that it must be something else.

To make a long story short, the cause of the problem was bad data in table A. It had been imported from a PC legacy database and contained two entries for each bank instead of the single entry which should have existed. This caused each user account to be returned twice because it joined with two entries in the bank table instead of just one. The problem was resolved by cleaning up the data.

The really scary thing about this experience is that the results of the query had been incorrect all along. The query had always been returning twice as many rows as it should have been. This situation was only noticed after the "order by" clause was included. Prior to being sorted, the duplicate rows had been there, but they weren't noticed because the result set was very large. A large volume of data being returned has the capability to camouflage errors by overwhelming the user.

13.1.1.15.2 Internal Corruption of Data
The other potential source for inaccurate data is through the actions of the client/server system itself. Users enter records, transactions, etc., into virtually every client/server

system via applications. If the applications don't enforce a minimal level of quality on the data being entered, then the contents of the database won't be very trustworthy. It is the responsibility of the testing staff to be certain that this quality has been built into the system.

13.1.1.15.2.1 Referential Integrity Data that is initially accurate and valid in a client/server system can be rendered invalid by a poorly designed system. The developer and system designer can't assume that users will understand the theory behind referential integrity. A client shouldn't be allowed to be deleted from the system if it has corresponding records in the orders table, the accounts payable table, the accounts receivable table, etc. Before the client can be dropped, all tables which have the potential to create referential integrity problems should be checked.

Either the system must drop related records itself (via programming or triggers) or explain to the user what steps are needed before the desired delete operation can be completed. If the user is successful in causing these problems, it represents a flaw in the system design. The blame shouldn't (and can't be) blamed on user ignorance.

13.1.1.15.2.2 Data Boundaries and Dependencies Another method in which the client/server system should control data quality is when pick lists are used. Many fields have well-defined upper or lower bounds. Other fields have a dependent relationship with another field on the window. The GUI should enforce these boundaries and relationships. It is incumbent on the testing staff to make certain that this quality checking is being done.

Some examples of data fields which have defined boundaries are percentage fields. They must be between 0.00 and 1.00. Age values must be greater than zero and less than some upper limit. Depending on the application, this upper limit will vary. If the system deals with employees, then a reasonable upper limit might be 100. When dealing with medical data, a realistic upper limit might be 125. Salaries should be greater than the minimum wage.

Other data quality checks require the value in one field to be compared or related to values in other fields. Zip codes should be checked against either the city or state. A user shouldn't be allowed to enter a 99xxx zip code when the address already entered is in Delaware. Area codes should be verified against city or state values. These two examples are fairly generic, but each application will likely have many fields with this type of dependency. Each of these situations must be explicitly tested.

13.1.2 Testing SQL Statements for Accuracy

How can you make sure that your SQL statements are accurate? The answer, of course, is testing. This section is an attempt to present some SQL testing topics that should be considered before testing a client/server system.

13.1.2.1 When to Test SQL Statements. SQL statements need to be tested at the individual module level, i.e., during unit testing. These types of tests are not particularly conducive to scripts or automated test tools. Once testing has progressed to integration and system testing, then the focus of testing moves outward to larger pieces of the system.

13.1.2.2 SQL Testing Goals. When testing SQL statements there are two separate goals which must be achieved. Although unrelated, each of these goals is necessary for the queries to contribute to the success of the client/server system.

The SQL statements must be accurate. That is, they must perform the actions which they are supposed to. In the case of a SELECT statement, testing must verify that the correct result set is being returned. When UPDATE or DELETE statements are the object of the testing, then it must be verified that the appropriate rows are modified or deleted.

The second objective relates to the performance of the statement; specifically is the query efficient? How long does the statement take to execute? A query that works but takes an excessive amount of time will prove to be worthless in a production environment. Users will not regard the system as a success if it takes more than a few seconds to retrieve basic data.

The testing to verify these two goals is performed in a specific order. The first objective must be to verify that the statement is correct. Once the accuracy of the SQL code is ensured, then steps will be taken to check the performance of the statement. It doesn't make much sense to expend time and effort in order to make an incorrect SQL statement more efficient.

13.1.2.3 Test Databases. The two objectives listed above are disparate enough that they require different testing approaches. The most significant difference in testing approaches is that distinct databases are needed. Two databases are needed to accomplish both of the objectives. A small test database can be used when testing the accuracy of SQL statements. Performance-related testing requires a larger database.

To be perfectly accurate, separate small and large databases might not be required. All that is necessary is that two distinct sets (large and small) of tables are available when SQL statements are being tested. Many database systems allow multiple tables to have the same name if the owners of the tables are different. Frequently, two tables with the same name are referred to as private and public versions of the table. The developer "owns" the private copy of the table and the DBA "owns" the public version. If this capability is available under the RDBMS system being tested, then the individual developer or tester can reference the private (small) version of the table for the first testing step and the public (larger) version for the second phase of testing.

13.1.2.4 Small Database.   Testing the accuracy of SQL statements requires that the tester be very familiar with both the expected results of the statements and the contents of the database. Only by knowing both of these areas can the tester verify that accurate result sets are being returned.

An example of statements and database contents will probably be beneficial at this point. Assume that two SQL statements are being tested. The first is supposed to return the list of all customers who have placed an order in the last 90 days. The second is intended to return customers who haven't placed an order in at least 90 days. The following two SQL statements fulfill these two requirements.

```
SELECT DISTINCT a.acct_number, a.acct_name
FROM account a, transaction t
WHERE a.acct_number = t.acct_number
    AND t.trans_date >= DAYS(TODAY(*), -90)

SELECT a.acct_number, a.acct_name
FROM account a
WHERE DAYS(TODAY(*), -90) > (SELECT MAX(t.trans_date)
                             FROM transaction t
                             WHERE a.acct_number = t.acct_number)
```

Test data must exist in the database that will be returned by each of these SQL queries. Additionally, there should be companies which fulfill neither situation. An outline of the data requirements for these tests includes the following:

1. Accounts that have only transactions more recent than 90 days.

2. Accounts which have only transactions older than 90 days.

3. Accounts with transactions in both time periods.

4. An account with a single transaction which is exactly 90 days old.

5. Accounts with no transactions at all.

The question of whether accounts with no activity should be included in the second report might be open. This decision will have a definite effect on how the query statement will be coded. Accounts with absolutely no transactions represents an outer join situation. The system specifications should dictate how this possibility should be handled. A question such as this should not be left to individual developers or testers to resolve on their own. They may not think of this situation, but primarily there is no guarantee that their decision would parallel what the users expect.

Companies which fall into all five categories are needed to adequately test these two SQL statements. In order to effectively test these queries, the tester will probably need to create customers from scratch specifically for these tests. Only by knowing what customers and transactions exist can the tester be certain that the correct rows are being returned.

The need to be extremely familiar with the data explains why the large database can't be relied upon during the initial phase of testing. The developer isn't likely to know all of the data which is in a very large database. Additionally, if the large database is being used by other developers, then it will likely be very volatile. Rows which were in a common database yesterday may not be in it today. In any event the tester will have trouble verifying that the results are correct if a large database is used when testing these statements.

13.1.2.5 Large Database.   A large database is necessary to determine if the queries are being processed efficiently. The reason that a different database is needed is because even the most inefficient SQL statement will perform acceptably if the tables being accessed have only a handful of rows. If the tables have very few rows, there may not be more than a fraction of a second difference between the most efficient and least efficient SQL statements. It is only when the size of the database is expanded that these efficiency differences are noticeable.

This test database must be sized to be as large as the maximum projected size of the production system. Many systems start up with a relatively small database and continue to grow as data is entered into them. In time they grow to their maximum production size. Performance testing must be performed on a database which has been sized to the final configuration. If this isn't done, then performance may be adequate when the system first goes online but degrades as the database grows. While this may defer problems for a little while, it would be much better to test on the full-sized database and avoid performance problems altogether. Section 15.1.2.3 provides information on tools which help to create a production-sized database.

Performance testing on a production-sized database may turn up the need for additional indexes, keys, transaction logs, or tables which need to be denormalized. This database will also turn up accuracy problems which won't appear in a small database.

When should efficiency testing be done? As usual the answer is as soon as possible. The earlier problems with the database are exposed the easier and cheaper it will be to correct them. There will be times when the correct solution is to simply add an index to a table. Creating an index on a table can be done at any time and requires no changes to any applications. Unfortunately, most database performance problems require solutions which are much more complicated than this. Frequently, the correction to a poorly performing query involves modifying one or more database tables. An existing table might need to be split into two tables or two existing tables may need to be combined into a single table. Completely new tables might also be required.

Other performance problems are solved by modifying the SQL statements. SQL, like most computer languages, allows the programmer to get the same results in more than one way. One method may be more efficient, but the correct result can be achieved by many, alternative statements. A quick example involves the SQL statement which selects all accounts with orders in the last 90 days. The original solution was:

```
SELECT DISTINCT a.acct_number, a.acct_name
FROM account a, transaction t
WHERE a.acct_number = t.acct_number
    AND t.trans_date >= DAYS(TODAY(*), -90)
```

An alternative statement which will return the same result set is:

```
SELECT a.acct_number, a.acct_name
FROM account a
WHERE DAYS(TODAY(*), -90) < (SELECT MAX(t.trans_date)
                             FROM transaction t
                             WHERE a.acct_number = t.acct_number)
```

Although they both return the same results, which one is more efficient? There are two ways to determine the answer to this question. The first method would be to run both queries and bracket them with statements which measure the amount of time they take to execute. Most RDBMS systems provide function calls which return the amount of CPU time and the number of disk I/O operations performed. By running both queries a number of times and averaging their results, the developer can determine which SQL statement is the most efficient.

The other technique to determine which statement is more efficient is to use a capability which is built into most database systems. Most RDBMS systems will allow the developer to view the query plan which is going to be used. A query plan defines exactly how the data will be extracted from the database. It includes details such as which indexes (if any) will be used, what kinds of sorts and joins will be performed, and what temporary tables will be created. Developers and testers need to become familiar with how to read and understand query plans. They must be able to recognize a plan which indicates that a truly bad query is being processed.

One last suggested solution to a poorly performing SQL statement is to move it into a stored procedure. While stored procedures don't represent a panacea, there are many situations where they will create a marked improvement in performance of a query. There are two primary reasons that explain the efficiency of stored procedures. A stored procedure generates less network traffic than an SQL statement which originates on a user workstation. Since stored procedures reside in the database there is no need for client-to-server communications. The second reason is that stored procedures are compiled the first time they are used. Subsequent executions of the stored procedure don't require the compilation process to be repeated.

13.2 Testing Databases

Databases aren't the monolithic objects which many developers and management personnel assume them to be. Cutting-edge databases include a large amount of internal knowledge and functionality. These items need to be specifically addressed during the testing effort. It isn't reasonable to assume testing on applications, transactions, or the user interface will be adequate.

13.2.1 Stored Procedures

Stored procedures are collections of SQL statements and conditional logic statements which reside in the database. They can be called by code or other stored procedures. From a testing point of view, the main advantage of using stored procedures is that SQL statements become centralized in a single location. Centralizing SQL statements allows the testing staff to focus on a single collection of statements instead of testing the same (or almost the same) functionality spread throughout the system. This advantage is a very significant one which shouldn't be minimized.

There are at least two approaches to testing stored procedures. The first is to remove the outer "shell" of the stored procedure and test it as simply a collection of SQL statements. This approach has the advantage of being simple to implement, and it will work for most stored procedures.

Needless to say, some stored procedures include more than simply SQL code. Most RDBMS systems allow stored procedures to include a fairly comprehensive collection of conditional logic statements. Stored procedures have the capability of becoming almost as complex as programs or subroutines.

Another drawback to simply testing the SQL statements within a stored procedure is that this doesn't test the parameters being passed to it. Much of the flexibility of stored procedures comes from their ability to receive and react to parameters passed to them. This allows them to perform slightly different functions for different callers. Testing must be done to make certain that parameters are handled correctly within stored procedures.

The other approach towards testing stored procedures is to utilize a debugging tool which specifically addresses stored procedures. The debugging capabilities of such a tool allow the tester to step into the statements of the stored procedure. They offer functionality much like debuggers in PowerBuilder and Visual Basic development tools.

Some of the capabilities of one debugging tool include:

1. Single step through stored procedure statements.

2. Flow of control within a stored procedure can be jumped to a specified line.

3. Breakpoints can be declared in the stored procedure. Breakpoints can be conditional or unconditional.

4. Local variables, global variables, and procedure parameters can be viewed and modified.

5. The status, result set, and current position of all declared cursors can be displayed.

6. Nested calls to other stored procedures can be skipped over or stepped into.

7. Triggers on database tables can be stepped into.

8. Procedure parameters can be stored in a text file and re-used later.

9. Procedure text is automatically indented and color coded for easier comprehension.
10. The ability to view the structure of database tables and indexes is provided.
11. Contents of database tables can be viewed and modified.
12. Data from tables can be exported into ASCII and spreadsheet formats.
13. Reports can document table structures, table data, stored procedures, triggers, and views.

13.2.2 Triggers

Triggers are specialized stored procedures which execute ("fire") under specialized circumstances. The circumstances that cause triggers to fire are queries which modify database tables. A trigger can be written to fire when a single, specified table has rows inserted, deleted, or updated. A trigger can in turn call stored procedures or cause other triggers to be fired.

Testing triggers can be accomplished in several ways. The first would be to perform an action that causes the trigger to fire and observe the results. For example, a trigger might be created on the account table to delete related rows in the transaction table when an account is deleted. A record in the transaction table that has no corresponding record in the account table is called an orphaned record. Orphaned records violate the principle of referential integrity.

Testing this trigger would involve deleting rows from the account table and verifying that those transaction records with the same account number are deleted. Accounts with zero, one, and more rows in the transaction table would need to be deleted during this testing. It would also be advisable to perform a count of the rows in the transaction table before and afterwards to make certain that only the expected rows have been deleted.

Another method of testing triggers would be to use a debugging tool. The debugger outlined in the section on stored procedures also provides the capability of testing triggers. A breakpoint on the trigger being tested would be set and the appropriate modification would be made to the base table. By stepping through the trigger, it could be determined whether it is functioning correctly.

From an administration and testing point of view, triggers are valuable for the same reasons that stored procedures are valuable. They provide a means of defining logic in one place and have it initiated when certain events occur from anywhere in the system. Testing a single trigger is easier than searching through hundreds of windows and thousands of lines of code attempting to find which one left an orphaned row after a delete operation.

13.2.3 Rules

Database rules are a method which allows control over what values can be inserted into columns of database tables. Rules are a powerful technique for enforcing data validity in a client/server system. Unfortunately, not all database systems provide the capability of defining rules. A rule can be defined such that only "F" or "M" can be inserted into a column titled gender. Another rule can require that an age value be between 1 and 120. Other rules could require that a U.S. state value be one of the fifty USPS state abbreviations or that zip codes be legitimate.

Testing rules essentially boil down to attempting to insert bad data into the database. This can be done by utilizing an application to create or modify records. It can also be done via an interactive SQL session. If testing is done with the application being developed, make sure that understandable error messages are being presented to the user. An explicit message that only the values "F" and "M" are allowed in this field is required. Don't reference rule names or any other internal logic in the message which the user sees. Keep it simple.

The alternative to using rules to enforce data validity is to add logic to all applications and windows which accept user input. This will result in code being duplicated in many places.

If rules are used, the amount of code and testing can be pared down. For example, assume that a gender field exists in a table. Data validity could be enforced by creating a single rule on that column or by adding logic to each of the many screens that list that column. Which requires more logic? To test the rule, the tester only has to attempt to input an invalid value from any application. Testing data validation which is included as part of the application requires that every single window accessing this column be tested.

It should be obvious that testing a single rule is significantly easier, faster, and more accurate than testing a large number of windows. Multiply this by the number of fields and windows which need to be tested and the discrepancy grows.

Rules are also significantly more productive if the data validity requirements should happen to change. If a fifty-first state were added to the Union, then all data validation on the state field would need to be updated. Either the single rule would be changed and tested, or all of the screens would need to be changed and tested.

13.2.4 Primary Keys

Primary keys serve a dual purpose in a relational database. The first purpose is to enforce uniqueness among rows in the table. If the unique identifier in the account table is account number, then declaring a primary key on that field will prevent multiple rows with duplicate account numbers from being included in the table.

Testing primary keys is a two-step process. The first step is to identify what constitutes a unique identifier of rows in each table. This column or combination of columns is then declared to be the primary key in the database table.

This step isn't as easy as it might appear to be. There will be tables in which the primary key won't be obvious. A simple example is the transaction table described earlier. Its columns include an account number, a transaction date, a transaction amount, and a merchant ID. The account number can't be the primary key because that would limit accounts to a single transaction. Combining other columns would have similar limitations.

Some tables won't have a combination of columns which guarantee a unique identifier for each row. In these cases an additional column, called a surrogate key, can be added. This is a value, frequently an ascending number, generated specifically to be a unique identifier of each row in the table. When a surrogate key is being generated for each row, then additional testing must be included to focus specifically on this value.

The second step in testing primary keys is to attempt to violate the uniqueness of the primary key. The tester can attempt to add a record with a duplicate key value. For example, a new account could be added which has the same account number as an existing row. Another test would be to attempt to modify a current record to change its key value to be the same as another record. Any attempts to perform the above should meet with failure.

13.2.5 Foreign Keys

Perhaps the most basic concept in a relational database is that tables are related to each other. The transaction table and the account table are related because records in the transaction table refer back to records in the account table. A foreign key is a value in one table which uniquely identifies rows in another table. For example, the transaction table contains the column acct_number. Acct_number is the primary key in the account table.

Foreign keys are used in relational databases to enforce referential integrity. If records in the account table are deleted, then the system must make certain that related records in all other tables are deleted as well. This can be accomplished through triggers, constraints, or application code, but it must be consistently applied. If it isn't applied consistently, then the database will eventually generate invalid data.

Testing foreign keys involves a combination of studying the database design and actions to verify that the enforcement technique has been implemented correctly and thoroughly. The database design must be examined to make certain that all tables with this type of relationship have been identified. Once they have been identified, then the chosen technique used to enforce the relationship must be applied in all locations. Testing foreign keys involves deleting records from one table and verifying that corresponding records are dropped from related tables.

13.2.6 Constraints

One definition of the word constraint is "a limitation or restriction." That definition describes exactly what a table constraint is; it is a restriction placed on the table. A table constraint restricts what values can be placed in the table's columns. While each database system varies, table constraints come in four general types. Each of these types is described in the following paragraphs.

Check constraints can be created to restrict the values which can be inserted into columns. A check constraint could be created to restrict values in a field to "F" and "M." Check constraints are very similar to database rules that were described earlier.

Foreign key constraints restrict values in columns to match values in a primary key of another table. A foreign key constraint could be used to force all values in the transaction table's acct_number column to appear in the account table.

Action can be declared to take place if a change is made which would violate a foreign key constraint. If a row in the account table is being modified or deleted, this would have the potential to violate a foreign key constraint in the transaction table. Potential actions on tables with a foreign key constraint include cascading the delete to related rows in the transaction table or modifying the foreign key value in the transaction so the constraint isn't violated.

Primary key constraints enforce uniqueness of the primary key in a database table. The account table could have a primary key constraint declared for the acct_number column. This would guarantee that each row in the table has a unique account number. Each table can have only a single primary key.

The final form of constraints is a unique constraint. A unique constraint can be declared for one or more columns which uniquely identify a row in the table. Unique constraints are similar to primary keys, but there can be more than one unique constraint declared for a table. An example of a unique constraint might exist in an employee table. The primary key of this table would be employee number. Each employee also has a Social Security number which is unique. A unique constraint could be declared on this field to ensure that each employee's Social Security number is unique.

Testing of constraints involves verifying that constraints are defined correctly. The second step is testing to make certain that they do what they are supposed to do. Testing actions would involve the following:

1. Attempting to insert rows into tables which violate check constraints.

2. Attempting to modify current values such that a check constraint would be violated.

3. Deleting rows which would violate foreign key constraints and verifying that appropriate actions are taken by the database engine.

4. Modifying values such that foreign key constraints are violated and verifying that appropriate actions have been taken by the database engine.

5. Attempting to insert rows which would violate the primary key constraint on the table.

6. Modifying values such that the primary key constraint on the table is violated.

7. Insert a row in a table which would result in a unique constraint being violated.

8. Modifying a value in a column such that the unique constraint is violated.

13.2.7 User-Defined DataTypes

Some relational database systems allow the declaration of local, user-defined data types (UDT). There are usually some limitations in how different from traditional data types the UDTs can be. UDTs are an attempt to make it easier to set up and reference specialized data which is used throughout a database.

If the client/server development project takes the opportunity to create and employ a user-defined data type, then this object must be tested thoroughly. Part of the testing should center on insuring that the data type was set up correctly. Later testing needs to make certain that developers understood, correctly used, and referenced this object.

13.2.8 Indexes

The primary use of an index is to enhance performance when accessing rows in the database. Suppose the system needs to provide a report based on the transaction table. The purpose of this report is to summarize the number and total transaction amount by merchant code. As the table currently exists, the database engine would have to perform a full table scan on the table to find all transactions for a given merchant. If the table grows to a significant size, this query would require a great deal of disk activity. An index on the merchant ID field could be added on this column. This index cuts down enormously on the effort required to fulfill requests based on a column which has had an index defined for it.

An *index* is a separate table based on one or more columns of a specific base table. The saying about a free lunch applies to indexes as much as anything else. Being a separate table, indexes require disk space. The wider the index and the more rows in the base table, the more space the index will require. Indexes also require a certain amount of maintenance. Each time a row is inserted, deleted, or modified in the base table, the index needs to be updated. The overhead incurred by placing an index on a frequently modified column may outweigh the potential benefits.

A properly designed database will include indexes on a large number of tables. Testing for indexes amounts to making sure that all columns which require indexes have them, and columns which don't require indexes don't have them. Indexes are appropriate for columns that are frequently referenced in the where clauses of SQL statements. Another candidate is a column that is joined with other columns in SQL statements. Indexes on columns which don't fit this description won't provide any performance improvement. Once an index has been declared, the database maintains it and determines if it will be used in query plans.

13.2.9 Replication

Replication is the ability to copy changes made in one database to one or more other databases. This feature is useful when the organization has a decentralized system. The advantages of creating decentralized databases include greater local control of the data, lower telecommunications costs, and better system performance. The ability to replicate databases is becoming a feature which more RDBMS systems are including.

Some of the basic terms and concepts in replication technology include the following:

- Asynchronous. The ability to log SQL commands for later transmission and processing at the second database.
- Bidirectional. When data changes can be made at either the publisher database or the subscriber database.
- Heterogeneous. Implies that the databases involved are different products, i.e., Oracle, Sybase, Informix.
- Heteromorphic. The data elements being replicated have different names on each database.
- Publisher. The originator of the replicated database changes.
- Push replication. The publisher site controls the replication process by "pushing" data out to subscribers.
- Pull replication. The subscriber site controls the replication process by "pulling" date from publisher.
- Refresh. Occurs when one or more tables are completely replicated.
- Subscriber. The receiver of replicated database changes.

When database replication is included in a client/server database, the process needs to be explicitly tested. Tests should be run which assure that changes to all publisher databases are replicated correctly to all subscribers. The timing of when replication activities take place should also be checked. Data collision (i.e., what happens if a particular row is changed in multiple databases) is an area which also needs to be thoroughly tested. Replication activity between heterogeneous databases (i.e., an Oracle database replicating to an Informix database) is another area where problems can occur. If replication is made to multiple databases, then each subscriber should be tested to assure that it received all changes it expects. The impact of data replication on system performance needs to be investigated. Poor communications between the different locations can cripple the replication process. The quality of communications connections should be tested when the system is established and periodically thereafter.

13.2.10 Backups

Any data which is deemed to be valuable enough to be put on a client/server system is valuable enough to be backed up. The plan for backing up the system should be devised and tested long before the system goes into production. In addition to being common sense, maintaining adequate backups is a legal obligation for some systems. There is no excuse for not knowing exactly what is being backed up and how frequently this is being done.

There are at least two kinds of backups which can be done. A full system backup (also called an offline backup) requires that the system be shut down before the backup is begun. Once the system has been properly shut down, the operating system is used to make backups of all pertinent files. A full backup should be done periodically. Full backups are frequently performed weekly or monthly.

Online backups (also called daily backups) can be done while the system is up and running. The RDBMS package copies data to a special type of backup file. Online backups frequently back up just the data which has been changed since the last backup.

While every database system is different, most vendors recommend a combination of online and offline backups. Offline backups are done periodically, while online backups are done more regularly. The combination decided upon attempts to minimize impact on the system while ensuring that the system can be completely rebuilt if the worst case should happen.

The backup plan needs to be tested thoroughly. It is surprising how something as seemingly simple as a backup can go wrong. Some potential problems are:

1. The backup files exceed the capacity of the storage device.
2. The backup process can't be completed in the scheduling window allotted to it.
3. The system isn't taken down cleanly or completely before a full backup is started.
4. The tape drive used to back up the system breaks down or produces a tape which can't be read.
5. Backup tapes are improperly labeled or overwritten.
6. The timer or scheduling function which should initiate the backup doesn't.
7. The backup doesn't include everything it should.

While it's the most obvious component, the database isn't the only object which needs to be backed up. Other objects that must be backed up to ensure continuity include:

- Source code files.
- Executable files.
- Initialization (INI) files.
- Online help files.
- Icon files.
- Images used by the system, e.g., .TIF files.
- DLL (dynamic link library) files.
- Report files.
- System documentation.

13.2.11 Recovery Procedures

Data recovery procedures go hand-in-glove with backup procedures. Performing backups is wasted effort if there is no method for restoring the data that has been saved.

A critical aspect of the recovery procedure is the quality of its documentation. It isn't rocket science to predict that if (when) the system crashes things will be chaotic. The atmosphere will be extremely tense and there will be tremendous pressure to get the system up and running. In the confusion it would be very easy for further damage to be done to the system if people panic.

Not all recoveries are identical. The first step in the recovery process should be to ascertain exactly what needs to be recovered. Some situations require that only the most recent online backup tapes be reloaded. Others would require that the most recent full backup be loaded and all subsequent daily backups be loaded. Complete documentation should exist for every possible recovery procedure.

The acid test of the backup and recovery procedures would be to take a full backup of the system and attempt to rebuild the entire system on a different hardware platform. This should be done using just the output of the backup procedures and following to-the-letter the recovery procedure documentation. If the procedures are deficient or incorrect in any manner, then corrections should be made and the test repeated.

13.3 Data Dictionary

While not specifically a test tool, a complete data dictionary provides valuable information about the data that is referenced in a client/server system. It can go a long way towards avoiding errors in the first place and resolving them quickly should an error occur.

Basically, a data dictionary is data about the system's data. Some of the basic information which is maintained about each data field in the data dictionary includes:

- Name of field.
- What other names is this field known by?
- What is the definition of the data field (i.e., a description in lay terms of the field)?
- Data type of field (integer, character, float, currency, date).
- Size of the field (24 characters, 4-byte integer).
- Originator of field, i.e., where does the data come from?
- Where is this field used, e.g., which reports, table, windows, etc.?
- What users receive copies of these reports?
- Which programs or applications use this field?

The information kept in the data dictionary that is of particular interest to the testing staff is a little more specialized. These items include:

- Can the field contain a NULL value?
- What are the permissible values for the field (e.g., M/F, Y/N, etc.)?
- Is this field dependent upon values in another table (e.g., account # in account table)?
- Are the values for this field contained in a lookup table (e.g., a table of state names)?
- What data entry mask should be associated with this field?

During initial phases of testing, the testers will have questions about data fields that must be answered to properly design tests. To develop a thorough, complete set of tests the tester has to know what the ranges of permissible values are. He or she will also need to know whether the field can contain a NULL value or not. Developing and maintaining a complete data dictionary places all the answers to these questions in a single place. While the task of developing the dictionary might be daunting, it will more than pay for itself in improving system quality, reducing time spent researching problems, and resolving disputes about the system's data.

The data dictionary will also prove extremely useful when a test database is being built. During this activity it is crucial to know what are permissible values, what dependencies exist, etc. Maintaining information of this type in a single, easily accessible location will allow test databases to be built more quickly and more accurately.

The alternatives to using a data dictionary to answer these types of questions aren't promising. One solution would be to spend time searching out and asking everyone on the project the questions. Much time would be spent and the consistency and quality of such answers would be dubious. Another alternative would be for the tester to guess at the answers. Obviously, guessing at the permissible values or whether a field should contain NULLs isn't a good idea. This approach won't prove conducive to thorough, accurate testing.

CHAPTER 14

Security

When I was a kid, my father frequently would say, "Locks are to keep the honest people honest." He meant that if professional thieves really wanted to break in and steal something from your house or business, they would find a way to do it. Locks were simply a means to make it more difficult for ordinary people to become thieves.

Implementing security in a client/server system is also an exercise in keeping the honest people honest. The security in most computer systems, client/server and otherwise, isn't strong enough to deter an accomplished, dedicated computer criminal. Evidence supporting this statement is the number of computer break-ins experienced by the military, NASA, etc. The security system is to keep the average user and opportunistic criminal at bay.

A secondary effort of the security system is to make the cost of breaking into the system so expensive in time, resources, and risk that even professional criminals will move on to easier pickings. If it takes a supercomputer to break into your system, it isn't likely that a criminal will attack it.

The time it takes to break a code is also an implicit factor in its safety. Breaking any encryption algorithm is possible if enough time and effort is invested. It might take an array of computers years to accomplish it, but every code can be broken. The important question is, "What is the message worth once the code is known?" If the code is changed frequently, then knowing today's code won't be of any appreciable value two months from now.

If security is built into a client/server system, then it must be tested to make certain that it has been implemented completely and correctly. This chapter describes methods in which security is implemented in client/server systems and methods for testing the security.

14.1 The Need for Security

It's probably an understatement to say that the world today is not a safe place. It seems that even things which are locked up and bolted down are still frequent targets of thieves, saboteurs, and vandals. This statement is as true for computer systems as anything else. In fact, since computers frequently contain valuable information they are often high-profile targets.

As information becomes both the backbone and lifeblood of modern corporations, it becomes vital to protect that information. The word "protect" has a number of meanings in the context of computer systems. The first meaning is that the data must be safeguarded from illicit alteration. It needs to be protected from being modified by those who have no need to modify it. If this type of protection isn't firmly in place, an accounts payable entry could easily be altered to have an extra zero or two added.

Protecting the data also extends to denying access to people who shouldn't have it. The people in this instance might be external to the organization, or they might be members of the organization who have no need or right to see all of its data. All companies probably consider their payroll information to be at a very high security level. Other data is equally valuable, if not more so. Data on such areas as customer lists, price agreements, discounts from suppliers, marketing plans, details about planned acquisitions and mergers would all be highly sensitive and valuable in the hands of competitors.

A final level of protection means that legitimate users of the system need to have access to that system at all times. Denying the users access to the system and its data could easily cripple a corporation. Imagine what would happen if the broker in a brokerage firm couldn't access their accounts when the stock market is in session. What if doctors couldn't retrieve patient records in a hospital. It doesn't take much of an imagination to envision a company being driven out of business by the loss of access to a critical computer system.

14.1.1 Understanding Why Security Penetrations Occur

The first step towards making a system secure is to try to understand the mentality of those who would break into it. The motivation for penetrating a computer system ranges greatly from individual to individual. Potential interlopers are dangerous no matter what their motivation. Each type of computer criminal should be taken seriously, and the system should be built with each potential threat in mind.

14.1.2 Who Is Trying to Break in?

The popular conception of a hacker being a teen or preteen with a home computer and too much time on his hands isn't necessarily the most accurate portrait of a computer criminal. While there certainly are computer criminals who fit this mold, they aren't necessarily the most prevalent or the most dangerous. Who are the likely persons trying to break through a system's security? The answer to this can be broken down into two types of people: internal and external. The following list provides some examples of individuals in an internal group.

- Disgruntled employee.
- Employee with debt/gambling/habit problems.
- Ex-employee with a grudge.
- Consultant or vendor.

An external group might include the following:

- Criminals.
- Competitors.
- Industrial espionage
- Terrorists.
- Hackers.

The goals of criminals in each category varies widely. The goals of internal threats are generally:

- Revenge, i.e., getting even for a real or perceived injustice.
- Profit, i.e., transferring funds from the victim to themselves.

External threats have the following goals:

- Profit, i.e., transferring funds from the victim to themselves.
- Fraud, e.g., fraudulent transactions intended to profit the criminal or harm the victim.
- Sabotage—denial of service to legitimate users by crashing or overloading the system.
- Intelligence gathering by a competing company or government.
- Illicit use of computer time or other resources.
- Theft of proprietary software.

Recent studies have indicated that perhaps the greatest threat to an organization's computer systems are its employees. Security built into client/server systems must recognize and deal with this threat. Many companies think their employees are trustworthy and would never act against the organization. Unfortunately, the reality is that many employees feel little allegiance to their employer. Employees with substance abuse or gambling problems are extremely likely to exploit a trusted position in order to gain funds to further their addictions. Other employees with little loyalty to an organization wouldn't think twice about taking advantages of their position to enrich themselves at the company's expense.

14.1.3 How Do They Attempt to Break in?

There are many methods by which intruders will attempt to gain entry into a system. The list of these methods is only limited by the imaginations of computer criminals. A few methods are listed here, but don't be deceived into thinking that these are the only techniques which can be used.

14.1.3.1 Impersonation.   Perhaps the most common method of breaking into a system is to impersonate a legitimate user. This form of intrusion can't be prevented by any amount of testing. The best that the system can do is to implement a secure and complete security system and train users not to reveal their passwords to anyone. Post-its stuck to users' terminals just might represent the biggest threat to computer security in history.

The corporate culture should encourage users to report suspicious activities which might be attempts at compromising system security. Frequently, systems display login messages indicating the time and date when the user last logged into the system. If the user notices that the last login time isn't what she expected it to be, then she should report this. Login messages also frequently display the number of failed login attempts which have occurred. If the user knows that his last login attempt was successful, then it's a safe assumption that someone else tried to log in as him. Changes to their customizations of an application might also indicate that an intruder is using their account. Changes in the data which shouldn't have occurred is yet another clue.

14.1.3.2 Using an Idle Terminal.   Even easier than impersonating another user is simply sitting down at another user's terminal when it is idle. Users regularly bring up client/server applications, log into them, use them for a while, and then move onto another application. Later in the workday they leave their desk, office, or cubicle. Other users or absolute strangers can easily sit down at another user's PC and view or modify data on the application during the legitimate user's absence.

The easiest way to thwart this security violation is to design, implement, and test automatic log-off logic in every application running on a client/server system. If the user doesn't perform any terminal activity for a prescribed time period (e.g., five minutes) the user is logged out. While this doesn't totally eliminate the risk of an idle terminal being used, it would cut down on the problem significantly.

14.1.3.3 Intercepting Network Communications. The cables which carry communications between the machines in a client/server system are quite vulnerable to intruders. They can be tapped fairly easily. It wouldn't be difficult to tap a network cable and monitor all of the data which is transmitted across it. This would provide an easy method for obtaining account numbers, passwords, confidential data, etc.

Vandalizing the cabling of a network used by a client/server would be easier yet. Cutting an Ethernet cable would take only a few seconds. This wouldn't provide the perpetrator with data, but it could effectively shut down the client/server system. It could preclude the use of the system for users in that area for an extended period of time.

The solution to network communications problems is to establish security for the physical network itself. The closet which contains LAN hardware and cables should be physically secured. Cables should be shielded by metal conduit instead of simply running bare cables through the ceiling. Telephone patch panels where communications connect to the outside world should be in locked rooms.

14.1.3.4 Directly Accessing Data Files. Most users probably don't realize (or care) that relational database systems store tables in disk files. These files may be created and accessed through the operating system, or they may be created and accessed directly by the database software. In either case the data which makes up the database is sitting on a disk drive somewhere. The access to these files must be tightly restricted. While it would be extremely difficult to insert false data into the files, it wouldn't be terribly difficult to interpret these files if they could be accessed.

Most relational database packages establish security on the data files they create. Normally the owner of the database is the only account which can directly access these files. All other accounts are forced to access them by going through the database engine. This form of security should be verified by running tests which attempt to violate the sanctity of these files.

Accounts which have system administrator (or super-user) privileges can access any file on most operating systems. If criminals were able to obtain this level of privilege they could easily read, modify, or delete database files. In most cases altering these base files would result in a corrupt database. Legitimate users would then be prevented from using the system until the database was restored. Passwords of administrator accounts need to be protected at all costs. No one should be given super-user privileges or accounts of this type unless there is a justifiable reason.

14.1.3.5 Dumpster Diving.   It is decidedly low tech, but a wealth of information can be gleaned about an organization by going through its trash! Some types of data which pertain to a client/server system include source code, directory listings, account numbers, passwords, IP addresses, etc. Why bother breaking into a computer system if all the confidential data it contains is thrown out in the trash every night at 11 P.M.?

Guidelines about how confidential materials should be disposed of must be established. Shredding this material is a relatively easy technique for much of it. Other items, such as user manuals, large listings, etc., aren't as easily disposed of. Paper isn't the only material which is tossed out. Diskettes, tapes, and old hardware also goes out the back door on a regular basis. Procedures need to be created and adhered to or all the security on the client/server system itself is just a waste of time.

Testing this portion of the system involves following up on people's adherence to the standards. The security administrator should make unannounced visits periodically and examine what is being thrown away by system users, developers, and administrators. More than likely, the nightly trash will contain information which would be of great interest and assistance to someone trying to break into your system.

14.1.3.6 Hardware Theft.   Computer hardware is getting smaller and smaller every day. Laptops are little larger than notebooks, and desktop machines can be only a little larger. Stealing a client machine is an easy way to obtain a tremendous amount of information about the client/server system. Data from client/server systems is often exported to word-processing documents, spreadsheets, and personal databases. Initialization files (*.INI) frequently contain account numbers and passwords.

Security can be heightened by making users aware of the value of the data on their machines. Emphasize that laptops shouldn't contain highly sensitive or confidential information. Passwords should never be included in initialization files, scripts, or batch files.

If possible, the contents of the hard drives in laptop machines should be encrypted. Without the proper password or key, the contents of the disk is unusable. While security measures such as these won't replace the hardware, at least it can minimize the damage if a machine is lost or stolen.

14.1.3.7 Gone But Not Forgotten.   Data on a computer which appears to have been removed frequently is still there. The most familiar example of this concept is the DOS delete statement. The deleted file isn't really gone; it has only been removed from the File Allocation Table (FAT). Any number of utilities can be used to resurrect this file and the data it contains. The practice applies to hard drives, network drives, and floppy diskettes. Any of these media might be the avenue for confidential data to be leaked if the user doesn't realize that deleting a file doesn't truly destroy it. In order to truly delete the data, the drive would have to be overwritten, reformatted, or physically destroyed.

Computer tapes represent yet another method by which the unscrupulous can obtain access to "deleted" data. Tapes which are re-used or used for scratch purposes still contain the data which was last written onto them. This data can be read by the next person using the tape. This can be foiled by overwriting a tape with garbage or random strings when the current user is done with it.

Memory space allocated by a program is another situation where data appears to be deleted, but in fact might not be. An application may allocate memory from the stack, write sensitive data on this memory block, and later deallocate the space. After the block is returned to the memory manager the data is still sitting at that address. It's very possible for the next program which allocates memory to read the memory block granted to it and acquire confidential data left there by the previous user. Many operating systems include a secure version of the allocation or deallocation function which will wipe the area clean before giving it to another user.

Testing should be performed to make certain that the above examples of "deleted" data won't violate the security of a system. Allocated memory areas need to be wiped clean before they are released. Deleted files need to be purged before the area is available to other users.

14.2 Potential Weaknesses of Client/Server Systems

Many traditional systems had the dumb terminals hard-wired directly to the mainframe computer. This isn't the case with client/server systems. A local area network (LAN) or wide area network (WAN) is the customary connection between a client machine and the server. This significantly looser collection is extremely flexible and provides support for enterprisewide computing. This very openness, however, creates additional risk. It opens the door for communications to be intercepted, duplicated, or otherwise abused.

Each of the major components in a client/server system have their own potential security weaknesses. Security implications of these components will each be addressed in the next few sections. The components which are addressed include:

- The database.
- Application software.
- Database server.
- The relational database system.
- The application server.
- The network.
- Client workstations.

14.2.1 Security Imposed at the Database Level

Perhaps the first place to focus on security improvements is at the database level. There are numerous advantages to be gained by implementing security at this level. The first advantage is that security imposed at the database level will be consistent across all applications in a client/server system. Since all applications access the database through the RDBMS engine, any security imposed at the database level will be applied to all users no matter what tool or application they use to access the database.

All of the mainline relational database management systems provide a number of tools and techniques to enable security to be enforced. Some of the techniques include granting permissions to individuals and groups, creating views, and using stored procedures. Each of the techniques is defined in later sections.

If security is implemented at the database level, there will be fewer gaps in the security. When security is implemented via individual applications, it isn't likely that each application will have the exact same method of applying security. Some applications will be more comprehensive than others. This inconsistency leads to security exposure and risks.

Testing the security of a client/server system will be different depending on how security has been implemented. If the code and techniques are different for each application, then each of these applications must be thoroughly tested from a security perspective. When security is imposed at the database level, it is applied to all applications identically and needs to be tested only a single time.

Another advantage of imposing security at the database level is that it relies upon fewer people to implement. Instead of requiring each developer to know and understand the security design, it is put into place by a small number of database administrators (DBAs). This minimizes the exposure due to inexperience, incompetence, and deliberate attempts to violate security.

Implementing security is a time-consuming job, but over the life of the client/server system, maintaining a system's security will take even more time and effort. If security is handled by each distinct application, then the effort to maintain the security system will be higher. Each time a user is added, deleted, or changes responsibility then her security entries in each application will have to be examined and possibly updated. The likelihood of mistakes being made are quite high with this approach. Contrast this with the simplicity of updating each user's changes at a single point.

14.2.1.1 User Accounts.   The bedrock of security implemented at the database level is the user account. Each user should have an individual account. There are few justifications for users sharing a single account. The DBA or security administrator creates accounts for each bona fide user of the system. Along with each account there is an associated password.

When each new user is added to the system, a default password should be assigned to them. This password shouldn't be obvious or predictable. A default password should be good for only a single login, and then the user must modify it. This requirement is being done for two reasons. The first reason is that now the user has a secure password. It's a password which not even the security officer or system administrator knows.

There is the possibility that another person could find out the new account and password before the legitimate user does. If this were to happen, the intruder would be required to modify the password when the account is first used. When the legitimate user logs on for the first time, he/she won't be able to use the password supplied by the security administrator. This would certainly raise questions about the condition of the account. The user should contact the security officer, and he/she will modify the password and investigate how the account could have been violated.

It should go without saying that account IDs and passwords should never be revealed by the users to anyone else. Passwords shouldn't be written on yellow stickies and attached to the monitor. Users might be amazed to learn that hiding their password on the underside of the keyboard isn't an approved practice. Nor is writing the account number and password on the desktop calendar.

It may sound obvious, but deleted or inactive users should be disabled immediately by the security administrator. This includes users who voluntarily (or otherwise) leave the organization, go on extended vacations, or are temporarily reassigned to other areas. Leaving active accounts on the system while the users are gone (temporarily or permanently) is simply an invitation to abuse. The amount of time to remove or inactivate such accounts is minimal.

Testing isn't likely to determine whether every account has been set up correctly. This is because user accounts will be created throughout the useful life of the system. It certainly doesn't stop when the system is installed and moves into production. What actually gets tested here is whether the procedures have been set up properly or not. The steps to create new user accounts need to be documented. These procedures need to be tested to make certain that they are both accurate and complete. They also need to ascertain that users aren't given privileges and capabilities outside the scope of their area or responsibility.

14.2.1.2 User Account Restrictions. A number of RDBMS packages allow restrictions to be placed on user accounts. An account can be restricted to accessing the database on certain days of the week or certain hours of the day. Other restrictions include the terminal from which the account can access the database. These capabilities can be used to restrict access to the system to normal working hours. Nighttime or weekend activity will be prevented. Attempts by users to violate these restrictions should be logged and investigated.

This might appear to solve many security-related problems, but it does introduce some operational ones. There will almost definitely be times when users will have a legitimate need to be on the system at odd times. Periods of high activity, such as month-end and year-end closing, immediately come to mind. If access restrictions are imposed, then users need to be able to contact someone and gain access at times when there is a legitimate need for it.

One question which should be asked is how sessions which span this transition are handled. What happens if a user logs into the system during the permissible time period and maintains the connection into the off hours? Will the system terminate the session immediately or allow it to continue indefinitely? The answer to this depends on the RDBMS package being used.

If this feature of the database system is going to be used, then it must be sufficiently tested. Test staff will have to attempt logging onto the system during the restricted hours to verify that this form of security is enforced. The ability to access the database during restricted time periods indicates that this form of security hasn't been implemented properly. Sessions which transition between accepted and unacceptable times must also be tested.

14.2.1.3 Permissions and Grants.

Once a user account has been created, the next action is to define what capabilities this account will be given. In a relational database environment, permissions are given to users via a "grant" statement. Grants can be divided into two types. The first type of grant enables the user to execute system-level commands. The second type of grant gives users the ability to access objects, primarily tables, which they don't own. Each type of grant will be described more thoroughly in the following sections.

14.2.1.3.1 System Privileges

RDBM systems typically provide a long list of system-level commands which are available to users. A few examples of these commands include the ability to create and drop tables, indexes, stored procedures, triggers, views, users, databases, roles, etc. These commands bestow the grantee with a great deal of power. It should be apparent that most of these privileges should be restricted to a very small number of accounts. Normal users would never need to create databases, views, triggers, stored procedures, etc.

Some of these privileges will be needed by the typical user to perform their daily tasks. Some RDBM systems include a "create session" privilege. Without this privilege the user won't be allowed to sign onto the system. Temporary tables are frequently created on behalf of users when they generate reports or perform other queries. If a user needs to generate reports, then she must be given the ability to create tables.

Testing must be performed to be certain that users have the privileges they absolutely need, but nothing more. This testing can be accomplished by creating a typical user account and attempting to perform all operations the user would expect to perform. This should include searching for data, inserting records, printing reports, etc.

14.2.1.3.2 User Object Permissions   The other form of grant allows users to access objects which they don't own. Typically the objects being referenced are tables, but they can include views, stored procedures, or specific columns within tables. The owner of the object is generally the only account with the ability to grant access privileges to those objects. The capabilities which can be granted on these objects typically include:

- Select.
- Insert.
- Update.
- Delete.
- Execute.

Testing should be done to make certain each user has access to only the objects they need to access. Furthermore, users should have the minimum level of access required to perform their jobs. A user which only views data shouldn't be given insert, update, or delete access to database tables.

Some systems allow a user account to be able to grant access privileges to other users. For example, user "Smith" could be given access to insert, delete, and update a given table. Smith is also given the ability to grant the same access capabilities to other users. Smith would be able to grant Jones permission to access the table.

There are a few instances where this ability would be well suited. A supervisor or department head could be granted this ability over data in her area. She would then be able to grant access to people she deems suitable. In this manner the DBA or security administrator isn't involved for every data access decision.

Be extremely careful if this capability exists and is used. The preceding example describes an appropriate situation for this ability. It shouldn't be granted to ordinary users, only to the people who "own" the data. This ability could easily be used to subvert system security.

14.2.1.4 Roles/Groups.   While the ability to grant rights to individual users is a powerful capability, the number of grants required can quickly become overwhelming if the system grows beyond a certain size. Assume a system has a total of 100 tables, views, stored procedures, and other objects. Further assume that this system has 1,000 users. Neither of these sizing estimates are out of the ordinary for a client/server system. If anything this database object estimate is very much on the low side. A more realistic number would be several times the estimates provided. The worst-case scenario would be that the DBA would need to create a grant allowing every user access to every database object. This works out to be 100,000 grant statements. While the worst-case scenario probably wouldn't occur, it would still be a tremendous amount of initial work and maintenance to grant each user permission to access even half of the tables.

Fortunately, relational systems have implemented a method so the DBA can avoid granting access to every object for each user. This technique involves dividing the user community into distinct groups which have the same security needs. Examples of such groups could be data-entry clerks, administrators, read-only users, etc. A group or role is defined for each class of user. Privileges needed by the group would be granted to the role or group. The final step would be to define the group to which each user is assigned.

Following the example in the opening paragraph of this section there would be far fewer grants required with the use of roles or groups. Assume that five security groups are defined. Grants to the tables would be assigned to these groups. The worst case for the number of grants would be 500 (5 groups times 100 tables), but more likely the average would be 50—75. It's true that 500 is not a small number of grants to maintain, but compare this to the previous worst-case scenario of maintaining 100,000 grants.

Each group needs to be tested to make certain the users in that group don't have access beyond their needs. The tester should log in as each role and run through a series of tests. Each test would include attempts to view, modify, add, or delete data which the group shouldn't be able to access. The ability to perform these actions constitutes a breach of security.

This security testing activity can be automated fairly easily. A security database needs to be created. This database would include records which are distributed such that each security group is able to see a certain set of records. Using a capture and playback test tool, the tester would step through each window in the applications checking for situations which allow a security group to view data or windows it shouldn't have access to. The test script captures this activity so it can be easily duplicated in the future.

Testing security is much simpler when roles are employed. If roles aren't used, then security testing needs to be performed to test the access which each individual user has in the system. When roles have been implemented, then security testing only needs to be performed once for each security group. Without the use of groups, testing would need to be repeated each time a user is added to the system. When groups are used, security testing is only done when a group is added or the group has its security access modified.

All users should belong to one of the defined security groups. If they aren't assigned to one of the preexisting groups, then one of two things will happen. The first possibility will be that the user won't have any privileges. The second possibility would be that the user might end up having excess privileges. Testing should be performed on an ongoing basis to verify that every user belongs to a security group.

14.2.1.5 Views. A view in a relational database system can be thought of as a virtual table. To the user, a view has the same look and feel as a table. Views have columns and rows and are queried in the same manner that tables are queried. The difference is that views themselves contain no data because they are defined in terms of underlying (base) tables. Views can be thought of as a mask which allows the base table(s) underneath them to show through. A view can be defined to include a subset of the columns in a single table, or it can include columns from multiple tables.

Views can be used to implement security in several ways. The first is that a view can be used to restrict the columns which a user is able to see. A "personnel" table might exist in the system which includes basic biographical information on a company's employees.. The personnel table might also include salary or performance data columns. All users would be allowed to see the basic biographical data. Access to the remunerative data would most likely be severely limited. Very few users would be allowed to see data of such a sensitive nature.

A view could be created which would include all of the nonfinancial columns in the personnel table. All users would be given access to this view. A smaller group of users would be able to access the base table and its more sensitive information.

The SQL code to create this style of view is:

```
CREATE VIEW employee_bio
AS SELECT emp_name, emp_id, emp_dept, emp_location
FROM personnel
```

The use of views to limit the columns in a table a user may access can be thought of as a vertical access restriction to the table. Views can also be used to restrict the rows in a table which a user sees. This can be thought of as a horizontal restriction to the table. A horizontal view can be used to restrict a user's access to the department, orders, time frame, etc., that that particular user needs to access. The statement to create a view to accomplish this will differ slightly between RDBMS packages, but would be along the lines of:

```
CREATE VIEW personnel_sales_dept
AS SELECT *
FROM personnel
WHERE dept_id = "sales"
```

There are many situations where the ability to allow a user to see a horizontal slice of a table is needed. A user might need to be restricted to accessing rows in their own department, records older than one year, salaries of employees making less than themselves, etc. Grants are not able to provide the capability to restrict users to horizontal slices of the database. This makes the ability of views to enable horizontal views extremely valuable.

If views are being used in a client/server system to implement security, then they must be tested. Testing views should be accomplished by two approaches. The first test would be to desk check the SQL code which creates each view. Examine the "create view" statement to be certain that it references only the tables and columns it should.

The second test is to grant access to the view to security groups and verify that users in these groups only see the data they are intended to see. An SQL test script can be executed which attempts to access data in the rows which haven't been granted to the current user. Success during attempts to see this data means that the view has been improperly defined or granted to the user's security group.

Once a view has been created, it should be protected from being modified. The SQL statement which creates it should be maintained by the Configuration Management team on disk volumes which aren't accessible to normal users. The ability to modify a view, either vertical or horizontal, could easily enable a user to violate system security. Views shouldn't be named in a manner which indicates that the object is a view. Knowing which objects are views and which are tables could easily prompt attempts to access data which users don't have access to.

14.2.1.6 Stored Procedures. *Stored procedures* are blocks of SQL statements which are defined at the database server level. They are invoked by applications running at the client level. Stored procedures can be used to enforce security by restricting access to tables by users. A stored procedure can be created to access a table in a certain way, for example, to insert rows into the table. The stored procedure could perform a certain amount of validity checking before it actually performs the insert operation. It could also insert rows in related tables. Permission to execute that stored procedure can be granted to users. The application would call the stored procedure and pass data which is to be inserted into the table. This would allow the user to insert rows into the table in a controlled manner. They could perform the tasks they need to without directly being given the ability to insert into the table.

Testing should be performed to validate that users have only the access to the stored procedure they require. Under no circumstances should anyone other than the DBA have the ability to delete, modify, or create any stored procedures. This ability could conceivably be used to circumvent security. Testing this aspect of security can be accomplished by logging into an interactive SQL session as each security group is attempting to delete, modify or create stored procedures.

A short SQL script could be written which attempts to perform these forbidden operations. The tester could log in as a user in one of the security groups and run this test script. The expectation is that all of these operations will fail due to the group's limitations. If any of the SQL calls is successful, then that security group has system privileges which it should not have had. The grants given to that group need to be reevaluated. This script should be run regularly and the results examined.

14.2.1.7 Synonyms. The concept of providing synonyms is available in a number of relational database systems. A synonym is an alternative name for a database object such as a table, view, stored procedure, etc. Synonyms are used to allow developers to use names which are shorter or more meaningful than what the object might be actually named.

If multiple objects with the same name exist, then how does the system know which object should be accessed? A search hierarchy is normally used to determine which object will be used. Each RDBMS has its own hierarchy, but the following list is fairly typical:

1. An object with the name owned by the user would be referenced first.

2. An object with the name owned by the database owner would be the second choice.

3. Any other object with the name which the user has permission to access.

While synonyms can be extremely convenient, it's quite possible that this convenience can be used to thwart system security. Suppose an application running on a client/server system is used to insert confidential information into a database table. Suppose a criminal created a private table which had the same columns as the real table. Suppose further that this criminal also was able to create or modify a synonym so SQL operations were applied against his table instead of the expected table. Without knowing what is happening, legitimate users could be reading from and writing to the wrong table. They could be misled by viewing incorrect data. They could also be inserting legitimate, confidential data into a table owned by a criminal.

Security testing should verify that no one except the DBA(s) has the ability to create synonyms. As the above example describes, this privilege isn't one which users need or should be granted. The SQL test script described in Section 14.2.1.5 could be expanded to make certain users don't have this ability. An example of some statements which could be included in this script are provided in Table 14.1.

14.2.1.8 Resource Quotas.   Most database packages allow the database administrator to limit the amount of system resources which each user can consume. Some of the resource usage which can be constrained include:

1. Disk space.

2. CPU time that a session can use.

3. CPU time per database call.

4. Connect time for a session.

5. Logical reads per session.

6. Concurrent sessions per user.

7. Memory buffer space.

TABLE 14.1

SQL Security Test Statements

```
create table test_table as (col_1 integer, col_2 char(24));
alter table real_table add new_column integer;
drop table real_table;

create synonym test_synonym for real_table;
drop synonym real_synonym;

create user new_user identified by password;
drop user real_user;

create view test_view as select * from real_table;
drop view real_view;
```

Some database systems won't terminate a query until it actually exceeds a quota. Other systems with more sophisticated query planners will estimate the resources each query will consume. If it projects that a particular query will exceed a quota, then the query won't be initiated. The latter system is more desirable because it prevents a lot of resources from being used before the system terminates the query due to a quota violation. Check the documentation of your database system to determine how it implements quota limitations.

Implementing quotas to limit the amount of system resources a user can consume may not sound like a security issue, but it is appropriate to include here. One method of violating a system's security is to deny its use to legitimate users. If a system doesn't impose resource limits on users, it would be trivial for a user to initiate activity which results in the system being paralyzed. This could easily have the effect of denying use of the system to legitimate users.

The testing required to verify that resource quotas have been properly implemented should be fairly easy. Simply create SQL statements which generate huge amounts of activity. Creating a Cartesian product involving two large tables will almost certainly exceed most logical read quotas. Signing onto the system multiple times as the same user will exceed the concurrent sessions quota. Perform these and similar activities and verify that the RDBMS quotas are enforced.

14.2.2 Security Imposed within Applications

Another common approach for applying security is to build security into the individual applications themselves. This approach has its pros and cons. Overall security certainly can be successfully implemented at the application level. One downside is that security is duplicated in each application. This can present problems if the number of applications is large and the development staff is limited.

The methods by which this is achieved vary, but basically they are used to restrict what the users can be and do. Security implemented by applications can and should be tested thoroughly. Essentially, these security tests involve attempts to access data and windows which users have no right to access. Successful attempts represent failures in system security.

14.2.2.1 Login Attempts. Restricting access to the application is the first and probably most important method of enforcing security in an application. All applications need to have a login screen through which users log into the system. The login screen should require them to enter their login ID and password. Some systems require that users provide a server and a database name. The application should in turn attempt to connect to the database using these values. If the connect operation is successful, then the user is able to enter the application. If the connect failed, then the user is denied access.

The number of failed login attempts which are allowed should be limited. Allowing an unlimited number of login attempts makes it easier for a system cracker to use a programmed method to repeatedly log into the system. Three attempts seems to be a reasonable number to allow users. If the user can't successfully log in after three attempts, the application should be terminated. Furthermore, after a certain number of failed attempts the system should not accept any additional login attempts from that workstation until a security officer reviews the situation. This prevents a hacker from simply running a password-cracking program which tries all possible password combinations.

The information returned to the client machine after a failed login should be minimal. Don't inform the criminal that the login account is OK but the password is wrong. Simply return the message that login/password is incorrect. Telling exactly which was wrong is providing valuable information which can be used to get around the existing security and just serves to weaken the system security.

Testing user accounts should include attempts at logging in with a valid account number but invalid passwords, valid account numbers with no password, etc. The tester should also press the CTRL/ALT/DEL key combination during the login. A well-designed login window shouldn't be tricked by any of these attempts.

14.2.2.2 Passwords. The application or the RDBMS should require that users periodically change their passwords. The frequency depends on the perceived value of the data. A period of 30 days seems to be fairly common. New passwords should pass certain criteria before they are accepted. Minimal criteria for acceptance should include the items listed in the following paragraphs.

Passwords must be longer than a specified minimum length. This length might be six characters or it might be eight characters. As passwords increase in length, the number of attempts it takes to guess it increases significantly. Each additional character in the password increases the number of possible passwords by a factor of at least 36 (26 characters plus 10 digits).

Can a user immediately re-use the same password? It wouldn't be inaccurate to say that most users are creatures of habit. If they were given the choice they would most likely never change their passwords. Given the option they would choose to use their existing password as the new password. The security system should prevent them from doing this. The current password shouldn't be available for re-use for a minimum of 30 days.

A password should be required to include a mixture of alphabetic characters and digits. It would be preferable that the digit(s) be positioned in the middle of the alphabetic characters instead of added onto the beginning or ending of the string. Too many users pick a password and then tack the month at the end of it. Each month their password changes by just a single character. This pattern is pervasive and can easily be guessed by a hacker.

Does the system prevent users from picking simple, easily guessed passwords? Users will frequently choose a password which is fairly obvious. If a password is too easy, then it's almost like not having security at all. Some general guidelines on what should not be allowed as passwords include the items listed in Table 14.2.

The application shouldn't maintain a separate list of user accounts and passwords internally. The shortcoming of this approach is that it

TABLE 14.2 Passwords Which Shouldn't Be Allowed	Login ID
	The month of the year
	Days of the week
	Any derivation of the user's name
	The default password, i.e., originally assigned password
	Spouses' names
	Social security numbers
	Children's name
	License plate numbers
	Derivation of the company name
	Any words found in an English dictionary
	Names of locations
	Names or nicknames of local sports teams
	Address of the facility

won't be secure compared to using the login security of the database package. Most RDBMS systems do a very good job of protecting account numbers and passwords. The passwords are kept in an encrypted format to prevent prying eyes from seeing them. If accounts and passwords are maintained in an application, then this data must be adequately protected by the application.

Testing a system's security in respect to passwords should contain a certain minimal number and types of tests. These tests should parallel the list of suggested password considerations listed in the previous paragraphs. The examples in Table 14.3 constitute a baseline for password testing. Any successes during these testing activities constitutes a security flaw. The system needs to be modified to prevent this from being allowed.

14.2.2.3 Navigation-based Security.   The basic principle when designing application navigation as a means of enforcing security is that the user can't access what they can't see. If a user can't possibly access the windows which display and edit salary information, then that user won't be able to view or edit this data via the application. There are two primary methods of implementing security in applications: building one application for each security group versus designing an application which dynamically adjusts itself to users.

14.2.2.3.1 Separate Applications for Each Security Group   The most basic method of enforcing security through application navigation is to build a separate application for each security group. Each distinct application would include only the screens available to the security requirements of the users who will be using it. Users would be authorized to

TABLE 14.3	Attempt to create a password with fewer than the required minimum number of characters
Testing Password Processing	Attempt to set the new password to the same value as the old password
	Set the password to all characters
	Set the password to all digits
	Pick a repetitive password such as "AAAAAA"
	Pick a day of the week
	Pick a month of the year
	Attempt to use the user's name as the password
	Attempt to use the user's name plus a digit as the password

log onto just the application which includes the aspects of the system they require. Attempts to log onto other applications would result in a login failure.

The obvious drawback to this approach is that it constitutes a tremendous amount of work. If there are five security groups, then there would be a need for five distinct applications. The work to build the five separate applications would be greater (although not likely quintuple) than the amount of work to build a single application. Additional work would also be required to document all the applications and train users.

Maintaining this environment would involve additional effort. Any software errors uncovered would have to be corrected in each application which they affect. There will very likely be slip-ups in which corrections won't be made to all affected applications. This will result in frustrated users and a black eye for the MIS group. The configuration management group would constantly be behind the curve in updating all of the executables.

The number of distinct applications required isn't likely to remain steady. As new users are added or the tasks of existing users evolve, the current applications would have to be reviewed and likely enhanced. New users would require new combinations of functionality which no current group has. Completely new applications would likely be required on a regular basis. This combination of needs would keep developers extremely busy even before significant enhancements to the application are considered.

Since each application is distinct, each would have to be tested separately. Testing scripts created for application "A" might or might not be applicable on application "B." It's more likely that separate testing scripts would need to be created and maintained for each application. Large collections of test scripts used to run regression testing and system load testing would definitely need to be built and maintained separately for each application.

All in all, this approach has few advantages and a great number of drawbacks. The maintenance overhead would be considerable. It should only be considered when the capabilities of the different user groups have little or no overlap. One situation which could justify separate applications is when one application is needed for general users and a second is created just for administrators of the system.

14.2.2.3.2 Dynamic Applications   A more generalized approach to imposing security via application navigation is to build a single application and dynamically alter it to suit the security needs of the current user.

The security group to which the user belongs would dictate exactly how the application appears. This would enable developers to focus on a single application instead of diluting efforts maintaining multiple versions of similar applications.

14.2.2.3.2.1 Dynamic Menus   Most GUI development environments allow menus to be built dynamically at run time. Menu items are used by the application to control application navigation. Dynamic menus are perhaps the most frequently employed method of dynamically customizing an application for multiple security groups. As each window is loaded, logic in the application accesses a security table to determine what menu items the user (or the user's security group) is allowed to access. The appropriate menus are built and then the window is displayed.

The advantage of this approach is that users aren't able to see functions or windows which they aren't authorized to access. If ineligible, users can see grayed-out (i.e., disabled) menu items for windows they can't access, it might lead to curiosity and attempts to get around the system's security. Preventing them from knowing that other functions exist will help to prevent security violations.

There are some disadvantages to this method of security implementation. The first is that the application will need to be somewhat more complicated than an application which is more static. The logic to determine which menu items the user is allowed to access needs to be designed, coded, and tested. This represents additional time and resources needed to develop the system.

Another drawback to this approach is that it will require additional processing time when the application executes. It takes additional CPU time and disk I/O transfers to access the security tables, calculate which items should be included, and dynamically build the menus. During this period of time, the user is kept waiting.

A final disadvantage is that it somewhat complicates the testing efforts. Distinct security testing must be performed for every security group in the system. Each window which every group can navigate to must be tested. Menu items on every window must be examined and executed to make certain that each security group is able to access only the windows they are allowed to access.

Capture and replay test tools can be used to record test scripts specifically geared towards application navigation. The scripts can simply walk the application through all menu items and windows for each security group. No functionality of the windows would be tested by these scripts. These test scripts could be saved and used during system testing, load testing, regression testing, and security testing. Capture and replay tools make the task of testing easier, but it still needs to be done.

The mechanism by which users are assigned to a security group must also be tested. This might be performed by a separate utility program, or it might be a window in the main application which is accessible to only the system administrator. No matter where it exists or how it is initiated, it needs to be tested to make certain it doesn't contain any errors. Errors in this application could easily result in severe security breaches by allowing users access to windows they shouldn't access. It could just as easily result in users being denied access to the windows in the application they should be able to reach. Neither of these types of errors will win the developers or testers any friends in the user community.

Just as an aside, the table(s) which contain security-related data should be protected against all update activity. If criminals gain access to these tables, they would be able to empower anyone to access any table or window in the system. One way of auditing access to these tables would be to create a trigger on them. Any time a row is inserted or updated, the trigger would create a row in a separate audit table. This row would contain details such as the date and time of the activity, the ID of the initiator, the windows and tables affected, and the access granted. The security administrator should review this log on a regular basis. Attempts to modify these tables should set off some very loud alarm bells within the system or security administration group.

14.2.2.3.2.2 Disabling and Hiding Buttons Dynamically altering the properties of buttons is another frequently utilized technique for controlling application functionality and navigation. The attributes of buttons can be dynamically modified depending on whether the current user is able to exercise the functionality behind each particular button. The security group of the current user determines which buttons on each window are enabled, disabled, or invisible. Just as in the creation of dynamic menu items, database tables would contain specifications on what buttons should be available to each security group.

Disabling or hiding buttons is also commonly used to control functionality on specific windows. If the user is able to edit the data, then an edit button is visible and enabled. If the user is allowed to delete data, then the delete button is visible and enabled. Users which don't have these privileges either wouldn't see the buttons or would see buttons which have been disabled.

Security enforced by button manipulation must also be adequately tested. It requires that the tester open every window and verify that the appropriate buttons are enabled. This activity must be performed for each security group. A capture and replay test script should be created for each of these tests. This script could be re-used for system, regression, and security testing.

14.2.3 Security at the Database Server

The database server is the nexus of any client/server system. The source of data is on the database server and the majority of all communications goes to or from this server. Since it is such a focal point, security on the server must be correspondingly higher than at the client level. In spite of the server being the focus of so much attention, it isn't very difficult to design security for the server.

14.2.3.1 Physical Security.   Physical access to the server should be adequately secured. The server should be located in a locked room. The reason for this is that servers, like all computers, are prone to tampering when they are in the boot process. They can be booted in single user mode and modified during the boot process. Preventing unauthorized personnel from physically accessing them will prevent unnecessary and risky reboot operations.

If the intent of criminals was to disrupt the system and deny users access to it then being able to get their hands on the server would allow this to be done. The server could be powered down, disconnected from the network, physically damaged, or disrupted in any number of other ways if access is possible.

14.2.3.2 Server Account Security.   Accounts on the server should be limited to those which are absolutely necessary. In general, users of a client/server system have little or no need for an account on the server. They normally log onto their client machines and connect directly to the database. Only a few situations would require that users have a server account.

It may sound obvious, but all default accounts created when the system is built should be deleted or inactivated. Vendors, both hardware and software, routinely create administration, test, and diagnostic accounts on new systems. All of these represent potential security hazards and should be eliminated immediately! If need for the account arises at a later time, then it can be added.

No one should be allowed to log directly onto the server other than the DBA and the SysAdmin group. Even the DBA might be able to perform his or her tasks remotely. The fewer people who actually log onto this machine the fewer security lapses there will be and the easier it will be to determine what the cause is when one occurs.

Testing to be performed on the server must include attempts to gain access to the server. The tester should attempt to log onto the server using commonly named accounts. Some examples are root, guest, test, etc. These accounts shouldn't exist. If they must exist then their passwords should be modified frequently. Tools are available which help in this area. Section 14.5 describes some of the capabilities of tools of this nature.

14.2.3.3 Securing Backup Tapes. Backup tapes must be physically secure. The data held on a tape is usually comprehensive enough to enable the system to be completely rebuilt. If this is the case then more than enough information resides on the backup tapes to provide computer criminals with the files and data they are seeking.

14.2.3.4 Power Supply. The power supply used by the server should also be controlled. If the power is cut to the server, then use of the system would be denied to legitimate users. Placing an uninterruptible power supply (UPS) within the secured server room will prevent this type of exposure. The UPS unit chosen must have enough capacity to supply power to all hardware which is deemed essential. This might include the server CPU, monitor, external disk drives, and external tape drives.

The UPS should provide enough time for users to gracefully exit the system. A client/server system which is truly crucial should have alternate power supplies which come online if the normal power goes out. Current UPS systems are intelligent enough to recognize that they are running low on power. When this threshold is reached, they send a signal to the server via an RS-232 link. The server must then shut the system down gracefully in the remaining time.

Testing must be done to verify that the UPS and the shutdown logic will function as advertised. UPS testing should include the steps listed in Table 14.4. Obviously, this type of testing must be done at a point when the system hasn't yet gone into production.

Testing in this area is essential because unpredictable events will eventually occur. One system I worked on had just added a UPS for the database server. The assumption was that the system was now bulletproof. Unfortunately, one night about midnight the cleaning crew unplugged the UPS, which wasn't in a secure room, so their vacuum cleaner could be plugged in. When they plugged the UPS back in, the prongs didn't quite make contact with the outlet. The UPS hummed along for the promised two hours. Then the system went down. As I recall, that was also the one day on which the database wasn't backed up. You're never as bulletproof as you think you are, but you'll never know it in time if you don't test for it.

14.2.4 Secure Versions of Database Systems

The RDBMS system being used may provide a secure version of the package. Oracle, for example, has a secure version of its database product, Trusted Oracle 7. This could be used instead of the standard commercial package in situations where security is of the utmost importance. Systems dealing with military data or financial data are two typical examples.

Trusted Oracle 7 provides multiple levels of security within a database. This scheme is called *multilevel security* (MLS). It controls access to individual rows of data by dynamically attaching a label to each row. The label represents the security level of the user who created the row. At no point can a user with a lower security level access that row. The only users who are able to reference this row are the users with a security as high or higher than the originator.

TABLE 14.4

UPS-Related Testing

1) Log several users onto the system

2) Pull the plug on the UPS unit.

3) Observe how long the UPS runs before it reaches a low power threshold.

4) Does it generate the appropriate signal to the server?

5) Were the users made aware of the situation? How? Should they have been?

6) Has the UPS reached a critical low power threshold?

7) Did the server gracefully kill the remaining user sessions?

8) Did logic on the server shut down the database server properly?

9) Was support personnel paged, e-mailed, or otherwise notified?

10) Did the system come back up gracefully?

11) If alternate sources of power (e.g., generators) exist, did they come online at the proper time?

The security label and the implicit processing which is used to check the security level is transparent to the user. Testing to verify that security has been implemented correctly would entail creating test data for each security level. A tester would log into the system at all security levels to determine whether data at higher levels of security can be accessed. This could be done via SQL scripts like the one outlined in Table 14.1.

14.2.5 Application Server Security

The application server also needs to be secure. The steps which should be taken to ensure its security are very much like the steps taken for the database server. This server also needs to be physically protected. It should be in a locked server room, perhaps the same room that the database server is in. It needs to have an uninterruptible power supply (UPS) to supply it with AC power.

The number of accounts on the application server should be severely limited. The ability to do that represents a serious lapse in security. Access to any disk file on this server should be limited to execute only. Gaining access to an account or disk files on this machine would enable a criminal to modify the applications or business rules being run.

14.2.6 Network Security

The network is quite possibly the component of a client/server system which poses the greatest security threat. The reason for this is that in order for it to connect the server and the client machines it must be open, i.e., connected to a network. Openness is dangerous. All sorts of devious minds are looking for the opportunity to create havoc on your client/server system. Network security is primarily an exercise in making the network available to legitimate users without putting out the welcome mat for unwanted parties.

One of the biggest threats to security is transmitting passwords, account names, and other confidential information in a format which is understandable to anyone who wants to intercept these messages. Are transmissions between the client and server machines encrypted? Make the data cost more to break into than it's worth. There are a number of good encryption packages available. Some of them (e.g., PGP—Pretty Good Privacy) are available for downloading free off the Internet.

The security area is almost like a cat-and-mouse game between system crackers and system administrators. Security flaws in operating systems are uncovered and exploited by crackers. Flaws and configuration problems in operating systems offer a cracker an opportunity to gain access to your system. Fixes to protect against these flaws are regularly identified and distributed. Installing the latest system patches will reduce the exposure to this danger. Procedures should be created and followed to make certain that patches are applied on a regular basis.

Another frequent method of violating network security is to exploit improperly configured network services. These services include finger, ftp, showmount, DNS, mail, sendmail, whois, tfpt, rpcinfo, and uucp. Finger is a potentially dangerous service because it can provide a cracker with a wealth of information about account names, home directories, last login times, etc.

Is it possible for someone to position a sniffer device on the network? This type of electronic eavesdropping could provide the listener with a wealth of information. Passwords, logins, addresses, etc., would all be potential information available to the intruder.

The final word in network security testing is to find whatever information and help is available. A number of tools are available to assist network and system administrators in setting up and testing secure systems. A number of these tools are described in Section 14.5. Become familiar with the information that is available as well as the tools.

14.2.7 Security on the Client Workstation

Programs can mimic the login window of the application in order to capture a legitimate user's password. The program intercepts the password, reports a login failure, and terminates itself. The user will assume he or she has incorrectly entered his or her ID or password and try again. The second time the user will connect to the application, but by that point the pseudo login program already has the logon ID and password.

If the criminal has access to users' workstations, this type of program can be planted. How can this be prevented? One solution is to run applications off a network drive which have severely limited write access. This would prevent any pseudo login programs from being written to the network drive.

Another way of preventing this type of security violation would be to control the desktop environment of the typical users. The ability to add icons would be restricted. All icons would be defined by LAN administration or security personnel. This would prevent a criminal from adding a password-grabbing program onto a user's workstation.

14.3 Other Security Violations

As if the previous potential security gaps aren't enough to worry about, there are still others. The following sections describe additional potential client/server security problems.

14.3.1 Protecting Source Code

Access to source code can provide a tremendous assistance to any criminal wishing to penetrate a system's security. Without the source code, a trespasser has to probe through a system to find its flaws. If a trespasser is able to obtain a copy of the source code, then he or she can scrutinize it for potential gaps or flaws in security.

Make sure adequate security is provided for the system's source code. Don't allow source code to reside on client machines or on the server. It should be located only on a workstation belonging to the configuration management group. This particular machine should have extremely limited access. If this machine can be disconnected from the network most of the time, that would provide additional security for the source code.

Users of the client/server system will require "execute" access to a number of EXE and DLL files. A truly ingenuous computer criminal will probably be capable of reverse engineering these types of files. If these files can be placed on the network drive and be public execute but not public read, it would give additional protection for the files and the system.

Testing activities should be directed towards attempting to access source code files. If they can be accessed by the testing staff then the security on them isn't adequate.

14.3.2 Idle Terminal Logoff

Users of client/server systems have a tendency to open up all the applications they use regularly once and keep them open as long as they can.

Normally, they close applications only when they start experiencing memory shortage difficulties. The problem with this type of behavior is that the applications are frequently left running when the user is no longer at his or her terminal. This can happen if the user walks away from a logged-in terminal to consult with a colleague or go on break. It can also happen if the user forgets or neglects to log out of the system at night.

An unattended terminal represents a severe security violation. An unauthorized user could seize that opportunity to access sensitive data. The data could be copied, deleted, added to, or modified. A criminal could also use this occasion to modify executable files. A virus, Trojan horse, or password-sniffing program could easily be slipped onto the system in less than a minute.

Security logic which detects an idle terminal is needed. This software can be built right into the application. Some of the popular GUI development packages make it fairly easy to install this type of logic. Both Power-Builder and Visual Basic make it easy to implement idle terminal logoff logic. It frequently takes the form of a timer which expires in a configurable amount of time, say five minutes. Each time the user interacts with the application via the keyboard or mouse, the timer is restarted at five minutes. The timer expires only if the user doesn't press a key or move the mouse for the specified amount of time.

When the idle terminal timer expires, there are two possible actions. The first possibility is that a login type window is displayed on the terminal. This window requires that a password be correctly entered to get back to the application which was running. The password required to restore the application can be the same as the password originally required to enter the application. If the same password isn't required, then the requirements for this password should be no less stringent than the original password's requirements.

The other possible action for an idle terminal is to close down the application. The current window could be closed or the entire application could be terminated. This is a more severe course of action which isn't likely to be popular with users, but it provides significantly more security.

The logic which automatically logs out users needs to be tested thoroughly. It must be verified that this security measure isn't being thwarted by screen savers or background programs running on the terminal. This can be tested by setting the timeout value to a reasonable period, bringing up the application, and verifying that it does indeed log the user off the system. Some automatic logout logic gives users the chance to maintain their session by performing some activity. If logic of this nature was included in the system, then it too must be tested.

Testing must also be performed to verify that an auto logoff functions correctly no matter what the user is doing in the application. The user might be in the middle of inserting new data and neglect to click the save button. The idle terminal logic should roll back this or any other type of transaction which is in progress. This can be tested by opening the application, beginning the data entry activity, and then allowing the idle timer to expire. Log back into the application and verify that the transaction was rolled back.

Is it possible for the user or a system hacker to initiate a program which tricks the application into thinking an idle terminal is still active? This program could periodically enter characters in the window, tab the cursor from one field to another, or reposition the mouse cursor. The intent of such a scheme might be to avoid auto logoffs. Run tests which verify that the logoff logic isn't fooled by a program of this type.

14.3.3 Trap Doors, Logic Bombs, and Trojan Horses

System and applications developers are in the perfect position to build trap doors, logic bombs, and Trojan horses into a client/server system. A *trap door* is a method to gain access to an application or system without going through normal login or authentication procedures. Developers may create trap doors to enable them to make corrections or modifications to the system quickly. Vendors may create and leave trap doors in a system to allow them to run remote diagnostic programs.

Trojan horses are programs which gain access to the system by hiding inside other, seemingly legitimate programs. An example might be a utility which is loaded onto the system to defragment disk drives. The utility might indeed defragment the disk drive, but it also makes other, undesirable modifications to the system. It might, for example, create a new account, give a specific user administrator privileges, or copy the password file to a public location.

A *logic bomb* is a piece of code which directs the system to perform specific functions after a certain time period has expired or after the program has executed a set number of times. Many anecdotal stories exist about software developers who plant logic bombs into their products to ensure that they receive payment from their customers. After the system has been in place for a set period of time, say 90 days, an obscure error message is presented. The user is forced to contact the developer for instructions on how to handle this undocumented situation. If the client hasn't paid the developer for the system, then the developer demands full and complete payment before he or she "assists" with this problem. If payment has been rendered, then he or she provides the code which deactivates this problem.

While it would be extremely difficult to guarantee that none of the above occur, there are methods of reducing the probability of this type of activity on the part of your developers. Some of these methods could be considered testing, while others deal more with operational or cultural aspects of the development environment.

Performing code reviews during the system's development exposes every developer's code to other people. It would be very difficult, but not impossible, to hide these covert activities during a code review session. Knowing that their code will be examined by a number of other developers and management will tend to stifle the urge to plant this type of code.

Pay special attention to the login logic when performing a code review. This is where trap doors are most likely to be hidden. Any code dealing with undocumented parameters in this area should raise a red flag.

A lack of documentation in the source code being developed may simply be an indication of a developer's laziness or dislike of an unpleasant chore. It might also indicate that the developer doesn't want to document code which isn't doing what it is supposed to be doing. A lone, undocumented section of code should be examined with particular vigor. Unfortunately, this doesn't mean that all documented code is trustworthy. Comments in code can easily be inaccurate or misleading.

Code which appears to be excessively "clever" should be examined more closely than normal code. In this case, "clever" might mean code which seems to be a little too complicated for the task at hand. It might be code which uses system function calls which don't seem quite necessary. It might be a "case" statement used to handle what could be handled by a simpler IF_THEN_ELSE statement. Even if it doesn't represent a security violation, "clever" code has a tendency to be more error prone than most code, especially if it is inadequately documented.

Use of undocumented parameters in calls to any function (system or local) should be questioned. It might be that these calls are doing something which they shouldn't be doing. Even if the code isn't violating security, it isn't a good idea to rely upon undocumented features. The current version of the function might work, but there is no guarantee that later releases of this function will continue to support an undocumented capability. By the time the next version is released, it is very likely that the original developer who used the feature will have forgotten about it or will have moved onto another project or company. The result will be that something which used to work successfully mysteriously no longer works. I promise you that many hours will be spent tracking this kind of error before the cause is determined.

Configuration management is the practice of controlling the software as it moves from the development group to production. Implementing sound configuration management can prevent the original code from being surreptitiously modified along this journey. Good configuration management (CM) practices include placing tight access restrictions on the disk drives or volumes where trusted code resides. Only CM personnel should be able to access code once it has been turned over to them by the developers.

Just as random drug tests can reduce drug use, so can random code inspections cut down on security violations. Let it be known in advance that random windows, functions, etc., turned over to the configuration management group will be examined with a fine toothed comb. Don't dwell on this; just establish it as a policy and make sure it is enforced. Since less code is developed by client/server development packages, this inspection won't be as onerous as it might sound.

Regular comparisons [file size, date/time last written, binary/hex comparison, or cyclic redundant character check (CRCC) values] of production code with backup versions or configuration management versions of the same files should be performed. The sizes and CRCC values of these newly built files should then be compared with executables and libraries on the production system. Discrepancies can indicate unauthorized modifications, patches, viruses, etc., which are threats to security.

Periodically all executables and libraries should be rebuilt from trusted source code. This is a step further than just comparing sizes, dates, and CRCC values. Again the sizes and cyclic redundant character check (CRCC) values of these newly built files should then be compared with executables and libraries on the production system. Discrepancies can indicate patches, viruses, etc., which are threats to security.

14.3.4 Viruses

Viruses are an important security concern. While viruses aren't normally associated with data being stolen, they frequently destroy data or deny access to the system by legitimate users. Antivirus software should be run regularly on both the server and client-level machines.

Viruses come in two main classes. The first class of viruses are referred to as "file infectors." Viruses of this type attach themselves to ordinary program files. Normally, the types of files they attach to are .COM or .EXE programs. Each time an infected file is executed, it infects additional files.

The second type of virus is a system or boot record infector. These viruses infect the code found in system areas of the disk. Normally the areas infected are the DOS boot sectors on diskettes or the master boot record (MBR) on hard drives. Each diskette inserted into the disk drive is a victim for infection.

14.3.4.1 Source of Viruses.   Viruses don't spontaneously appear on a client/server system. They are loaded onto the system through the action of someone. Viruses can be spread maliciously, but normally this is done inadvertently by a user or developer. Users may have downloaded a game or tool from a bulletin board system (BBS), and they bring it in to the office. They might also unknowingly pick up a virus on a diskette from their home computer or a co-worker's computer and infect their own computer.

Each shop should develop a policy which describes what software can be loaded onto the system. Obviously, a policy which states that nothing should be loaded onto the system is optimal from a security standpoint. Unfortunately, this policy stands very little chance of being taken seriously and even less of chance of being enforced. The next best alternative would be to emphasize how important it is to screen all diskettes which are inserted into any workstation in the system.

All diskettes should be virus checked before being inserted into a disk drive. Set up and publicize the existence of computers which are available exclusively for scanning floppy diskettes. If people don't realize that they exist, then they can't take advantage of them. Since new viruses are being developed all the time, make sure that the latest version of virus-checking software is being used.

14.3.4.2 Antivirus Products.   Since people aren't normally fastidious about testing their diskettes, this isn't likely to totally prevent viruses from infecting your computer system. If viruses can't be prevented from infecting the system, the next best step is to minimize the damage they are able to do. This can be accomplished by running virus detection software on all client machines on a regular basis. This software detects, identifies, and removes viruses before they can do much damage.

A number of products are available which promise to keep your client workstations virus free. Among them are:

- Dr. Solomon.
- McAfee.
- Norton Antivirus.

Every organization which utilizes any computers should acquire an antivirus product and implement it. Since existing viruses are constantly being modified and new viruses are continuously being created, it is necessary to acquire and install updates on a regular basis.

14.4 Other Testing Security

Security testing is different from other testing in a number of ways. To thoroughly perform security testing requires a tremendous amount of experience. Internal testing can be done, but a system which requires the highest possible level of protection should involve experts in its security-testing process.

Another difference is that security testing should be viewed as an ongoing activity instead of a one-time event. Most testing of a client/server system is done once. Unless some aspect of the system is changed (e.g., application software, RDBMS software, hardware, network) then testing isn't repeated. Security testing must be ongoing because hackers continuously develop new attacks on computer systems. Complacency in this area can result in a system becoming vulnerable to such intrusions.

14.4.1 Tiger Teams

The term "tiger team" is given to a group of penetration experts who are deliberately asked to attempt to breach the security of a system. They usually represent a group of outside experts brought in to test security of a system which requires the highest level of protection possible. This might be justified if the system is critical to a company's operations or it contains extremely valuable information.

A tiger team is provided minimal information about the system they are trying to breach. This is done to duplicate the knowledge that other

system crackers would begin with. If the tiger team is successful in penetrating the system, then its security was vulnerable. Unfortunately, if
they aren't able to gain access to the system, it doesn't guarantee that the
system is absolutely secure.

When should a tiger team be scheduled to attempt to penetrate a
system? It doesn't make much sense to bring a group of outsiders
into the testing phase until the internal people have tested the system's security. It's better for the in-house testers to find as many
shortcomings as they can and address them. Only then should outsiders make their attempts. If they are engaged prematurely, they will
undoubtedly uncover the problems the local testers would have
found. This represents a waste of their time and energy, both of
which are expensive commodities.

14.4.2 Security Team

Establish a security team which handles ongoing security problems.
This could include virus outbreaks, potential system break-ins, and
ongoing security testing. The security team (also referred to as the crisis management team) should consist of team members with a variety
of backgrounds and experience. Skills which would be useful in the
group include a manager, a system programmer or system administrator, an auditor, and a representative from the law enforcement field.
The time to establish a security team is not after a break-in has
occurred.

Users should be made aware of who is on the security team. If
they notice anomalies in the system, they should report them to the
security team. Examples of anomalies are login messages which
report unsuccessful login attempts which the user knows he or she
didn't make. The last login date and time might also indicate that
someone has successfully logged into the system masquerading as
them. If applications take considerably longer than expected to complete, it might signify that other programs are running or that the
database has been adversely modified.

The security team should be proactive as well as reactive. They
should be continuously testing the system's security and obtaining
and installing a security-related operating system and network software patches. Monitoring the system's logs and audit trail files should
be a regular function for this group.

14.5 Third-Party Tools to Enforce or Test Security

There are a number of tools which are available to help in either setting up a secure client/server system or testing the security of an existing client/server system. The products listed below are meant only to be representative of what is available on the market. The fact that a product has been included is not to be construed as an endorsement of any particular product or vendor.

14.5.1 PowerCerv's PADLock

PADLock (PowerBuilder Application and Data Lock) is a third-party tool from PowerCerv which allows a security administrator to create and administer security for PowerBuilder-based applications. It eliminates the need for developers to build security into their PowerBuilder applications.

A point-and-click method is used by PADLock to administer security. The security administrator runs each PowerBuilder application for which security is being defined. All objects to which access is being limited are selected. The types of objects for which security can be specified include windows, window controls, menus, menu items, user objects, DataWindows (intelligent grids), DataWindow columns, DataWindow rows, and DataWindow cells. The security administrator then identifies which user or group of users are to be given access to each of these objects.

Objects which users don't have access to can be made invisible or disabled. Users can be granted read-only or edit privileges on objects. Access data is stored by PADLock in a database. Since it is data-driven, there is no need to recompile and redistribute applications if security is changed.

PADLock will function on client/server systems which use Power-Builder and the following databases: Sybase DBLib, MS SQL Server, Oracle, Sybase SQL Anywhere (Watcom), and Informix.

14.5.2 SATAN

One security-elated tool which has received a tremendous amount of publicity recently is the Security Administrator Tool for Analyzing

Networks (SATAN). SATAN is a testing and reporting tool which draws together information about network host computers. Information is gathered about specified hosts and networks by examining network services (e.g., finger, NIS, ftp, rexd, and NFS). This data is reported in a summary format or in a rule-based system to help investigate potential security problems. Some of the security vulnerabilities which SATAN probes for include the following:

1. NFS export to unprivileged programs.

2. NFS export via portmapper.

3. Unrestricted NFS export.

4. NIS password file access.

5. rexd access.

6. Sendmail vulnerabilities.

7. TFTP file access.

8. Remote shell access.

9. Unrestricted X server access.

10. Writable FTP home directory.

11. wu-ftpd vulnerability.

SATAN was designed as a security tool for system and network administrators. Unfortunately, it can provide the same information about a system's weaknesses to a potential system criminal. The vulnerabilities which SATAN reveals are not new, but the ability to locate them with an easy-to-use tool increases the exposure of sites which haven't properly addressed security. System and network administrators should acquaint themselves with SATAN and other related security tools. They need to assure themselves that their systems aren't vulnerable to the problems which tools of this nature identify.

14.5.3 SQL<>SECURE Password Manager

When users log directly onto a server, it is the operating system which authenticates that the user's identification and password are valid. The task of verifying a new password is also performed by the operating system. A robust operating system will check the new password for adherence to certain standards. These standards frequently include minimum length, nonblank passwords, easily guessed passwords, attempts to reuse the same password, etc. If the new password doesn't meet the standards, then the operating system won't allow the user to modify his or her password to the proposed new one.

In many client/server applications, the user never logs onto the server's operating system. The user actually logs into the database directly from the client workstation, bypassing the operating system at the server level. When the user changes his or her password, this is also done via the database management package. Most database systems don't include the same level of password checking that operating systems do. They don't always require the new password to meet minimum length standards, nonblank requirements, etc. This deficiency can result in weak or absent passwords on users' database accounts.

If the database system doesn't perform checking on new passwords, then this function must be performed by another program. The choices facing the developer of a client/server system are to build this functionality into the application or acquire and implement a third-party tool which does it. Password Manager from BrainTree Security Software provides this. Some of the functions which Password Manager include are:

■ Verifies that new passwords meet security standards before they are accepted. Standards might include minimum length, reuse checks, dictionary checks, easily guessed passwords.

■ Records the data, time, and source of password change operations.

■ Can synchronize the user's operating system password to the new database password.

■ Can synchronize passwords between multiple databases.

■ Can disable accounts which haven't been used for a specific time period.

■ Can disable accounts after a set number of login failures.

Password Manager applications run on MS-Windows, Motif, Macintosh-based systems. These applications can be run stand-alone, integrated into local applications, or invoked via a user-callable API.

14.5.4 Password Crackers

A *password cracker* is a utility or program which has been specifically designed to guess a system's passwords. These programs have a list of commonly used account names and passwords. Using these values, they attempt to gain access to systems. The password list might include every word in an English language dictionary.

Tools of this nature are readily available on the Internet. Security testing must include the steps to acquire and use tools like this. If you don't test your system for vulnerabilities, then system crackers certainly will do the testing for you!

14.6 Summary

A lot of security and security testing boils down to being proactive instead of reactive and paying attention to details. Security testing must be done as early as practical. Once the system goes live, the security flaws will be there for anyone to exploit. If they exist, it won't take long for someone to spot them and take advantage of them. Reacting to such an intrusion is very much a case of shutting the barn door after the horse is gone.

One way of almost guaranteeing that a system's security will be poorly implemented is to do it at the last minute. It will almost certainly lead to cracks, gaps, oversights, etc. Security needs to be designed and developed in parallel with the design and development of client/server systems and applications. If security is shoehorned in at the last minute, then testing must be especially vigorous and vigilant to catch the holes which will undoubtedly exist.

A good deal of security in a system is instituting and following procedures which are little more than common sense. Procedures such as physical security, changing passwords, not loading questionable software, not writing down one's password, shredding confidential documents, etc., represent a tremendous improvement in the security of a system. Testing these procedures isn't something that is done just during system testing. It's an ongoing process in which everyone plays a part. Users, developers, system administrators, and managers all need to follow the rules to help safeguard the system.

Don't overlook the possibility that criminals might attempt to gain access to the system outside of the applications being developed. This might be via an interactive SQL session. Another method might be to attach to it via an ODBC tool like Microsoft Access. They might attempt to bypass the RDBMS and access disk files directly. Putting the security into the database instead of the application will provide protection against this type of security breach attempt.

CHAPTER 15

Odds and Ends

There are a significant number of other client/server-related testing topics which need to be discussed but aren't large enough to require an entire chapter. This chapter is an attempt to shed some light on some of these topics. In spite of the brevity of the material devoted to them, each of these topics is certainly important.

15.1 Batch Processing

It may come as a surprise to some, but client/server systems haven't done away with the need for batch processing. Even on the client/server paradigm, there is still the requirement to handle large processing jobs. These requirements can include data being imported from other systems, producing extremely large reports, cutting monthly checks, periodic archival of data, month-end processing, etc.

15.1.1 Where Is Batch Processing Performed?

Batch jobs are frequently executed on the server instead of on a client machine. It makes sense to run them there for several reasons. The most significant reason for executing batch jobs on the server is to minimize the network activity generated by the job. A batch job will likely process tens or hundreds of thousands of rows from the database. It isn't efficient to move the data from the database server across the network to the client, process it, and then move it back across the network to the server. Imposing this load on the network would have a noticeable effect on system performance experienced by other users of the client/server system.

Another reason for running batch jobs on the server is that the job will be completed more quickly on the server. The explanation for this is that servers typically have better hardware. The typical server's CPU will be significantly faster than the average client machine's CPU. Servers with multiple CPUs are becoming more common. Most server machines have significantly more memory than the average client workstation. This combination of hardware will help ensure that lengthy batch processing will complete more quickly on a server than on a client machine.

The server is likely to have an operating system more suited to multiprocessing than the client machine. Most servers in client/server systems are running an operating system such as UNIX or Windows NT. The typical client machine is running Windows 3.1 or Windows 95. These systems aren't designed to run multiple processes the way UNIX and Windows NT are. Jobs run on operating systems designed for multiprocessing are less likely to hang up or abnormally terminate.

As mentioned earlier, batch jobs will be expected to run for considerable periods of time. Running batch jobs on a client machine will effectively tie up the machine for lengthy periods of time. This will result in the client machine being either unavailable or available in a severely degraded performance mode. Most users wouldn't be happy to have their personal machines locked up or slowed down for the better part of a day.

Once batch jobs are kicked off, it is imperative that they complete successfully. If a payroll processing job doesn't complete in time there will be a lot of unhappy employees. Client machines aren't as likely to be on a UPS as the server is.

Network interruptions would jeopardize the batch process. If the network experienced problems while data was being sent between the server and the client machine, it could introduce errors or cause the job to be aborted. Running batch jobs on the server takes the network out of the picture. This results in a lower risk of failure for the batch processing.

15.1.2 Testing Batch Processes

Testing batch processes is significantly different than the testing done elsewhere in a client/server system. Batch processing is unlikely to include GUI interfaces or other accouterments normally associated with client/server systems. Testing of the batch processing is more like traditional programming than it is similar to testing GUI interfaces.

There are a number of points which must be included when the test plans for batch processing is developed. The items which are necessary are outlined in the following sections.

15.1.2.1 Batch Job Initiation. Batch processing requires that jobs somehow be kicked off. This initiation might be a manual process, an automated process, or a combination of the two. No matter how it is done, the initiation process must be tested to make certain that it works. Testing each of these three methods is slightly different. A brief outline of each is described here.

15.1.2.1.1 Manual Initiation If the initiation process is a manual one, then procedures to perform it must be developed, tested, and published. These procedures should tell the user exactly what needs to be done, what order it must be performed in, and when it should be done. They should also include information on how the user can verify that the batch process has been successfully started.

Testing a manual process consists of attempting to initiate it by strictly following the written procedures. It would be much more effective to have a user instead of a programmer or other developer-type person be "driving" this test. This will help to flush out ambiguities, misunderstandings, or steps which might have been overlooked. Someone who is too familiar with the process would be more likely to take the correct steps in spite of slightly flawed documentation.

15.1.2.1.2 Automatic Initiation   When the batch job initiation is automated, the testing is different but should be just as thorough. A job might be initiated by the cron facility in UNIX, the Enterprise Manager on a Microsoft SQL Server system, or a third-party scheduling package. Tests must make certain that the appropriate jobs are scheduled on the right days at the right times.

A number of questions should be asked and investigated before entrusting job scheduling to an automated process. Among the potential situations which need to be tested are the following:

- Is the scheduling process automatically restarted after a system reboot?
- Will the scheduling process be properly handled after a server crash?
- What rescheduling is done if the server crashes while a batch job is running?
- Can the scheduling logic generate an alert (e-mail or page someone) if a process isn't initiated?
- Does the account which scheduled the process have adequate access to all required files?
- What security is in place to prevent someone from meddling with the scheduling queue?
- Will the biannual shift to and from Daylight Savings Time be handled correctly?
- How far in advance can jobs be scheduled? Can it handle quarterly and yearly scheduling?

15.1.2.1.3 Manual and Automatic Initiation   Situations which combine manual and automated initiation of batch processes can become fairly complicated. The user might have to run one or more manual processes to set up data or verify the validity of the data being processed. At a later time, the batch job would be automatically initiated to perform the actual processing.

When there is a mixture of manual and automatic job initiation, testing must expose problems when one step doesn't take place in the expected sequence. Besides the questions and test scenarios that were raised in the two previous sections, the following should be examined or tested:

- Can the batch job recognize that necessary manual steps didn't take place?

- How would the batch job handle this situation?

- Do both the manual and automatic processes log problems to the same place?

- Is it possible for steps be performed out of sequence? Will this be fatal?

15.1.2.2 Testing Parameters. Batch processes frequently need some type of input to control the processing they will perform. The parameter might be passed to the process when it is initiated. Alternatively, the parameter value(s) might reside in a known location such as a file or database table. Examples of the types of values which might be supplied as parameters include a date, a date range, a department number, a calendar quarter, a starting sequence number, minimum amount of checks to cut, an age value of people or bills, etc.

Testing in relationship to parameters needs to verify a number of things. The first test is that both the scheduler (manual or automatic) and the batch process agree on the location of the parameters. They will both be referencing the same database table, row in a table, disk file, subdirectory, etc. They both need to be able to access that location, whether it is a file or a database table.

The number of parameters involved needs to be identical between the scheduler and the batch process, as does the order of the parameters and the datatype of each parameter.

Testing that the parameters are correct might seem to be overkill or trivial at first glance. It won't seem that way when a batch process doesn't run to completion because the parameters supplied to it were wrong. Or worse yet, it runs to completion but processed the wrong month's data. Either of these situations will have you, your users, and your management fuming.

15.1.2.3 The Window in Time.   Most batch processing is scheduled to execute during a certain window of time. This window is normally from the time when users get off the system for the night until they reappear the following morning. The time frame from midnight until 6 A.M. is a fairly common window for batch processing. System activity is oftentimes at its lowest point during this time period. This allows batch processing to obtain and hold more system resources (database locks, tables, memory, disk I/O, CPU time, etc.) without impacting other users on the system.

Many systems are experiencing a severe shrinking in the duration of this window. Some sites no longer have or never had a window which could be exclusively dedicated to batch processing. The shrinking window phenomena is caused by a number of things. Users might be working around the clock. The organization might have gone international. This would require supporting users in different time zones around the world. It will always be business hours to someone somewhere in the world.

The impact of not completing batch processes during the available window can be severe. Users will undoubtedly be impacted. Their response time will probably be significantly worse than they are accustomed to. Reports or data which are needed might not be available at the start of the business day. The worst-case scenario would be for deadlocks to occur when users start logging onto the system. This could crash user applications or, worse yet, crash a batch process which has been running for a number of hours.

Performance-related testing must be done to determine if the available time window is sufficient to run all the necessary batch jobs. If batch processing can't be completed in the available time window, then steps must be taken to make it finish in that amount of time. Steps which need to be taken will be different on each client/server system. What is appropriate for one environment won't be acceptable on another system, so any solutions implemented must take local requirements into consideration. A few possible solutions to this problem are listed in Table 15.1.

15.1.2.4 Test Data.   Batch processing is a specialized enough activity to warrant its own set of test data. This data should be geared towards the type of processing and tests needed for batch processing. The first step towards this goal is to create a sufficient amount of test data. If the production environment produces 100,000 bills a month during a batch process, then testing with 100 bills is both inadequate and dan-

TABLE 15.1

Potential Steps to
Speed Up Batch
Processes

Reduce the amount of batch processing by performing some tasks during normal business hours.

Start batch processing earlier in the window.

Divide batch processing into smaller units to distribute it across multiple days.

Make batch processing more efficient by using set processing instead of row by row processing.

Verify that the database engine isn't performing table scans when indexes could be used.

Make certain that tables' primary keys are appropriate.

If clustered tables are possible in the RDBM system, explore the possibility of using them.

Add indexes to the database tables to speed access to them.

Update database statistics used by the RDBMS to optimize queries more frequently.

Extract subsets of database tables into temporary tables and use them instead of full-sized tables.

Install additional memory in the server.

Defragment disks and database tables.

Distribute the database tables across more disk drives to reduce head contention.

Change the database to use raw files if this is an option under the RDBMS being used.

Replace the current server with a more powerful one.

Add additional CPUs to the database server.

Take steps to tune the database engine.

gerous. It's inadequate because it won't test all possible data variations. It's dangerous because it might produce misleading expectations concerning how long it will take to process the production number of records.

All tables which are referenced by the batch process need to be fully sized. Assume a batch process produces credit card billing statements. The tables involved include an account table, a transaction table, and a merchant table. The number of rows in the production tables might be 1 million for the account information, 20 million transactions in the transaction table, and the merchant table might include over 1 million merchants. The join necessary to produce each customer's bill involves each of these three tables. If any one of them is inadequately sized, then the resulting query won't accurately reflect what production performance will be.

Unfortunately, the best of screening processes is still likely to let in an occasional piece of inaccurate or incomplete data. When users are confronted with bad data, they can use their judgment and experience to decide how to deal with it. If they still can't handle it, they can call in a higher authority. Batch processes can do neither. They have no judgment on which to base their actions. The best to expect from batch processes is to recognize bad records and kick them out to a bad record file. An entry should also be written to the log file. Batch processes can't be allowed to pause when bad records are encountered. Doing this will almost certainly prevent them from completing within their time window.

A circumstance which certainly can occur is for a batch process to be initiated and not have any data to process. Either no parameters were supplied to it, the parameters were wrong, or the expected data isn't where the process expected to find it. The error-handling capabilities of the batch process should be able to handle this situation. The best solution would be to generate an alert so the problem is addressed before the batch processing window concludes. A less desirable method of handling this problem is to ignore it.

15.1.2.5 Testing/Verifying That Results Produced Are Correct. Amidst all of the batch-processing testing, it would be easy to overlook testing designed to verify that records have been processed correctly. This testing is probably the most important of all. To design these tests, the tester must have access to the system documentation which specifies what the batch process is supposed to do. If the process is designed to calculate payroll and cut checks, then the specifications should list all of the deductions which apply.

The size of the tables used when performing this particular testing would likely be fairly small initially. The tester would be examining records on an individual basis, checking for their accuracy instead of the quantity. Once the accuracy of the processing has been verified, then the quantities of data would be increased.

15.1.2.6 Log Files.   Since no one will be watching a batch process as it runs, it must somehow log its activities. Normally, log files are produced to document what activities have taken place. The exact format of logs will vary from system to system. They may be entries in a database table, or they may be produced in the form of a text file. No matter what their format, these logs need to chronicle such details as when the process started, who started it, what parameters were passed to the process, when the process completed, how many records were processed, and what errors it encountered. Other details might include summaries of the amounts of dollars or other units processed.

Accuracy and completeness of the log files is extremely important to batch processing. It provides one of the few means of tracking what happened and, more importantly, what didn't happen. If problems have occurred during batch processing, the logs will guide administrators in correcting the situation. This might require that portions of the batch job be rerun, all of it be rerun, etc.

The logic which generates log files must be tested just like all other processing. Tests should include deliberately setting conditions so the batch process will fail every conceivable way. After each such failure, the log files need to be examined to make certain they accurately captured and reported the problems encountered.

15.1.3 Drawbacks of Executing Batch Processing on the Server

Running batch jobs on the server does have some disadvantages. The primary disadvantage is that it requires both the developers and the testers to be able to function on yet another platform. Both developers and testers must become familiar with another editor, user interface, etc. While this offers them the opportunity for growth, it certainly will affect their productivity at the onset of their efforts.

Another impact of dealing with multiple platforms is how it affects the tools used. Tools which might be available for the client machine's environment might not be available for the server environment. Many of the GUI-based tools mentioned so far in this book won't run on a UNIX system. This might require that additional tools be acquired, installed, and learned. Obviously, this represents additional outlays in terms of dollars and time.

Testing batch processing is complicated by the fact that the language used is probably different from what is used elsewhere in the system. The dialects of languages such as SQL and C are subtly different between different vendor's packages. This subtly can easily lure the developer into thinking they are identical and that development can be done on either platform. Problems generated by this situation aren't likely to manifest themselves until the process is actually moved to the final computer platform and executed there. For this reason, development and testing must be performed on the platform where the batch program is to be executed.

15.2 Data Conversion

Client/server systems are frequently built to replace an existing system. The existing system, often referred to as a legacy system, is frequently mainframe based. The new system is usually intended to perform the same basic functions, but with a graphical user interface. When a client/server system is replacing a legacy system, there is usually a requirement that data from the old system be converted and available in the new system. This is a pretty reasonable assumption. The legacy system contains all of the data used to run the current system, and that data needs to be transferred to the new system.

This effort is never trivial and can be especially complicated if the "database" of the old system isn't really a database. Frequently it is a collection of text files, each of which is roughly the equivalent of a table. A recent survey found that 85% of corporate data is stored in nonrelational structures. Testing of the client/server system must encompass testing the data conversion process when that activity is included in the project effort.

15.2.1 What Legacy Data Conversion Includes

Converting from a legacy system to a relational database is at least a two-step process. The first step is to map the existing data into the new database. This step should be done in parallel with the design of the new database. By doing these tasks at the same time, it will be easier to identify fields which have been overlooked and incorporate them into the new database. If the mapping is done at a later time, then the new database won't be solidified until the mapping is completed.

During this first step, it would be beneficial to document the nature and usage of database tables. Examples of what should be identified include how many rows are expected in the table, how frequently rows are added, the source of incoming records, and how many rows are inserted at a time. Identifying which tables are static in nature and which are more dynamic is also a useful piece of knowledge.

The second step is to actually write programs which extract data from the legacy database and insert it into the new database. This effort will be more difficult and probably much more time-consuming than the first step.

It would be advisable to write a number of individual conversion programs instead of a single, monolithic conversion program. There are two good reasons for doing it this way. The first is efficiency related. A single conversion program will likely run for a long time to convert the entire database. What if only a single table needs to be completed at this time? Why run an all-encompassing conversion program to convert a single table?

The second advantage of creating multiple conversion programs, each with a specific function, is that this approach will prove to be much easier to test. If the data in table "x" is wrong, then the error must be in the one routine which inserts or updates data in "x." The alternative would be to search a huge program and attempt to track logic in it. Modularity won't guarantee that conversions will be error-free, but it can make locating errors significantly easier.

15.2.2 Conversion Problems

Data conversion is a dirty and difficult job. Some of the primary reasons for this are listed in Table 15.2. Explanations of these problems are presented in the following paragraphs.

15.2.2.1 Legacy Databases Evolved Instead of Being Designed. I don't think it would be an exaggeration to state that flat-file databases generally evolved instead of being designed. This statement isn't intended to be an insult of any kind. Systems evolve to meet the changing needs of the organization. As the systems evolve, so too must the data files which support them. Frequently, additional columns are added. Existing columns are resized and relocated.

In many cases new files are added instead of modifying existing files. This is done so existing code which referenced the original files

TABLE 15.2

Conversion
Difficulties

Legacy databases evolved instead of being designed

Differences in datatypes

Inadequate documentation

Fields which have more than one meaning

Fundamental incongruity between relational databases and records in flat files

Database rules are buried in the program's procedural code

Differences in the meanings of zeroes and spaces

Processing date values

wouldn't need to be modified. New programs are developed to reference the additional data files. This situation represents complications for the conversion process because it needs to combine the two parts of the record.

15.2.2.2 Differences in Datatypes.   There are fundamental differences between the data types which are available on legacy systems versus those included in relational databases. Some typical legacy data types include packed decimal, display, numeric, and computational. The data types which are available in most relational databases include integer, real, date, time, char (character), varchar (variable character), and BLOB (binary large object).

Most of the time, it is reasonably easy to convert from one world to the next, but occasionally there are difficulties. Packed decimal is one of these difficulties. Since there is no packed decimal datatype in relational systems, it must be converted to something more conventional. The conversion can be done by a "C" program and the value inserted into the relational database.

Another problem is that flat files frequently include bits which are used as flags. A particular bit might mean that the account is active. A second bit flag might indicate that the account has no outstanding credit problems. Unless the database is extremely well documented, the meanings of each of the individual flags can only be found by digging through the code.

Implied decimal points represent yet another complication. A value might be stored as an integer, but the code which processes it handles it as if there were a decimal point. This technique is frequently used to avoid the rounding problem when dealing with monetary values. The implied decimal point may not be documented. Only by examining the code is it apparent that the value is in fact a real datatype and not an integer datatype.

15.2.2.3 Inadequate Documentation.   More often than one would like, the documentation of a legacy database or file system is nonexistent, missing, incomplete, out of date, or poorly written. Too often the true meaning of database fields must be extracted from the legacy system's source code at a high cost in time and frustration. When this is the case, it becomes extremely difficult to make sure that the conversion process is error free.

Legacy systems which have been in place for decades have undergone many, many modifications. Most of them probably weren't reflected in

the system's documentation. In many cases the programmers who originally developed the system or maintained it during its lifetime may no
longer be around. These both compound the inadequate documentation problems.

15.2.2.4 Fields Which Have More Than One Meaning. Fields in
flat files are frequently used to represent more than one value. One
system being converted had two values packed into many of its fields.
One particular field was extremely odious. If the value in this field
was less than or equal to 1231, then it represented a date, but if it was
greater than 1231, then it was a ship number. Dual usage at this level
can drive the staff programming the conversion effort crazy.

Often a second field (type code) determines what a field (ID) represents. For example, the ID field might contain either a customer ID
number or a supplier ID number, depending on whether the type code
is zero or one. Processing logic must check these flags or run the risk of
adding a supplier to the customer account table.

This problem is even more confusing when values of two different
datatypes inhabit the same field. One value might be an integer and
the other incarnation might be a character string. Again, a bit flag
would dictate which format is used to interpret the field. When this is
the case, the conversion program may be forced to read everything in
as a string and then convert it to other types of data when it is
required.

**15.2.2.5 Fundamental Incongruity Between Relational Databases
and Flat Files** There are often fundamental differences between flat
files and relational database tables. One of the most basic differences
has to do with the duplication of data. Relational databases tend to be
fairly well normalized. Essentially, this means data isn't duplicated
unnecessarily. A table of credit card transactions doesn't contain the
name or address of the credit card holder. This information is in
the account table. Including it in the transactions table would duplicate
the name and address on every transaction record. This represents a
tremendous waste of space as well as potential integrity problems.

Flat files frequently duplicate data to a much greater degree. If the
transaction table were stored in a flat file, it might include the card-
holder name and address. This duplication of data needs to be
removed from the flat file when it is converted to a relational database.
The extra steps require additional coding, additional processing, and
additional testing.

15.2.2.6 Data Rules Are Buried in Procedural Code.   Data rules represent an understanding of what the data means and how it is to be processed. Some of the earlier examples of multiple values being held in a single field represent data rules. Legacy systems don't often document data rules explicitly. The rules on these systems tend to be embedded in the program's procedural code.

It's extremely difficult to program the conversion logic if the data rules aren't well defined. Testing to determine whether the rules have been followed is just as difficult without a clear understanding of the same rules. Unfortunately, this is the situation which presents itself when converting legacy data in many cases.

15.2.2.7 Differences in the Usage of Zeroes and Spaces.   Many flat files are fairly loose when distinguishing what is a zero and what is a blank character value. Frequently, fields which contain numeric values allow leading blanks to represent zeroes. In some cases an entirely blank field is used to represent a value of zero. If this is the way the data is interpreted, then the conversion programs must follow the same conventions when interpreting data values.

15.2.2.8 Processing Date Values.   Flat text files express date and time values in an incredible variety of formats. Table 15.3 provides a listing of just some of the formats which are likely to be encountered when dealing with legacy files. Further permutations might include separator values which are represented by hyphens, slashes, periods, colons, or other characters. The conversion programs must recognize that these are date fields and convert whatever value exists in the field to an appropriate date.

In Table 15.3, MM stands for a two-digit month value (01, 02, ..., 12). DD stands for a two digit day value (01, 02, ..., 30, 31). YY stands for a two-digit year value. MON represents a three-character month value (JAN, FEB, ...). HH, MM, and SS stand for two-digit values for the hour, minute, and second, respectively. DOW is a three-character value for the day of the week (MON, TUE, ...).

15.2.3 When to Convert

Ideally, the data conversion would be performed very early in the project. There are two excellent reasons for starting this effort so early. First

TABLE 15.3	MMDDYY
Date and Time Formats	MMDDYYYY
	DDMMYY
	DDMMYYYY
	MONDDYY
	MONDDYYYY
	MMYY
	MMYYYY
	MONYY
	MONYYYY
	HH:MM:SS
	Julian Date
	seconds since midnight
	tenths of seconds since midnight
	DOW

of all the converted data provides the most realistic test data for the database. What could be more realistic than actual, live data? If this data is available early enough, then there will be no need to acquire and use a data-generating-type test tool.

Actually, in some cases the data might be too realistic. If the data is considered to be extremely sensitive, then it might need to be filtered or sanitized before it is made available to the development and test staff. Financial data or salary-type information might fall into this category.

The second advantage to early conversion is that the quality and accuracy of the conversion process will be better the earlier it is done. The earlier the conversion is completed, the more its output will be used and tested before cut-over takes place. If this data is used during the majority of the testing, then it will be critically examined many, many times. Each time a developer runs into a problem, he or she will examine the data to see if it is the cause of the difficulty. Any errors in the data actually caused by the conversion process will be quickly pointed out to the conversion team by developers and testers.

15.2.4 Conversion Documentation

The conversion process needs to be extremely well documented. As each field is mapped from the legacy database to the relational database, there needs to be documentation of this mapping. This is needed in the event that there are questions or problems with the converted data. The documentation will allow the source of the data to be traced back to the original data files.

15.2.5 The Final Conversion

There are likely to be a number of test and intermediate conversion iterations of the database from the legacy system to the new system. Errors in data and problems identified in this cycle will be used to continuously refine the process. Each conversion iteration will hopefully be more accurate and go more smoothly than the preceding iteration. As each conversion is executed the amount of time to set it up and run it should be documented. Hopefully, this time period will be declining as the process becomes more practiced and smoother.

The smoothness of the conversion process becomes crucial when the final conversion is to be performed. This is important because it is usually desirable to minimize the time between when the legacy system is shut down for the last time and when the new system is brought online permanently. The sequence is normally for the old system to be turned off, the data to be converted and loaded into the new system, and then the new system is brought online. Having a smooth, well-documented conversion process with accurate timing estimates will make this process much easier for all concerned.

The final database conversion process shouldn't require any specific testing. It represents the culmination of all testing done up until this point in time. If the previous test conversions haven't gone smoothly, then you shouldn't be performing the final conversion.

15.3 Performance and Optimization

The performance of a client/server system is definitely an area which needs to be tested. If the performance doesn't meet the specifications or isn't considered acceptable, then users and management will likely consider the system to be a failure no matter how sophisticated and error free the system is. If it takes 10 minutes for each screen to come up, then users are not going to be impressed with the screen, no matter what data is on that particular screen.

Performance testing must be started early in the development cycle. The reason for this is that performance problems are frequently caused by very fundamental errors or mistakes. The database might be poorly designed, the RDBMS package being used might be ill-suited to the environment, the application coding might be inefficient, or inadequate hardware might have been acquired. All of these problems are fixable, but they can't be corrected in the blink of an eye. If the performance problem isn't noticed until after the system goes into production, then the users are going to have to live with it until corrections can be made. It would be so much better if the performance problem were noticed well in advance and corrective action taken before the system goes live. Everyone's lives (users, management, developers) would be much easier if things were done in this order.

Some performance-related areas which can be addressed and tested are outlined in the following sections. One thing to keep in mind is that there generally isn't a silver bullet which will solve all of a system's performance problems. A number of little things should be considered, tested, and tweaked. Don't expect any one modification to do it. Another thing to keep in mind is that performance testing and tuning isn't a one-shot operation. A client/server system is an evolving organism. Settings which are optimal initially might not be optimal after the system has been up and running for a year.

15.3.1 Application Design

It's no accident that the first area mentioned for performance testing is application design. Industrywide experience is that this is the area where most significant performance improvements will be gained. Your first and foremost efforts to improve system performance should be directed towards the application design and coding. Some of the situations to test for are outlined in the following sections.

15.3.1.1 Concurrency Control. Some performance-related problems will slow a system down, but a concurrency problem is capable of completely locking up a client/server system. Concurrency problems occur when multiple users attempt to access the same database resources, usually tables, at the same time. Some operations, such as reads, are nonexclusive requests. The database engine will allow multiple nonexclusive users to be performed simultaneously. Other operations, like updates, require exclusive access to at least part of the database table. Multiple users cannot perform exclusive operations simultaneously.

Unit testing won't experience concurrency problems because it is usually performed by a single user at a time. Integration testing will most likely experience these problems for the same reason. Only stress testing or system testing will have any chance of catching concurrency problems. They will only expose it if the number of simulated users or transactions pushes the system to a relatively high level of activity.

If testing didn't expose all concurrency problems or this type of testing was never done, you don't have to worry about finding these problems. The system's users will find these problems for you. When their systems lock up indefinitely, the support staff will be informed very, very quickly. Of course, the users and their management will likely be looking for someone's head.

If concurrency problems reach a peak, then some users will be informed that their transactions have been picked to be the victim of a deadlock situation. Not only does this slow down that particular user, but it is likely to annoy them greatly. Depending on how the application has been coded, the user might be required to repeat any data which was entered before the deadlock occurred.

If the application was developed without including checks on the return codes, then the user might not be made aware that this situation has occurred. From the user's perspective, everything seemed to go just fine. The system didn't inform the user that there was any sort of problem. In fact, the record wasn't inserted into the system at all. This type of situation will leave users with a very strong distaste for the system.

Most RDBMS systems provide utilities which can help confirm that concurrency problems are occurring. Examine the SQL sessions which are currently open but stalled. Their status will probably indicate that they are waiting for a database lock. If it's possible to view the SQL statements they are waiting on then do so. The tables referenced in these statements are the ones which are currently locked by other users.

The correction to these types of problems isn't easy or simple. Applications need to be rewritten to hold table locks for shorter periods of time. Sometimes the culprit is code which processes the data a row at a time (see Section 15.3.1.4 for an explanation of this topic). Another solution might be to move major processing activities to times when the system is less heavily utilized, i.e., run those massive reports or load processes as a batch job at night. Redesigning database tables may also rectify these problems. There isn't a single cause or a single solution to this predicament. The best solution is to run stress tests to help expose and solve the problem before the system goes into production.

15.3.1.2 Transactions. One of the tasks which must be performed during system design is to identify and refine elements of work done by the users which must be performed as a unit. These are referred to as transactions. Code must be written in such a way that it ensures that transactions either run successfully or are completely backed out. A transaction can't be partly performed. They are an all-or-nothing sort of situation.

When a transaction is underway, it frequently obtains an exclusive lock on more than one database table. Until the user completes this transaction, no other user will be able to access those tables. If the application is written incorrectly, then the user can keep a transaction open indefinitely. A properly written application won't allow a user to do this. Correctly written code takes the duration of a transaction out of a user's control.

There is no easy way to guarantee that transaction processing has been coded correctly. The best method of reaching this goal is to institute peer code reviews. The more people who look at the code, the less likely it is that bad practices like this will make it to the completed system.

15.3.1.3 Query Optimization. Two SQL query statements which perform the same operation can take drastically different amounts of time and resources to complete. The difference is strictly in how well each of them has been written. One query statement might reference extraneous tables, use unnecessary subselects, include system functions which slow things down, or have unneeded statements in the where clause.

How can inefficient statements be found? One way they can be identified is to perform code inspections and walk-throughs. One aspect of the inspection process each module undergoes would be to examine the efficiency of the SQL statements included in it. The developer would be required to present both the SQL code and the query plan the database engine produces when it executes each SQL query. If the code is outrageously inefficient, then all of the eyes and brain power assembled at a code inspection meeting should quickly spot the deficiency.

A second method of finding SQL statements which need some TLC is to enable some form of profiling. Profiling techniques are discussed in Section 15.3.1.5.1. Unfortunately, this method is reactive instead of proactive. It would be better to find them during a code inspection. This is because if inefficient code is found during a code inspection, the developers who wrote the code will hopefully learn something from the exercise. Ideally, they would improve their practice of the art and not write such inefficient code in the future. Nipping bad habits in the bud will improve the quality of SQL code they write during the remainder of the project and hopefully their careers.

Statements which are guilty of being inefficient need to be rewritten ASAP! Every development shop needs an SQL guru—someone who prides himself or herself on being able to write extremely productive, efficient SQL statements. Let the guru examine especially wayward statements and work her magic on them. If your shop doesn't have an SQL guru then grow one or hire one!

15.3.1.4 Set Processing Versus Row Processing.

Relational databases deal with sets of data. A query statement whether it is a select, update, or delete statement affects all rows in the table which meet the statement's where clause. Traditional data processing frequently dealt with flat files. This type of processing logic opened a file and dealt with the records one at a time. The first record was read, processed, and written to an output file.

The fundamental differences between these two approaches are the reasons why many client/server applications are slower than they could be. The developer didn't know how, wasn't trained, or didn't choose to think in a "relational" manner.

A very simplistic example can help to illustrate the situation. Assume that Congress has passed a law hiking the minimum wage from $4.75 to $5.25 per hour. All employees on the payroll who are making minimum wage will be given a raise on a certain date. There are any number of SQL statements which could be used to perform this type of operation. Figures 15.1 and 15.2 provide example solutions from each end of the set versus row spectrum.

The query in Figure 15.1 updates all salaries which were at the old minimum wage to the new minimum wage with a single SQL statement. Another advantage to this approach is that all of the processing is performed on the server. None of the rows get moved across the network from the server to the client machine for processing.

Figure 15.1
Set Processing
Solution

```
UPDATE employee

SET salary = 5.25

WHERE salary = 4.75;
```

Figure 15.2 reads every row in the employee table one at a time into local variables. Each salary is then tested to see if it is equal to the minimum wage. Those rows that include a salary equal to the minimum wage are changed in the database individually via an update statement.

Assume the organization has 1,000 employees and half of them are making minimum wage. The first approach issues a single SQL command and all processing is done on the server. The second approach will read all 1,000 rows across the network, test each of them, and issue 500 update statements back across the network.

Which will be faster? Obviously the first approach will be much faster and more efficient. How much inefficient code of this nature will it take to bring a client/server system to its knees? If the tables being dealt with are large, it might only take a few queries like this to have an impact of a system's performance. How much code like this is in your client/server system?

How can row-by-row processing be found? The same techniques that were used to find other forms of inefficient queries can be used. The best method is to catch them during development by instituting peer code reviews. Hopefully, as such code is reviewed, everyone will improve their SQL skills. The second best method is to find them by running profiling tools on the finished applications. This method is reacting instead of proacting. While it is better to discover inefficient code than leave it in place, this method of handling the problem isn't as desirable as the first method.

15.3.1.5 Tools. Tools are available to stress test client/server systems and its database. These tools essentially generate or simulate the activities of a large number of users. By using such a tool, the testing staff can accurately model what the performance of the system will be when 10, 100, 1,000 users have logged on. Employing these tools will expose performance-related problems before it's too late. Plan on acquiring one of these tools early and using it often.

There are other types of performance-related tools which can be used in a client/server project. Some of these tools are discussed in the following sections.

Figure 15.2
Row at a Time
Solution

```
SELECT:employee_id=employee_id,:salary=salary

FROM employee

{

        IF salary=4.75 THEN

                UPDATE employee

                SET salary=5.25

                WHERE employee_id=:employee_id;

        END IF

}
```

15.3.1.5.1 Profiling Tools   A profiling tool is one which attempts to identify which particular applications and specific parts of an application are generating the largest amount of system activity. They might produce statistics listing the number of times a particular function was called, how much clock time was spent in each function, and the number of disk accesses each function generated. By reviewing this information, the test staff will know which parts of the system are the most offensive and they can direct their collective efforts towards those pieces first.

Profiling tools can be either purchased or developed locally. It isn't very difficult to implement a home-grown version of a profiling tool. Code needs to be added to each application which captures and logs performance related information when the application is started. For finer granularity, each window or function in the applications would capture this information. The particular pieces of data which should be gathered include the clock time when the module was entered, the CPU time used by the process up until this point, and the number of disk I/O operations performed by this process up until this point. When processing in that module is about to conclude, then similar statistics would be gathered again. By comparing the two sets of data, it can be determined what resources were consumed in the module. This data could be inserted into a database table, and reports or screens would be designed to extract the data.

Third-party profiling tools provide essentially the same information. The method which they use to extract data will be significantly more sophisticated. The tools frequently tap into the communications which take place between processes running on the client and those on the server. By analyzing these messages, the tool can provide a great deal of information, including specific SQL statements being executed, without requiring that the applications include profiling source statements.

15.3.1.5.2 Performance Analysis Tools Mercury Interactive produces tools specifically for performance analysis and tuning of data access operations. Versions of their *SQLInspector* tool are available for the following database products:

- *SQLInspector for Microsoft Jet* for Microsoft's Jet Database engine.
- *SQLInspector for ODBC* for ODBC API calls.
- *SQLInspector for SQL Server dbLib* for DB-Library accesses to Sybase or Microsoft SQL Server.
- *SQLInspector for Oracle OCI* for Oracle OCI functions interface with Oracle7 Server.

SQLInspector allows the users to be fairly selective regarding what data will be logged. The user can specify that either one specific program be tracked or all programs be tracked. The type of data being collected can be limited to just the SQL script, the SQL script and the result code, or all of the messages sent between the client and the server.

If the user chooses to collect extended data (i.e., all of the data) then he or she also specifies which types of SQL commands will be logged. A laundry list of available commands are listed and the user can choose that one, several, or all of them be traced. Figure 15.3 is a screen shot of the windows which present the user with choices controlling what data will be tracked.

Each version of SQLInspector intercepts messages sent between the client processes and the database engine. All messages are written to a log file. Some of the types of details which Inspector allows you to view include the function call name, parameters, execution time, and error codes returned by the server. This information can be used to help locate bottlenecks in the system's performance and debug transaction errors. The viewer can be searched to find specific messages. Figure 15.4 is a screen print of the SQLInspector Log Viewer.

15.3.2 Database Design

Once applications have been examined and found to be reasonably well written, the next potential area for improvement is the database design. There are a number of features of a relational database which can be

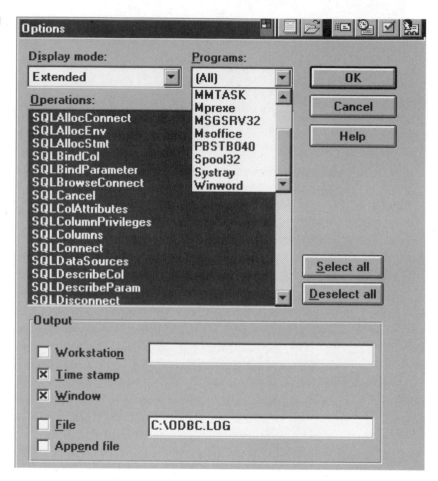

Figure 15.3
SQLInspector Options
Window

changed or added which will significantly improve the performance users will experience. The following sections describe some changes which can be made.

15.3.2.1 Indexes. An *index* is a database structure, actually a table, which is used to speed access to another table. A database table which contains data on employees might include a department code. If a report needs to include all employees in the Engineering department, there are two ways this can be accomplished. The first method would be for the database engine to scan the entire table and return the rows which have the value "engineering" in the department column.

The second method would be to create an index on the department column. This index table will have one row for each row in the employee table. Each row has two columns: the department and a pointer to the corresponding row in the base table. Access time is significantly reduced by selecting all "engineering" entries in the index and using the pointer to obtain the full employee record.

Indexes can improve performance significantly, but they do involve a price. An index takes a certain amount of disk space. Indexes also have to be maintained. Every time a row in the base table is inserted or deleted, the index table must be adjusted. If a row in the base table has a change to the column upon which an index is based, then that change will also need to be made to the index. All of the maintenance of an index is done automatically by the database engine.

15.3.2.2 Clustering. There are many times when two or more tables in a database are accessed together. An example might be a client table and an address table. Every time a row from the client table is read, a row from the address table will also be read. When this situation is true, then the two tables can be physically stored together. This concept is called *clustering*. By storing the two tables together, the number of I/Os needed to access them will be minimized.

While clustering can yield performance improvements, be careful that the technique isn't overused. Clustering together tables which aren't

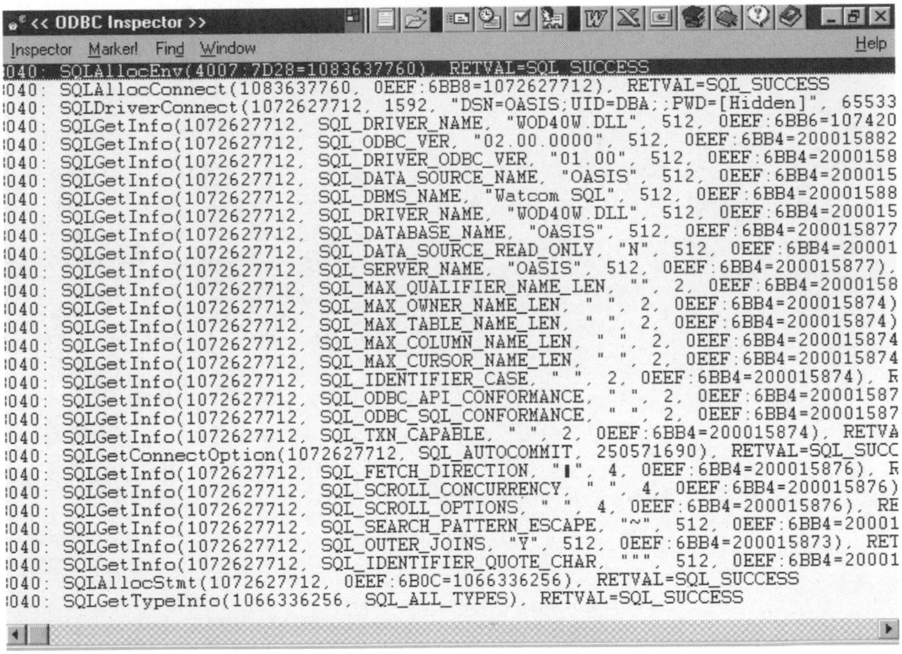

Figure 15.4
SQLInspector Log Viewer

really that closely connected won't yield performance gains. In fact, the net result might be a performance decrease.

15.3.2.3 Denormalize the Database.

The process of breaking down the database into separate tables is called "normalizing" the database. There are a number of rules or "forms" used to perform this process. These rules won't be discussed in this text. While undergoing the process to "fully normalize" a database is valuable, there are times when it has a negative effect on system performance. The gist of what happens is that the database is broken down into many, many tables. To access data in a format which users need, these tables must be joined back together within SQL statements. The join operations aren't without a performance overhead.

If the database being used seems to require that every SQL statement join many tables, then perhaps the database needs to be denormalized. This process redesigns tables so that not as many join operations are required.

15.3.2.4 Refreshing Statistics.

All of the indexes in the world won't be of any use if the database doesn't have current statistics on the table. The database engine uses these statistics to determine which, if any, index should be used. If the statistics on a table are out of date, then the index might not be used. Statistics should be refreshed on a regular basis. This can frequently be done during lull times by setting up batch jobs to do it.

15.3.3 Hardware

One potential solution to performance-related problems is to throw hardware at them. Additional hardware resources can improve the performance of a system very quickly. The advantage of this solution is that it can be implemented fairly quickly. The disadvantage is that it can get to be expensive. Determining exactly where the bottlenecks are will take some investigating. If a system isn't I/O bound, then adding disk drives to it won't offer any improvement at all. It will be a complete waste of time and money. Adding hardware can be done at the server level, the client level, or both. Each of these are discussed in the following sections.

15.3.3.1 Server Hardware.

An insufficient amount of memory on the database server can cause a client/server's performance to be less than it should be. If there isn't enough memory available, the operating system might have to move cache areas to disk, and the database engine won't be able to hold much data in cache. Both of these situations will increase the amount of disk I/O which is performed. Disk activity on a server is the absolutely slowest form of processing.

Additional disk drives being added to the server can also have a noticeable improvement on system performance. If the database is distributed across more drives, then there will be less head contention for the drives. This means that the disk heads won't be jumping around on the drive. Placing overhead objects such as recovery logs, control files, and redo logs onto dedicated drives will also gain performance improvements.

If the bottleneck is the speed of the CPU, then a faster CPU could be installed. A multiprocessor server could also be acquired. Before going to this expense, make certain that the current operating system and database engine can take advantage of multiple CPUs. It would probably present political problems to spend a large amount of money buying an expensive CPU and not see any performance improvement.

15.3.3.2 Client Hardware.   The hardware which is most likely to improve the performance at the client level is to add memory. A minimum amount of memory for a client/server workstation should be 16MB. Less than this will result in unreasonably slow performance for the system.

Another likely candidate for improvement on the client machine is the network card. If the network card is slower than the network will support, then overall performance will be slower than it could be.

15.3.4 Database Engine

The database engine is the focal point for most of the processing on a client/server system. If the proper database package wasn't chosen or it has been installed incorrectly, then performance can be severely degraded. The following items should be examined.

15.3.4.1 Is the Correct RDBMS Being Used?   Relational database systems come in a number of sizes. Some are suitable for single user, desktop applications. Others are suited for use by a single department, say up to 100 users. Others are industrial-strength products capable of supporting thousands of users. If a client/server system has been developed which relies on a database system incapable of supporting the user base, then performance will never be good. As additional users are added performance will continue to degrade. If this is the situation, it would be better to quickly install a database package which was developed to support the number of users on the system.

15.3.4.2 RDBMS Tuning.   For most client/server systems, the last place to look to improve performance should be tuning the RDBMS system itself. There are two reasons for this. First of all, most relational systems do a fairly good job of setting the initial parameters. The vendor has a lot of experience with a lot of clients and the settings were made with all of that experience taken into consideration. The default parameters should provide acceptable performance under most conditions.

The second reason for not attempting to tune the RDBMS package is that if it is done poorly, then performance is likely to get significantly worse. DBAs and other types frequently leap into this area and make changes which they haven't researched thoroughly enough. They may not realize the implications of tuning adjustments they are about to make. None of these parameters should be modified without a great deal of consideration, experience, and training.

15.3.5 Network

The network represents a bottleneck in many client/server systems. Everything which is transferred between the client machines, the database server, and the application server (if one exists) must travel across the network. If there are network-related problems, then every part of the system will be affected. Aspects of the network which can be investigated are described in the following sections.

15.3.5.1 Minimizing Network Traffic.   One technique for handling potential network problems is to decrease the traffic which goes across the network. Even when the network is fairly slow, the impact can be mitigated if the absolute minimum number of messages are sent across it.

If the client/server system being developed involves distributed databases, there are techniques to minimize the amount of network traffic. One technique is to partition the data between databases such that local data is positioned on a local server. Another technique is to replicate data locally so that users access local data instead of remote data whenever possible.

A "fat client" positions all of the application-executable and DLL files on the client machine. By having those files on the client machine, there is no need to transport these sizable files across the network. While fat clients impose a certain amount of additional administrative overhead, they can make a significant reduction in the amount of network traffic.

15.3.5.2 Optimizing the Network. No matter what type of network is used to support a client/server system, it can encounter problems. It is important for the network manager to monitor the performance on a regular basis. This is needed to correct network performance problems before they become severe.

The first step which must be done to optimize the network is to understand what activity is taking place on the network. Tuning the network is highly dependent upon the type of network involved. There are some measurements which apply to all types of networks. Some of these performance-related measurements are listed here.

1. How many packets during normal operations are zipping across the network and which stations are generating them?
2. How much memory is being allocated to network-related processes?
3. What percentage of the system's capacity is being utilized?
4. What is the average response time?
5. Is the response time increasing?
6. What percentage of transmissions are being retransmitted?
7. What percentage of blocks being read are coming from the cache?
8. The average and maximum packet size being transmitted.

Once measurements have been taken, the next step is to analyze the data. At that point decisions can be made regarding what changes to make to, hopefully, improve network performance. The changes that are made must be carefully noted. If performance gets worse instead of better, these modifications will need to be backed out.

Many network packages come with their own monitoring tools. Other easily used tools are available from third-party vendors which can be used to analyze traffic on the network. These tools show how many packets are flowing across the network and which stations are generating them. A network analysis tool should be acquired for the particular type of network being used.

15.4 Code Management and Version Control

The objective of testing the software in a client/server system is to identify, locate, and correct all software errors. Once errors are successfully fixed, the updated code needs to be installed on all versions of the source code. Different versions of the software exist for a number of reasons. These reasons include the need to support different client platforms (e.g., Windows 3.11, Windows 95, Macintosh, UNIX), different levels of testing being performed, or customized versions of the client/server system. If the corrected software isn't distributed to all the sets of source code, then the error will still exist on some machines. It's very possible that the flawed version will inadvertently be copied onto other machines. If the error isn't discovered during the remaining testing efforts, then users will very possibly encounter this error when the system goes into production.

It isn't productive, politically correct, or professional to expend the resources to correct a problem and then falter when it comes to completely eliminating the bad software. Unfortunately, too many development organizations fumble the ball when it comes to properly managing software being developed. The result can be errors which reoccur and must be "fixed" over and over again. This takes time and effort and detracts from the ability to remain focused on fixing other errors.

Code management and version control software can help to make certain that changes to the software are properly installed, maintained, and distributed. At first glance it might not seem that code management and version software qualifies as a test tool. The view can be taken that any tool or product which helps eliminate errors should be included in the category of test tools. If this broader point of view is subscribed to, then software configuration management (SCM) products certainly fall into the test tool category.

15.4.1 Software Configuration Management Capabilities

There are a large number of configuration management tools available on the market. Some development environments include rudimentary SCM features within their systems. Each vendor's method of providing management functions is slightly different, but they are all basically the same capabilities. Some of the major capabilities which software configuration management tools provide are listed in Table 15.4. Each of these capabilities is described in a following section.

15.4.1.1 Check In/Check Out. The concept of checking in and checking out software modules allows multiple developers to work on a project without overwriting one another's work. Developer A checks out module XYZ. He or she is free to make whatever changes he or she needs to make to this module. Other developers are able to look at the current version of this module but can't make changes to it until developer A checks it back in. At that point another developer can check out that particular module.

If this level of control isn't in place, then two developers might end up modifying a module at the same time. The version of software would depend on who performed the last write. This would result in any number of problems. Corrections made to the software by one of the developers would possibly be overwritten, resulting in the recurrence of an error which should have been eliminated.

A number of software development environments include check in/check out functionality in the enterprise or higher-level versions of the tools. PowerBuilder and Visual Basic are among the development tools which include this capability. Check in/check out is a fundamental method of preventing errors from being included or reintroduced into software modules. All development projects should acquire and utilize basic check in/check out protection.

15.4.1.2 Revision History of Changes. Modules in all software development efforts experience a large number of changes. Client/server systems are no different from other software projects. It becomes important to know what changes have been made to each of the modules in a project. Software updates may need to be applied to a number of modules, and there needs to be a way to determine which of those modules have been modified.

TABLE 15.4

Software Configuration Management Capabilities

Check in/check

Revision history of changes

Assemble new builds

Archive source code

Allow backtracking

Supports multiple versions

Configuration management software tracks changes to the software it is managing. It documents what changes were made to each module, who made them, and when. It also tracks what versions the changed modules have been incorporated into.

15.4.1.3 Assemble New Builds.   A "build" is the act of creating a new executable program from all of the source code modules which make it up. Client/server projects undergo a large number of builds during the development lifetime. A new build is created to make use of software modules which include available new features, better performance, or correction of errors. The new builds are then tested and evaluated. Errors discovered or enhancements which are desired are included in the source code, and the iterative process continues.

Since the number of builds created is significant, it becomes necessary to optimize this activity to the greatest extent possible. Builds need to be as consistent as possible. The latest version of each software module needs to be included in each build. Any compilation errors which occur need to be logged and corrected. Once all errors are corrected, the compilation process needs to be performed successfully from beginning to end.

As the development effort continues, the amount of software will grow. By the time the completion is nearing, the number of modules included will be a sizable number. It isn't necessary that each and every module be recompiled. The only modules which truly need to be compiled are the ones which changed and the ones which include changed modules. Configuration management packages keep track of which modules have changed and which are dependent upon the ones which have changed. This enables them to compile the minimum collection of modules necessary.

Documentation needs to be created and kept on each new build. If errors or other problems occur, it will be necessary to determine when a build was created. Other details which will be needed are the list of modules that were included in the build. The fixes corrected and the features that should be included in the build would also be useful information. A final piece of data which will prove very useful is to know which sites, machines, and directories this build was deployed to.

15.4.1.4 Archive Source Code.   Accidents happen. This is true even (especially?) on software development projects. Hardware can crash, back-up tapes sometimes prove to be unreadable, files are deleted by accident, disks can get reformatted, and source files can be overwritten by mistake. Any of these disasters can cause source code or executables to be inadvertently lost. Client/server development projects are difficult enough to complete without having to deal with problems such as these.

Software configuration management products can help to protect against the loss of project files. They can be used to back up project files on a regular, recurring basis. If the unthinkable should happen and files are lost, then SCM tools can be used to quickly and reliably restore the project to where it was just prior to the point in time when things disappeared.

15.4.1.5 Allows Backtracking. Some, but not all, errors are made when source code is developed. A significant number of errors in software are introduced when modules are initially written. An error might occur when an enhancement is being added. It might occur when another error is being fixed. It could conceivably occur when code is being moved from one module to another. No matter what the circumstances leading up to the problem, there will without a doubt be an instance where an error is introduced into the software during every client/server development project.

How can the situation be prevented? Because we're all human, it isn't possible to completely prevent this type of error from happening. If it can't be prevented for occurring, then the next best thing is to help get over such a problem when it occurs. Software configuration management products have the ability to help minimize the effort it takes to correct these errors. Assume a certain error is found in build number 124 of a system. If this problem wasn't occurring in build number 123, then it is a fairly safe assumption that one of the changes introduced the problem. An SCM package should be able to list the exact source code changes which make up each build. It shouldn't take long to examine these changes to identify which one is capable of creating the new error.

15.4.1.6 Supports Multiple Versions One of the identifying features of a client/server system is the heterogeneous nature of its hardware. The system will very likely be deployed to a diverse assemblage of client hardware. The hardware might include PCs running Microsoft Windows, Macintosh machines, or UNIX boxes running X-terminal emulation. There is a high likelihood that the software deployed to each of the machines will have to be different.

Many client/server systems are deployed to multiple sites. Each site could represent a different client or a different division of the organization. The greater the number of sites to which a system is deployed, the higher the certainty that software customizations will be required.

Maintaining different versions of software can become tedious and difficult. This is true whether it is done to support different platforms or custom versions of the software. Code management products provide facilities to assist in this area. They allow different versions of the project to be defined. Changes to specific source modules will be made in all projects which include that particular source module.

15.5 Testing Third-Party Applications

Many client/server systems aren't developed internally by an organization. A significant number of large client/server systems are being purchased from vendors or custom built for an organization by a consulting firm. The system being developed might require specialized expertise which the organization doesn't have. Management may not be interested in scaling up their MIS department to meet the requirements of a large development effort. Management may simply be unwilling to take on the development costs and risks associated with a client/server project.

No matter what the reason for going outside, a client/server system acquired from an external vendor needs to be tested just as thoroughly as a system which was developed internally. Much of the testing process that is necessary is the same for both types of systems. The biggest difference is that the vendor rather than internal personnel will be making the software corrections.

However, there are some aspects of the testing which must be handled much differently. These differences and the reasons behind them are outlined in the following sections.

15.5.1 Test Early

If a client/server system is being custom built, then it is especially important to begin the testing as early and vigorously as possible. In fact, there are a number of reasons why testing these systems early and thoroughly is even more important than testing a system which was developed internally.

15.5.1.1 Reduces Rework Required.   Many times what the client or users consider to be an error is really a misunderstanding. The root of the misunderstanding might be an ambiguous specification, a poorly worded memo, confusion over terms used, or something similar. If the vendor thinks that the fault lies with the client, then the vendor may attempt to bill for the time it takes to correct the situation. The vendor may or may not be successful in this billing, but either way, if the problem is uncovered earlier it can be resolved quickly and more cheaply.

15.5.1.2 Warranty. Most vendors will provide a warranty on their products for only a certain period of time. If the client wants support after that period, then they must purchase a separate support agreement. If the client doesn't intend to purchase on-going support, then they need to identify and inform the vendor of errors as quickly as possible.

15.5.1.3 Turnaround Time. The time it takes to fix a problem if a vendor is involved is very likely to be longer than if the development was done internally. One reason is that the vendor will have a number of competing uses for their resources, especially their people. Enhancing their current product line is one use of resources. Deploying the current product to other hardware and software platforms is another. Building the next generation of the product is a third. Expanding into completely other areas might be yet another. Correcting software errors is only one activity, and it might not be the highest priority.

Another reason that the turnaround time tends to be longer is that the process of reporting errors is likely to be more formalized. There will be more forms and steps required to identify, report, prioritize, and approve software changes. Formalities tend to take more time.

Vendors will likely have a number of clients who have purchased their products. Proposed changes to fix a problem at one site can't be made in a vacuum. Each fix will need to be evaluated to assure that they won't adversely affect another client who has installed the product.

All of the above explain why turnaround time will likely be longer if a vendor is involved. They each serve to emphasize the importance of finding and reporting errors before the system goes into production. If a show-stopping error occurs on a production system, there will be serious repercussions. It is so much smoother to find errors before this occurs.

15.5.1.4 Going Out of Business. It isn't a pleasant topic to dwell on, but every year many companies declare bankruptcy or otherwise go out of business. There is a possibility that one of the unfortunate companies will be the vendor which provided your client/server system. If this should happen, the damage can be minimized if all or most of the errors in the system have been identified and corrected.

While the topic of going out of business is being discussed, it's an opportune time to discuss putting source code in escrow. Many vendors are unwilling to release the source code of their products. If the vendor takes this position, it is important to have the source code placed in escrow. This will allow your organization to get the source code in the event that the vendor goes out of business or otherwise fails to perform. Consult an attorney familiar with this area of law to obtain legal advice on this topic.

15.5.2 Document Errors Thoroughly

Any errors encountered during the testing process must be documented thoroughly. The tester who discovered the error must be extremely complete when documenting and describing the error. Without a thorough understanding of the problem, the vendor may not be able to reproduce it. If that is the case, the vendor may not be willing or able to pursue the problem.

15.6 Managing Databases

References made to the database associated with a client/server system are usually singular in nature. People speak of the database as if there is only a single database involved. This is probably far from accurate. In a development effort there is a definite need for a number of databases. Depending on the phase of the project, there may be up to three different classes of databases being used. The three classes of databases are presented in Table 15.5. Further details on how and when each class of database is used are provided in the following sections.

15.6.1 Development Databases

Databases which support a client/server project during the early development phase tend to be fairly malleable. The design hasn't been fully

TABLE 15.5 Classes of Databases	Development
	Quality Assurance
	Production

solidified yet. Since this is the case, the steps required to make changes to the design of database tables needs to be fairly relaxed.

Frequently during the early phases of the project, developers are referencing distinct databases. Each developer might be changing its database tables to accommodate changing user requirements. These changes can occur quickly or slowly and steadily. If all developers on the project were required to update their modules to meet these changes as they occur, then much of their time would be spent on this task. It is much more efficient for the changes to be restricted to just the one developer until they have stabilized. At that point they can be distributed to all other developers on the project.

Another reason for developers working in separate databases is that developers prefer to have a great deal of control over their test data. If all developers are referencing the same database, then they will all be sharing test data. Changes in the data made by one developer will affect tests made by other developers. This can lead to a great deal of trouble, including time spent chasing down puzzling "errors" which were caused by changes made to the test data made by another developer.

Some database systems allow different schemas to exist within a single database. Each developer could have his or her own schema. This would allow two different developers to use a single table name and actually be referencing two distinct tables. This solution is actually better than creating separate databases because the overhead is reduced significantly.

15.6.2 Quality Assurance

The folks in Quality Assurance will insist on their own database, and they should get one. The tables in the QA database need to be extremely tightly controlled. No ad hoc or spontaneous changes can be made to these tables. Every change being made must go through the proper channels and be thoroughly documented.

The data in the QA database must also be more static in nature than development databases. It will be used during the testing of all modules in the system. The data in this database must be roughly as voluminous as the production database will be. The distribution or variety of entries must also reflect what is expected in the production database.

Since tests will modify the data, there needs to be mechanisms in place for restoring the QA database to a known state. This method of restoring databases might include statements which perform bulk loads of data from text files. Another alternative is to take snapshots of the database before tests are run. Once the testing is complete, the snapshot can be used to roll the database back to its original starting position. A third method might be to use third-party tools which have been developed for loading test databases.

15.6.3 Production

It should go without saying that the production database is even more tightly controlled than the QA database. Any alterations made to it must already have been thoroughly tested in the development and quality assurance databases. If and when changes are made, they need to follow strict operational steps to implement. These steps might include the following:

- Justifying the change to management.
- Verifying that the proper testing has been done.
- Backing up the current production database.
- Coordinating the change with the user community.
- Taking down any affected applications.
- Implementing the change.
- Verifying that the change was made correctly.
- Bringing the affected applications back on line.
- Informing the affected users.

To minimize the impact on the users, there might be restrictions on when changes can be made. Certain periods of the month might be off limits. Normally, this would include the last few and the first few work days of each month. This is because many systems experience a great deal of activity during the last few days of the month and need the first couple of days in the following month to close it out.

Other organizations may prohibit changes from being made on certain days of the week or times during the day. The day-of-the-week restriction might be in place because fewer support personnel are available on that and the following day. Time restrictions usually reflect a desire to minimize user disruption during busy times of the day.

Not only is the design of the production database frozen to developers, but the contents of the database are also off limits to them. Developers should have no opportunity to interact with the production database. It only takes a small mistake in an SQL statement to alter a large number of rows, delete rows, or drop tables. Any testing that developers do must be done on development databases.

Another reason for limiting developers from accessing the production database is strictly security based. In an interactive SQL session, a knowledgeable developer could easily violate security. Data could be viewed, altered, or inserted which could lead to illegal activities. For these reasons there is normally an impenetrable barrier between developers and production data.

15.7 Tools for Building Test Databases

To a very large degree, testing performed on a client/server system is only as good as the test database is realistic. A "realistic" database is one which is comparable in size (i.e., number of rows) and complexity (i.e., diversity of entries) to the database which the system will ultimately have when it is fully deployed and developed. An unrealistically small test database won't yield accurate timing prediction. Similarly, a test database which is constructed of homogeneous (i.e., heavily duplicated) data won't push testing to its limits.

15.7.1 Database Size

It has been stated in other sections, but it is worth repeating that a test database must contain roughly the same number of rows as the production database is projected to contain. If this sizing isn't similar, then any performance or stress testing done won't be accurate or reliable. SQL queries won't take the same amount of time. Queries won't attempt to obtain the same number of database locks. Temporary tables won't be anywhere near the same size. Each of these elements will drastically affect the amount of time it takes to complete SQL queries.

Putting aside performance for a moment, there are other reasons for sizing the test database properly. Predicting how long it will take to back up the database will be easier and more accurate if testing is done on a full-sized database. The size and number of tapes required for the backup can also be verified if preliminary backup operations are done on a realistic database.

How much disk space is going to be needed by the production database? Estimates can be made, but how reliable will they be? Have all factors been taken into consideration when these estimates were made? Were all indexes and their requirements accounted for? Was the estimate made using a realistic fill factor for the tables? Was fragmentation of the disks taken into account? How much space should be allocated for system logs? Have the tables and indexes been properly distributed across all available disk drives? Is adequate temp space available?

If and when a database recovery operation is necessary, you won't want to guess at the recovery procedures. They must all have been documented and thoroughly tested beforehand. How long will it take to recover the database from backup tapes? It would be extremely difficult to predict this without actually running through the process once. An unrealistic database won't give an accurate indication of how long a recovery operation will take.

How long will it take to update database statistics? This operation is vital to assure that the database engine is performing SQL queries in the most efficient manner. If the test database isn't large enough, you may be lured into false assumptions regarding how long this will take, how frequently it should be done, and how much space the histograms generated will require.

This section has attempted to raise a great number of questions about the database and its size. Many of these questions can't reliably be answered until a production-sized database is created and populated. Waiting until the system goes into production to answer such fundamental questions is a terrible mistake. As my father was fond of saying, "It's an accident waiting for a place to happen."

15.7.2 Table Dependencies

Unfortunately, manually generating data for a sizable, complex database requires a significant investment in time and energy. In most client/server databases, there are a great many dependencies which relate the tables together. Very few tables in a relational database truly stand alone. Most are related in some way to one or more other tables. Some of the more central tables will be related to a number of tables. Test data being created must adhere to these complex relationships.

Some of the examples in this book dealt with credit card transactions. Tables referenced in these examples included bank, account, and transaction tables. Rows in the account table each have a bank number in them.

This bank number must exist in the bank table. Rows in the transaction table contain account numbers, and each account number must exist in the account table.

This is where the examples stopped, but there are a large number of supporting tables which weren't discussed. A merchant field exists in the transaction table, and each merchant number must exist in the merchant table. Many of the tables contain address-type information. Addresses refer to cities, states, and zip codes. Each of these values are likely to be related to a table of the same name.

There are many tables which will exist in client/server databases. Virtually all of them are related in one way or another. Test data being generated must reflect these relationships. It isn't enough to generate a series of ascending numbers or random strings and call it representative test data. The test data must include all of the complexities and subtleties which exist in real data. Anything less runs the risk of leaving questions about the validity of the testing.

15.7.3 Keys and Uniqueness

In addition to the relationship requirements, there are other considerations when creating test data. The overwhelming majority of relational database tables are created with a primary key. This key can consist of one or more columns which uniquely identify each row in the table. Test databases must fulfill the uniqueness requirement of primary keys.

Other columns besides the primary key might be required to be unique. An employee table, for example, might contain a column for the employee ID number and the employee's social security number. The employee ID might be the unique primary key of the table. Since social security numbers are defined to be unique, the table will (or should) have a constraint on this column which enforces uniqueness. All data inserted into this table must adhere to these constraints.

15.7.4 Data Generating Tools

The preceding sections cover the bad news. The good news is that there are test tools available which can assist the test staff in creating test data. Previous sections have explained that test data can't simply be a random collection of numbers and character strings. Data in associated tables must be related based on the common columns or keys. The distribution of data in the database must be reflective of the actual values expected to be inserted into the system. Tools are available which can meet these requirements.

15.7.4.1 Distribution of Data.   One tool which can generate test data is BenchWorks by INFOgy, Inc. One of many capabilities of Bench-Works is the ability to generate data for populating tables according to the developer's statistical requirements and constraints. BenchWorks allows the test staff to design data with customized characteristics in each column in a very concise manner. Test data can be broken down into three rough types: character, numeric, and data. BenchWorks has functions to control the distribution of values for each of these datatypes.

15.7.4.1.1 Character Data   Character data can be generated for CHAR or VARCHAR data types. Data for character-based columns can be generated defined by "Min String Length" and "Max String Length" parameters. The generated data may consist of alphabetic characters, digits, or a mixture of each type.

15.7.4.1.2 Numeric Data   The distribution of numeric data in a test database is extremely important. It needs to accurately reflect what the production data will look like. Some of the data columns will need to be strictly sequential. An example of such a column would be an order number, an employee number, or a transaction number. Other columns' data might need to be randomly distributed between two extremes, but centered around a known value. An order amount, for example, would always be greater than zero, less than $1,000,000.00, and average about $1,000. Still other columns might be represented by completely random distribution of data. An example of this might be a randomly generated verification code.

BenchWorks provides functions to generate data in a number of distribution patterns. These functions can be used to meet all of the requirements outlined previously. Some of these functions are listed in Table 15.6.

Most of these functions allow parameters to be specified which control or limit the data distribution. The most common parameters which can be specified are values to limit the start and end values of the distribution pattern. Another parameter, variation, is available to control the number of distinct patterns that may occur.

TABLE 15.6

BenchWorks
Distribution
Functions

Ordered sequences of unique elements

Random sequences of random values

Cyclical distribution of the specified data type

Uniformly distributed random sequences

Sequences with a Gaussian distribution with maximum in the center of the specified range

Exponentially distributed sequences

Integer-valued Poisson distributed sequences

Continuous-valued Gamma distributed sequences

A random sequence of elements enumerated by the user with frequencies for each element in the distribution specified

Random sequence of elements enumerated by the user with the exact number of occurrences of each element specified

15.7.4.1.3 Time and Date Data Many database tables include fields which hold date-oriented data. Date values are created in Bench-Works as a character string. The exact format of these strings is "YYYY:MM:DD:HH:MM:SS." When the data is to be inserted into the database, the string is converted to a date via a conversion function from the database package.

15.7.4.2 Data Integrity. Data integrity within BenchWorks includes verifying that constraint specifications have been adhered to when data is inserted into the database. One type of constraint is the requirement that each value in a column be unique within the table. This constraint is frequently imposed on a primary key which shouldn't be duplicated, such as an employee ID number. If a column has been specified to be unique within a table, then BenchWorks won't attempt to create and insert rows with duplicate values for that column. All values generated by BenchWorks for that particular column will be unique.

Another type of constraint on a column can be that the column is declared to be a foreign key. This requires that any value in this column must already exist in the table to which this column is associated. For example, an address table might have a column name "state." The state column would be declared to be a foreign key of a table named "state." The state table will be loaded with 50 rows, one for each of the U.S. states. No value in the state column of the address can contain a value which isn't present in the state table. An attempt to insert such a value, e.g., "ZZ," would be rejected and an error message would be returned to the caller.

A third type of constraint is that values in a column cannot be NULL. Columns which are primary keys or foreign keys aren't allowed to be NULL. The database design will likely contain other columns which shouldn't be allowed to contain NULL values. An example might be the department number an employee is assigned to. Everyone must be assigned to a department. BenchWorks would not attempt to insert rows with NULL values in that particular column and table.

15.8 Date and Time Testing

Date and time data is used by almost all client/server systems. Most database tables which hold transaction-related data will have at least one date or date/time-related column. This field may represent the date and time that the transaction was entered into the system. The limits or duration (e.g., begin date and end date) of an entity may be recorded. A date when the record should be archived or purged might be stored. There will be very few client/server systems which don't include at least one date value.

Date-related data and logic must be tested. Since some situations (e.g., leap year) don't happen frequently, they must be explicitly examined in the testing activity. A few of date and time relation testing situations are described in the following sections.

15.8.1 Multiple Time Zones

Many client/server systems have been built to support many branches of an organization. As companies expand domestically and internationally, it's very likely that the client/server system will be deployed across a number of time zones. When this occurs, then a time-related problem can become important. If users are entering data into the system from multiple time zones and a time value needs to be included in a record, what time should be used? The time at the office where the insert is being performed? The time at the home office of the organization? Greenwich Mean Time (GMT)? The same question exists in regards to date values. If the date is different between different sites, which date should be used when data is entered into the system?

There are any number of possible solutions to these time-related questions. Three potential solutions are to convert all date and time values to a standard (global) time zone and store that value. A second solution would be to store time and date in the local time and also store a value which indicates the time zone of the location which created the record. A third solution is to store both the local and common global time with the record.

Do local workstation initialization files (*.INI) include a time zone parameter? This might be the avenue used to control the conversion between local time and global time. If this type of parameter is used, then it must be tested. At some point in time, the install process must determine what the local time zone is. This can be obtained from client workstation operating system (Windows 3.11, Windows NT, etc.), or the user can be queried for this piece of setup data. No matter which method is used to identify the local time zone, it has to be tested.

From a testing point of view, it doesn't really matter what solution is used. That decision is a quandary for the designers. What matters is that the solution which has been chosen has been adequately tested and found to be working correctly. If a global time is being used, then all conversions to and from that global time should be tested and verified to be working correctly.

Testing should include inserting records into the database from workstations which are emulating different time zones. Particularly, tests should include insert operations from the present time zone, the present time zone plus one hour, and the present time zone minus one hour.

Another set of tests should verify that a difference of dates can be handled. This will occur when the local time has advanced past midnight into the next day and the global time isn't there yet. It can also happen when the local time is far enough behind the global time to be in the previous day. Tests should include inserting records from a location which is currently in a different date then the global time. Both of the situations should be tested, i.e., test where the local time is yesterday and tomorrow from the global time perspective.

Differences in dates can also cause the two time values to have differences in the month or year units. A difference in these units will happen on a regular basis, i.e., the last day of every month and the last day of every year. Can the system handle these situations? This, too, needs to be tested.

15.8.2 Daylight Savings Time

Daylight Savings Time complicates the date and time issue considerably. Not all countries in the world switch to Daylight Savings Time at the same time each year. There are countries which never go onto Daylight Savings Time. Within the United States there are entire states which don't shift to Daylight Savings Time. Arizona is an example of a state which doesn't undergo this twice-yearly clock shift. The conversion process must be cognizant of what states and countries go on Daylight Savings Time and on what day of the year. This needs to be thoroughly tested for each country and time zone in which client machines will be located.

15.8.3 Leap Year

One last time and date related testing requirement is leap year. In many situations, leap year related logic is an afterthought. Such an offhand dismissal of the topic can come back to haunt a system. Logic and/or calculations to determine how many days are in this year's month of February occur every year. Every four years the answer is different, so logic must properly recognize this. Programmers and testers may not take the time to thoroughly test the logic because the next leap year seems so far in the future. It will arrive a lot sooner than you expect.

15.8.4 Year 2000

I would be remiss if I didn't mention the looming problem with the year 2000. Most client/server systems are likely to be using the internal date datatype provided by the RDBMS package. If date values are being stored in datatypes other than date, then all four year digits should be stored. With the current costs for disk storage, it isn't worth saving two bytes by only storing the final two bytes of the year value.

CHAPTER 16

The Future of Client/Server Systems and Testing

To write the last chapter of this book, I contacted a number of companies which market test tools geared towards client/server systems. I wanted to obtain their insight on what the future holds for client/server systems and the tools used to test them. Representatives from almost every vendor seemed more than happy to discuss this subject with me. The following chapter summarizes their thoughts on this important topic.

The top two items mentioned by vendors dealt with the Internet and performance. Every vendor mentioned the Internet (or intranets) as the most significant factor in the future of client/server systems. An overwhelming majority mentioned the performance of client/server systems as an important topic.

The other topics discussed, while important, had nowhere near the consensus among vendors that these two points did. The other topics mentioned have been listed in no particular order.

16.1 Web-based Applications Which Run on the Internet or an Intranet

Every vendor I talked to mentioned that the Internet, intranets, or Web technology will have a tremendous impact on the future of client/server systems. Client/server systems will increasingly be deployed on either the Internet or an intranet. There are a number of reasons for this projection.

16.1.1 Advantages of Combining Client/Server Systems and Web Technology

Utilizing the Internet or intranets solves a number of the problems associated with client/server systems. Many client machines already contain Web browser software. If a client/server system can be accessed via a Web browser, then there is no need to deploy any software to the client machine.

If the application is modified, then no software needs to be updated on each client's workstation. The next time the user logs onto the system, he or she will access the most recent version of the software. Normally, this situation represents a significant administrative problem for the organization.

Increasingly, users of client/server systems will come from outside the organization. An Internet-accessible, client/server system fits into this trend. The alternative to an Internet-based system would require that the application be deployed to potential users.

16.1.2 Disadvantages of Combining Client/Server Systems and Web Technology

Web browsers are becoming more differentiated from each other. Each vendor is trying to make its product "better" than the others. This trend is likely to continue. The effect on testing is that Internet applications will need to be tested to verify that they work properly on different browsers. As the number of distinct browsers grows, it will be difficult, if not impossible, to certify applications on all of them. The developing organization will have to select a subset of browsers and verify that their applications work properly on this group. Tools will be needed to minimize the amount of manual effort required when doing this task.

If a user of a client/server system encounters an error, it is a fairly easy task determining who the error should be reported to. The user calls the MIS department or whoever else is in charge of supporting the application and informs them of the situation. Internet users encountering similar errors aren't likely to know whom to call. Nor would they be, for the most part, willing to make the effort. To get them to report errors, the process must require minimal effort on their part. A method for reporting errors must be available or embedded in the application.

Web-based applications will be as difficult or more difficult than client/server systems are to test. Additional complications are:

- The same event-driven, nonprocedural code.
- Multivendor deployment environment.
- Deployment environment changes constantly.
- The number of users changes drastically.
- Immature technology.
- An additional point of failure, i.e., the Web server.
- Components are more likely to have been supplied by a third-party vendor.
- Tremendous negative exposure if the application crashes.

16.1.3 Web-oriented Test Tools

Test tools which will thrive in the future need to be extended to include the ability to test Web-based applications. Complications in this goal:

1. Test tools need to be able to properly identify and process objects that don't have winhandles like the current generation of client/server objects.
2. URL links need to be properly handled.
3. Automatic link verification. If a link has changed or died, the test tool must recognize the situation.
4. Applets have brought active content to browsers. Many of the properties of an applet aren't visible. Test tools must be able to test such programs.

Stress testing and load testing will be just as important on Web applications as they are on client/server systems. The unpredictable level of hits will complicate predicting performance. The system should be engineered to handle the maximum anticipated load.

16.2 Performance

The second most often mentioned point during discussions with tool vendors was the performance of client/server systems. Each vendor seemed to include a comment that users don't think client/server systems are fast enough. It appears that the user community in general applauds the power and user friendly interface which most client/server systems provide. The only frequently mentioned short-coming is that too many client/server systems are sluggish.

Too many stories were related to me about client/server systems which didn't or almost didn't get off the ground because of their poor performance. The performance of a new client/server system needs to be accurately predicted before deployment. Once a system has been deployed, it is much more difficult and time-consuming to make the changes required to improve the system's performance. Even more important, if a poorly performing client/server system is deployed, then you've already acquired a black eye in the minds of the users.

16.2.1 Test Tools

Test tools are currently available which can help predict a client/server system's performance. Unfortunately, they aren't always used properly or early enough. There are several reasons for this. First of all, client/server development is a fairly new field. Many organizations, including management and developers, are still gaining much-needed experience. They may not understand the importance of beginning the testing extremely early in the development schedule.

A second reason why these tools aren't used broadly enough is that they are still fairly immature. The tools themselves need improvement. Specifically, the tools required to generate a realistic test database require either a great deal of experience or a fairly strong statistics background.

Tools will also be needed in the future to accurately pinpoint where performance bottlenecks will be. If a projection is made that the system will be I/O intensive, then faster or a greater number of disk drives can be acquired. If the bottleneck is predicted to be in the network, then the system can be tuned to minimize the amount of data passed across it.

16.2.2 Performance Will Become Increasingly Important

The significance of system performance will become increasingly relevant in the future. A number of considerations will align to make performance even more crucial in the future. Some of the points are:

1. Future systems will be required to support more users.
2. Future databases will become significantly larger.
3. Future applications will be more complex.
4. Future datatypes will include multimedia, i.e., audio and video.
5. Web-based systems will experience extremely wide ranges of user hits.

Faster hardware will help alleviate the performance problem, but it doesn't represent the only solution. Client/server systems will have to be designed better from the outset to maximize their performance. Performance-related testing will need to be scheduled early in the system development cycle to identify potential bottlenecks as early as possible.

16.3 A Single Testing Platform

The ability to test numerous clients and multiple operating systems from a single testing platform is a goal many vendors are heading for. The prospect of directing all testing from a single workstation has a number of advantages.

Testing is easier if it can be accomplished from a single workstation. There will no longer be the need to load software onto multiple test workstations. The testing staff will no longer need to utilize one test workstation for Windows-based clients and another for MOTIF-based clients. This will make the test staff more productive.

A single testing platform will be more efficient. Testing staff will no longer need to acquire and learn multiple tools, languages, or approaches. A single tool implies a single language. Allowing the test staff to master a single tool instead of forcing them to have a working knowledge of a number of tools will result in greater efficiency, fewer errors, and better testing.

Re-use of test plans, test scripts, statistics, and other by-products of the testing process will be higher if a single tool is used. If test scripts can be executed on multiple client environments, it will result in greater productivity and more consistent testing.

16.4 Full Life Cycle of Software

Future tool-related products will attempt to wrap all phases of software development and testing into a single, continuous process. These phases will include system design, requirements specification, system development, test creation, and test database creation. Output from the earlier activities will be used to drive the later activities. One example of this would be that the system specifications would generate test plans and test data. This would enable a consistent and complete set of test scripts to be created.

16.5 Prominence of QA Group

As the value of producing quality software becomes more apparent to the organization, the recognition given to the Quality Assurance (QA) group will rise. In too many organizations, the QA group is held in very low esteem. Many developers would rather quit than be assigned to the testing department. If quality software is going to be produced, this attitude has to change. It can only change if management's perception of this group improves.

Far from being at the back of the pack in terms of technology, the QA group is (or should be) leading the organization. To properly test a client/server system, QA professionals need to have a higher level of skills, know more languages, and be able to work with more products than any other group. Management will recognize that a well-trained, experienced QA group is a valuable asset. When this occurs, QA professionals will no longer be considered "poor cousins" to the rest of the MIS department. They will be appreciated and compensated accordingly.

16.6 Multitiered Client/Systems

Multitiered client/server systems are becoming the norm for large-scale, mission-critical client/server systems. The operative question is no longer, "Should we move to a multitiered architecture?" The move to multitiered systems is all but inevitable for mission-critical client/server systems. Now the questions being posed are:

- How many application servers should there be?
- How can users or specific applications be partitioned between applications servers?
- What is the impact of putting all Financials users on one server and all HR (Human Resources) users on the other?

16.7 Increasingly Complex Client/Server Systems

Client/server systems in the future will be bigger and better! More users will access these systems. They will have more data, more screens, and more complicated processing. Unfortunately, along with "bigger and better" comes greater complexity.

Along with the increasingly complex systems is the problem of determining where an error is occurring. We're moving into a world where you will have to work hard just to determine which computer the problem is occurring on. This isn't meant to be a flip statement. If data on a screen or in a report is incorrect, what computers are the possible causes of the problem? The following represent some very realistic possibilities for the source of the problem.

- The fault could be within the report or window running on the user's workstation.
- It could be a stored procedure in the database which gathers the data.
- A business rule running on an application server could have logic problems.
- Invalid data could have been loaded into the database by an import process.
- Security considerations could be preventing the user from seeing all of the pertinent data.

16.8 Definition of Testing and Errors Will Broaden

Currently, many people (users, management, and developers) think of system testing and errors in too narrow a sense. Their definition of an error is if the system hangs or crashes. While a system hang or crash certainly is an error, there are many other types of errors which occur besides these. A broader definition of errors needs to be considered. This definition would have to include:

- Logic errors.
- Inefficient application design (i.e., a nonergonomic user interface).
- Security violations.
- Performance problems.
- Missing functionality.
- Confusing or cryptic error messages.

- Inadequate or misleading help screens.
- Insufficient documentation.

16.9 Packaged Applications

Packaged client/server systems will proliferate in the future. Companies are opting to purchase prebuilt client/server systems from vendors instead of going the route of custom building them. Management, in many cases, has evaluated the situation and decided that the risk and potential outlay to develop a system from scratch is too great. Purchasing a system from a vendor is seen as being safer and more likely to deliver a functioning system for a set price.

The success of applications such as PeopleSoft, SAP, and Oracle Financials are evidence of this trend. More and more companies are choosing vendors such as these for large client/server systems. Packaged applications have been designed to be extremely flexible products. They enable the client to tailor the system with a high degree of customizations during or after installation.

At least one test-tool vendor predicted that in the future, packaged applications will become increasingly specialized. Systems will be developed to address specific markets, e.g., pharmaceuticals, insurance, and legal systems. The concept of prepackaged boutique or niche client/server systems isn't out of the question.

A trend towards packaged applications doesn't in any way diminish the need for testing. The organization purchasing a package system will still need to thoroughly test the system. Testing is needed regardless of whether it was purchased or developed in-house. These systems will be tested specifically for performance tuning, stress testing, and logic errors. Any customizations which were made to the system will need to be addressed during the testing process.

Once a packaged system has been installed, the testing doesn't necessarily stop. Many packages consist of multiple modules (a Human Resources module, a Payroll module, an Accounts/Receivable module, etc.). If additional modules are later added, there would need to be performance testing to determine whether the current hardware would be capable of supporting the expansion. Testing would also be in order if a new department was going to be added to the system.

One vendor indicated that in 1995, 0% of their sales were for testing packaged applications. By 1996 approximately 10% of their sales were used for that purpose. He estimated that 33% of their business would come from this source in 1997. Clearly the trend of applying test tools to packaged applications is on the rise.

16.10 Automated Data Generation Tools

Relational databases associated with client/server systems in the future will continue to grow. It doesn't take a genius to make this prediction. Currently there are many databases which are in the hundreds of gigabytes range. A few organizations have databases that are in the terabyte range. It is very likely that future databases will dwarf these. This growth is caused jointly because companies are gathering more data and retaining more data.

There are size thresholds which severely affect the performance of databases. Testing with a database sized below a threshold won't predict what the database's performance will be once it crosses the threshold. This will force the growth of test databases to correspond to the size of production databases.

How will a testing staff in the future create enough test data to populate a 100GB database, given the requirements that test data must have roughly the same quantity and similar diversity as the production database has? This task simply can't be done manually! Creating test data to run performance tests on very large databases won't be possible without automated tools.

Data-generation tools in the future will need to improve in a number of ways. First of all, the next generation of these tools will be easier to use than the current products. Future products will need to be used by staff with less engineering and math backgrounds. The tools should be easy enough to allow less experienced staff to utilize them. This could be accomplished by allowing the user to create a few records into the database. The tool could then create test data by extrapolating from the sample data.

Another method for creating a suitably sized database would be to extract the information directly from the system design specifications. These tools would extract sizing and other data requirements from the system's design documents. Once this information was known, it would create the database according to these specifications.

16.11 Enterprisewide Repository of Error and Test Data

It will be desirable to have a single repository which contains enterprisewide error and test data. This will yield a number of advantages. A larger body of data, including historical data, will allow better predictions to be made. This will enable management to better assess the status and progress of projects.

This repository will need to be able to interact with a number of test tools. Or rather, test tools will need to be able to access the repository. Several vendors mention that future tools will be capable of sharing data with each other. Creating a standardized, industrywide testing database is a noble goal. But past experience shows that it will be some time before such standards can be hammered out. It will take even more time until all the industry players market tools which meet the standards.

16.12 Test Tool Improvements

Test tools will need to become easier to use. Currently, creating a benchmark is more of an art than a science. The next generation of test tools will lead users through this process. The wizards of today are capable of creating only the most basic scripts. Future tools will be capable of automating much more of the testing process. They will enable less experienced users to be as proficient as the best testing staff of today.

Individual test tools will become better integrated. The tools need to be able to talk to each other. This can be accomplished in two ways. Some vendors will purchase other companies in order to make their suites complete. Other vendors will team up in order to provide complete solutions to their customers. Each of these methods are currently happening in today's test-tool market.

Test tools will become risk identifiers. These tools will help managers evaluate if the system is ready for production. Such tools could also be used to shape the testing schedule. If only a limited time is available for testing, they could predict which tests should be run in that time period to maximize testing.

16.13 Larger Systems Will Force More Testing

Many of the client/server systems installed today are considered mission critical. If the system goes down, the company suffers. If the system stays down long enough, the company could fail. This trend will continue in the future. In fact, as the number of users increases, the costs of a mission-critical system failing will become astronomical. If several thousand users are on a system, it would be unthinkable to have all of them idled. This reality will force management to recognize that testing, including performance testing, can't be trimmed just because the project is behind schedule, over budget, or testing seems to be expensive.

The enormous costs of deploying a client/server system to a large user base will justify fixing problems, including performance problems, before the system is deployed. This, too, will force management to recognize that testing isn't optional. Thorough testing, quite simply, is something which can't be bypassed.

16.14 Experience of the User Population Will Mature

Any new technology goes through a period before it is completely accepted by its intended users. Today's test tools are no different in this regard than FORTAN compilers were two (three?) generations ago. It takes time before the marketplace becomes educated about and comfortable with new methods and new products. Test tools are currently going through this maturation process.

Tools which test GUI front-ends are further along in this process than other tools. The marketplace comfort level for systemwide test tools and performance test tools isn't as far along as GUI test tools. How will people become more comfortable with this type of tool? It will require a combination of education, experience, and success stories.

16.15 Configuration Problems

Problems with configuring client/server systems are troubling a great many sites. Once a client/server system is up and running, it can be difficult to keep it functional. Some of the common problems are:

- Continual new versions of the product are released.
- DLLs are being overwritten.
- Uninstalls don't always work properly.
- Incompatible versions of DLLs and other modules exist.

This situation will only get worse as more software is loaded onto users' workstations. The solution to this is better configuration management procedures. The administrators of a system need to better track what has been installed on each of the servers and client workstations. Tools must be developed to better administration personnel in this process.

16.16 Where Will the Expertise Be?

As client/server systems become increasingly complex, it will take an extremely well-trained technical staff to develop and support them. There is a trend in American business for organizations to focus on their "core functionality." This means that airlines will focus on transporting passengers via their planes and banks will focus on providing financial services to their clients. Running a computer system (client/server or otherwise) may not be considered part of their core functionality.

As a consequence of these two trends, the future may see a great deal more outsourcing of development and support of client/server systems. Expertise in client/server systems could accumulate at consulting companies which declare client/server technology to be their "core functionality." This assessment is really no more than a prediction that the current trend of outsourcing will continue.

INDEX

S

About the Author

Kelly C. Bourne (Omaha, Nebraska) is a software developer and consultant with extensive experience in client/server systems, GUI systems, and relational databases. He has written many articles for *DBMS, Database Programming and Design,* and *Oracle Review.*